THE CATHOLIC EDUC

MUSI
SECOND YEAR

Teachers Manual

By

JUSTINE WARD

Illustrations by Frances Delehanty

CHURCH MUSIC ASSOCIATION OF AMERICA
2025

Music Second Year
by Justine Ward

Second edition, 1936

First reprint edition, CMAA, 2007
Second reprint edition, 2025

Church Music Association of America
405 E. Laburnum Ave., Suite 3
Richmond, Virginia 23222

ISBN 978-1-962440-24-0

PREFACE TO THE NEW EDITION

Music Second Year is designed to meet the needs of the children of the second grade. The work is presented in a Teacher's Manual, a set of charts and a Children's Manual of melodies, songs and liturgical chants.

The material has been revised and, in certain respects, completely recast according to the principles which were applied to Music First Year,[1] to which this volume is a sequel. Both books give the children a knowledge of modern music without neglecting to lay a solid foundation for the liturgical chant of the Church. It is evident that a child whose early impressions of music have been confined to the rhythmic and modal system of the past few centuries, whose taste and technique have been orientated toward secular music only, will find it difficult in later years to turn with conviction toward the melodies which the Church has placed before us as the highest type of musical prayer. We need a broader conception of modality and a broader conception of rhythm, and these should be placed before our children while they are still plastic and free from musical preconceptions. Their taste must be directed toward a type of beauty which cannot easily be loved unless, first, it be known.

Such, then, is the task that has been undertaken in the revision of these books. For many years the material has been subjected to careful laboratory tests which have not been limited to a single nation nor to a single type of school. The result of this broader rhythmic and modal treatment has proved more effective, not from the liturgical standpoint only, but even from the standpoint of music in general.

During the first year, development rather than growth has been stressed, and the study of a repertoire reduced to a minimum, since mental development must precede mental growth. When development is at its maximum, growth is at its minimum and conversely. In music, as in other branches, any attempt to bring about premature or excessive growth will result in an arrested mental development. Those teachers who have applied this principle during the first year will begin to reap their reward during the second, for as the developmental process nears completion, rapid growth sets in. Until that time the teacher should aim at a vital assimilation of fundamental musical experiences and their translation into action and into creative effort. The child is satisfied with the use of tones and rhythms which delight him for their own sake. He does not crave for songs as such.

Already the children have received accurate sense training, both visual and auditive; sensory motor training has been given, the children's powers of observation and memory were stimulated as well as their imagination and creative powers. All this work should be carried on and perfected during the second year. The children will be capable of more correlation, they will grasp simultaneously the several elements in a musical composition: melody with rhythm and both of these with staff notation. A beginning should be made toward the correlation of verbal rhythm with musical rhythm, and the children's compositions should include the setting of a given text to music. The study of musical form is further developed and examples are given for the guidance of teacher and pupils.

Music is not an occult art. It can be grasped by every human being provided it be taught according to the laws of sound psychology. Thus, a new truth, in music, can become

[1] Catholic Education Press, 1933.

functional only on condition that there be *preparation, correlation with what has gone before*, and *action*, for a child can grasp little save through his actions. In these books we have provided a wealth of suggestions for the stimulation of self-activity. These the teacher must apply in such a fashion as scrupulously to refrain from substituting his own mental energy for the mental energy of the child. The latter is the living artizan. It is he who must express his musical ideas, and these must remain the *thoughts of a child*, not a mere mechanical imitation of adult standards.

Each musical truth must be reduced to practice before the pupils can be entrusted with the next truth. By practice we mean the breaking up of the elements, their combination in various ways, their application in a personal manner. Only in so far as a truth is thus assimilated does it become part of the mind itself and partake of its growing impulse. Knowledge, on the contrary, which is merely memorized provides no principle of growth, but, like all dead matters is subject to decay.

While the first book dealt principally with the major mode, the second deals with the minor mode, both natural and harmonic. The two Gregorian modes based on *Re* are introduced in correlation with the minor, just as the two modes based on *Sol* were presented in correlation with the major. The practice of free rhythm is developed side by side with measured rhythm, and both by means of gestures and movements of the body. A wealth of mediaeval folksongs are included, many of them in the ancient modalities and a considerable repertoire of Gregorian Chants, all of which would have been inaccessible to the children without this richer rhythmic and modal background.

It has been proved that this book, in its revised form, is well within the power of the grade teacher to impart to his pupils. It is indeed of the highest importance that this matter should be handled by the regular class teacher, whether our ultimate aim be general culture or a specific preparation for the liturgical chant of the Church. Where can we find an army of professional musicians willing to devote their time, day by day, to the gradual evocation of that tiny germ of beauty which lies hidden in the soul of each child? Where among musicians, will we find a knowledge of child psychology sufficient to restrain his desire to impose his doctrine from without? Where will we find the knowledge and patience with which to correlate music with the other subjects that are imparted? The grade teacher alone can meet the test. I insist on this point, for if music is to be transmitted from generation to generation as an essential part of the cultural and religious inheritance of each child, it cannot be treated as an isolated subject. An isolated truth will never become functional. Music must be taught, if at all, in close correlation with the other branches of knowledge, by the same teacher who imparts them and in the regular school hours. Thus the musical future of our children is in the hands of the grade teacher. This has been our *credo* from the beginning, and after twenty years of experience in the field, this faith has been fully justified.

In all the Gregorian numbers, and indeed throughout the book, the rhythmic doctrine taught is that of Solesmes, and my special gratitude is due to the RR. Benedictine Fathers and their editors Messrs. Desclee & Cie. for their kind permission to make use of the rhythmic signs of Solesmes.

Rome, 1935. JUSTINE WARD.

ADVICE TO TEACHERS

As in the First Year, the Book is divided into chapters each one of which corresponds, approximately, to a week's work. A daily period of twenty minutes is assumed.

Intonation and *rhythm* are approached separately when new problems are presented. Where no new difficulties are involved, pupils should be encouraged to grasp the two elements simultaneously.

Staff notation is presented by means of the C clef in various positions. The children will read from the C clef, while the modern key signatures are added for the information of the teacher. Simple melodies on the staff should be read at sight, whereas those which offer difficulties of interval or of rhythm should be prepared by naming the notes in strict time before attempting to sing the melody.

Words and Music.—The relation between words and music, rhythmically and melodically, should be brought out during the second year. Suggestions for this work will be found on Page 16.

INTONATION EXERCISES

The pupils should sing at the precise moment when the teacher points to a note and should stop singing when the pointer is raised. This rule must be rigidly enforced. Thus each note or group of notes will be detached from what precedes and from what follows, and the brief moment of silence gives the pupils time to *think ahead*, to conceive mentally, the sound that is to be sung next. The result is a firm, definite attack of each tone or group of tones. As soon as a sound has been sung, it should be forgotten in order to concentrate upon the *note ahead*, whether this be a help-note or a sound to be sung. A few voices, indeed a single voice which clings tardily to the previous note can ruin the work of a whole class. The pupils must understand that they must *think before singing*, and that they must *think forward*, never backward. This rule applies exclusively to the *Intonation Exercises*. In all other work (Vocal Exercises, Rhythmic Exercises, Melodies and Songs) this detached, staccato manner of singing is not applicable, for the notes must be treated, not as isolated units, but as forming part of a group or a phrase. All such exercises, then, must be sung *legato*.

Help-notes.—The use of help-notes should be encouraged, since the power to *think* a note without singing it, a note on which another depends, is the source of power and accuracy in reading music. In finding the help-notes, the children should not be hurried. The help-note should occupy as much time as a note to be sung, and the children must have confidence that sufficient time will be given them, lacking which, they will make no effort to *think* the desired tones. Gradually the process becomes more rapid when the habit of hearing notes without singing them has been well formed. In the early chapters of this volume, the exercises are devised with this purpose: to give a certain dexterity in *thinking without singing*, while dealing with familiar melodic material. This mastery over the help-note will prove invaluable later in the year when applied to new problems.

Throughout the Second Year, whenever an interval proves difficult, the teacher should supply the appropriate help-note, whether the manual does so or not. Moreover, when the children fail to sing true to pitch, the remedy should be sought in supplying help-notes which will correct the fault.

RHYTHM

In studying the *Rhythmic Exercises*, the Gestures of the First Year should be used. Where the rhythmic designs contain a complicated arrangement of eighth notes which tend to retard the Rhythmic Gestures, these problems may be *prepared* (as a sort of analysis) by beating time lightly while reciting the rhythmic design. As soon as the problem is grasped, the beating of time should be abandoned and the rhythmic gesture substituted.

The value of the gestures consists in the fact that they bring about a coordination and control of the motor impulses. Through their use, the children obtain, not merely a mechanical metrical accuracy (which can be obtained by beating time) but a *true sense of rhythm*, a sense which gradually becomes instinctive and automatic. This object will not be attained if the children make the gestures in a hesitating manner. That is why it is preferable to allow the beating of time during the process of metrical analysis. When this object has been attained, the rhythmic gesture should be used, since it serves to lift these metrical fragments into their true position in the musical phrase.

These gestures should be used by the teacher when giving metrical dictation.

Metrical dictation should never be given *on the harmonium*. The sounds of this instrument are not sufficiently neat. The metrical dictation should be given in one of the following ways:

(*a*) By the teacher's own voice.

(*b*) By tapping lightly and clearly with the fingers.

(*c*) By using a small drum or other instrument of percussion.

Any one of these methods is effective if well employed. The principal object of the exercise being to give the children a quick and accurate perception of metrical details, it follows that the models put before them must be precise and perfect.

In the *Vocal Exercises* and the *Songs*, the gestures should be reduced in size, that they may not interfere with the perfection of the voice production, and, as a general rule, should be made with the right hand only. Alternation should be encouraged, between the two halves of the class: one half singing, the other half making the rhythmic gestures, with reversal of the functions at a point agreed upon in advance.

STAFF NOTATION

The exercises in *Staff Notation* are of three categories. The first type are purely *eye-training:* the notes are to be named but not sung, in response to the tap of the pointer. The tempo should be approximately Metronome 60, becoming swifter with practice. Whatever be the tempo, the pulse must be regular and metrically accurate.

The exercises of the second type are to be *sung*. They follow the exercises of the first type. The Diagrams on the Staff serve for both types of exercise, as well as for rapid visualization.

The staff exercises of the third type consist in a simultaneous grasp of interval, rhythm and notation. Entire melodies are presented where all the elements, melodic, rhythmic and of notation, are already familiar. These melodies should be sung at sight, slowly at first but always evenly, then at the proper tempo.

Other melodies on the staff will require preparation, as regards interval, or rhythm, or both. Where there is a difficult interval, the teacher should prepare it in advance on the fingers or on the blackboard. Where the difficulty is one of rhythm, a metrical schema of the whole melody should be put on the board and it should be studied as a rhythmic exercise before attempting to sing the melody. Where the metrical difficulty is less great, the melody may be studied as follows: Read the names of the notes without singing in strict time. Repeat, with rhythmic gestures. Sing the melody slowly. Repeat in the proper tempo with gestures.

MELODIES AND SONGS

The number of melodies and songs included in the second year book is greater than is strictly necessary, and greater, also, than can be studied in the course of the week's work outlined in the chapters. We have purposely included these songs and melodies in order to provide a choice. Moreover, where, as is often the case, this volume is used by older children, the number of melodies illustrative of the material is not too great. For the little ones, then, the teacher will make a choice, and will not attempt to render all the songs and melodies embodied in the second year book.

These melodies are so graded that they contain no difficulty which has not previously been prepared in the Intonation and Rhythmic Exercises. They are not, however, used merely to illustrate a technical point. Their main purpose is to form the taste of the children and to stimulate their imagination. Almost all these melodies are ancient folk-songs from various countries. A few are the work of child-composers. The most notable are taken from the Gregorian repertoire.

COMPOSITION BY THE CHILDREN

The children should be encouraged to compose melodies—with and without words—not with the idea of developing great composers of music in the primary grades of our schools, but simply as expression, and a precious aid in developing the child's musical taste and temperament. Until a child has learned to use tones and rhythms as he would use the colors in a box of crayons, he remains outside the realm of musical delight. The compositions, to be sincere, must be the compositions *of a child*, and not a mere imitation of adult concepts. The child will need guidance, however, as well as stimulation. The following principles will aid the teacher in this delicate task:

1. The spontaneity of the child should not be crushed but, on the contrary, stimulated. If we begin by imposing a set of arbitrary rules for the progression of tones, for the length of phrases, for the likenesses and contrasts that must appear in a melody, this will intimidate and discourage, and the child, thus hedged about with inhibitions, will cease to make any personal effort and will string notes together mechanically according to the imposed will of the teacher.

2. Yet the child's taste must be guided toward higher standards of beauty.

These two principles may appear contradictory, but they are no more so when applied to music than when applied to any other branch of education. The task of combining them is delicate and requires tact and good pedagogy.

In the first year, the dramatization of a story was suggested as one of the means of stimulating the children's desire for expression. This desire once awakened, various methods were suggested for drawing their attention to those devices of symmetry, of balance, of contrast (melodic or rhythmic) which give character to the phrases of a melody. In using the devices mentioned above, it is important to have obtained the confidence and enthusiasm of the children before drawing their attention to these counsels of perfection. The proper moment for such suggestions is when the children are already eager to compose melodies, not while they are still timid and hesitant. Some teachers, over-anxious for rapid results, place on the board a framework of bars into which the children are asked to compose a melody. This is tantamount to *imposing a form before there has been an idea.* Such practice will defeat its own ends, since it will not stimulate the child to use his own powers.

Models.—One of the greatest aids to the formation of taste is the placing of beautiful models before the children. These models should be free from rhythmical or melodic errors, and be of simple and noble inspiration. Such models are provided by the melodies used in the manuals, which should be sung in preference to melodies composed by the teacher or the pupils. Such models have their effect upon the compositions of the children, indirectly.

Direct Aid.—Such aid should be two-fold: melodic and rhythmic. When a beautiful melody has been sung by the class, the children's attention can be drawn to certain features of interest: repetition (either exact or approximative), contrasts of melodic direction, contrasts of rhythm. Another way of using the melodies is to place the first phrase on the board, and ask the children to write an answering phrase. When a number of these have been composed and a selection made, then the children may be encouraged to sing the melody as it is written, comparing the composer's ideas with their own. They will sing it with more interest and curiosity after having made efforts at personal composition. Another way to use the models is to place on the board the principal parts of the melody, leaving certain passages blank for the children to fill in. After which, they will sing the melody itself as given in the manual.

The most valuable aid, however, is provided in the rhythmic designs; the combining of several rhythms by repetition or by contrast. The children are free to arrange the various designs according to their fancy and compose the melodic setting to bring about a sense of unity or of variety. Each chapter provides material for such work. By this means a sense of form is built up, gradually, from within.

When composing melodies, the children should sing a whole phrase softly to themselves before writing anything on the board, to avoid the temptation of writing a series of meaningless figures without musical significance. It must be done softly, in a whisper, so that the class work may not be disturbed. Later, when the habit of *hearing without singing* has been developed, this preliminary treatment of the phrase may be suppressed.

Improvisations develop spontaneity while *written compositions* develop judgment and provide an opportunity for constructive criticism by the teacher.

The improvisations may take the form of a *Musical Conversation* between two or more children, or a child may improvise the entire melody, a system which many teachers prefer. In either case, the improvisation should be:

(*a*) *Melodic,* but should take on a more rhythmic character than the improvisations composed during the First Year.

(*b*) *Rhythmic.*—Designs merely pronounced and accompanied by the appropriate gesture.

(*c*) *Melodic and Rhythmic* in the sense that each phrase of the melody will be sung with the appropriate rhythmic gesture.

The children should be encouraged to use longer phrases than during the first year, and—while the melodies retain the character of an improvisation—certain *habits of thought* can be cultivated without loss of spontaneity.

Their attention should be drawn to the fact that a musical theme can be answered in several ways:

We can say "yes" or we can say "no."

When we want to say "yes," *we repeat the same thing,* either exactly, or in somewhat the same fashion. (Note examples of answers affirmative or negative in the melodies of the manual.)

When we want to say "no," we make a change. The change can be melodic or rhythmic, or both together.

Examples

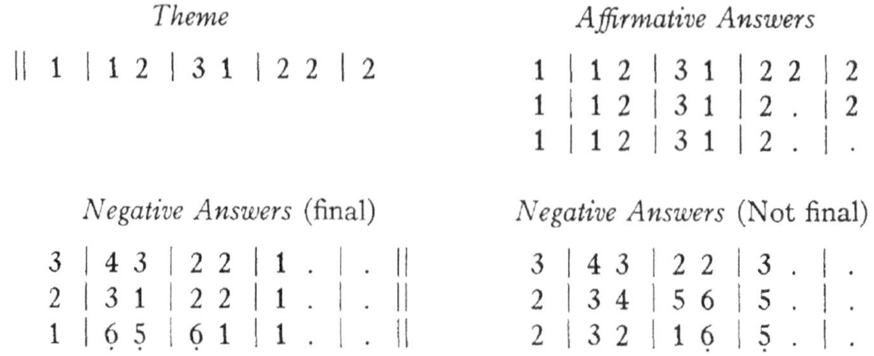

Theme

|| 1 | 1 2 | 3 1 | 2 2 | 2

Affirmative Answers

1 | 1 2 | 3 1 | 2 2 | 2
1 | 1 2 | 3 1 | 2 . | 2
1 | 1 2 | 3 1 | 2 . | .

Negative Answers (final)

3 | 4 3 | 2 2 | 1 . | . ||
2 | 3 1 | 2 2 | 1 . | . ||
1 | 6̣ 5̣ | 6̣ 1 | 1 . | . ||

Negative Answers (Not final)

3 | 4 3 | 2 2 | 3 . | .
2 | 3 4 | 5 6 | 5 . | .
2 | 3 2 | 1 6̣ | 5̣ . | .

These answers, affirmative and negative, make no use of rhythmic contrasts. The following answers change the design of the rhythm:

Theme

|| 1 | 1 2 | 3 1 | 2 2 | 2

Affirmative answers with slight variation

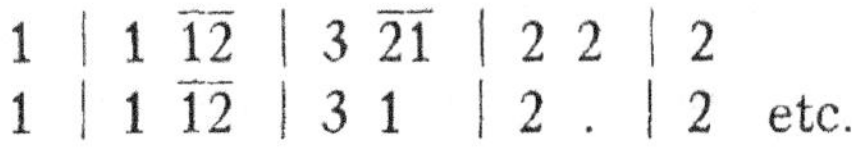

1 | 1 $\overline{12}$ | 3 $\overline{21}$ | 2 2 | 2

1 | 1 $\overline{12}$ | 3 1 | 2 . | 2 etc.

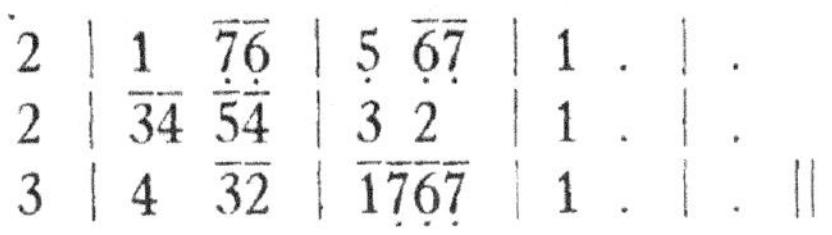

The notes with ictus are the same as in the theme

Negative answers (final)

2 | 1 $\overline{76}$ | 5 $\overline{67}$ | 1 . | .

2 | $\overline{34}$ $\overline{54}$ | 3 2 | 1 . | .

3 | 4 $\overline{32}$ | $\overline{1767}$ | 1 . | . ||

Negative answers (not final)

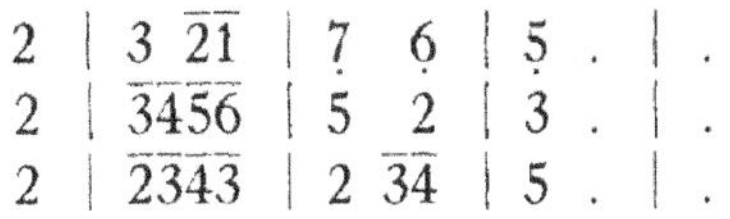

2 | 3 $\overline{21}$ | 7 6 | 5 . | .

2 | $\overline{3456}$ | 5 2 | 3 . | .

2 | $\overline{2343}$ | 2 $\overline{34}$ | 5 . | .

Thus, a musical theme can be answered affirmatively or negatively. The negative answer can be a contrast of melodic direction without change of rhythm, or can embody a change of rhythm also.

When we have decided whether to say "yes" or "no" to the theme given, we can *repeat* affirmatively or negatively.

We will take the same theme as an example. (*a*)

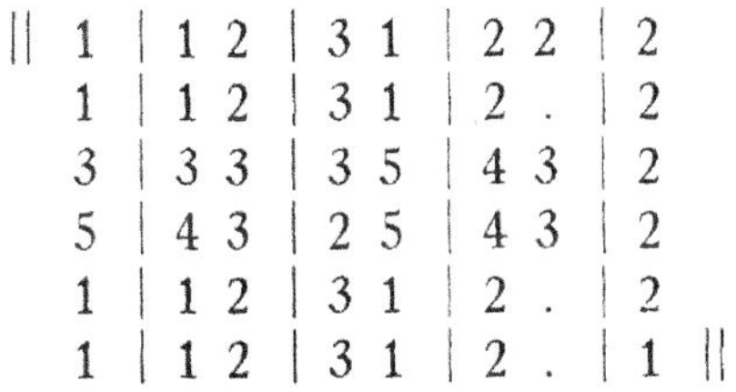

|| 1 | 1 2 | 3 1 | 2 2 | 2 — *Theme A.*

1 | 1 2 | 3 1 | 2 . | 2 — *Affirmative answer a.*

3 | 3 3 | 3 5 | 4 3 | 2 — *Contrast B* can be repeated or not, in whole or in part.

5 | 4 3 | 2 5 | 4 3 | 2

1 | 1 2 | 3 1 | 2 . | 2 — *End with a return to A + a.*

1 | 1 2 | 3 1 | 2 . | 1 ||

In this melody we have a theme, an affirmative answer: (*A + a*)
Then a contrast repeated in part (*B + b*)
An affirmative ending repeated twice (*A + a*)
This is the simplest possible form (*Aa Bb Aa*).

Taking the same theme, we will give a negative answer: (*A + B*)

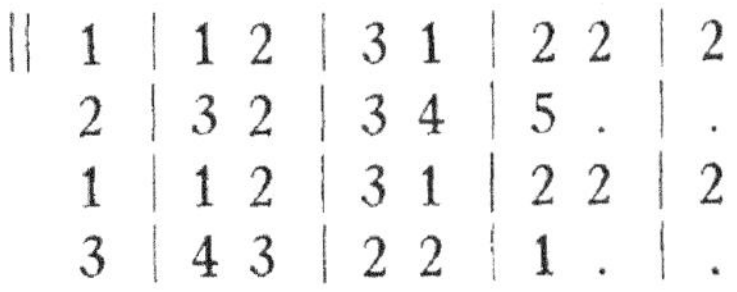

|| 1 | 1 2 | 3 1 | 2 2 | 2 — *Theme A.*

2 | 3 2 | 3 4 | 5 . | . — *Negative answer B.*

1 | 1 2 | 3 1 | 2 2 | 2 — *Repetition A.*

3 | 4 3 | 2 2 | 1 . | . — *Negative ending C.*

These simple ideas of likeness or contrast are basic in the art of composition, and should be presented in the simplest possible form. Some themes adapt themselves to one treatment, others to another. In the course of these pages, suggestions will be made for the development of these ideas and their adaptation to the material embodied in the chapters.

Structural Tones Characteristic of the Modality

Each Mode has certain structural tones which must be brought out in order to affirm clearly the modality in which we are writing. These tones must predominate in the *theme*, and wherever a sense of *repose* is sought. These structural tones are as follows:

Major Mode: do, mi and *sol.*
Modes of Sol: sol, ti and *re.*
Minor Mode: la, do and *mi.*
Modes of Re: re, fa and *la.*

When the first note of each measure is a structural tone, we affirm our modality. When, on the contrary, we build a phrase on a series of non-structural tones, we produce a sense of contrast.

Non-structural Tones

Major Mode: re, fa, la, ti.
Modes of Sol: fa, la do, mi.
Minor Modes: sol (se), ti, re, fa (fe).
Modes of Re: do, mi, sol, ti, (teu).

The phrases may move in scale progression or in chord progression, while affirming the modality, provided the first note of each measure (or of the majority thereof) is a structural note of the mode.

Examples

|| 5̣ | 1 2 | 3 4 | 5 5 | 5 — Theme on structural tones of Major Mode.

|| 1 3 | 3 5 | 6 5 | 5 . | — Theme on structural tones of Major Mode.

|| 6̣ | 6̣ . 7̣ | 1 2 3 | 3 . 2 | 3 . — Minor Mode.

|| 6̣ | 6̣ 3 | 3 2 | 3 . | 3' 6̣ | 6̣ 3 | 3 2 | 3 . | . — Minor Mode.

|| 5 | 5 . 6 | 7 . 1̇ | 7 . 6 | 5 . 5 | 2̇ . 6 | 2̇ . 1̇ | 2̇ . . | . .

Modes of Sol

Process of composition.—First there must be an *idea.* In developing that idea, there must be something that repeats itself, like the weaving of a pattern.

We must find the same thing, exactly repeated, or similar in certain respects to the original theme. That is what creates a sense of *unity*. There need not be absolute identity: a design may appear in an enlarged form or in a reversed direction, or transferred to a different part of the scale.

Then there must be a *contrast*. A good melody must contain a surprise for us, somewhere. *One* surprise is usually enough. A good surprise, melodically, is to move from one part of the scale to another, from the lower pentachord to the upper tetrachord, or vice versa. Another surprise is to change from the progression of the scale to the progression of the chord, or vice versa; or from the suggestion of one chord to the suggestion of another. (None of these devices should be employed *often*.) These are melodic surprises.

Rhythmic surprises are pleasant if there be not too many. Each phrase must have a form that will please the ear, and it must have a pleasing relation to the other phrases of the melody. This does not mean that all the phrases should be of similar length and similar rhythmic design. Variety is interesting provided there be a sense of architectural balance and proportion conveyed. In this sense of balance, we must not forget the art of *pausing*. Silence is as eloquent as sound—in its proper place. No melody is complete without its moments of rest. The importance of the pause should be in proportion to the length of the phrase and the character of what we have expressed musically. During the pause we have time to grasp what has been said and to prepare for what is to come. Moreover, apart from the aesthetical value of the pause, we must consider the physical need of proper breathing. These things the children should be aided to discover for themselves, by timely suggestion or, if need be, by criticism. The pauses need not all be of the same length. Usually the final pause and the central one are longer than the intermediary pauses. An examination of the melodies in Music First and Second Years will illustrate these points.

The correction of errors.—Certain errors must be corrected lest a false form should remain before the class. Among such errors are: incorrect cadences (see Music First Year, Chapter 20, page 169) and incorrect placing of the bar lines. A bar line must always be placed to the left of a long note. The rhythmic designs will aid the children in this respect, especially when accompanied by the appropriate gestures.

USE OF THE HARMONIUM

As in the First Year, the teacher will use the harmonium as follows:

Before beginning to sing a line of an intonation exercise, or vocal exercise.

Before each phrase of an ear test, finger dictation, or visualisation exercise, the teacher will play the first tone on the harmonium, repeating with his voice the name of the tone "*Do*" or "*sol*" or "*la*," as the case may be.

At the end of each line, or dictated phrase, the teacher should play the tone on which the phrase ends to verify the pitch.

Some teachers neglect this proper verification. Others use the harmonium to excess, following the voices of the children note by note. This custom is not to be encouraged. The children become over dependent on exterior aid instead of using their own volition. They relapse into the passive attitude of listeners. Thus, the harmonium if used to excess, prevents the formation of good musical habits and renders the children parasitical. There is a second disadvantage in the fact that the harmonium, being a tempered instrument, can provide only an *approximate model* of the correct relation of the tones and half-tones. In the pentachord: 1 2 34 5, for instance, the three whole tones are *not equal*, and should not be sung so. A voice singing true to pitch will be *more true* than the harmonium. If the teacher will verify the extremities of the pentachord (*do* and *sol*) in whatever tonality he desires, these extremities will be relatively true even on the harmonium: the relation between the tonic and the fifth, the tonic and the fourth, the tonic and the octave being those which deviate the least from true pitch on the tempered instrument.

Thus if the children are singing the major pentachord (1 2 3 4 5) the notes 1 and 5 may be controlled on the harmonium, but it would be unwise to follow the voices, note by note, along the various steps of the pentachord. In the minor pentachord (6̣ 7̣ 1 2 3), the tones 6̣ and 3 may be verified. In the whole scale, 1 and 8 for the major; 6̣ and 6 for the minor.

ORDER AND SEQUENCE IN A LESSON

The plan of a lesson, in the second year, differs very little from that of the first year, save that the periods of mental concentration can be longer. There must always be an alternation between the exercises requiring concentration and those where there is relative relaxation, that no time may be wasted. The interest of the children in problems of a purely musical nature is much greater in the second year than in the first. To hold this willing attention, the teacher will do well to present something *new* at each lesson, or some old thing *in a new way*. The children should expect to find a surprise in each lesson.

Each lesson will contain:

1. *Vocal Exercises.*

2. *Intonation Exercises*, both in numbers and on the staff.
3. *Rhythmic Exercises*, developing powers of execution and of observation, (with and without gestures).
4. *Rhythm and Melody* (being phrases illustrative of the rhythmic designs studied during the chapter).
5. *Melody and Rhythm* (being phrases devised for the assimilation of the material embodied in the Intonation Exercises).
6. *Ear training* (*a*) Melodic
   (*b*) Rhythmic
   (*c*) With melody and rhythm.
7. *Visualization* from diagrams in numbers or on the staff, from the fingers, or from phrases written and erased from the black-board.
8. *Aural memory*, phrases sung once and repeated with backs to the board or chart.
9. *Melodies and Songs* from number notation and from the staff for the cultivation of taste.
10. *Composition* (written or improvised). These should be used several times a week as home work, and occasionally in class.
11. *Composition of melodies to simple little poems.* (Occasionally.)

These elements will not be used in the order given above, but they will be arranged in such a manner as to alternate the periods of greatest concentration with those of relative relaxation as described in detail in Music First Year.

When improvising, the children should use the names of the notes, at times; at others, they should sing on a vowel sound. The former habit develops greater accuracy; the latter, greater spontaneity.

PLAN OF A LESSON

We repeat the advice given in the first year: the teacher should make a definite plan of the music lesson in advance as regards the material to be covered and the manner in which the various points of the lesson are to be fitted together. Evidently, a good teacher will not be a slave to the preconceived plan when at work with the children, but the plan is essential to good teaching. At the end of the class a record should be kept of the matter actually covered in the lesson. In this manner, the time is used to the best advantage, without useless repetition on the one hand, or, on the other, those fatal gaps that remain unfilled and that make further progress impossible.

WORDS AND MUSIC

There is a stage where the use of words can be a help in understanding a rhythmic problem, rather than the reverse. The teacher will be the best judge of the proper time to introduce the work suggested below.

Rhythm of words (without melody).

An attempt at correlation between the various rhythmic designs as applied to music and to language can enrich both studies provided there be sufficient time in the school curriculum for this study.

1. A single word.
2. A single word repeated.

In English, the accented syllable usually corresponds with the rhythmic *ictus*.[1]

It takes at least two units (two syllables) to make the briefest possible rhythm. We will begin with words of two syllables.

Form a	*Form b*
1 1	1 1
a- dore	an- gel

Place a bar line to the left of the accented syllable.

Once the bars are in place, we can add length as above.

Repeat each of these words, giving length only to the last:

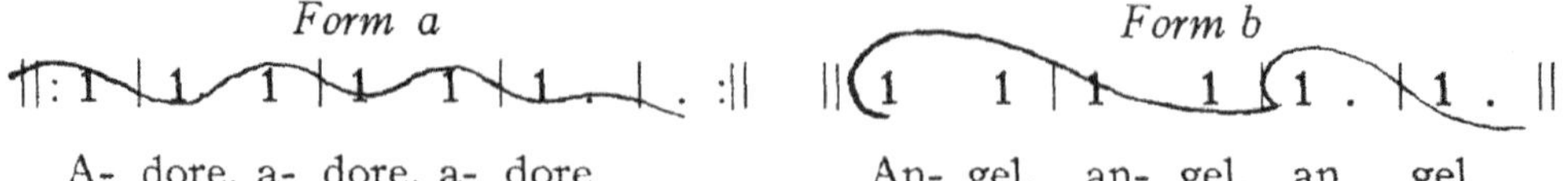

The children should find other words which can be rhythmed like each of the above forms. Thus:

[1] The first "beat" of a measure.

(*a*)	(*b*)
Parade	Father
Admire	Mother
Redeem	Music
Believe	Loving
Obey	Active
Delight	Rapid

Words of *Form a* are complete in themselves because, being astride of the bar line, their last syllable falls on a structural or ictic note, a note to which we can give *length*—two dots of prolongation to the final note to form a definite cadence of ending.

Words of *Form b* fit within a measure. The last syllable is, so to speak, *in the air*. In order to form a cadence or ending, we are forced to prolong *both syllables* of the final word.

In setting words to music, the custom of our day is to place the accented syllable of the word on the ictic note of the melody. For the moment, the children should apply this principle of the coincidence of the accented syllable with the ictic note.

When the accented syllable has been placed to the right of the bar line, the syllables may be lengthened without disturbing the relation between the accent and the rhythmic ictus, thus:

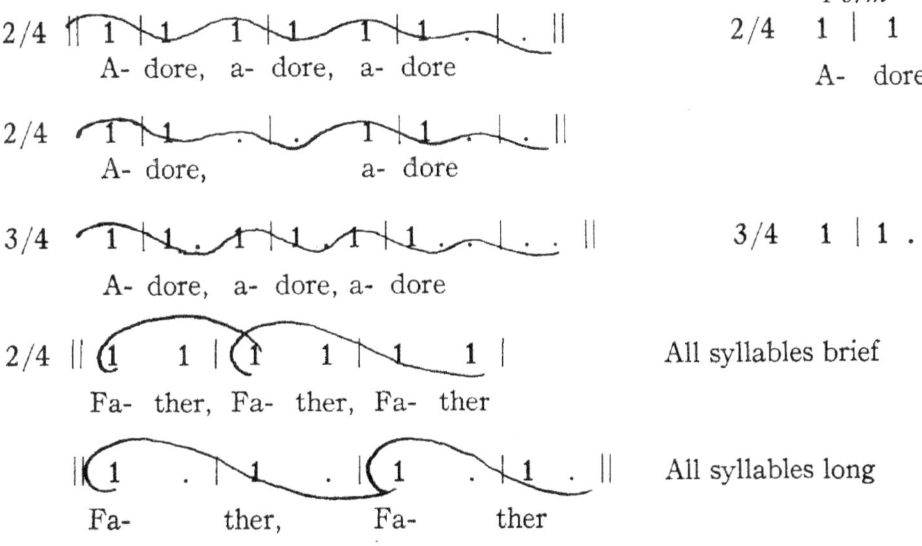

pages: to make the accented syllables of the text correspond with the ictic note of the melody. They may use 2/4 or 3/4 time.

WORDS OF MORE THAN TWO SYLLABLES

Since the same principle applies to these longer words, and also to the combination of monosyllables with longer words, a few examples will suffice, without attempting to cover this matter in an exhaustive fashion.

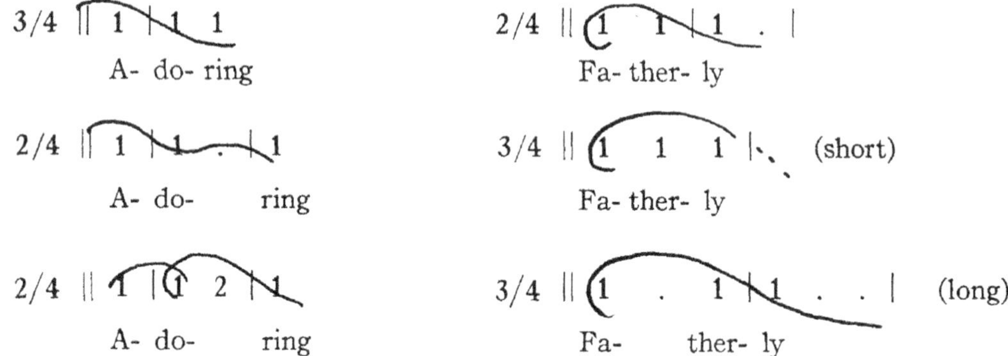

Once more these dots of prolongation can be replaced by tones in the melody.

Monosyllables take on the rhythm of their surroundings, as in the following phrases:

Each of these rhythmic designs should be repeated with gestures. Then the children may compose a melody—spontaneously.

WORDS OF THREE SYLLABLES

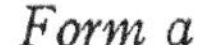

Form a

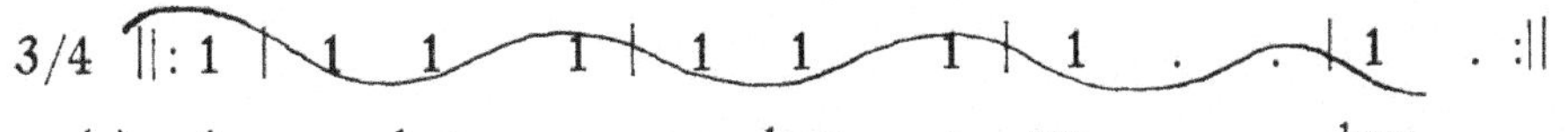

(*a*) A- wa- ken, a- wa- ken, a- wa- ken.
(*b*) Good mor- ning, good mor- ning, good mor- ning.

2/4 ||: 1 | 1 . | 1 1 | 1 . | 1 1 | 1 . | 1 . | . :||

(*a*) A- wa- ken, a- wa- ken, a- wa- ken.
(*b*) Ex- cuse me, ex- cuse me, ex- cuse me.

b represents brief words rhythmed like a word of three syllables.

Form b

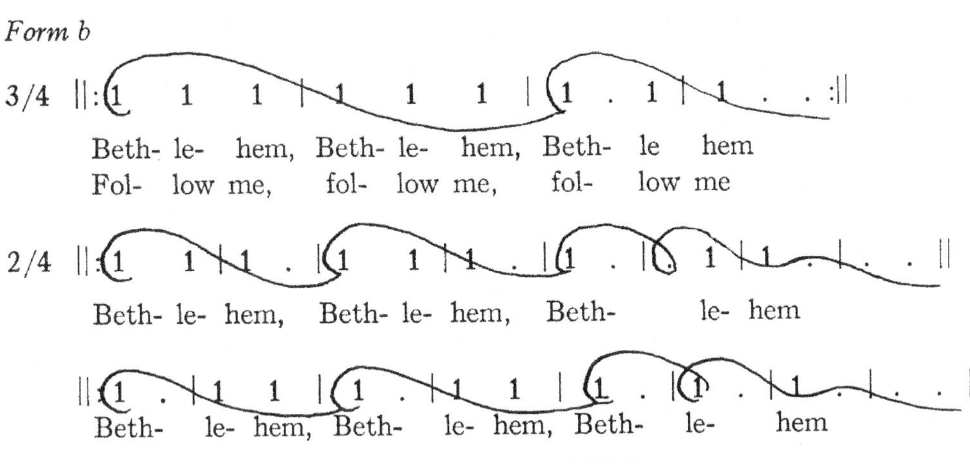

FOUR SYLLABLES

Long words and short. Same rule. Place bar to left of accented syllables

Form a

Mys- te- ri- ous
In Pa- ra- dise
An an- gel bright
A cloud at rest

Form b

Ex- cla- ma- tion
Guar- dian an- gel
I shall find him

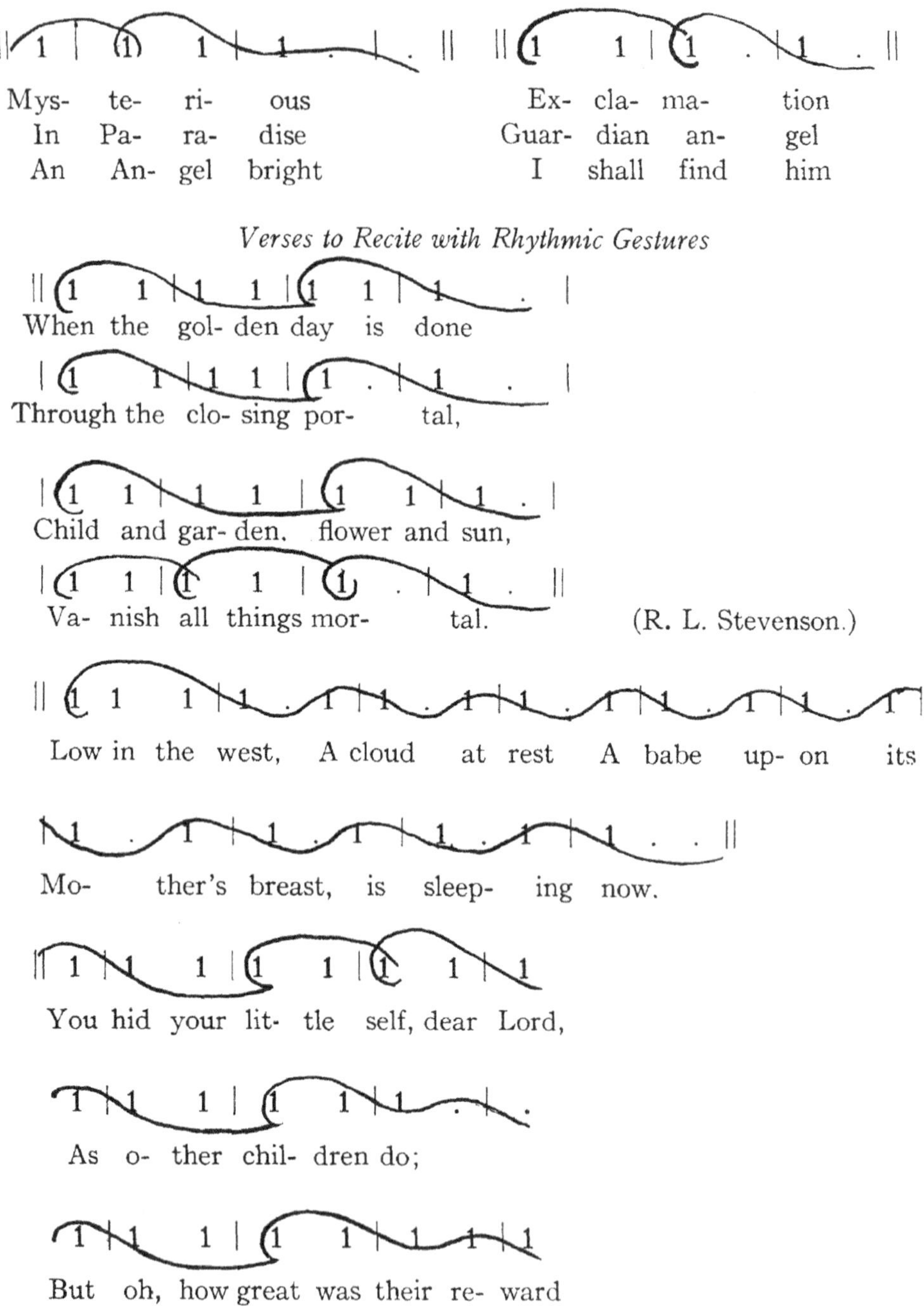
Mys- te- ri- ous
In Pa- ra- dise
An An- gel bright
Ex- cla- ma- tion
Guar- dian an- gel
I shall find him
Verses to Recite with Rhythmic Gestures
When the gol- den day is done
Through the clo- sing por- tal,
Child and gar- den. flower and sun,
Va- nish all things mor- tal.
(R. L. Stevenson.)
Low in the west, A cloud at rest A babe up- on its
Mo- ther's breast, is sleep- ing now.
You hid your lit- tle self, dear Lord,
As o- ther chil- dren do;
But oh, how great was their re- ward

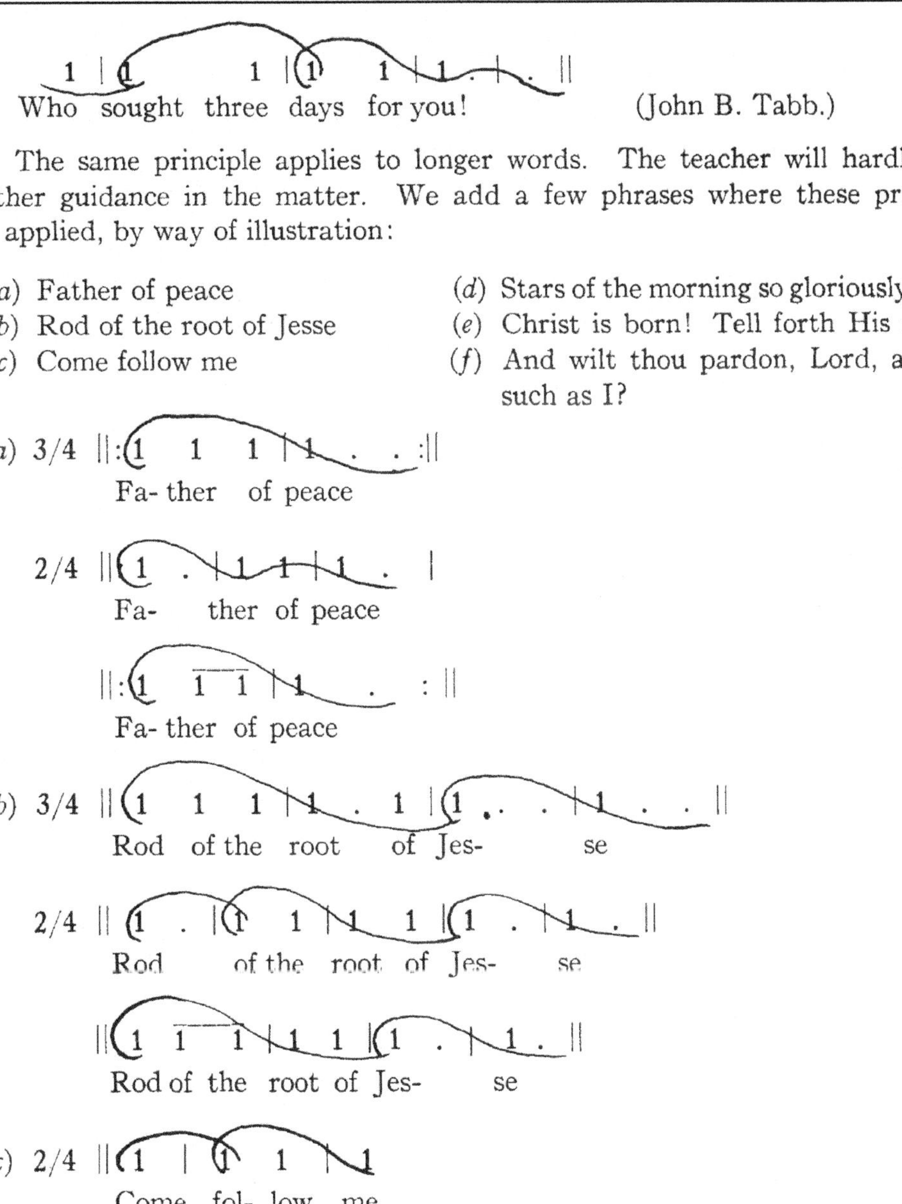

(John B. Tabb.)

The same principle applies to longer words. The teacher will hardly need further guidance in the matter. We add a few phrases where these principles are applied, by way of illustration:

(*a*) Father of peace
(*b*) Rod of the root of Jesse
(*c*) Come follow me
(*d*) Stars of the morning so gloriously bright
(*e*) Christ is born! Tell forth His fame!
(*f*) And wilt thou pardon, Lord, a sinner such as I?

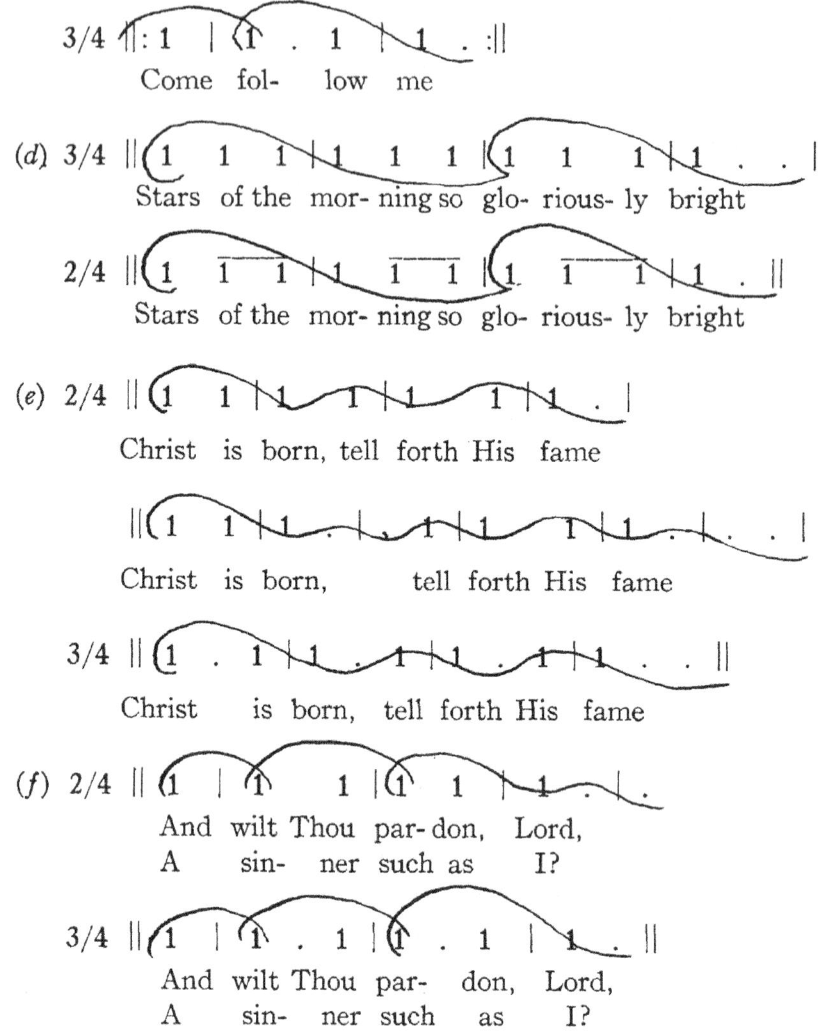

After working out on the board a few examples of this sort, the children will learn to scan a line correctly at sight. Exercises in rapid visualization should be employed, using words and rhythmic gestures. Later, the children should not only *write* melodies to little poems, but should even improvise the music to simple phrases, at sight. The teacher will be careful to select phrases that do not offer difficulties or rhythmic irregularities during the early stages of the work, lest confusion be caused.

The rhythmic recitation of a line is the first step toward the improvisation of a melody. The child repeats the line softly several times, choosing the rhythmic treatment he wants to give it. After repeating the line softly and rhythmically, the melody should form itself spontaneously translating the child's own feeling for the text. At first the teacher should not interfere with this process. Later suggestions may be offered regarding *the melody of words and phrases*. Encouragement and stimulation will produce better results than dry criticism; a set of iron-clad rules will completely paralyze the child's creative musical instinct.

When the teacher feels that the moment has come to open the children's eyes to certain fundamental laws of beauty in this respect, he may develop the following ideas:

1. The *accented* syllable (or the accent of the most important word in a phrase) should be placed at the summit of the melody, a rise in pitch being the most eloquent manner of giving that syllable its due importance. A diagram can be put on the board as follows.

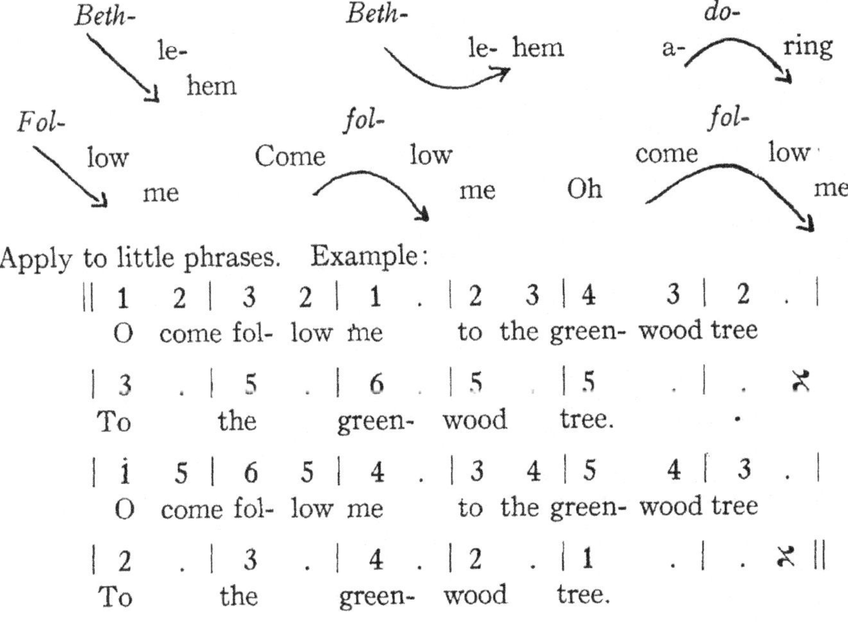

In this example, the accented syllable of each word is raised in pitch above the other syllables. It is not necessary that all should be raised in this manner; indeed such a thing would become monotonous. The important thing is to give melodic prominence to the *most important* word, and let the melody rise toward the accent of that word.

Example

Christ is born! Let all rejoice! Which word do we want to place in bold relief? We can sing:

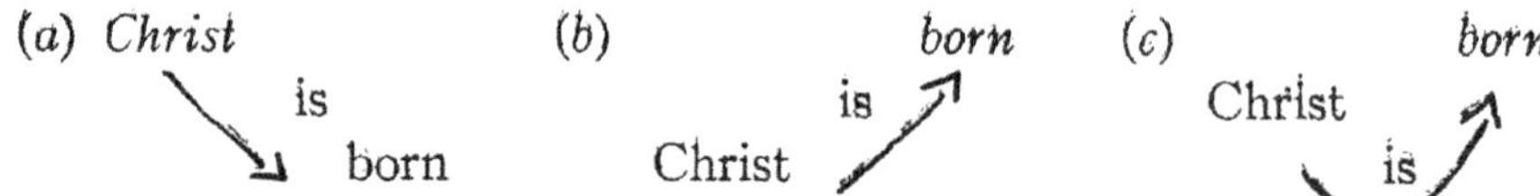

According to the sense we wish to give to that phrase we will compose our melody:

(*a*) || 5 3 | 1   (*b*) || 5 6 | 1̇   (*c*) || 3 1 | 5
Christ is born   Christ is *born*   *Christ* is *born*

Either one would be correct. When that first theme is settled we must link to it the end of the phrase: "Let all rejoice."

Three themes

(*a*) || 5 3 | 1   (*b*) || 5 6 | 1̇   (*c*) || 3 1 | 5
Christ   born   Christ born

All three themes follow the chord line. We should either continue along the same chord line, or else use the scale line. As our affirmation is definite in direction, we should turn in order to make a curve, thus:

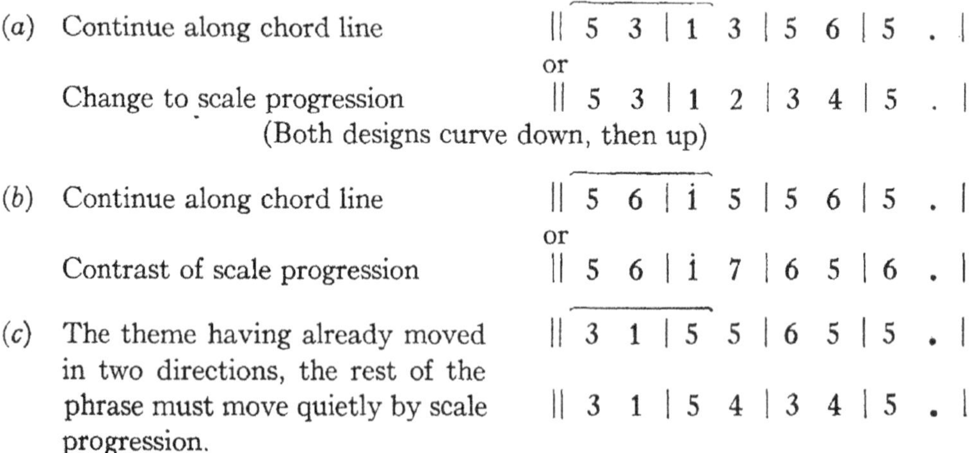

(*a*) Continue along chord line || 5 3 | 1 3 | 5 6 | 5 . |
or
Change to scale progression || 5 3 | 1 2 | 3 4 | 5 . |
(Both designs curve down, then up)

(*b*) Continue along chord line || 5 6 | 1̇ 5 | 5 6 | 5 . |
or
Contrast of scale progression || 5 6 | 1̇ 7 | 6 5 | 6 . |

(*c*) The theme having already moved in two directions, the rest of the phrase must move quietly by scale progression. || 3 1 | 5 5 | 6 5 | 5 . |
|| 3 1 | 5 4 | 3 4 | 5 . |

These are the most common rules for melodic progression.

In this case, to make the idea plain, we have chosen only the first half of the phrase "Christ is born," composed three themes, and made the rest of the phrase conform to the beginning.

A better way would be to think of the *whole phrase:* "Christ is born, let all rejoice." Let the child repeat the phrase gently and decide *which words* are to receive the melodic accent. This will at once give a sort of melodic diagram of the phrase as a whole.

|| 5 3 | 1 2 | 3 4 | 5 . | (*Christ* and *rejoice* have the melodic accent.)
Christ re- joice

|| 5 6 | 1̇ 5 | 6 5 | 5 . | (*born* and *all* have accent.)
born all

|| 3 1 | 5 4 | 3 4 | 5 . | (*Christ, born* and *rejoice.*)
Christ born re- joice

This habit of giving the significant word a rising melody should be cultivated in the children. Let them feel that language itself possesses a germinal melody. With their cultivated sense of rhythm, this cultivated sense of the melody of language will become natural and instinctive and will have an excellent influence on their reading and pronunciation.

In course of the chapters, we will insert little phrases which adapt themselves to the rhythmic designs that are being studied during the week that the children may have the joy of the two-fold rhythmic experience—the purely musical rhythm and the verbal rhythm. The teacher may use these little phrases as a basis for composition of melodies, as home work for the children. Such home work delights the children.

We have gathered together, in this introductory part of the book, the suggestions for the correlation of rhythm and language, with the idea that the teacher will be more free to introduce the subject at the point where it will be most helpful.

VOCAL EXERCISES

Review the Vocal Exercises of the First Year.

1. Use the syllable *Nu* (noo) on single, sustained tones, then on phrases sung legato.

2. Use the syllables *Nu-o* and *Nu-o-a*, as described in the first year, on single, sustained tones, then on longer phrases.

In pronouncing the consonants "N" or "M" the children should not be permitted to *close their teeth*. This bad habit produces a forced and ugly tone.

As soon as this review has accomplished its purpose, namely, a good tone production, forward, light, and without strain, the exercises of the Second Year should be studied. The following principles should be kept in mind:

(*a*) Each day, the vocal exercises should be introduced by a few single tones sung on the syllables *Nu* and *No* (from A to E). The syllables *Mu* and *Mo* may also be used. This assures a forward resonance.

(*b*) This should be followed by one or two tones on which the whole series of syllables, *Nu-o-a-e-i* or *Mu-o-a-e-i*, will be sung.

(*c*) After this preparation, the direct attack of the various vowel sounds, as embodied in the vocal exercises of the second year, should be studied.

(*d*) In case the tone production should suffer or the resonance of the voices diminish in singing the exercises of the second year, a temporary return to the syllable "*Nu*" should be used as a remedy.

(*e*) There should be no rigidity of throat, lips or tongue, nor any muscular strain whatever. Everything must function simply, naturally, and with the utmost flexibility.

(*f*) In breathing, the children should make *no movement* of the shoulders. They should *not be encouraged to think* that the important thing is the volume of air introduced into the lungs. The important thing is *the use to which we put our supply of air!* An exaggerated supply of air is difficult to control. On the other hand, it is astonishing how long a phrase can be sung with a relatively small supply of air provided we put this supply to good use. The ideal, as usual, is somewhere between the two extremes. We must have enough air, otherwise singing becomes impossible, and not too much, otherwise breath control becomes difficult.

In presenting the single tones during the period when the Major Mode is being studied in the Intonation Exercises, these tones should be presented in the order of the Major Pentachord. When the Seventh or Eighth Modes are being studied, they will follow this order. When, on the contrary, the Minor Mode is being studied, the single tones of the vocal exercises should move along the minor pentachord (6̣ 7̣ 1 2 3).

In order to aid the perfect correlation between vocal exercises and intonation exercises, the exercises are given in three forms—major, minor and eighth mode—marked *a*, *b* and *c* respectively. The teacher will use the form which is adapted to the work in intonation of that lesson.

VOCAL EXERCISES OF THE SECOND YEAR

No. 24a. Major form *No. 24b. Minor form*

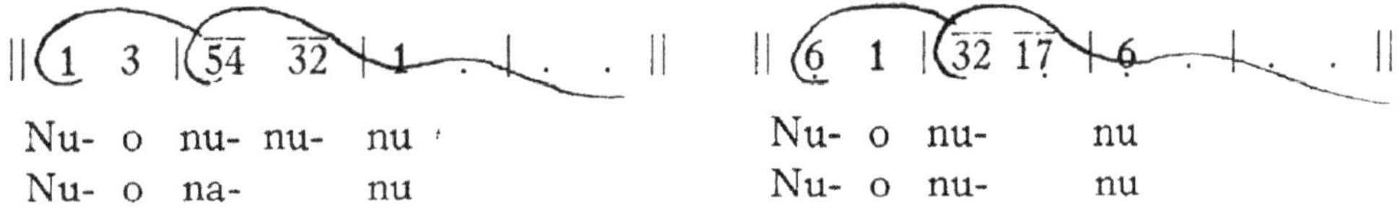

No. 24c. Modes of Sol

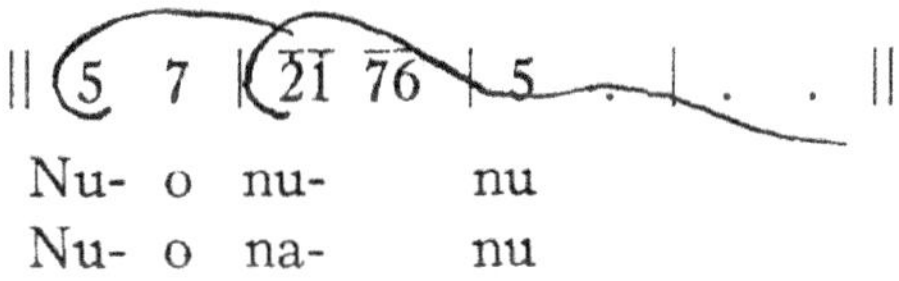

No. 25a. Major form
(A♭, A, B♭, B, C)

No. 25b. Minor form
(Gm, G♯m, Am, B♭m, Bm, Cm, Dm)

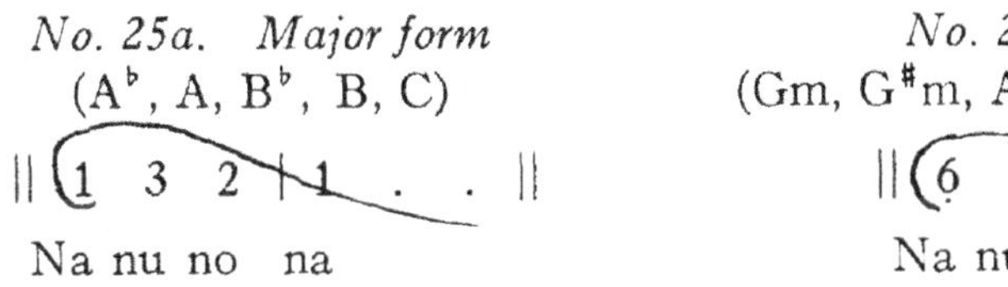

|| 6 1 7 | 6 . . ||
Na nu no na

No. 25c. Modes of Sol

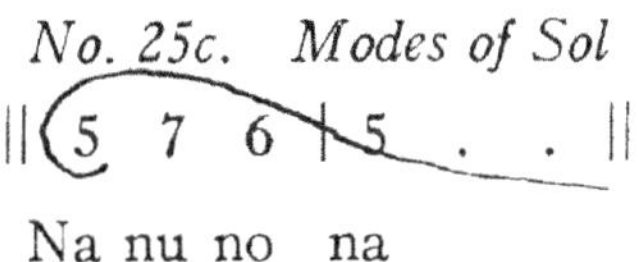

No. 26a (As No. 25) *No. 26b* (As No. 25 except omit *Dm*)

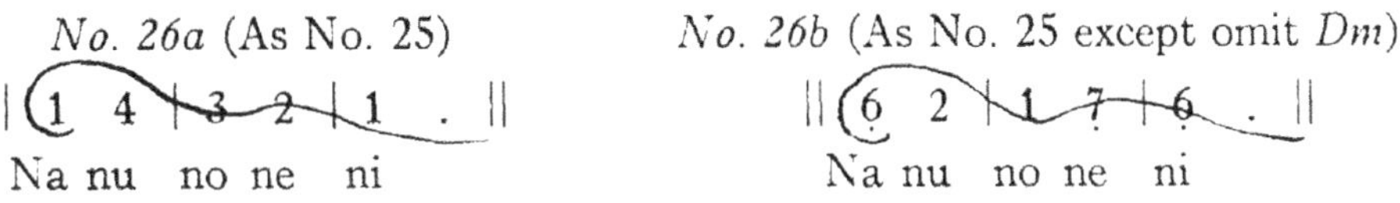

No. 26c

|| 5 i | 7 6 | 5 . | . . ||
Na nu no ne ni

No. 31a

|| 12 34 | 54 32 | 17 65 | 6 7 | 1 . ||

Nu ——— nu ———
No ——— no ———
Na ——— na ———
Ne ——— ne ———
Ni ——— ni ———

No. 31b

|| 67 12 | 32 17 | 6 54 | 3 45 | 6 . ||

Nu ——— nu ———
No ——— no ———
Na ——— na ———
Ne ——— ne ———
Ni ——— ni ———

In addition to the exercises given above, suggestions will be made in the course of the chapters for special exercises to develop some particular point in connection with the intonation work of that chapter. The exercises listed above should be covered during the year for the general development of the vocal qualities required, namely: a clear articulation of all vowel sounds following the syllable *N* or *M* which, as it were, push the tone forward and high.

When the children are able to sing all the vowel sounds, as embodied in the vocal exercises, with a well placed voice, the teacher may use other consonants, replacing the preliminary *N* or *M* by sounds which require a crisp, free motion of the lips and the tongue. It is difficult to fix arbitrarily the precise moment for the introduction of this work. If it be delayed too long, the lips and tongue will become lazy and, as it were, paralyzed in the "*Nu*" position. If it be introduced too quickly, the tone may lose its resonance. We can only give the general advice that other consonants should be tried as soon as the "N" and "M" are no longer needed to obtain the placing of the tone.

The consonants other than *N* and *M* should be pronounced in a whisper, without singing them. Later they should be sung. It is useful to alternate a consonant requiring flexibility of the *lips* with one which requires agility of the *tongue.*

B and *P:* are formed by the ***lips***. The passage of air between lips gently closed produces these sounds.

T and *D:* are formed by the ***tongue***. The passage of air between the tip of the tongue and the upper teeth produces these sounds.

R: must be formed, in singing, very far forward in the mouth, and not in the throat. This delicate rolling sound is produced between the tip of the tongue and the roots of the upper teeth.

An alternation of the two kinds of consonants will provide the maximum of flexibility in the use of the lips and of the tongue. Syllables such as the following should be recited rhythmically:

Ba-ta, Bra-ta, Pa-da, Pra-da, etc.

| 1 1 | 1 1 | $\overline{1\ 1}$ $\overline{1\ 1}$ | $\overline{1\ 1}$ $\overline{1\ 1}$ | 1 . | . . ||

Ba- ta ba- ta ba- ta ba- ta ba- ta ba ta ba.
Bra- ta bra- ta bra- ta bra- ta bra- ta bra- ta bra.

Other vowels and other consonants can be used. This rhythmic recitation, in a whisper should precede any attempt to *sing* these sounds.

Nothing should be said to the children about *lips* or *tongue*. To draw attention to these organs produces immediate rigidity. The pupils should be given exercises which require their use.

A good exercise, in this connection, is to allow one child to pronounce a sentence ***under his breath*** and see whether the other children can guess the meaning. A phrase conveying an order requiring action on the part of the one who "hears," makes this exercise a sort of game. In reality, it is an exercise in lip-reading. Many children speak with a certain rigidity of the lips, and the fault becomes a grave one when they sing. In all this work, a certain discretion must be observed, lest there be exaggeration, for any movement beyond what is natural and necessary for a neat articulation becomes a grimace, which is worse than the fault it seeks to correct.

CHAPTER ONE

Vocal Exercises. Syllable *Nu.* As in the first year.

Intonation.—Review of the Major Pentachord and Tetrachord, using *Diagrams 3 and 4* of the first year.

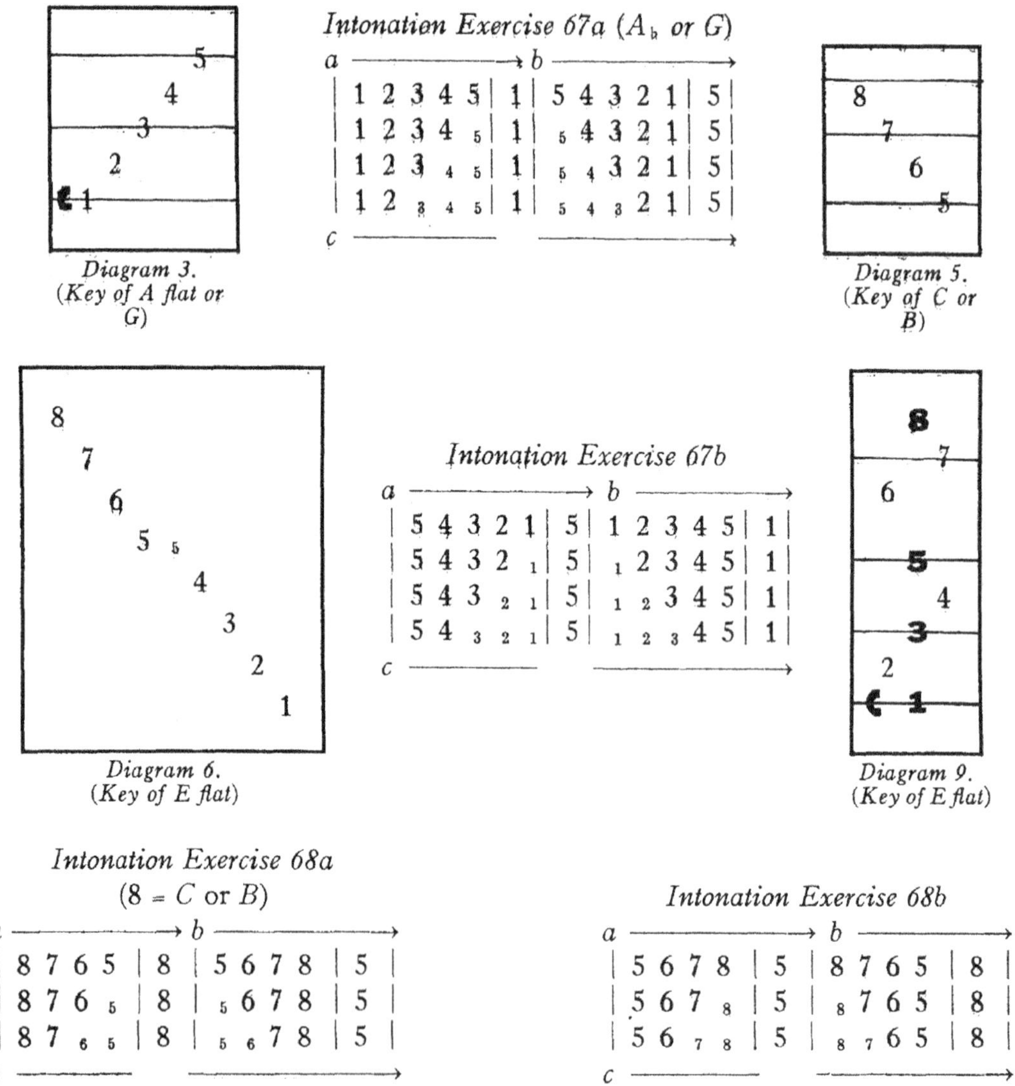

Diagram 3. (Key of A flat or G)

Diagram 5. (Key of C or B)

Diagram 6. (Key of E flat)

Diagram 9. (Key of E flat)

Intonation Exercise 67a ($A_\flat$ *or G*)

a ⟶ b ⟶

a		b	
1 2 3 4 5	1	5 4 3 2 1	5
1 2 3 4 5	1	5 4 3 2 1	5
1 2 3 4 5	1	5 4 3 2 1	5
1 2 3 4 5	1	5 4 3 2 1	5

c ⟶

Intonation Exercise 67b

a		b	
5 4 3 2 1	5	1 2 3 4 5	1
5 4 3 2 1	5	1 2 3 4 5	1
5 4 3 2 1	5	1 2 3 4 5	1
5 4 3 2 1	5	1 2 3 4 5	1

c ⟶

Intonation Exercise 68a

(8 = *C* or *B*)

a		b	
8 7 6 5	8	5 6 7 8	5
8 7 6 5	8	5 6 7 8	5
8 7 6 5	8	5 6 7 8	5

c ⟶

Intonation Exercise 68b

a		b	
5 6 7 8	5	8 7 6 5	8
5 6 7 8	5	8 7 6 5	8
5 6 7 8	5	8 7 6 5	8

c ⟶

Intonation Exercise 69a

(Key of E flat or D)

a →		b →	
8 7 6 5 4 3 2 1	8	1 2 3 4 5 6 7 8	1 8
8 7 6 5 4 3 2 1	8	1 2 3 4 5 6 7 8	1 8
8 7 6 5 4 3 2 1	8	1 2 3 4 5 6 7 8	1 8
8 7 6 5 4 3 2 1	8	1 2 3 4 5 6 7 8	1 8
8 7 6 5 4 3 2 1	8	1 2 3 4 5 6 7 8	1 8
8 7 6 5 4 3 2 1	8	1 2 3 4 5 6 7 8	1 8
8 7 6 5 4 3 2 1	8	1 2 3 4 5 6 7 8	1 8

c →

Intonation Exercise 69b

a →		b →	
1 2 3 4 5 6 7 8	1	8 7 6 5 4 3 2 1	8
1 2 3 4 5 6 7 8	1	8 7 6 5 4 3 2 1	8
1 2 3 4 5 6 7 8	1	8 7 6 5 4 3 2 1	8
1 2 3 4 5 6 7 8	1	8 7 6 5 4 3 2 1	8
1 2 3 4 5 6 7 8	1	8 7 6 5 4 3 2 1	8
1 2 3 4 5 6 7 8	1	8 7 6 5 4 3 2 1	8
1 2 3 4 5 6 7 8	1	8 7 6 5 4 3 2 1	8

c →

Intonation Exercise 33 and 35, First Year

(Key of E flat)

| 1 2 1 1 2 3 3 4 3 3 4 5 5 6 5 5 6 7 8 8 7 8   8 7 8 8 7 6 5 5 6 5 5 4 3 3 4 3 3 2 1 1 2 1 |

| 1 2 1   3 4 3   5 6 5   8 7 8   8 7 8   5 6 5   3 4 3   1 2 1 |

| 1 2 1   3 4 3   5 6 5   8 7 8   8 7 8   5 6 5   3 4 3   1 2 1 |

Notation Observation

Name the notes, then sing

Rhythmic Exercise 27

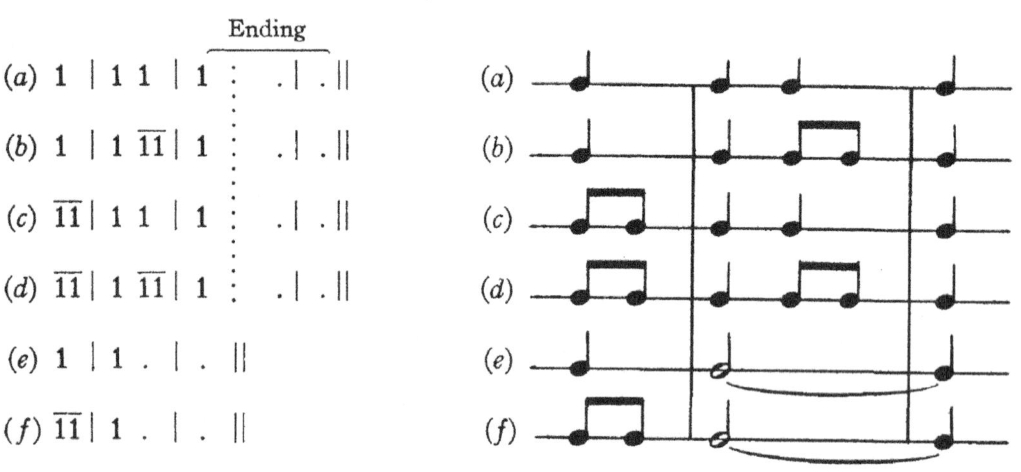

Phrases to Sing at Sight

One Design Repeated

Model b.—1 | 1 $\overline{11}$ | 1

|| 1 | 1 $\overline{12}$ | 1 2 | 3 $\overline{34}$ | 3
3 | 5 $\overline{65}$ | 4 3 | 2 $\overline{34}$ | 5
5 | 6 $\overline{54}$ | 3 2 | 1 . | . ||

Model b + b and b + e

|| 3 | 1 $\overline{12}$ | 3 3 | 5 $\overline{43}$ | 2
2 |. 2 $\overline{23}$ | 4 3 | 5 . | .
5 | 5 $\overline{67}$ | $\dot{1}$ 5 | 6 $\overline{54}$ | 3
3 | 2 $\overline{34}$ | 3 2 | 1 . | . ||

Model c.—$\overline{11}$ | 1 1 | 1

|| $\overline{32}$ | 1 1 | 1 $\overline{34}$ | 5 5 | 5
$\overline{56}$ | 5 4 | 3 $\overline{43}$ | 2 2 | 1 ||

|| $\overline{32}$ | 1 3 | 3 $\overline{34}$ | 3 5 | 5
$\overline{56}$ | 5 $\dot{1}$ | $\dot{1}$ $\overline{76}$ | 5 4 | 3
$\overline{32}$ | 1 3 | 5 $\overline{32}$ | 1 . | . ||

$\overline{32}$ | 1 3 | 5 $\overline{34}$ | 5 6 | 5
$\overline{56}$ | 5 6 | $\dot{1}$ $\overline{76}$ | 5 6 | 5
$\overline{34}$ | 5 3 | 2 $\overline{32}$ | 1 . | . ||

Model d.—$\overline{11}$ | 1 $\overline{11}$ | 1

|| $\overline{12}$ | 3 $\overline{32}$ | 1 $\overline{34}$ | 5 $\overline{56}$ | 5
$\overline{34}$ | 5 $\overline{34}$ | 5 $\overline{34}$ | 5 $\overline{67}$ | $\dot{1}$
$\overline{17}$ | $\dot{1}$ $\overline{76}$ | 5 $\overline{67}$ | $\dot{1}$ $\overline{76}$ | 5
$\overline{17}$ | $\dot{1}$ $\overline{56}$ | 5 $\overline{34}$ | 3 $\overline{12}$ | 1

|| $\overline{12}$ | 1 $\overline{34}$ | 3 $\overline{56}$ | 5 $\overline{32}$ | 1
$\overline{12}$ | 1 $\overline{34}$ | 5 $\overline{67}$ | $\dot{1}$ $\overline{76}$ | 5
$\overline{56}$ | 5 $\overline{17}$ | $\dot{1}$ $\overline{17}$ | 6 $\overline{56}$ | 5
$\overline{54}$ | 3 $\overline{43}$ | 2 $\overline{32}$ | 1 . | . ||

Model c + c and c + e. c + c and c + f

|| $\overline{32}$ | 1 1 | 1 $\overline{34}$ | 5 6 | 5
$\overline{34}$ | 5 6 | 5 6 | 5 . | .
$\overline{56}$ | 5 6 | 5 $\overline{17}$ | 6 5 | 3
$\overline{32}$ | 1 3 | 5 $\overline{32}$ | 1 . | . ||

Model d + d and d + f

|| $\overline{12}$ | 3 $\overline{32}$ | 1 $\overline{34}$ | 5 $\overline{34}$ | 5
$\overline{34}$ | 5 $\overline{17}$ | $\dot{1}$ $\overline{76}$ | 5 . | .
$\overline{17}$ | $\dot{1}$ $\overline{76}$ | 5 $\overline{67}$ | $\dot{1}$ $\overline{76}$ | 5
$\overline{56}$ | 5 $\overline{43}$ | 2 $\overline{32}$ | 1 . | . ||

Rhythm and Melody
(a + b + c + d + e + f)

|| 3 | 1 3 | 5
3 | 5 $\overline{43}$ | 2
$\overline{32}$ | 1 3 | 5
$\overline{34}$ | 5 $\overline{43}$ | 2
3 | 5 . | .
$\overline{32}$ | 1 . | . ||

|| $\dot{1}$ | 5 6 | 5
$\dot{1}$ | 5 $\overline{34}$ | 5
$\overline{34}$ | 5 6 | 5
$\overline{56}$ | 5 $\overline{34}$ | 5
$\dot{1}$ | 5 . | .
$\overline{17}$ | $\dot{1}$. | . ||

Prepare by reciting Rhythmic Exercise 27 with Gesture 1 or 2.

Notation, Rhythm and Melody

Name notes rhythmically. Sing

Designs Used to Form a Free Melody

|| $\overline{56}$ | 5 . | .
$\overline{32}$ | 1 $\overline{23}$ | 4 $\overline{32}$ | 3 . | 𝄽
$\overline{56}$ | 5 . | .
$\overline{32}$ | 1 $\overline{23}$ | 4 $\overline{32}$ | 1 . | . ||

Diagram 28b

From these exercises on the Pentachord and Tetrachord, pass to those on the whole scale and on the Compass Exercise.

Review the same material on the staff, with the *do clef* on the first line.

The same diagrams should be used for rapid visualization, both with numbers and with staff notation.

Rhythm.—Review *Simple Rhythm and Simple Time* from *Year I*, with *Rhythmic Movements 1 and 2.*

The new children in the class will use the designs with one note to a pulse. The children who have studied music last year will use each of the *Rhythmic Designs* in *Rhythmic Exercise 27* as follows:

(*a*) One design repeated until it becomes familiar, always with Rhythmic Gesture 1 or 2. Thus:

(*b*) ||: 1 | 1 $\overline{11}$ | 1 1 | 1 $\overline{11}$ | 1 :||

During this time, phrases conforming to this design should be composed. Dictation, observation, aural memory exercises—all should aid to form a solid and durable impression of that design. The same process will be followed for the others.

Dictation (Rhythmic only)

(*a*) *One design.*—The children say *which one?*

(*b*) *One design.*—The children write it on the board.

(*c*) *Two designs combined to make a long one.*—The children say *which two?*

(*d*) *Two designs.*—The children write them on the board.

Melodic Dictation will follow the principles outlined in the first year book.

Rhythmic dictation (without melody) as outlined above.

Melody and Rhythm (None for the new children). For the old students, such forms as the following:

Dictation: Melody and Rhythm

|| 1 | 3 2 | 1 $\overline{12}$ | 3 4 | 5 $\overline{23}$ | 4 $\overline{32}$ | 3

1 | 3 $\overline{32}$ | 1 $\overline{56}$ | 5 $\overline{43}$ | 2 $\overline{23}$ | 2 . | .

$\overline{32}$ | 1 . | . ||

The teacher dictates one line at a time, preferably with his voice (failing which, with the harmonium). The children write the phrases, or answer by singing the tones with their names.

Observation.—1. One Design Repeated.
2. Two designs alternated and repeated.

This exercise is planned to sharpen the children's perception regarding the relation of metrical designs to the fundamental rhythm.

1. The children make Rhythmic Gesture 1 or 2.

2. The teacher *taps a design* and repeats the same, in perfect time with the gesture of the children. (The various designs should be left before their eyes as an aid to the ear.)

3. Without interrupting their rhythmic movements, each child—as soon as the teacher's design is recognized—will say (as the case requires):

a | a a | a
b | b bb | b
cc | c c | c etc.

pronouncing rhythmically as above while fitting the design into the rhythmic movement.

At a sign from the teacher, the children stop repeating the design, but continue the rhythmic movement. Whereupon the teacher taps a *different* design. Once more the children recognize it, pronounce it by letter, rhythmically, fitting it into the gesture. Thus, alternately, the children *listen in silence*, recognize, and repeat.

When this has become relatively simple (and it will not take long), then *two designs*, alternated, and repeated, should be offered in precisely the same manner. Evidently the teacher must tap these designs with the utmost precision, briskly, and in time with the movements of the children. If the children should find this exercise difficult at first, it can be prepared by simple, imitative tapping of designs without the rhythmic gestures. Then the study should be made as outlined above.

Observation: two designs alternated (see p. 38)

Composition.—These same designs, a single design repeated, or several in alternation, can be used as themes for the children's compositions.

1. The child *chooses* a design.
2. He decides whether to repeat it or add another.

		Examples					*First line of Melody*
$(a + a)$	‖ 1	3 4	5 5	4 3	2		One design repeated.
$(a + b)$	‖ 1	3 4	5 3	5 $\overline{43}$	2		Two designs combined.
$(c + a)$	‖ $\overline{12}$	3 5	6 5	4 3	2		Two designs combined.
$(d + e)$	‖ $\overline{34}$	5 $\overline{34}$	5 6	5 .	.		Two designs combined.
$(c + c)$	‖ $\overline{12}$	3 5	5 $\overline{67}$	8 5	5		One design repeated.
$(d + c)$	‖ $\overline{54}$	3 $\overline{43}$	2 $\overline{32}$	1 1	1		Two designs combined.

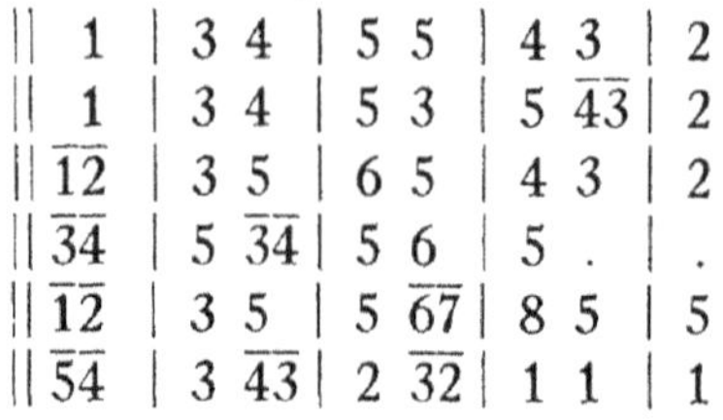

(The number of arrangements of this material is infinite.)
(These examples will illustrate the principle only.)

3. Having composed his first line, an answering phrase must be composed. The second phrase can vary from the first:

(*a*) By a *change of melodic direction.*
(*b*) By a *change of rhythm* (a contrasting metrical design).
(*c*) By a *melodic and rhythmic change.*

An example of each of these contrasts:

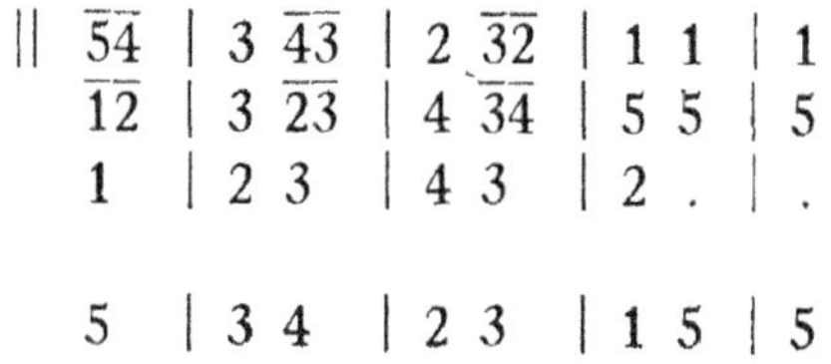

First line.	‖ $\overline{54}$	3 $\overline{43}$	2 $\overline{32}$	1 1	1	
Second line.	$\overline{12}$	3 $\overline{23}$	4 $\overline{34}$	5 5	5	Change of melodic direction.
Second line.	1	2 3	4 3	2 .	.	Change of melodic direction and rhythm.
Second line.	5	3 4	2 3	1 5	5	Change of rhythm.

Each of these examples assumes that the melody is to continue. In the *third line* there will be a *contrast* if the second has been similar to the first. There will be *repetition* (likeness) if the second has already provided a contrast. We give an example below, but suggest that the teacher examine the various melodies provided in Music First and Second Year for examples of contrasts and likenesses.

Melody with much unity and little variety.

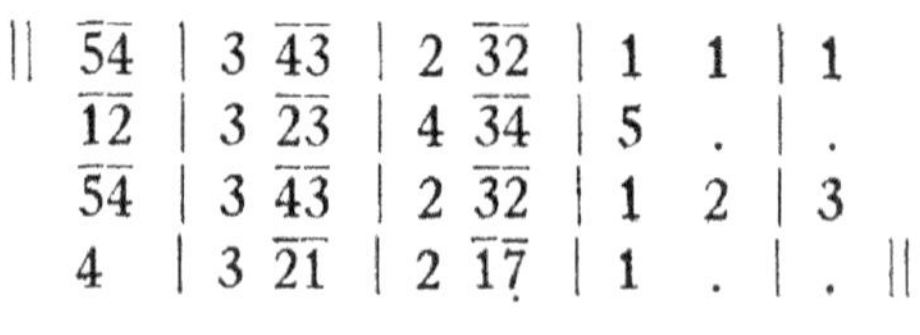

‖ $\overline{54}$	3 $\overline{43}$	2 $\overline{32}$	1 1	1
$\overline{12}$	3 $\overline{23}$	4 $\overline{34}$	5 .	.
$\overline{54}$	3 $\overline{43}$	2 $\overline{32}$	1 2	3
4	3 $\overline{21}$	2 $\overline{1\underset{.}{7}}$	1 .	. ‖

To give a melodic contrast without changing the rhythmic scheme, change *Line 3* to read as follows:

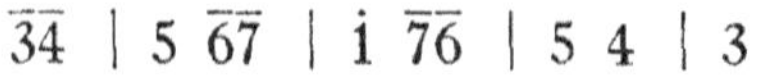

$\overline{34}$ | 5 $\overline{67}$ | $\dot{1}$ $\overline{76}$ | 5 4 | 3

If more rhythmic contrast is desired, the melody could be developed as follows:

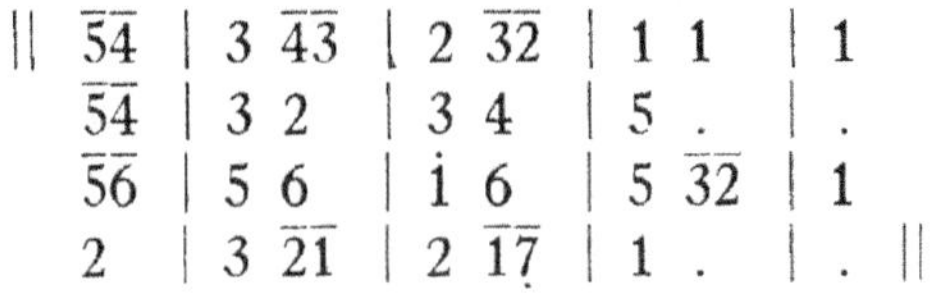

$$\begin{array}{llllll}
\| \; \overline{54} & |\; 3\;\overline{43} & |\; 2\;\overline{32} & |\; 1\;1 & |\; 1 & \\
\;\;\;\overline{54} & |\; 3\;2 & |\; 3\;4 & |\; 5\;. & |\; . & \\
\;\;\;\overline{56} & |\; 5\;6 & |\; \dot{1}\;6 & |\; 5\;\overline{32} & |\; 1 & \\
\;\;\;2 & |\; 3\;\overline{21} & |\; 2\;\overline{1\underset{.}{7}} & |\; 1\;. & |\; . & \|
\end{array}$$

The combinations are without limit *in themselves*, and the children may be encouraged to experiment. When they have tried various combinations, then the teacher may make suggestions along the following general lines:

1. There must not be *too many surprises* in a good melody. If we want a rhythmic surprise, let the melody move along rather quietly. If we want a melodic surprise (a change from the lower pentachord to the upper tetrachord, or a change from the scale progression to the chord progression) then we must keep our rhythm rather quiet.

2. Usually at the center and at the end (but *always* at the end) we feel the need of a design with a long cadence (*e* or *f* in the designs of this chapter). This sets before us the two halves of the melody and gives us time to breathe!

3. In the second half of the melody we must always provide something which brings back a memory of the first half. (See the designs of the First Year: *a b + a b; a a + b b; a b + b a;* etc.) It is not necessary to repeat exactly what has gone before, but a *reminder* of some part of the beginning knits the melody together.

Usually a few suggestions of this nature suffice. A set of fixed rules imposed by the teacher tends to kill the spontaneity of the young composers.

Improvisations.—Purely melodic, then melodic and rhythmic, then with rhythmic gestures.

Metrical conversations.—A child taps one of the designs, lightly (using the back of the hand on which to tap). Another child answers by tapping the same design, or another of his choice. From the tapping of a single design, the tapping of two designs will follow without difficulty. The tapping must be neat and strictly in time. The children may be allowed to tap one or more designs for the class to *guess which one.*

The teacher may tap or sing *recto tono* the rhythmic design of a song that the children know well. The child who recognizes the melody raises his hand and gives the name of the song.

Staff Notation.—The exercises are divided into those intended for eye training (rapid visualization and *naming* of the tones) and those which are intended for singing.

Melodies.—Where a melody contains difficulties of rhythmic designs (as No. 84 in this chapter) the teacher should put the rhythmic scheme on the board, and use it for rhythmic drill before singing the melody, thus:

Melody 84

|| 1 | 1 $\overline{11}$ | 1 1 | 1 . | .

1 | $\overline{11}$ 1 | 1 1 | 1 . | .

1 | 1 1 | 1 $\overline{11}$ | 1 1 | 1 . | .

1 | 1 1 | $\overline{11}$ 1 | 1 . | . ||

Such preparation will be found valuable as regards all staff melodies containing eighth notes, at least on the early part of the school year. It will take less time than would be required later to correct an error resulting from a vague grasp of the rhythm.

Where a melody contains a difficult interval (as No. 85: 3 6 5; and No. 86: 2 5) this difficulty should be prepared in advance on the fingers or on the board.

Plan of a Lesson.—As in the first year, the matter should be so presented to the children as to keep their interest and attention at the highest point. Consequently, the teacher will alternate the moments of intense concentration with those of action. The moments of attention are slightly longer during the second year than during the first.

Plan of a Lesson

1. Vocal Exercises.
2. Intonation from Chart, Blackboard and (or) fingers.
3. Rhythmic gestures, and tapping of designs.
4. Dictation (melodic on intonation material).
5. Vocal Exercises.
6. Singing of melody.
7. Observation and memory. (Numbers and (or) staff.)
8. Composition or improvisation.
9. Metrical conversation (tapping of designs).

The teacher need not follow this precise plan, but may vary it according to need, bearing in mind the general principles for the organization of a lesson already explained in the first year.

CHAPTER TWO

Vocal Exercises.—Syllable *Nu* (*noo*) as in First Year.
Intonation.—Review of Tonic chord and Compass Exercise (continued).

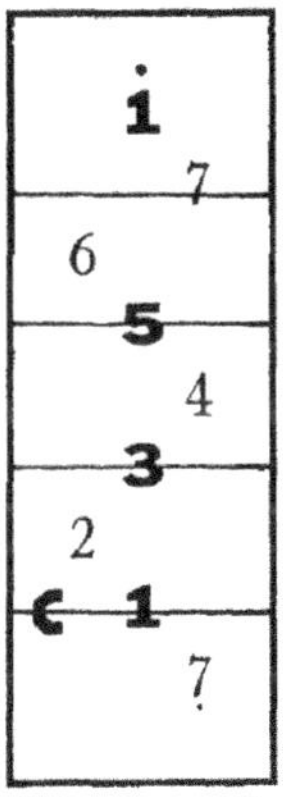

1̇
7
6
5
4
3
2
C 1
7

Diagram 29.

Compass Exercise (Key of G or A♭)

Use Diagram 29, also horizontal form

| 1 2 1 3 4 3 5 6 5 | 5 6 5 3 4 3 1 2 1 |
| 1 2 1 $_{3\ 4\ 3}$ 5 6 5 | 5 6 5 $_{3\ 4\ 3}$ 1 2 1 |

Compass Exercise (Key of C or D)

Use Diagram 29 also horizontal form

| 1̇ 7 1̇ 5 6 5 3 4 3 | 3 4 3 5 6 5 1̇ 7 1̇ |
| 1̇ 7 1̇ $_{5\ 6\ 5}$ 3 4 3 | 3 4 3 $_{5\ 6\ 5}$ 1̇ 7 1̇ |

Tonic Chord Review (Key of G or A♭)

Use Diagram 29, also horizontal form

(*a*) | 121 343 565 565 343 121 | 565 343 121 121 343 565 |
| 1_{21} 3_{43} 5_{65} 5_{65} 3_{43} 1_{21} | 5_{65} 3_{43} 1_{21} 1_{21} 3_{43} 5_{65} |
| 1 3 5 5 3 1 | 5 3 1 1 3 5 |51

(*b*) | 121 343 565 565 343 121 | 565 343 121 121 343 565 |
| $_{1}$21 $_{3}$43 $_{5}$65 $_{5}$65 $_{3}$43 $_{1}$21 | $_{5}$65 $_{3}$43 $_{1}$21 $_{1}$21 $_{3}$43 $_{5}$65 |

(*c*) | 121 343 565 1̇71̇ | 1̇71̇ 565 343 121 | (*Key of E flat*)
| $_{1}$21 $_{3}$43 $_{5}$65 1̇71̇ | 1̇71̇ $_{5}$65 $_{3}$43 $_{1}$21 |
| 1 3 5 1̇ | 1̇ 5 3 1 |

Intonation Exercise 70

Use Diagram 29, also horizontal form

12345 | 1 3 5 $_{1}$21 $_{3}$43 $_{5}$65 | 5 3 1 $_{5}$65 $_{3}$43 $_{1}$ 2 1 |
| 1 3 1 $_{3}$5 $_{1}$21 $_{3\ 4\ 3}$ $_{5}$65 | 5 3 5 $_{3}$1 $_{5}$65 $_{3\ 4\ 3}$ 2 1 |
| 1 $_{3}$5 $_{3}$1 3 43 $_{5}$65 | 5 $_{3}$1 $_{3}$5 3 $_{5}$65 $_{4}$3 2 1 |

Then two designs alternated and repeated

||: $\overline{11}$	| $\overline{11}$ $\overline{11}$	| $\overline{11}$' $\overline{11}$	| $\overline{11}$ $\overline{11}$	| 1'	:||	(*h* + *i*.)
||: $\overline{11}$	| $\overline{11}$ $\overline{11}$	| $\overline{11}$' $\overline{11}$	| 1 .	| .	:||	(*h* + *f*.)
||: 1	| $\overline{11}$ $\overline{11}$	| 1 ' 1	| 1 1	| 1	:||	(*g* + *a*.)
||: 1	| 1 1	| 1 ' 1	| $\overline{11}$ $\overline{11}$	| 1	:||	(*a* + *g*.)
||: $\overline{11}$	| $\overline{11}$ $\overline{11}$	| $\overline{11}$' $\overline{11}$	| 1 1	| 1	:||	(*h* + *b*.)
||: $\overline{11}$	| $\overline{11}$ $\overline{11}$	| 1 1	| 1 .	| .	:||	(*i* + *e*.)

The designs of Chapter One must be before the class as well as those of Chapter Two.

Rhythm and Melody

|| $\overline{12}$ | 1 $\overline{34}$ | 3 $\overline{56}$ | 5 . | .
$\overline{56}$ | $\overline{54}$ $\overline{32}$ | 1 2 | 1 . | . ||

|| $\overline{32}$ | $\overline{12}$ $\overline{34}$ | 5 6 | 5 . | .
$\overline{87}$ | 8 $\overline{56}$ | 5 $\overline{32}$ | 1 . | . ||

2 Designs

|| 2 | 1 4 | 3 6 | 5 . | .
$\overline{56}$ | $\overline{54}$ $\overline{32}$ | $\overline{12}$ $\overline{31}$ | 2 . | .
$\overline{23}$ | $\overline{43}$ $\overline{23}$ | $\overline{45}$ $\overline{67}$ | $\dot{1}$. | .
6 | 5 $\overline{12}$ | 3 2 | 1 . | . ||

3 Designs (Rigaudon, Rameau)

|| $\overline{54}$ | 3 1 | 1 2 | 3 $\overline{23}$ | 1
5 | 6 5 | 4 4 | $\overline{34}$ $\overline{32}$ | 1

Children should discover and indicate each design. Finish the above melody.

Rhythm, Melody and Staff Notation

Melody 87

Observation

Diagram 31

Study Melodies 88 and 89, Children's Manual, page 7.
Sing Song: The Annunciation, Children's Manual, page 6.

Vocal Exercises on the syllable *Nu* (No. 1, 6, 7, 11 and 12) of the first year. As soon as the tone is light and resonant, using the single tones, one of the longer exercises combining rhythm and melody should be sung.

Intonation.—Continue the review of the *Tonic Chord* and *Compass Exercise,* and in so doing, drill the children in the use of help notes, as a bridge from tone to tone, and from group to group. The diagrams enable the teacher to vary this work according to the capacity of his class.

The intonation work should be developed *in numbers and on the staff.*

Rapid observation should be developed with both forms of notation, as described in Chapter One.

Rhythm.—Three new designs, all beginning on the up-pulse, are added to those of last week. Each design must be studied and repeated with Rhythmic movement 1 or 2. Rhythmic ear tests must be given with *one design repeated; two designs alternated* and *repeated,* as described in Chapter One. Since the three new designs must be used in relation to the earlier ones, studied last week, the whole series (*a* to *i*) should be available that the children may be helped by the eye as well as the ear. We have included several examples of alternating designs as examples of the type of work suggested, but these examples are by no means all that can be done with the material.

Rhythm and Melody.—If the children hesitate, let them use these examples as a metrical exercise first, and when the rhythm is clear, sing the melody. This hesitation is more likely to occur with the phrases on the staff, rather than with those in numbers. It is always wiser to separate the difficulties rather than allow the children to become discouraged.

Staff Notation.—*Do* on the first line, to which we may add some work with *Do* on the second line if it can be done without producing confusion. (See Diagram 30, and Melodies 87 and 89). The children should transcribe some of the examples of *rhythm and melody* to the staff with *do* on the first line, then on the second.

The *tapping of designs* while the children make the rhythmic movements should be continued and developed, using the new designs as well as the old.

Melodic dictation will follow the lines of the review (*Tonic Chord*, and *Compass Exercise* in the *do-do* range).

The rhythmic dictation will make use of the new and old designs.

The experienced teacher will avoid giving a difficult interval when dictating a phrase with divided beat. The interval work should be established by means of *short phrases* dictated *without any rhythm;* and, little by little, with the notes rhythmed simply, thus:

Example of the Process

(*Interval 3 6 5*)

Dictation without Rhythm

```
| 1 2 3 4 5           |
| 1 2 1 3 4 3 5 6 5   |

| 21 43 65            |
| 1  43 65            |
| 1     3 65          |
```

Dictation with Rhythm

```
2 | 1   2 | 3   . | .
4 | 3   6 | 5   . | .
4 | 3   6 | 5   4 | 3   . | .
6 | 5   4 | 3   2 | 1   . | .
```

In general the rhythmic dictation with divided beat must be confined to the simple scale progression, depending on the tones of the tonic chord. Otherwise the children will be puzzled.

Dictation with Divided Beat

```
3  | 1   3  | 5
32 | 1   34 | 5
32 | 12  34 | 5

5  | 3   3  | 1
54 | 3   32 | 1
54 | 34  32 | 1 etc.
```

```
3  | 1   3  | 5   6  | 5
32 | 12  34 | 5   6  | 5
5  | 6   5  | 3   2  | 1
5  | 6   54 | 3   2  | 1
5  | 6   54 | 34  32 | 1 etc.
```

CHAPTER THREE

Vocal Exercises.—Syllable *nu* (*noo*) as in the first year. Also *nu-o-u* and *nu-o-a.*

Intonation.—Review of the *Fourth Compass Exercise.* (See Music First Year, Chapter 19.)

Diagram 10. (First Year)

Diagram 32b

Diagram 32a.

Intonation Exercise 43 (Key of F)

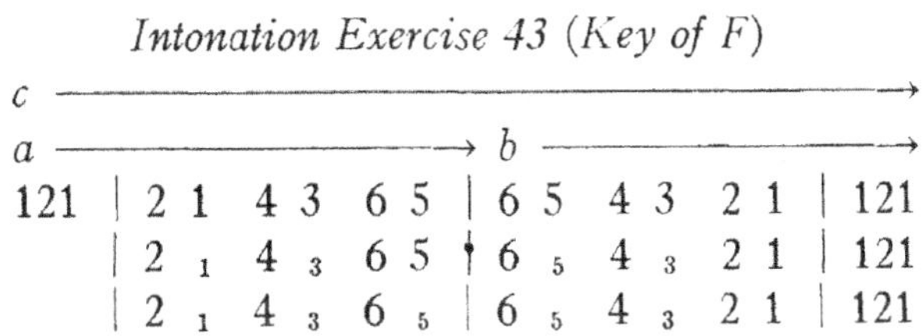

Intonation Exercise 71a (Key of F)

Use Diagram 10

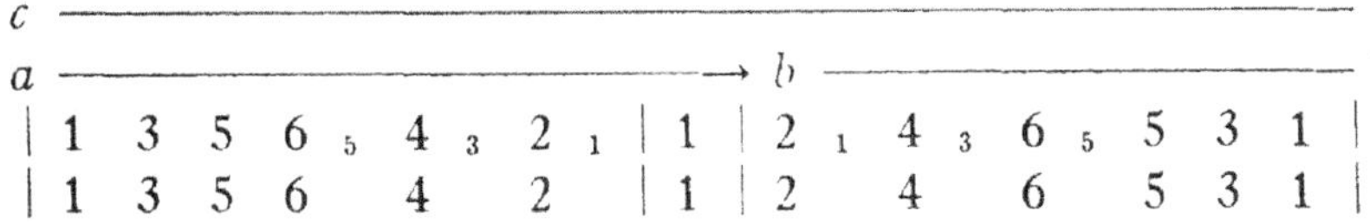

Intonation Exercise 71b

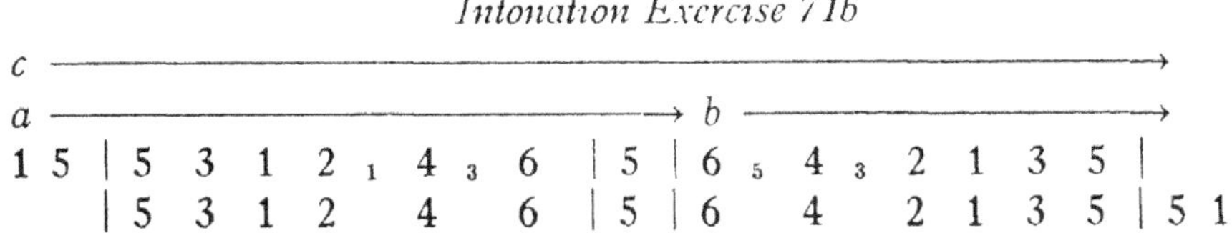

Intonation Exercise 72

Use Diagram 32a and b

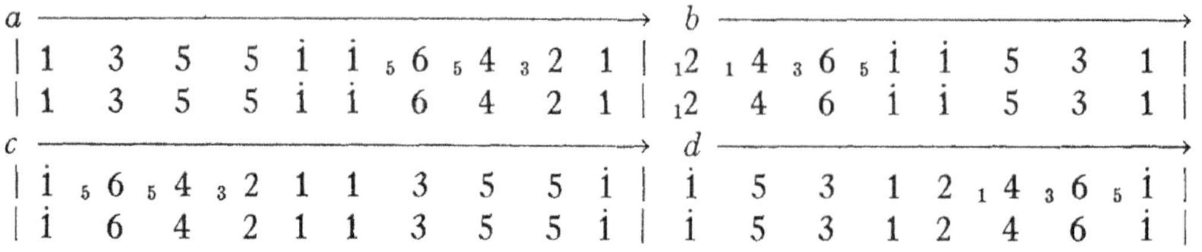

a → *b* →

| 1 3 5 5 1̇ 1̇ $_5$6 $_5$4 $_3$2 1 | $_1$2 $_1$4 $_3$6 $_5$1̇ 1̇ 5 3 1 |

| 1 3 5 5 1̇ 1̇ 6 4 2 1 | $_1$2 4 6 1̇ 1̇ 5 3 1 |

c → *d* →

| 1̇ $_5$6 $_5$4 $_3$2 1 1 3 5 5 1̇ | 1̇ 5 3 1 2 $_1$4 $_3$6 $_5$1̇ |

| 1̇ 6 4 2 1 1 3 5 5 1̇ | 1̇ 5 3 1 2 4 6 1̇ |

Intonation Exercise 73

Use Diagram 32a and b

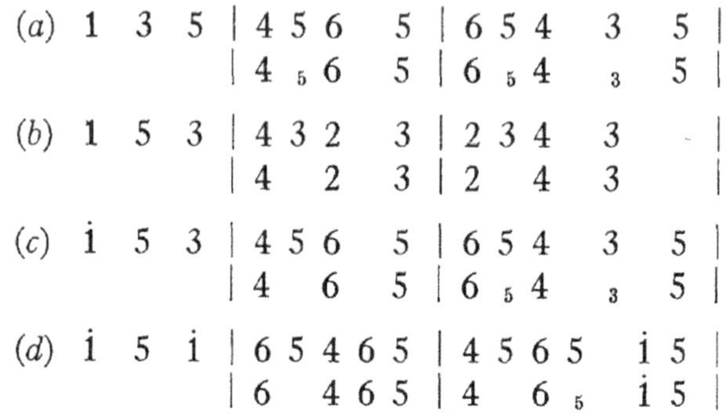

(*a*) 1 3 5 | 4 5 6 5 | 6 5 4 3 5 |

| 4 $_5$6 5 | 6 $_5$4 $_3$ 5 |

(*b*) 1 5 3 | 4 3 2 3 | 2 3 4 3 |

| 4 2 3 | 2 4 3 |

(*c*) 1̇ 5 3 | 4 5 6 5 | 6 5 4 3 5 |

| 4 6 5 | 6 $_5$4 $_3$ 5 |

(*d*) 1̇ 5 1̇ | 6 5 4 6 5 | 4 5 6 5 1̇ 5 |

| 6 4 6 5 | 4 6 $_5$ 1̇ 5 |

Build up each interval of a third as it appears on the diagram sustained by the proper help notes, according to the model given in Exercise 73.

Melody 90 (Catalan)

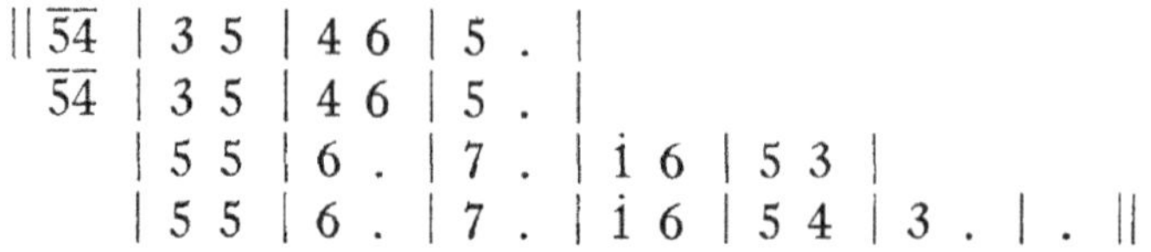

|| $\overline{54}$ | 3 5 | 4 6 | 5 . |

$\overline{54}$ | 3 5 | 4 6 | 5 . |

| 5 5 | 6 . | 7 . | 1̇ 6 | 5 3 |

| 5 5 | 6 . | 7 . | 1̇ 6 | 5 4 | 3 . | . ||

Melody 91 (Catalan)

|| $\overline{34}$ | 5 6 | 4 3 | 2 . | .

$\overline{23}$ | 4 5 | 3 2 | 1 . | .

$\overline{34}$ | 5 5 | 5 5 | 6 . | .

$\overline{23}$ | 4 4 | 4 4 | 5 $\overline{54}$ | 3 $\overline{32}$ | 1 . | . ||

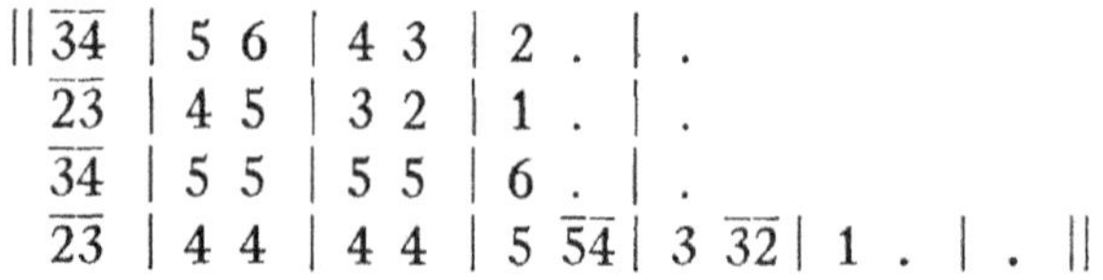

Melody 92

	: 3 1 5	6 . 4	5 . 5	3 1 5	6 . 4	5 . . :	
3 5 6	4 . 2	1 . 1	5 5 $\dot{1}$	6 . 4	5 . .
3 5 6	4 . 2	1 . .	5 5 $\dot{1}$	6 . 7	$\dot{1}$ . .	

Rhythmic Exercise 29

End

(*a*) ||: 1 1 | 1 1 :|| 1 . : 1 . ||

(*b*) ||: 1 1 | 1 . :||

(*c*) ||: $\overline{11}$ $\overline{11}$ | $\overline{11}$ $\overline{11}$:|| 1 . : . . ||

(*d*) ||: $\overline{11}$ $\overline{11}$ | 1 1 :|| 1 1 : 1 . ||

(*e*) ||: $\overline{11}$ $\overline{11}$ | 1 . :|| 1 1 : 1 . ||

(*f*) ||: 1 1 | $\overline{11}$ $\overline{11}$:|| 1 . : 1 . ||

(*g*) ||: 1 . | $\overline{11}$ $\overline{11}$:|| 1 . : 1 . ||

(*h*) || 1 . | . . ||

Use for rhythmic drill and dictation:

(*a*) One design repeated.

(*b*) Two designs alternated and repeated.

Rhythm and Melody (One design repeated)

Model d.—|| $\overline{11}$ $\overline{11}$ | 1 1 ||

||: $\overline{12}$ $\overline{34}$ | 5 3 | $\overline{12}$ $\overline{34}$ | 5 3 |
| $\overline{12}$ $\overline{34}$ | 5 3 | 4 2 | 1 . :||

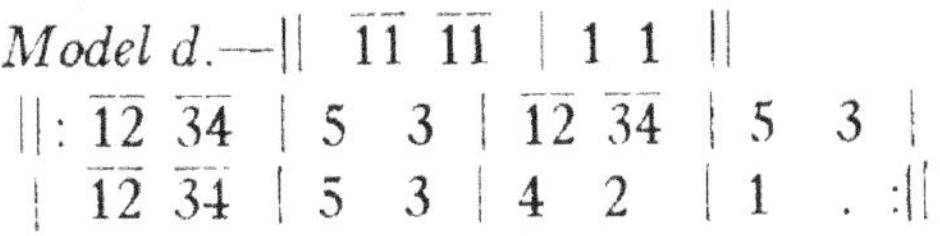

Sing briskly while beating time. Then with arsis-thesis.

Model a + c

Model c.—|| $\overline{11}$ $\overline{11}$ | $\overline{11}$ $\overline{11}$ ||

|| $\overline{56}$ $\overline{54}$ | $\overline{32}$ $\overline{34}$ | $\overline{56}$ $\overline{54}$ | $\overline{32}$ $\overline{34}$ |
| $\overline{5\dot{1}}$ $\overline{76}$ | $\overline{54}$ $\overline{32}$ | 1 . | . . ||

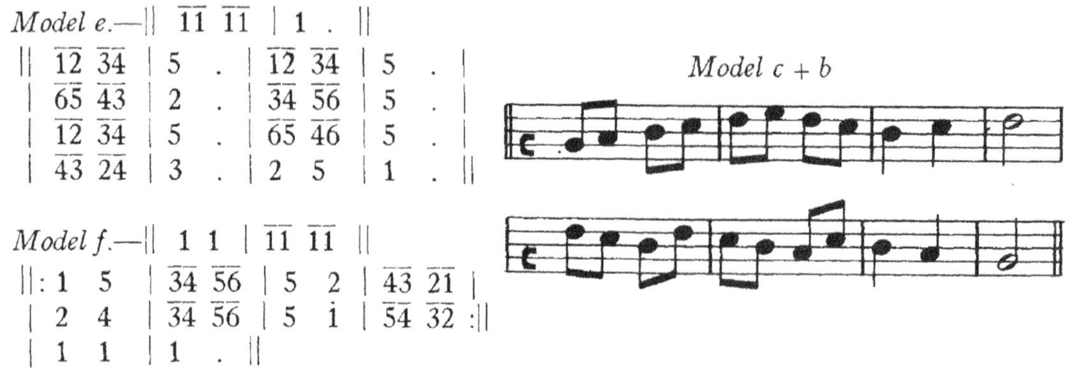

Examples of Two Designs

| 1 1 | 1 1 | 11 11 | 1 . | (*a* + *e*.)
| 11 11 | 1 1 | 1 1 | 1 . | (*d* + *b*.)
| 11 11 | 1 1 | 11 11 | 1 . | (*d* + *e*.)
| 1 1 | 11 11 | 1 1 | 1 . | (*f* + *b*.)
| 11 11 | 11 11 | 1 1 | 1 1 | (*c* + *a*.)
| 11 11 | 11 11 | 11 11 | 1 . | (*c* + *e*.)

1. Rhythmic recitation.
2. Observation.
3. Tapping fitted into rhythmic gesture.
4. Use in musical compositions.

Examples of Three Designs

| 11 11 | 1 1 | 1 1 | 1 1 | 11 11 | 1 . | (*d* + *a* + *e*.)
| 1 1 | 11 11 | 1 . | 11 11 | 1 . | . . | (*f* + *g* + *h*.)

Examples of Four Designs

| 11 11 | 1 1 | 1 1 | 1 1 | 1 . | 11 11 | 1 . | . . | *d* + *a* + *g* + *h*.)
| 1 1 | 11 11 | 1 . | 11 11 | 11 11 | 1 . | 1 1 | 1 . | (*f*, *g*, *e*, *b*.)

(The examples of Three and of Four Designs should be read rhythmically, beating time, then with arsis-thesis.)

The children should be encouraged to use *longer themes* for their compositions than during the first year. The following themes of two, three and four designs will serve as illustrations.

Themes Utilizing Two Designs

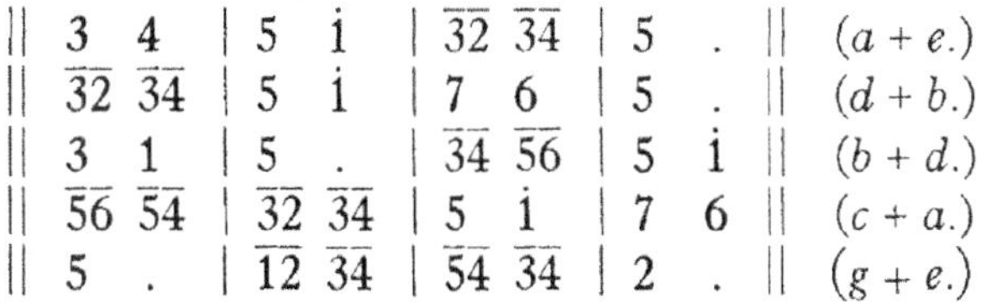

|| 3 4 | 5 1̇ | 32 34 | 5 . || (*a* + *e*.)
|| 32 34 | 5 1̇ | 7 6 | 5 . || (*d* + *b*.)
|| 3 1 | 5 . | 34 56 | 5 1̇ || (*b* + *d*.)
|| 56 54 | 32 34 | 5 1̇ | 7 6 || (*c* + *a*.)
|| 5 . | 12 34 | 54 34 | 2 . || (*g* + *e*.)

The children compose an answering phrase.

Themes Utilizing Three Designs

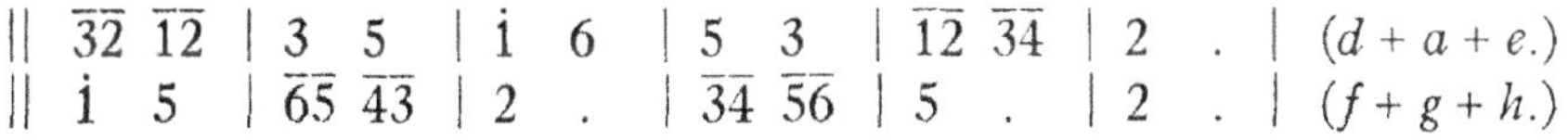

|| 32 12 | 3 5 | 1̇ 6 | 5 3 | 12 34 | 2 . | (*d* + *a* + *e*.)
|| 1̇ 5 | 65 43 | 2 . | 34 56 | 5 . | 2 . | (*f* + *g* + *h*.)

Themes Utilizing Four Designs

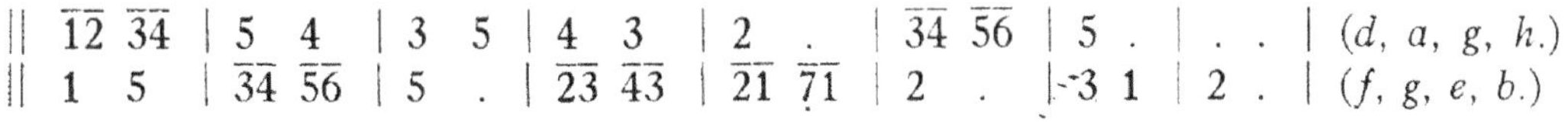

|| 12 34 | 5 4 | 3 5 | 4 3 | 2 . | 34 56 | 5 . | . . | (*d*, *a*, *g*, *h*.)
|| 1 5 | 34 56 | 5 . | 23 43 | 21 7̣1 | 2 . | -3 1 | 2 . | (*f*, *g*, *e*, *b*.)

When the theme consists of two designs, the children may be asked to improvise an answering phrase. When more than two designs are used, the theme will require a *written answer*, either made of similar designs or, preferably, of contrasting ones.

Rhythm and Melody

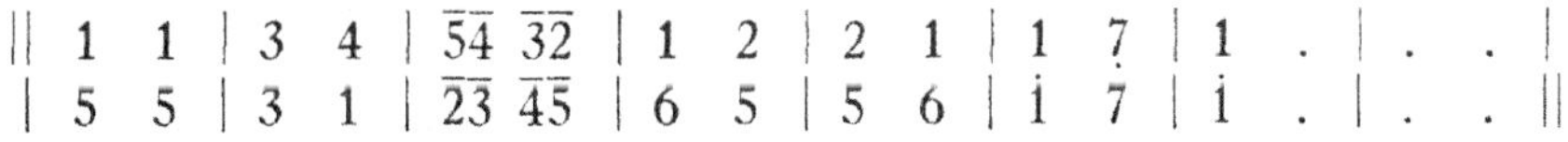

|| 1 1 | 3 4 | 54 32 | 1 2 | 2 1 | 1 7̣ | 1 . | . . |
| 5 5 | 3 1 | 23 45 | 6 5 | 5 6 | 1̇ 7 | 1̇ . | . . ||

Recite rhythmically with gestures. Then sing. Find *three* designs.

Gavotte

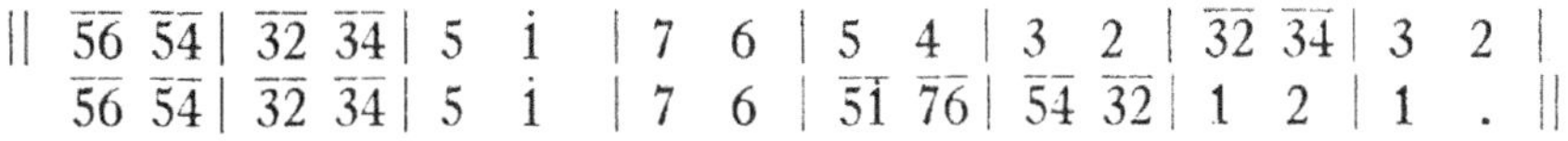

|| 56 54 | 32 34 | 5 1̇ | 7 6 | 5 4 | 3 2 | 32 34 | 3 2 |
56 54 | 32 34 | 5 1̇ | 7 6 | 51 76 | 54 32 | 1 2 | 1 . ||

Recite as above. Then sing. Find *four* designs.

Melody 93

(Key of D)

	54 34	5 67	1̇ 2̇	1̇ 7'	54 34	5 67	1̇ 6	5 .
56 54	34 32	1 2	3 3'	56 54	34 32	1 2	1 .
17 17	17 17	1̇ 6	5 .	17 16	56 54	3 2	1 .
12 34	5 5	6 71	5 .	1̇ 76	5 55	6 5	1 .	

Rhythm, Melody and Staff Notation

Study the following numbers from The Children's Manual:

Cock-a-doodle-doo, page 8.
Melodies 94 and 95, page 7.
A Welcome to Jesus, page 10.

Vocal Exercises, First Year, No. 13, 14 and 15, Syllable *nu*, and No. 19 on Syllables *nu-o-u* and *nu-o-a*.

Intonation.—Review of the *Fourth Compass Exercise*, using *Diagram 10* and also the horizontal form of the *Exercise No. 43*. The help-notes must be used until the intervals are well established and can be sung perfectly in tune, *Re* depending on *Do*, *Fa* on *Mi*, *La* on *Sol*. When this has been accomplished, gradually, by use of the diagrams, more independence should be sought, so that any *two tones* of the right hand column can be sung in connection with the intermediary tone of the left hand column. (1 3 5 6 4 5 4 6 5. 1 3 4 2 3 2 4 3 . etc.) The same principle applies to the study of *Intonation Exercise 72* which should be worked out first on *Diagram 32a*, then horizontally as in the exercise itself, and when the intervals have been perfectly established by means of the help-notes, then the right hand column should be studied more independently as described above.

Intonation Exercise 73 illustrates the process already described.

In composing melodies, the children should not be encouraged to use the chord 2 4 6 or 6 4 2 as a whole; still less, the chord 2 4 6 1̇ or 1̇ 6 4 2, but rather to use one or other of these intervals. See in this connection *Melodies 90, 94* and *95*. The study of the chord line with help-notes is merely an *exercise* to obtain a command of the intervals, but is not a counsel of perfection for the composition of melodies.

Rhythm.—Exercise 29 is practically a review of the forms of composite time studied in the first year. Each design should be read rhythmically with gestures, and repeated several times. Then two at least should be combined and repeated.

Preparation by Beating Time or by Tapping the Design.—The placing of four crochets under an arsis or a thesis (as in Designs *c*, *d*, *e*, *f* and *g*) offers a certain difficulty until the designs themselves become familiar. The result will be a slow and hesitant gesture, inaccuracy of movement and vagueness of metrical design. This should not be permitted. We must have perfect accuracy in the detail of the design before going farther. Thus, to prepare the difficulty, the teacher may allow the children to beat time "down-up, down-up"—but lightly and without rigidity, while they are working out the rhythmic designs. Or they may tap the design lightly with one hand on the back of the other hand. As soon as the design is clearly grasped, the gestures of composite time should be substituted for the tapping or for the beating of time. This applies to all rhythmic work from this point on: wherever it is necessary to reduce the design to individual "beats" it may be done, but always *as a preparation* for the composite time and the arsis-thesis movement. The technique of composite time will be reserved for phrases in which the interior details are already familiar.

In dictating rhythmic designs, the teacher may employ the tapping or the beating of time, until the designs are sufficiently clear to use the arsis-thesis movement. Usually the children *recognize* a design quite easily; the drill should be used for enabling them to *execute* designs rapidly and accurately.

Example of the Same Designs Treated as:

(*a*) *Simple Time*

(Beating time gesture)

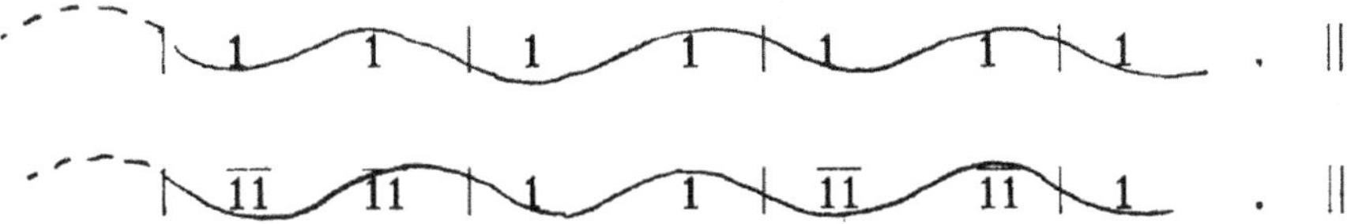

(b) Composite Time

(Arsis-thesis gesture)

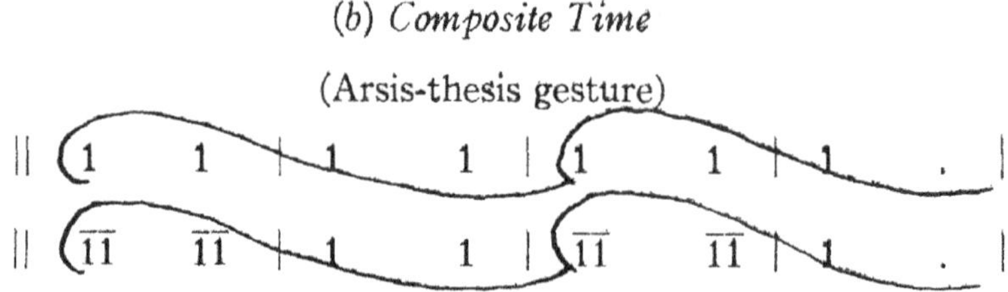

In *Rhythmic Exercise 29*, some designs are unfinished, simply fragments: (*a, c, d, f, g*). Under brackets we have added endings to these individual designs. When two designs are combined, these endings are not needed, for a design with an ending should always be chosen for the second of the two (*b, e* or *h*). But let us suppose that the teacher wishes to drill the children on *Design c* or *d, f* or *g*. The process would be as follows:

	Design		Ending	
(*c*)	||: 11 11	| 11 11 :||	1 .	| . . ||
(*d*)	||: 11 11	| 1 1 :||	1 1	| 1 . ||
(*f*)	||: 1 1	| 11 11 :||	1 .	| 1 . ||
(*g*)	||: 1 .	| 11 11 :||	1 .	| 1 . ||

The design itself is repeated rapidly and accurately, then the ending is added. These endings are, of course interchangeable. The only necessary thing is to provide *length* after the repetition of the design.

In the phrases under *Rhythm and Melody* a few examples will be found embodying a single design. It is best, however, to use these as little as possible, for the designs become interesting from a musical standpoint only when combined with others. The single designs are only a *step* toward the real object of this work: the building of a rhythmic vocabulary.

To provide variety in the work, let the children read rhythmically, with gestures, the designs indicated by the teacher. Thus:

Children stand at attention (for beating time or for chironomy):

Teacher: "*e* plus *b*". The children read these two designs rhythmically with gestures, three or four times at least.

The Rhythmic designs on the staff should be named rhythmically and then the melody should be sung slowly, without any gesture. Then the whole should be repeated, rhythm and melody, while beating time, then with arsis-thesis.

Dictation.—The melodic dictation will follow closely the work described under *Intonation*. Suggestions for this work are given in *Chapter 19* of *Music First Year*.

When the essential intervals of the *Fourth Compass Exercise* have been established by means of purely melodic dictation, a very simple arrangement using melody and rhythm may be proposed. There should be no use of the divided beat at first. The gesture of the hand should always accompany dictation of this sort:

Examples

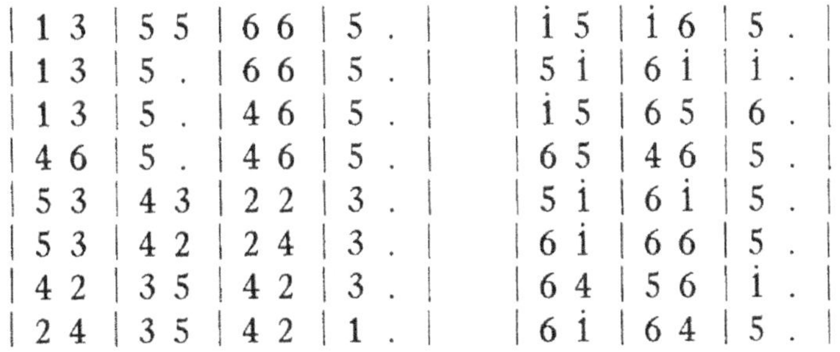

1 3	5 5	6 6	5 .	1̇ 5	1̇ 6	5 .
1 3	5 .	6 6	5 .	5 1̇	6 1̇	1̇ .
1 3	5 .	4 6	5 .	1̇ 5	6 5	6 .
4 6	5 .	4 6	5 .	6 5	4 6	5 .
5 3	4 3	2 2	3 .	5 1̇	6 1̇	5 .
5 3	4 2	2 4	3 .	6 1̇	6 6	5 .
4 2	3 5	4 2	3 .	6 4	5 6	1̇ .
2 4	3 5	4 2	1 .	6 1̇	6 4	5 .

When there is difficulty in hearing an interval, use the intervening note. Thus:

4 2 3 . : 4 3 2 3 . etc.

When crochets are used, they should bridge the intervals of a chord, very simply, thus:

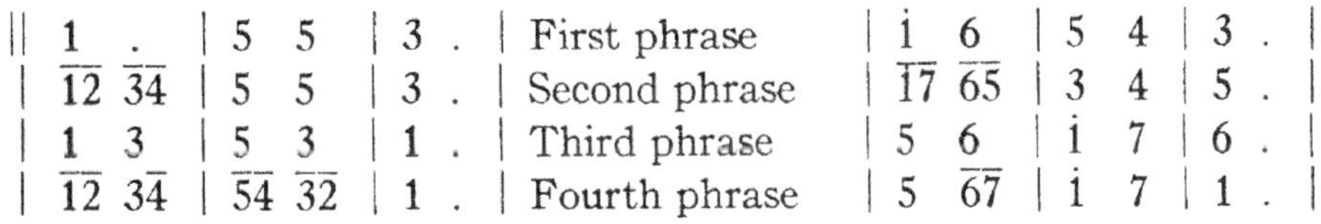

1 .	5 5	3 .	First phrase	1̇ 6	5 4	3 .
$\overline{12}$ $\overline{34}$	5 5	3 .	Second phrase	$\overline{1̇7}$ $\overline{65}$	3 4	5 .
1 3	5 3	1 .	Third phrase	5 6	1̇ 7	6 .
$\overline{12}$ $\overline{34}$	$\overline{54}$ $\overline{32}$	1 .	Fourth phrase	5 $\overline{67}$	1̇ 7	1 .

Thus: *difficulties of interval* should be dictated *without any definite rhythm*, slowly, evenly.

Moderately familiar matter can be given a *rhythmic form* but without the use of the divided beat.

Difficulties of rhythm (designs with crochets) must be dictated *without any melody*.

Where the intervals and also the rhythmic designs are familiar, then the crochets may be used in dictating, but always planning the examples in such a way as to build up the intervals in advance, and almost to solve the problem by the relation between the phrases dictated.

The rhythm of words may be approached on the board and also pronounced and rhythmed spontaneously. Thus:

|| 1 1 | 1 . | 1 1 | 1 . | (Designs *b* + *b*.)

Mat- thew, Mark, Luke and John

| 1 1 | 1 1 | 1 1 | 1 . | (Designs *a* + *b*.)

Bless the bed that I lie on

or || 1 1 | 1 1 | 1 1 | 1 1 | or | 1 . | 1 . | (Designs *a* + *a*.)

Je- sus, ten- der She- pherd, hear me hear me

| 1 1 | 1 1 | 1 1 | 1 . | (Designs *a* + *b*.)

Bless Thy lit- tle lamb to- night

Also any other verses that adapt themselves to the designs of the week.

Composition.—The children should be encouraged to write themes of two or even three rhythmic designs.

CHAPTER FOUR

Vocal Exercises.—Nu (No. 17 and 18, First Year).
Also: *Nu-o-a*, and *Nu-a-u*, No. 19 and 20, First Year. No. 24, Second Year.
Intonation.—Major Scale and Chord, Plagal Range.

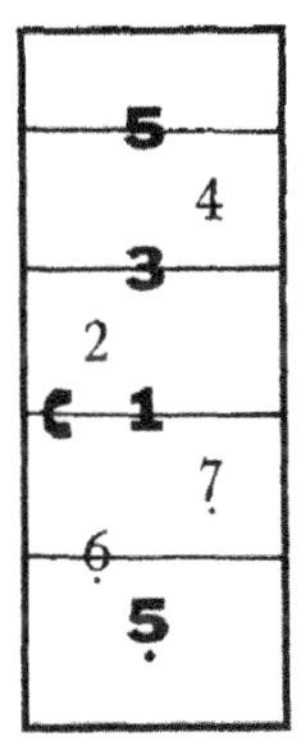

Diagram 13.
(Year 1.)

Review Plagal Range

12345 54321 1765 5671
Use Diagrams 13 and 33; also horizontal form for singing and observation.

Diagram 33.

Review Compass Exercises in Plagal Range

(Key of G or A♭)

| 121 343 565 565 343 121 565 121 171 |
| 1 3 5 5 3 1 5 1 |
| ₁21 ₃43 ₅65 ₅65 ₃43 ₁21 ₅65 ₁21 ₁71 |

Melody and Rhythm

	1 5	5 .	12 34	5 .			56 54	34 32	1 5	5 .
54 32	17 65	6 .	5 .		23 43	21 76	5 .	. .
5 1	2 .	12 34	5 .		12 34	5 3	12 34	5 5
54 32	17 67	1 .	. .			6 5	67 12	1 .	. .	

Review 3/4 Time, Simple.

(Gesture 3)

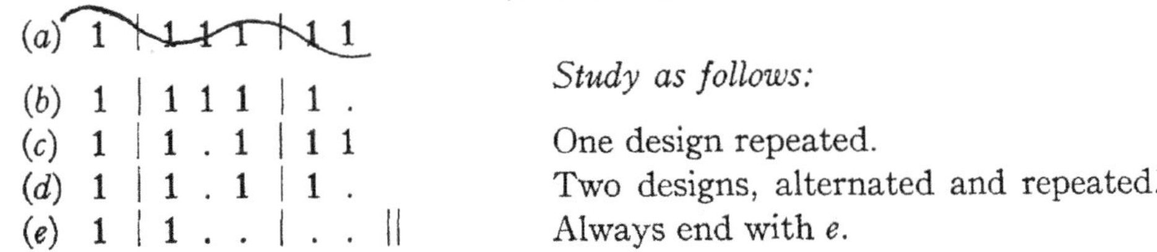

Study as follows:

One design repeated.
Two designs, alternated and repeated.
Always end with *e*.

Rhythm and Melody

1. ||: 5 | 321 | 22
5 | 321 | 2. :||
3 | 1.. | .. || End.

2. ||: 5 | 321 | 21
5 | 3.2 | 1. :||
2 | 1.. | .. || End.

3. ||: $\underset{\cdot}{5}$ | 123 | 2.5 | 3.2 | 1.
$\underset{\cdot}{5}$ | 1.2 | 325 | 3.2 | 1. :||
||: 5 | 3.5 | 3.5 | 432 | 31 :||
5 | 3.5 | 3.5 | 432 | $1\underset{\cdot}{5}\underset{\cdot}{5}$ | 1.. | .. ||

Rhythm 30

(*a*) | 1 1 | 1 1 |

(*b*) | 1 1 | 1 . |

(*c*) | 1 $\overline{11}$ | 1 $\overline{11}$ |

(*d*) | 1 $\overline{11}$ | 1 1 |

(*e*) | 1 $\overline{11}$ | 1 . |

(*f*) | 1 . | . . |

One Design Repeated

(*c*) ||: 5 $\overline{34}$ | 5 $\overline{34}$ | 5 $\overline{32}$ | 1 $\overline{\underset{\cdot}{7}1}$ |
| 2 $\overline{23}$ | 4 $\overline{23}$ | 4 $\overline{32}$ | 1 $\overline{34}$:|| 2 2 | 1 . ||

(*d*) || 5 $\overline{34}$ | 5 6 | 5 $\overline{34}$ | 5 6 |
| 5 $\overline{34}$ | 5 $\dot{1}$ | $\underset{\cdot}{5}$ $\overline{32}$ | 1 . ||

(*e*) || 5 $\overline{34}$ | 5 . | $\dot{1}$ $\overline{76}$ | 5 . |
| 5 $\overline{34}$ | 5 . | 4 $\overline{32}$ | 1 . ||

Two Designs Combined and Repeated

Always choose one with a cadence to combine with one which lacks a cadence.

(*c* + *b*)

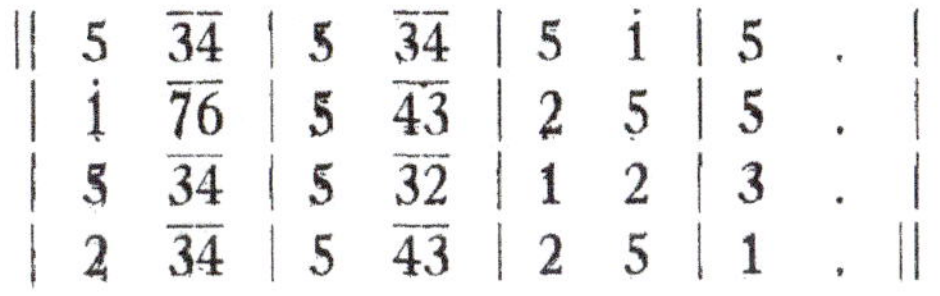

	5 $\overline{34}$	5 $\overline{34}$	5 $\dot{1}$	5 .
$\dot{1}$ $\overline{76}$	5 $\overline{43}$	2 5	5 .
5 $\overline{34}$	5 $\overline{32}$	1 2	3 .
2 $\overline{34}$	5 $\overline{43}$	2 5	1 .	

(*d* + *e*)

	1 $\overline{34}$	5 6	5 $\overline{34}$	5 .
5 $\overline{65}$	4 3	2 $\overline{12}$	3 .
2 $\overline{34}$	3 2	1 $\overline{\underset{.}{7}\underset{.}{6}}$	$\underset{.}{5}$.
$\underset{.}{5}$ $\overline{\underset{.}{6}\underset{.}{7}}$	1 2	2 $\overline{1\underset{.}{7}}$	1 .	

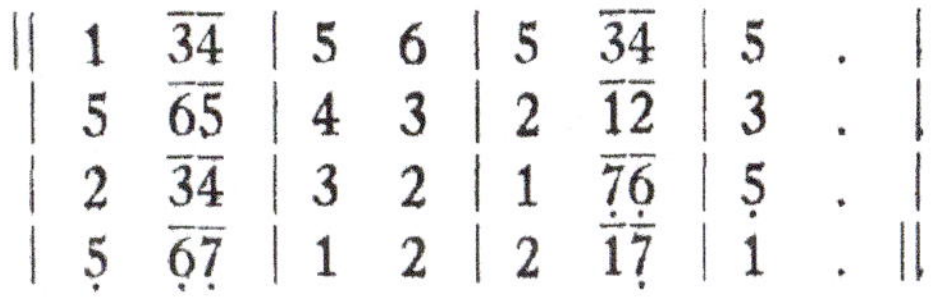

Three Designs Combined and Repeated

Always choose one with cadence for the last.

(*e* + *c* + *f*)

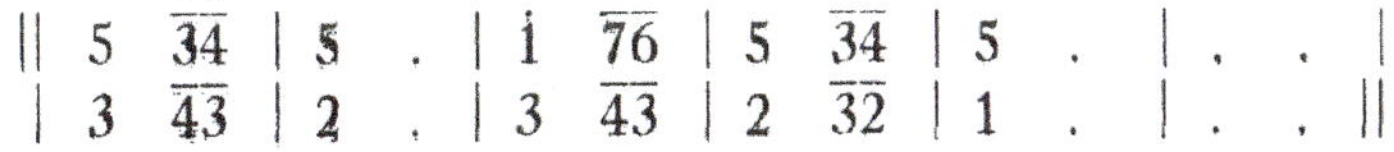

|| 5 $\overline{34}$ | 5 . | $\dot{1}$ $\overline{76}$ | 5 $\overline{34}$ | 5 . | . . |
| 3 $\overline{43}$ | 2 . | 3 $\overline{43}$ | 2 $\overline{32}$ | 1 . | . . ||

Four Designs (b + c + d: b + c + d + f)

|| 1 5 | 5 . | 3 $\overline{43}$ | 2 $\overline{12}$ | 3 $\overline{43}$ | 2 2 |
| 1 5 | 5 . | 3 $\overline{43}$ | 2 $\overline{12}$ | 3 $\overline{43}$ | 2 2 | 1 . | . . ||

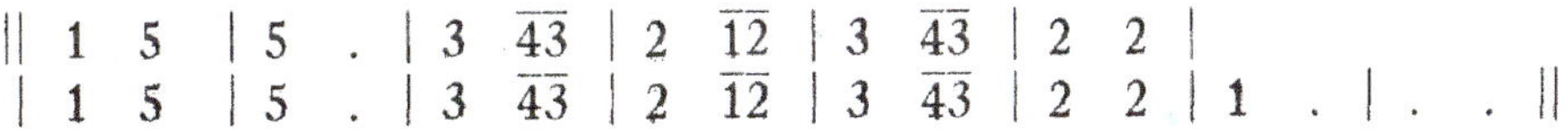

Observation

One Design Repeated. Two Designs alternated and repeated.

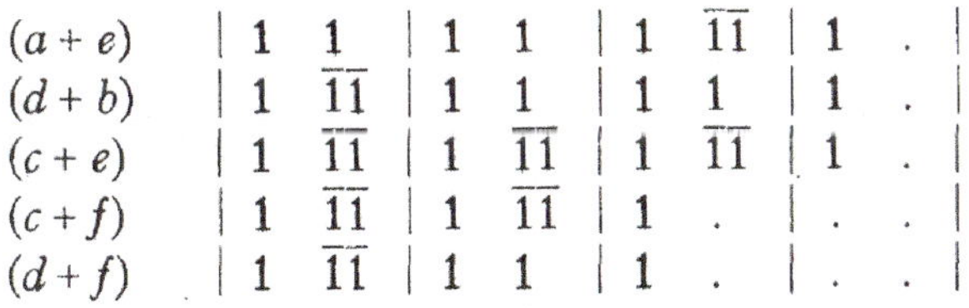

(*a* + *e*) | 1 1 | 1 1 | 1 $\overline{11}$ | 1 . |
(*d* + *b*) | 1 $\overline{11}$ | 1 1 | 1 1 | 1 . |
(*c* + *e*) | 1 $\overline{11}$ | 1 $\overline{11}$ | 1 $\overline{11}$ | 1 . |
(*c* + *f*) | 1 $\overline{11}$ | 1 $\overline{11}$ | 1 . | . . |
(*d* + *f*) | 1 $\overline{11}$ | 1 1 | 1 . | . . |

Always take a design with a cadence for the last one.

Themes for Melodic Compositions

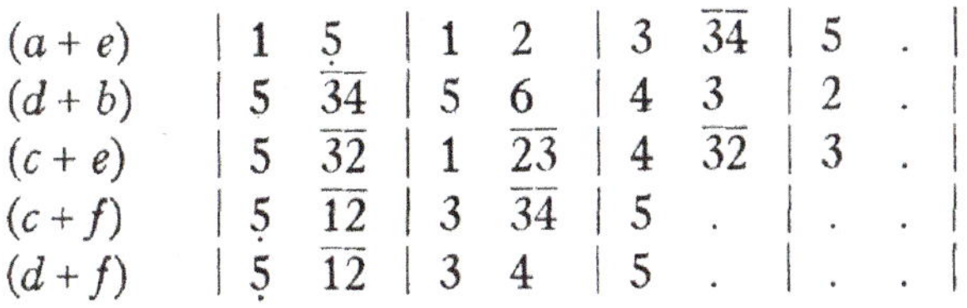

(*a* + *e*) | 1 $\underset{.}{5}$ | 1 2 | 3 $\overline{34}$ | 5 . |
(*d* + *b*) | 5 $\overline{34}$ | 5 6 | 4 3 | 2 . |
(*c* + *e*) | 5 $\overline{32}$ | 1 $\overline{23}$ | 4 $\overline{32}$ | 3 . |
(*c* + *f*) | $\underset{.}{5}$ $\overline{12}$ | 3 $\overline{34}$ | 5 . | . . |
(*d* + *f*) | $\underset{.}{5}$ $\overline{12}$ | 3 4 | 5 . | . . |

1. Answer in same design.
2. Answer in a contrasting design.

Themes for Melodic Composition

(Designs of Week 3 and 4)

I. || 5 55 | 6 6 | 54 32 | 1 2 | 5 . | . . ||
II. || 1 11 | 2 2 | 3 1 | 4 6 | 54 32 | 17 66 | 5 . | . . ||

In answering these themes: there must be *unity and variety.*
If the *variety* is in the *melody*, the rhythm should not change very greatly.
If the *variety* is in the *rhythm*, the melody should move quietly.

Example Theme I.	|| 5 55 | 6 6 | 54 32 | 1 2 | 5 . | . . ||
Answer a.	|| 6 66 | 7 5 | 67 12 | 3 2 | 1 . | . . ||
Answer b.	|| 5 55 | 6 6 | 7 5 | 1 . | 12 34 | 5 5 | 1 . | . . ||

Answer a provides a *melodic contrast* (following a different chord line), and therefore reproduces the same rhythmic designs as are contained in the theme.

Answer b begins by reproducing exactly the first statement, an octave below: and ends with a contrast that is both rhythmic and melodic.

Observation

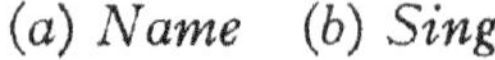

Study the following numbers from The Children's Manual:

Melodies 96, 97, page 11; *98, 99, 100*, page 12.
A Christmas Carol, page 14.
Immortal Babe, page 13.
The Root and the Flower, page 16.

Vocal Exercises.—Nos. 17 and 18 of the First Year (Syllable *Nu*). Also Nos. 19 and 20 on *Nu-o-u* and *Nu-o-a*. Also No. 24, Second Year.

Intonation.—Review of the *Major Scale*, *Chord* and *Compass Exercise* in the plagal range (5̣ – 5). Use the *Diagram No. 13*, then *Staff Diagram 33* which can be substituted as soon as the intervals have been solidly established by means of the number notation. Both diagrams should serve for rapid observation and memory work. The staff diagram should be used, also, for exercises in rapid *naming* of the notes without singing, in which case the notes can be used freely regardless of the interval. Any note should be named at once without hesitation.

Melody and Rhythm.—These phrases use the rhythmic forms studied last week. They illustrate the melodic material and should be sung as follows: 1. Without gestures. 2. Recited rhythmically while beating time. 3. Sung while beating time. 4. Sung with the arsis-thesis gesture. (Some of these lines would be expressed more correctly by one arsis and three thesis, or again by two arsis and two thesis, but these counsels of perfection should not be insisted upon until such time as the simple succession of arsis-thesis can be executed without hesitation.)

Rhythm.—Review 3/4 Time without divided-beat. *Gesture 3*, first without singing, in strict and rapid time, with a smooth curve free from angularity or jerkiness. Then the teacher may tap one of the designs in 3/4 time, fitting it into the children's gesture. The children recognize the design and pronounce it rhythmically while continuing the gesture. Then the phrases under Rhythm and Melody should be sung, repeating as often as the teacher thinks useful the part enclosed within *repeat signs*, and ending, always with a design having a long cadence.

A trained perception that functions easily and rapidly is more useful in music than the most profound calculation that does not function. In the use of these designs the teacher should encourage rapid perception of the design as a whole, and the use of only such things as can be handled with a certain ease and joy. Certain metrical and rhythmical truths must become almost instinctive, otherwise they will be of no practical use. Thus to vary the work, much observation should be carried out on the board: a design written and erased, then sung by the pupils; a design indicated on the chart, and sung several times with gestures by the children with backs turned to the chart; a design tapped by the teacher and repeated with gestures by the children. In each case the design should be repeated several times that it may make a deeper impression on the muscles and the mind. Then the children may use the designs to tap a "metrical conversation." When this becomes too simple, the same process can be applied to a conversation combining melody with rhythm. It is well to vary the type of exercise demanded, that each lesson may contain a surprise.

Rhythmic Exercise 30 continues the study of the divided beat in 2/4 Time. *Figures a, b* and *f* are already familiar. *Figures c, d* and *e* are the matter that require study, and this will follow the lines already described: One design repeated; two designs alternated and repeated, then, gradually, phrases of three designs and of four designs should be built up. 1. Beating time lightly but neatly. 2. Gesture of arsis-thesis. Designs such as *c* and *d* cannot be used at the end of a phrase: a design such as *b*, *e* or *f* is required at the cadence.

Theoretically, it is simpler to repeat one design than to combine it with others. Practically, that is to say musically, this is not always true. It all depends on the design itself. To repeat indefinitely a design such as *c* is extremely difficult because it provides no point of repose. It is a fragment which is more easily rendered when combined with a design providing length. This will be evident by the examples given below. No. 1 is far more difficult to sing than No. 2 or No. 3, though the former is composed of a single design and the latter, of several designs.

1. | 5 $\overline{34}$ | 5 $\overline{34}$ | 5 $\overline{45}$ | 6 $\overline{54}$ | 3 $\overline{12}$ | 3 $\overline{23}$ | 5 . | . . |

2. | 5 $\overline{34}$ | 5 . | 6 5 | 4 3 | 2 $\overline{12}$ | 3 $\overline{23}$ | 5 . | . . |

3. | 5 $\overline{34}$ | 5 $\overline{34}$ | 5 $\overrightarrow{32}$ | 1 . | 1 $\overline{\underset{\cdot}{7}\underset{\cdot}{6}}$ | $\underset{\cdot}{5}$ $\overline{\underset{\cdot}{5}\underset{\cdot}{6}}$ | 1 2 | 1 . |

The teacher will do well to remember this fact in giving examples for dictation and observation. On the other hand certain designs repeat themselves easily, among which are those which give a point of repose, such as *b* and *e*. In combining two designs the teacher should always select for the *second*, one with a point of repose. If three designs are combined, the third must provide a point of repose (or cadence).

Themes for melodic composition.—A good theme suggests a good answer. The children have now arrived at a degree of musical culture where their efforts at composition can be guided, to a certain extent; less by means of strict rules and inhibitions than by contact with fine models. Fine models are provided by the little melodies contained in each chapter. A few general principles of composition can be brought within the comprehension and experience of the children, however. Among them, the following:

1. *A theme that rises.*—Answer: a theme that descends.
2. *A theme that descends.*—Answer: a theme that rises.

3. *A theme that rises and descends.*—Answer: a theme that descends and rises.

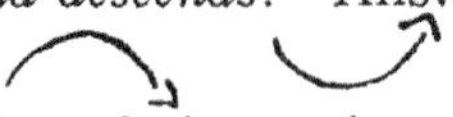

4. *A theme that descends and rises.*—Answer: a theme that rises and descends.

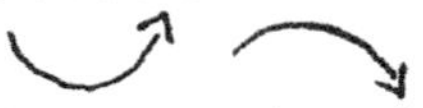

These are not rules, but general tendencies. They may be reduced to a Diagram of melodic direction.

5. A theme that remains approximately even may be answered by a contrast either descending or rising:

Theme. || 5 $\overline{34}$ | 5 $\overline{34}$ | 5 . | $\dot{}$ . . |

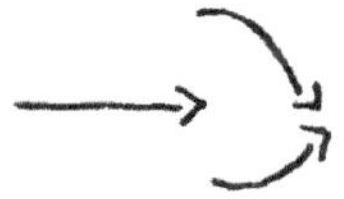

Answer:

1. | $\dot{1}$ $\overline{76}$ | 5 $\overline{32}$ | 3 . | . . ||

2. | 1 $\overline{23}$ | 4 $\overline{34}$ | 5 . | . . ||

or by a repetition of the motif on another degree of the scale:

Answer:

3*a*. | $\dot{1}$ $\overline{67}$ | $\dot{1}$ $\overline{67}$ | $\dot{1}$. | . . ||

3*b*. | 6 $\overline{45}$ | 6 $\overline{45}$ | 6 . | . . ||

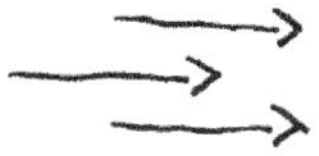

or by the same motif in reversed direction:

Answer:

4*a*. | 2 $\overline{43}$ | 2 $\overline{43}$ | 2 . | . . ||

4*b*. | 5 $\overline{65}$ | 4 $\overline{54}$ | 3 . | . . ||

These are purely melodic changes. The rhythmic design remains.

The answer, however, may embody a *change of rhythm*, and this is often the most interesting form of answer. The number of such possible changes is infinite. We give a few examples to illustrate the principle. We retain the same theme.

Answer:

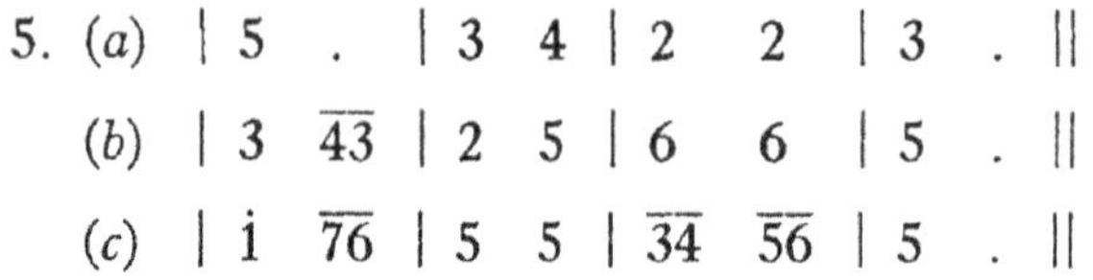

5. (*a*) | 5 . | 3 4 | 2 2 | 3 . ||

(*b*) | 3 $\overline{43}$ | 2 5 | 6 6 | 5 . ||

(*c*) | $\dot{1}$ $\overline{76}$ | 5 5 | $\overline{34}$ $\overline{56}$ | 5 . ||

The themes given on pages 63 and 64 should be answered in various ways, following the suggestions explained above. The teacher will judge whether to give the children several ideas at once or whether to let them work on one form of answer until it is clearly understood. This will depend, evidently, on the age and the aptitudes of the pupils themselves.

The children will then begin to wonder *what to do next?*

This depends upon what form of answer has been chosen. If the rhythm has been kept more or less similar during theme and answer, a change of rhythm usually appears in the remainder of the melody. On the contrary, if the rhythm of the answer has been in contrast to that of the theme, the third line of the melody will repeat (in whole or in part) the rhythmic design of original theme.

We think that a more detailed explanation at this point would tend to puzzle rather than guide the taste of the children. They should give their attention, at present, to composing answers to the themes provided in this chapter, and applying, in a general way, the suggestions made on pages 66 and 67.

Melody 96: Phrase 1: theme.
Phrase 2: answer with melodic contrast; original rhythm maintained.
Phrase 3: melody similar to Phrase 2, rhythmic contrast.
Phrase 4: melody moves quietly, rhythmic contrast toward cadence.

Melody 97: Phrase 1: Repeated twice, exactly. (Chord line.)
Phrase 3: Melodic contrast. (Active tones.)
Phrase 4: Melody reminds us of first line, rhythmic change toward end to make a nice approach to the cadence by prolonged notes.

In singing the melodies already studied as well as those to come, the teacher may ask the children questions to bring out their powers of observation: Where do we find contrasts? Likenesses? Are they melodic or rhythmic? This must be done with discernment and tact that the singing of the melodies may not lose its joy and become a dry technical drill.

Dictation

Melodic

(See Music, First Year Chapter 20 and 21.)

Rhythmic 2/4 and 3/4 Time

One Design.
Two designs.

Rhythm and Melody 2/4

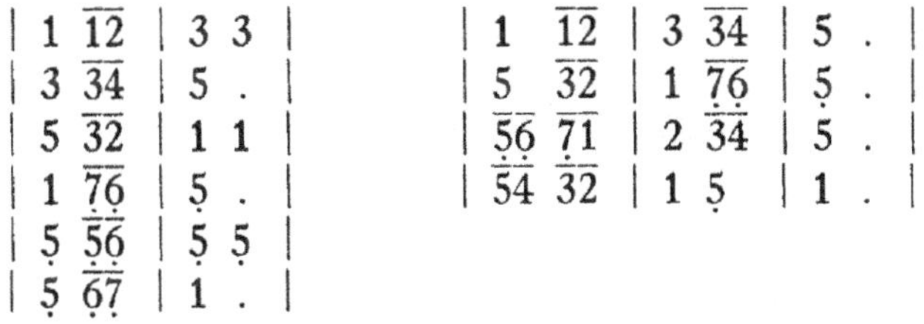

1 12	3 3
3 34	5 .
5 32	1 1
1 76	5 .
5 56	5 5
5 67	1 .

1 12	3 34	5 .
5 32	1 76	5 .
56 71	2 34	5 .
54 32	1 5	1 .

Rhythm and Melody 3/4

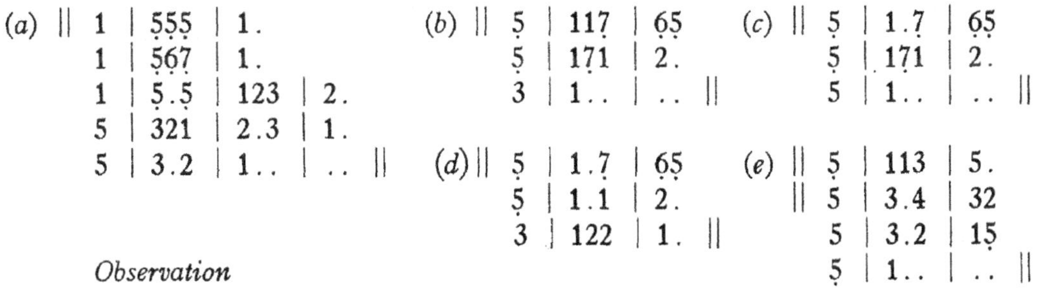

(*a*) || 1 | 555 | 1.
1 | 567 | 1.
1 | 5.5 | 123 | 2.
5 | 321 | 2.3 | 1.
5 | 3.2 | 1.. | .. ||

(*b*) || 5 | 117 | 65
5 | 171 | 2.
3 | 1.. | .. ||

(*c*) || 5 | 1.7 | 65
5 | 171 | 2.
5 | 1.. | .. ||

(*d*) || 5 | 1.7 | 65
5 | 1.1 | 2.
3 | 122 | 1. ||

(*e*) || 5 | 113 | 5.
|| 5 | 3.4 | 32
5 | 3.2 | 15
5 | 1.. | .. ||

Observation

| 121 565 123 |
| 121 565 12345 |
| 565 54321 |
| 565 34321 |
| 54321 565 |
| 565 343 121 5 |
| 565 121 343 5 | etc.

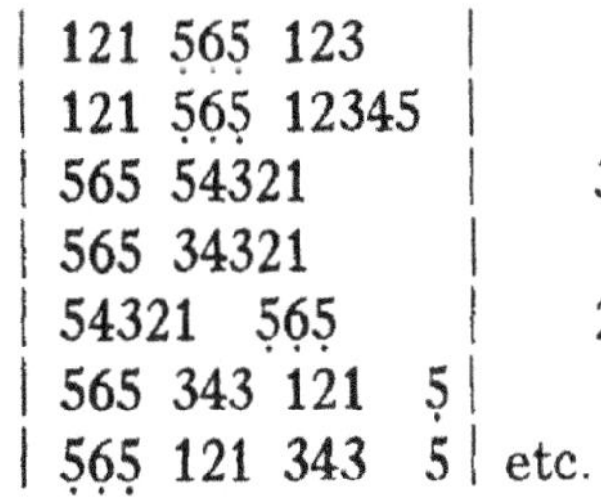

Themes for Musical Conversations

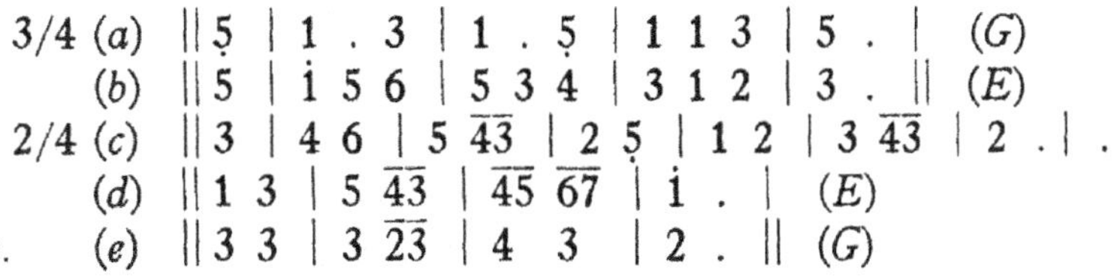

3/4 (*a*) || 5 | 1 . 3 | 1 . 5 | 1 1 3 | 5 . | (*G*)
(*b*) || 5 | 1 5 6 | 5 3 4 | 3 1 2 | 3 . || (*E*)
2/4 (*c*) || 3 | 4 6 | 5 43 | 2 5 | 1 2 | 3 43 | 2 . | .
(*d*) || 1 3 | 5 43 | 45 67 | 1 . | (*E*)
(*e*) || 3 3 | 3 23 | 4 3 | 2 . || (*G*)

Words: Rhythm and Melody

A development of the ideas (melodic and metrical) suggested in the last chapter.

1. *Melodic.*—Bring out the accents, or at least the most important ones, by a rise in pitch.

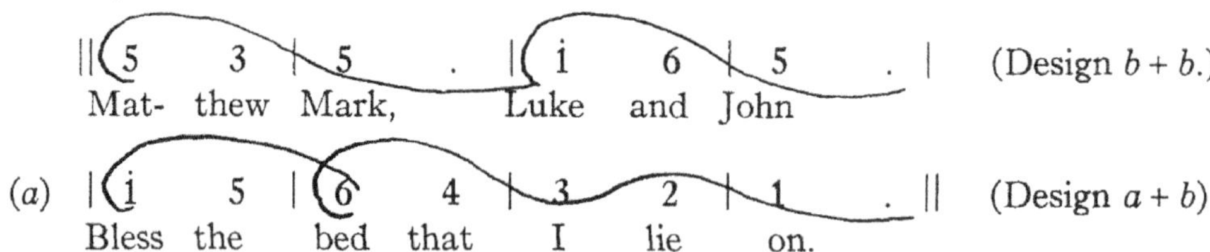

2. *Metrical.*—Replace the simple pulses by divided pulses in at least part of the melody, keeping the ictic notes as they are above.

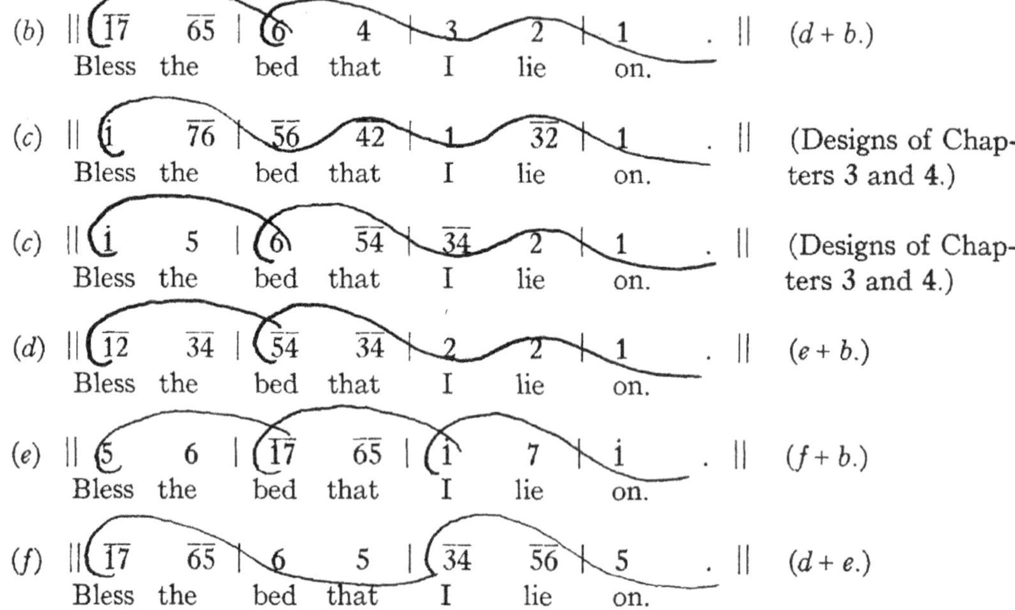

These illustrations are for the use of the teacher who will judge how many possibilities to put before the children. The principal point for the children themselves is to realize that the Designs can be applied to words as well as to melodies pure and simple.

CHAPTER FIVE

Vocal Exercises Nos. 19, 20 and 21.—Syllables *Nu-o-u, nu-a-u, nu-o-a-u, First Year. Nos. 25 and 26:* Syllables *Na nu no na* and *na nu no ne ni, Second Year.*

Intonation.—Major Mode, Tonic and Dominant chords.

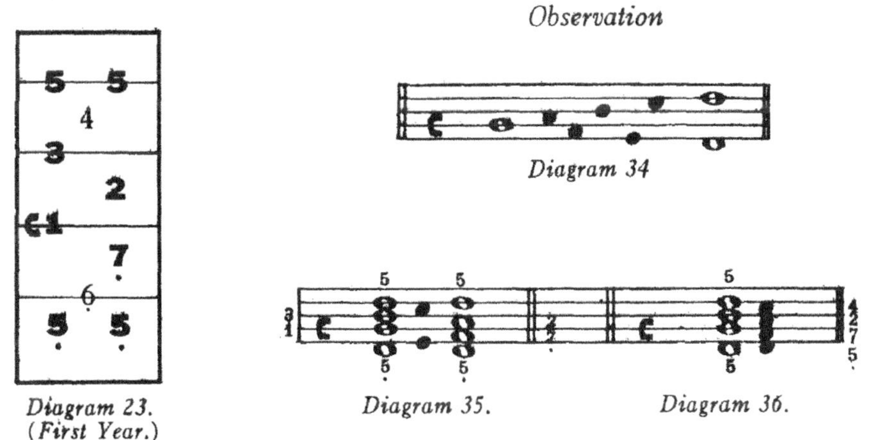

Diagram 23. (First Year.) *Diagram 34* *Diagram 35.* *Diagram 36.*

Review Int. Ex. 66 *a* and *b*, Year I, Chapter 28.

Intonation Exercise 74 (Diagrams 23 and 35)
(Key of C or D)

1 5̣ | 5̣ 1 7̣ 1 2 | 2 1 7̣ 1 5̣ | 1 2 | 2 1 7̣ 1 5̣ | 5̣ 1 7 1 2 |
| 5̣ $_1$ 7̣ $_1$ 2 | 2 $_1$ 7̣ $_1$ 5̣ | | 2 $_1$ 7̣ $_1$ 5̣ | 5̣ $_1$ 7̣ $_1$ 2 |
| 5̣ 7̣ 2 | 2 7 5̣ | | 2 7̣ 5̣ | 5̣ 7̣ 2 |
| 5̣ 7̣ 2 7 5̣ | 5̣ 1 | 2 7̣ 5̣ 7̣ 2 | 2 1

Intonation Exercise 75 (Diagrams 23 and 35)
(Key of A^b or A)

1 5̣ | 5̣ 1 7̣ 1 2 1 5 | 5 $_4$ 3 $_2$ 1 $_7$ $_6$ 5̣ |
| 5̣ $_1$ 7̣ $_1$ 2 $_1$ 5 | 5 3 1 5̣ | 5̣ 1
| 5̣ 7̣ 2 $_3$ 4$_3$ | 5 3 1 5̣ | 5̣ 1

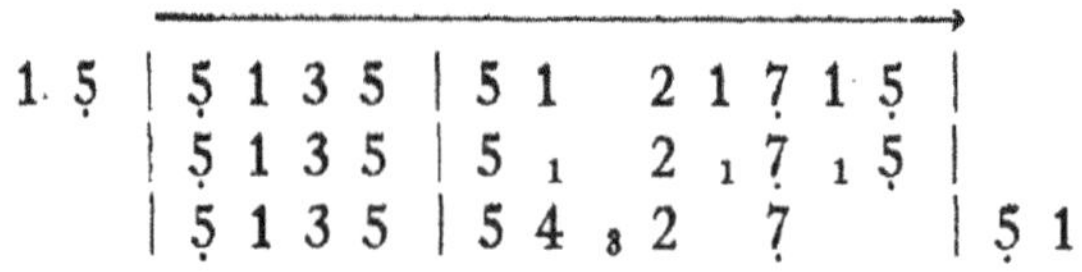

1. 5̣ | 5̣ 1 3 5 | 5 1 2 1 7̣ 1 5̣ |
| 5̣ 1 3 5 | 5 $_1$ 2 $_1$ 7̣ $_1$ 5̣ |
| 5̣ 1 3 5 | 5 4 $_3$ 2 7̣ | 5̣ 1

Use Diagram 23 for observation. Up one column, down the other.

Melody and Rhythm

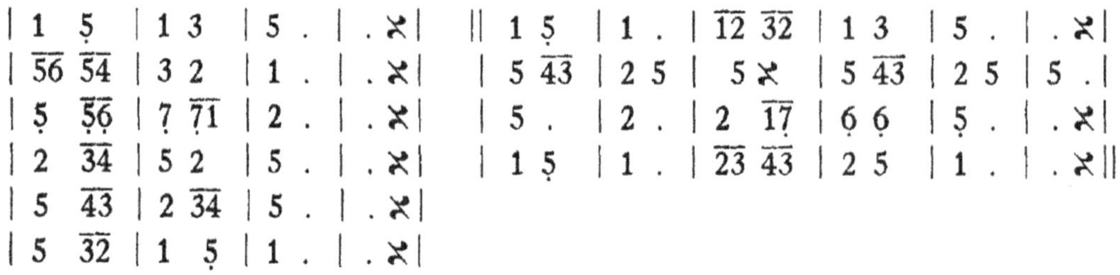

1 5̣	1 3	5 .	. x
56 54	3 2	1 .	. x
5̣ 5̣6̣	7̣ 7̣1	2 .	. x
2 34	5 2	5 .	. x
5 43	2 34	5 .	. x
5 32	1 5̣	1 .	. x

	1 5̣	1 .	12 32	1 3	5 .	. x
5 43	2 5	5 x	5 43	2 5	5 .
5 .	2 .	2 17̣	6̣ 6̣	5̣ .	. x
1 5̣	1 .	23 43	2 5	1 .	. x	

Melody and Rhythm

|| 5̣ | 1 . . | 2 . . | 3 1 5 | 4 2 7̣ | 1 3 1 | 5̣ .
| 5̣ | 2 4 2 | 5̣ . 5̣ | 1 3 1 | 5̣ . . |
| 5 | 4 2 5 | 3 1 5 | 5 . 2 | 2 3 4 | 5 . . | . . ||

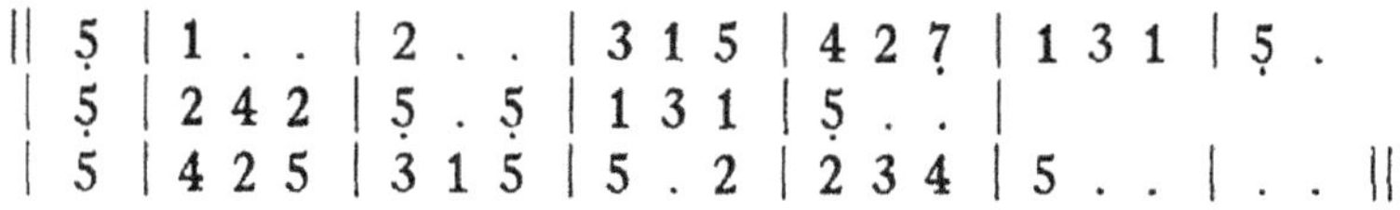

Intonation Exercise 76

(Key of A♭ or G)

(Use Diagram 36)

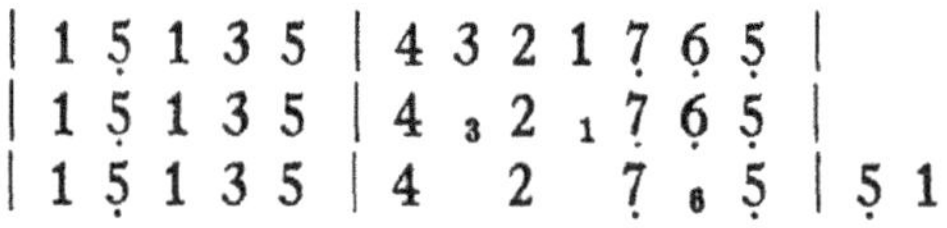

| 1 5̣ 1 3 5 | 4 3 2 1 7̣ 6̣ 5̣ |
| 1 5̣ 1 3 5 | 4 $_3$ 2 $_1$ 7̣ 6̣ 5̣ |
| 1 5̣ 1 3 5 | 4 2 7̣ $_6$ 5̣ | 5̣ 1

Intonation Exercise 77

(Key of A or A flat)

(*a*) | 1 5̣ 1 2 5̣ 2 3 5̣ 3 4 5̣ 4 3 5̣ 3 2 5̣ 2 1 5̣ 1 7̣ 5̣ 7̣ 1 |
| 1 5̣ $_1$ 2 5̣ $_2$ 3 5̣ $_3$ 4 5̣ $_4$ 3 5̣ $_3$ 2 5̣ $_2$ 1 5̣ $_1$ 7̣ 5̣ $_7$ 1 |
| 1 5̣ 2 5̣ 3 5̣ 4 5̣ 3 5̣ 2 5̣ 1 5̣ 7̣ 5̣ 1 |

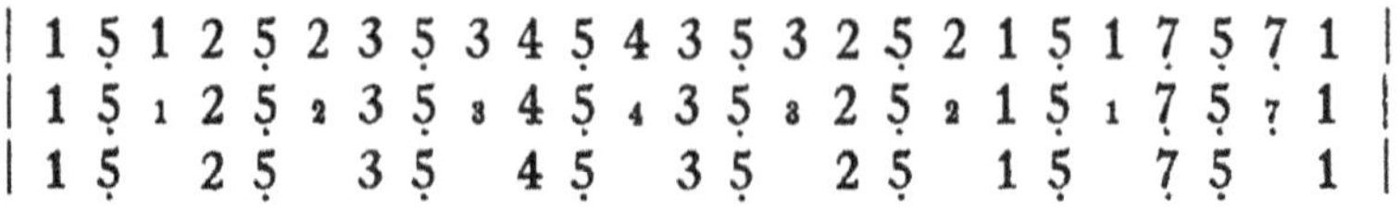

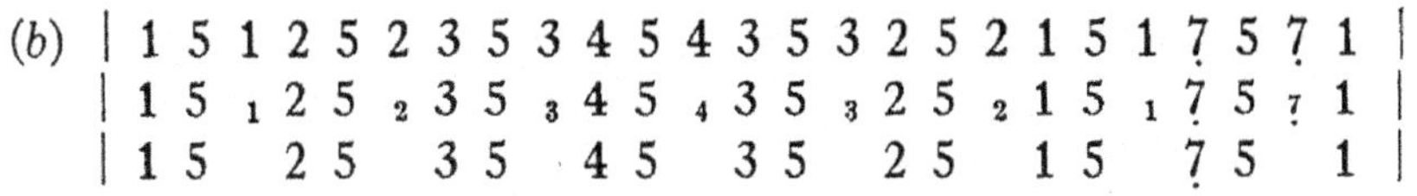

(b) | 1 5 1 2 5 2 3 5 3 4 5 4 3 5 3 2 5 2 1 5 1 7̣ 5 7̣ 1 |
| 1 5 ₁ 2 5 ₂ 3 5 ₃ 4 5 ₄ 3 5 ₃ 2 5 ₂ 1 5 ₁ 7̣ 5 ₇̣ 1 |
| 1 5 2 5 3 5 4 5 3 5 2 5 1 5 7̣ 5 1 |

Sing as written in numbers. Then from Staff Diagram 34.

Sing Melodies 101, 102, 103 and 104, *Children's Manual*, page 19.
Study one of the following Songs from the Children's Manual:

My Willow Tree, page 18.
High on the Hillside, page 20.
Marching Song, page 22.

Rhythm 31

Review Composite Time, 3/4

(Gesture 3)

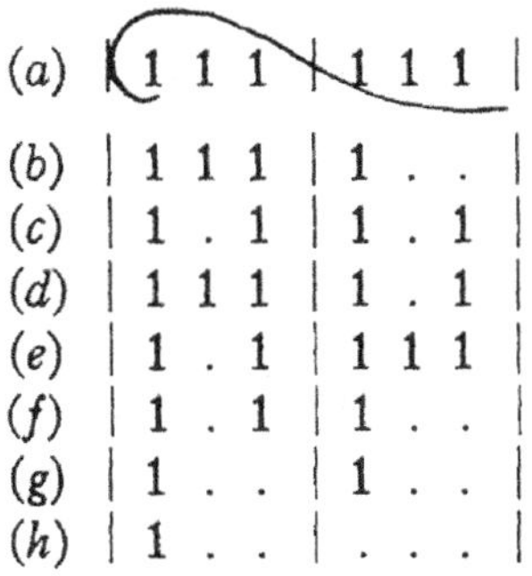

(a) | 1 1 1 | 1 1 1 |
(b) | 1 1 1 | 1 . . |
(c) | 1 . 1 | 1 . 1 |
(d) | 1 1 1 | 1 . 1 |
(e) | 1 . 1 | 1 1 1 |
(f) | 1 . 1 | 1 . . |
(g) | 1 . . | 1 . . |
(h) | 1 . . | . . . |

Repeat one design. For the end, add either *b, f, g* or *h*.
Then *alternate two designs, and repeat.* For the second, choose one with length.
Thus: *a + b, a + f, a + g, a + h*
c + b (or *f*, or *g* or *h*)
d + b (or *f*, or *g* or *h*)

This review should be made thoroughly, that the children be able to make the Rhythmic movement (Arsis-thesis) in brisk, smooth tempo, but without any jerks or angularities. When this result has been accomplished, the review has already served its purpose and it is not necessary to insist upon carrying out all possible combinations of the above designs.

A few phrases embodying rhythm and melody are given, but it is preferable, from this point on, to depend upon the Melodies in the Children's Manual for the application of the principles studied in the course of the chapters.

Rhythm and Melody
(Key of G)

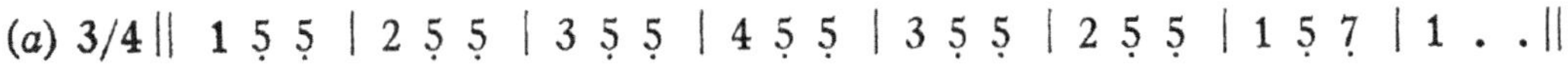

(a) 3/4 || 1 5̣ 5̣ | 2 5̣ 5̣ | 3 5̣ 5̣ | 4 5̣ 5̣ | 3 5̣ 5̣ | 2 5̣ 5̣ | 1 5̣ 7̣ | 1 . . ||

Rhythm and Melody

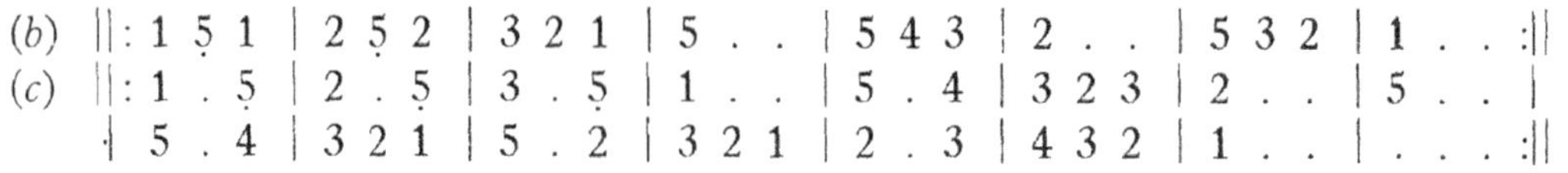

(*b*) ||: 1 5̣ 1 | 2 5̣ 2 | 3 2 1 | 5 . . | 5 4 3 | 2 . . | 5 3 2 | 1 . . :||

(*c*) ||: 1 . 5̣ | 2 . 5̣ | 3 . 5̣ | 1 . . | 5 . 4 | 3 2 3 | 2 . . | 5 . . |

| 5 . 4 | 3 2 1 | 5 . 2 | 3 2 1 | 2 . 3 | 4 3 2 | 1 . . | . . . :||

Observation and Dictation using the designs given above. (Rhythm **31**.)

Vocal Exercises of the First Year No. 19, 20 and 21, also 24 of the Second Year, for the placing of the syllables *Nu-o-u, Nu-a-u* and *Nu-o-a-u.* While studying the above, begin the direct attack of *Na* using the vocal exercises of the *Second Year Nos. 25 and 26* for the series *Na-nu-no-na* and *Na-nu-no-ne-ni.* The teacher will use all possible precautions that the tone shall not become throaty or nasal. (See the directions under *Vocal Exercises*, page 27.)

Intonation.—Review the *Tonic Chord* with the *Dominant Chord* in the plagal range using the Diagrams in numbers, then the Staff Diagrams. It is not enough to drill the children in the intervals embodied in the *Intonation Exercises of this chapter*, but they should acquire facility in singing the various intervals of these chords with freedom, this melodic material being a review of that covered in the first year. The chord of the *Dominant seventh* is presented in *Intonation Exercise 76* and on *Staff Diagram 36.*

Intonation Exercise 77 measures each tone of the scale from *low sol,* then from *high sol.* Sing slowly, verifying the pitch after each group, if necessary, thus:

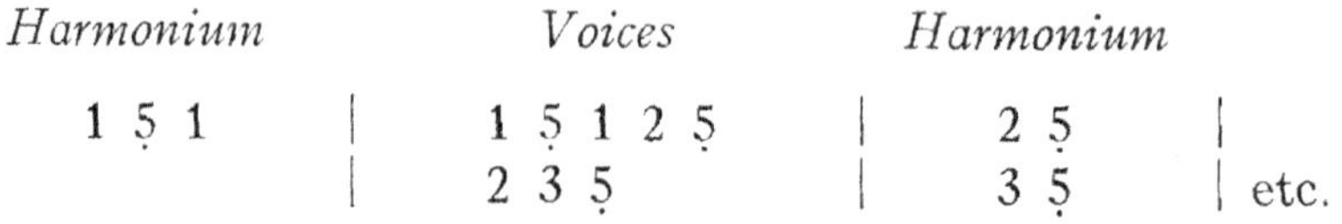

Harmonium	*Voices*	*Harmonium*	
1 5̣ 1	1 5̣ 1 2 5̣	2 5̣	
	2 3 5̣	3 5̣	etc.

If the pitch should be imperfect, the teacher will supply help notes on the board or through finger dictation: bridging over, through stepwise progression, those intervals which lack perfection, then resuming the exercise as it is written. Evidently the help-notes will rarely be needed, and then only to *correct an imperfection.* Inexactitude of pitch should always be corrected through building up a mental background (which is the function of the help-notes), rather than by the less laborious process of pure imitation. An impatient teacher will be tempted to play the passage or sing it correctly and thus obtain quick results at the expense of the child's inner development.

As the chords of the dominant and dominant seventh occupy the principal place in this chapter, the teacher would do well to draw the attention of the children to the fact that these intervals are used sparingly in the melodies. We find: 5̣ 2 or 5̣ 7̣ or 7̣2; often 4 2, but rarely the whole chord. We find fragments of the chord followed by passages in scale progression. Examine with the children the melodies of this chapter and others, for this discreet use of the dominant chord.

Rhythm.—Continue the review of 3/4 time—this time with composite time groups and the arsis-thesis gesture. Employ the designs one by one, then by twos, by threes, etc. Use rhythmic dictation of designs, observation, tapping, etc.

The Rhythm of words can be developed in 3/4 time as well as in 2/4 time. Thus:

2/4 || 1 1 | 1 1 | 1 1 | 1 1 | (or | 1 . | 1 . |)
Je- sus ten- der Shep- herd hear me hear me

| 1 1 | 1 1 | 1 1 | 1 . |
Bless Thy lit- tle lamb to- night

3/4 || 1 . 1 | 1 . 1 | 1 . 1 | 1 . 1 | (or | 1 . . | 1 . . |)
Je- sus ten- der Shep- herd hear me hear me

| 1 . 1 | 1 . 1 | 1 . 1 | 1 . . ||
Bless Thy lit- tle lamb to- night

The designs in 2/4 time can be used for replacing quarter notes with eighth notes, as described in the last chapter (p. 70).

In 3/4 time, the syllables can be sung to two notes as easily as to one long note: thus:

|| 5 . 4 | 3 . 2 | 3 . 4 | 5 . 5 |
Je- sus ten- der Shep- herd hear me

(*a*) | 5 . 4 | 3‿2 3 | 1 . 2 | 1 . . ||
Bless Thy lit- tle lamb to- night

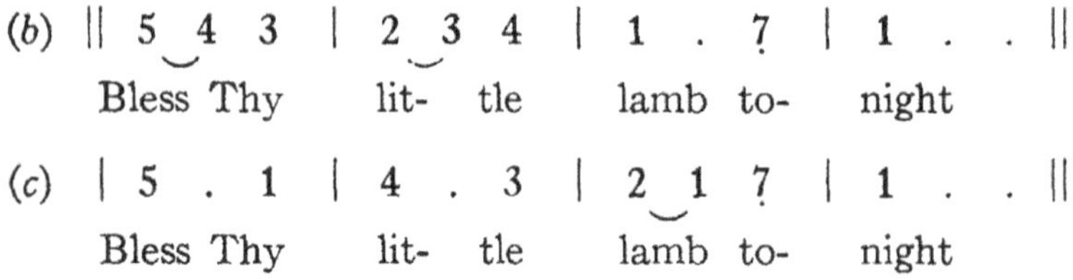

(*b*) || 5 ‿ 4 3 | 2 ‿ 3 4 | 1 . 7̣ | 1 . . ||
Bless Thy lit- tle lamb to- night

(*c*) | 5 . 1 | 4 . 3 | 2 ‿ 1 7̣ | 1 . . ||
Bless Thy lit- tle lamb to- night

Thus all the designs can be made useful even in the combining of words with melody and rhythm.

Let the children compose a melody for these words:

Jesus tender Shepherd hear me;
Bless Thy little Lamb tonight;
Through the darkness be Thou near me;
Keep me safe till morning light.

It may be in 2/4 or 3/4 time. It may use one design carried through all the lines (as far as that is possible) or vary the designs in order to make proper contrast. After they have tried to compose a melody to this verse, show them Song p. 86[1] where this verse is set to music, and let them sing it. Their own efforts to compose a setting will make the song as it is given the more interesting to the children. We suggest that songs that are given in this manual might often be built up in this manner: by allowing the children to try their own powers at composing at least a *part* of the song, before singing the real one given in the book.

Dictation

Melodic

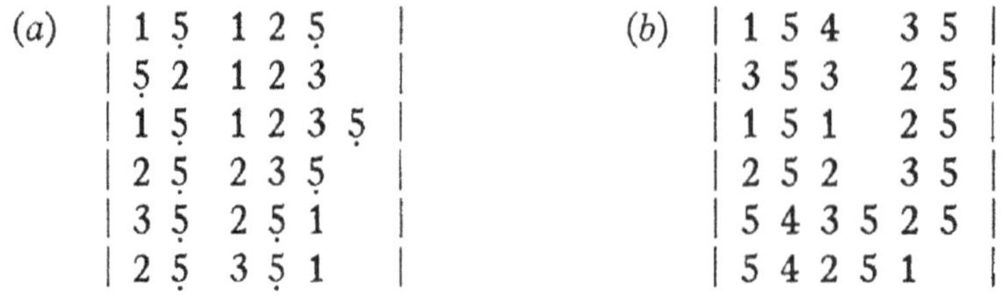

(*a*)	(*b*)
| 1 5̣ 1 2 5̣ |	| 1 5 4 3 5 |
| 5̣ 2 1 2 3 |	| 3 5 3 2 5 |
| 1 5̣ 1 2 3 5̣ |	| 1 5 1 2 5 |
| 2 5̣ 2 3 5̣ |	| 2 5 2 3 5 |
| 3 5̣ 2 5̣ 1 |	| 5 4 3 5 2 5 |
| 2 5̣ 3 5̣ 1 |	| 5 4 2 5 1 |

Melody and Rhythm

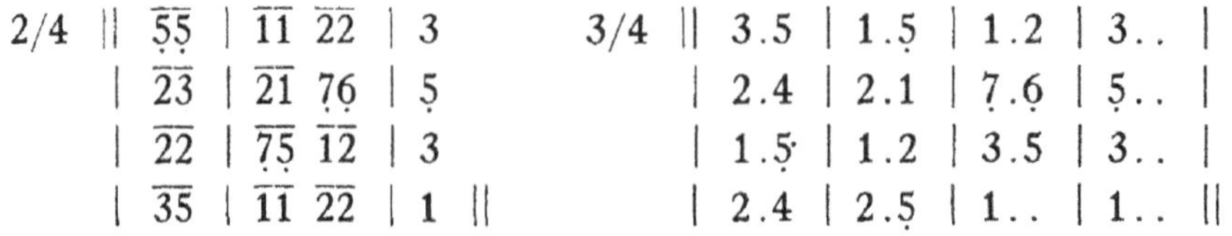

2/4	3/4
|| $\overline{55}$ (5̣5̣) | $\overline{11}$ $\overline{22}$ | 3	|| 3.5 | 1.5̣ | 1.2 | 3.. |
| $\overline{23}$ | $\overline{21}$ $\overline{76}$ (7̣6̣) | 5̣	| 2.4 | 2.1 | 7̣.6̣ | 5̣.. |
| $\overline{22}$ | $\overline{75}$ (7̣5̣) $\overline{12}$ | 3	| 1.5̣ | 1.2 | 3.5 | 3.. |
| $\overline{35}$ | $\overline{11}$ $\overline{22}$ | 1 ||	| 2.4 | 2.5̣ | 1.. | 1.. ||

[1] Children's Manual.

Phrases for Observation (Mozart)

15̣ 15̣ 15̣ 1.	
25̣ 25̣ 25̣ 2.	
31 31 31 3.	
42 42 42 4.	
3. .4 54 32 1.
13 53 15̣ 5̣5̣
4̣. 6̣. 5̣. 6̣7̣	1.	

Themes for Composition and Musical Conversations

3/4 || 5 | 5 . 4 | 3 4 5 | 2 . |
2/4 || 1 | 5 6̅5̅ | 4̅3̅ 2̅1̅ | 7̣̅1̅ 2̅2̅ | 5̣
2/4 || 3 2̅1̅ | 2 5̣ | 1̅3̅ 2̅1̅ | 7̣ 5̣ |
2/4 || 1 . | 7̣̅1̅ 2̅7̣̅ | 5̣ . |
2/4 || 1 1̅2̅ | 3 1 | 6̣ . | 2 1 | 7̣ 7̣̅7̣̅ | 1 2 | 5̣ . | . 𝄽 |
2/4 || 1̅2̅ 3̅4̅ | 5 5 | 5 5 | 3 1 |

3/4 || 3 3 3 | 3 . . | 3 3 3 | 3 . . | 3 3 3 | 3 . . | 5 4 3 | 2 . . |
3/4 || 1 . 3 | 1 . 5̣ | 1 3 5 | 5 . . |
3/4 || 5 . . | 3 4 2 | 3 . . | 1 2 7̣ | 1 . 𝄽 |
2/4 || 5 . | 1 3 | 2 4 | 3̅2̅ 1̅7̣̅ | 6̣̅7̣̅ 1̅2̅ | 3 4 | 5 𝄽 |
2/4 || 1 . | 3 4 | 5̅4̅ 3̅2̅ | 1 2 | 5̣ . | . 𝄽 |

This variety of themes provides a choice. It is not necessary that all be used.

CHAPTER SIX

Vocal Exercises Nos. 24c, 25c, 26c, 27c. Also Nos. 28a and 29a.

Special Exercise for Chapters VI and VII

(5 = G, A♭, A and B♭)

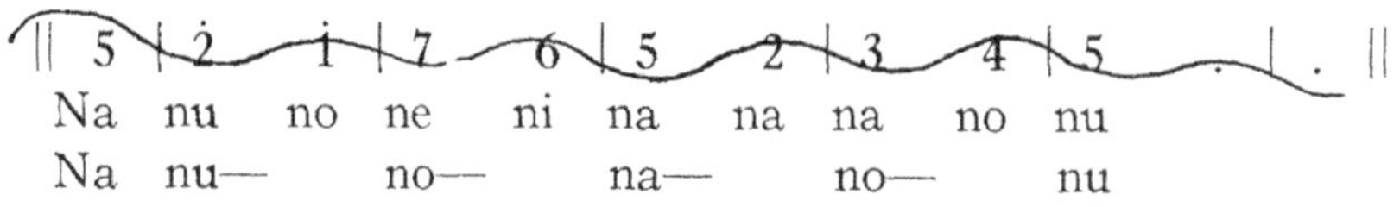

```
|| 5 | 2   1 | 7   6 | 5   2 | 3   4 | 5       | .  ||
   Na  nu  no  ne  ni  na  na  na  no  nu
   Na  nu—     no—     na—     no—     nu
```

Intonation.—Tonic and Dominant Chords in Plagal Range, and review of Mode VIII.

Intonation Exercise 78

(Key of G or A♭)

(Use Diagrams 23 and 35)

```
1 5 | 5 1 3 5   | 5 3 1 5   |
    | 5 1 ₃ 5   | 5 ₃ 1 5   |
    | 5 ₁ 3 5   | 5 3 ₁ 5   |
    | 5 ₁ ₃ 5   | 5 ₃ ₁ 5   | 5 1
```

Intonation Exercise 79

(Key of G or A♭)

(Use Diagram 36)

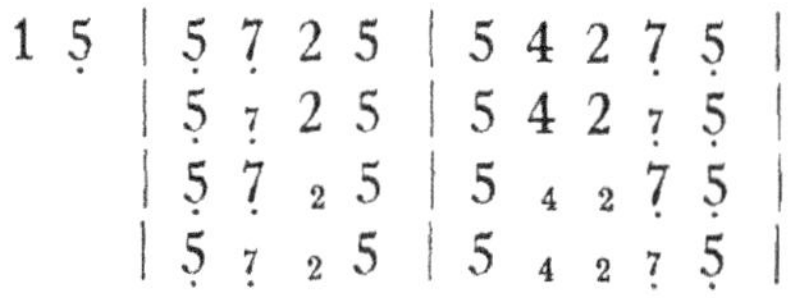

```
1 5 | 5 7 2 5   | 5 4 2 7 5   |
    | 5 ₇ 2 5   | 5 4 2 ₇ 5   |
    | 5 7 ₂ 5   | 5 ₄ ₂ 7 5   |
    | 5 ₇ ₂ 5   | 5 ₄ ₂ ₇ 5   |
```

Then, on Diagrams, Free Use of Intervals

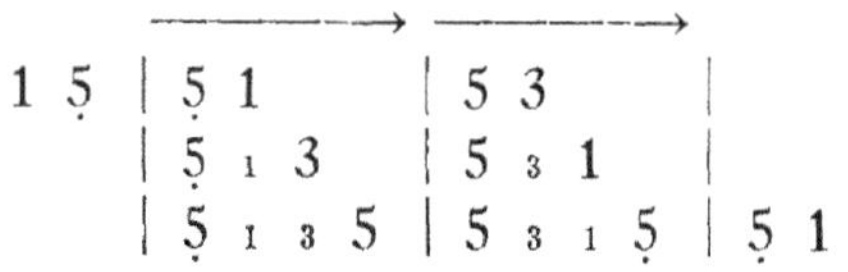

```
      ———————→   ———————→
1 5 | 5 1       | 5 3       |
    | 5 ₁ 3     | 5 ₃ 1     |
    | 5 ₁ ₃ 5   | 5 ₃ ₁ 5   | 5 1
```

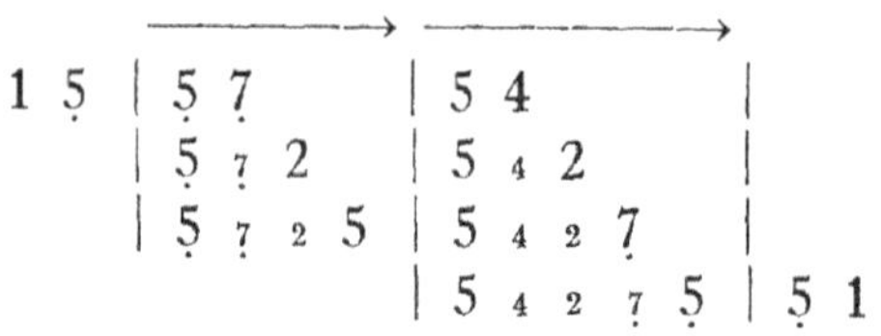

```
      ———————→   ————————→
1 5 | 5 7       | 5 4         |
    | 5 ₇ 2     | 5 ₄ 2       |
    | 5 ₇ ₂ 5   | 5 ₄ ₂ 7     |
                | 5 ₄ ₂ ₇ 5   | 5 1
```

Intonation Exercise 80

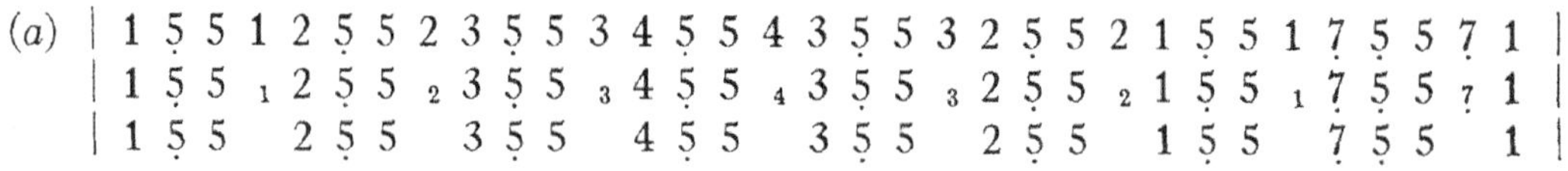

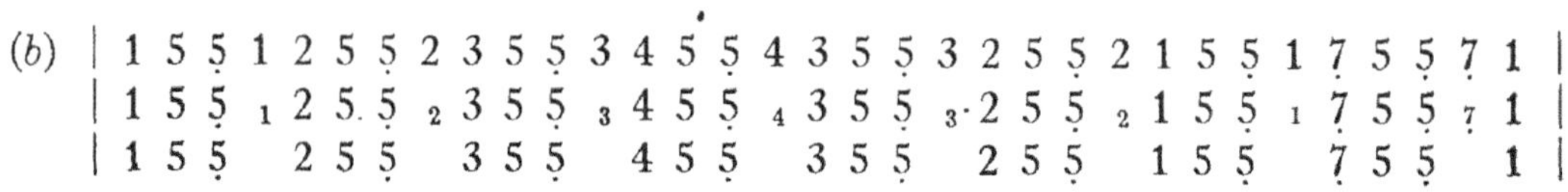

```
(a) | 1 5 5 1 2 5 5 2 3 5 5 3 4 5 5 4 3 5 5 3 2 5 5 2 1 5 5 1 7 5 5 7 1 |
    | 1 5 5 ₁ 2 5 5 ₂ 3 5 5 ₃ 4 5 5 ₄ 3 5 5 ₃ 2 5 5 ₂ 1 5 5 ₁ 7 5 5 ₇ 1 |
    | 1 5 5   2 5 5   3 5 5   4 5 5   3 5 5   2 5 5   1 5 5   7 5 5   1 |

(b) | 1 5 5 1 2 5 5 2 3 5 5 3 4 5 5 4 3 5 5 3 2 5 5 2 1 5 5 1 7 5 5 7 1 |
    | 1 5 5 ₁ 2 5 5 ₂ 3 5 5 ₃ 4 5 5 ₄ 3 5 5 ₃ 2 5 5 ₂ 1 5 5 ₁ 7 5 5 ₇ 1 |
    | 1 5 5   2 5 5   3 5 5   4 5 5   3 5 5   2 5 5   1 5 5   7 5 5   1 |
```

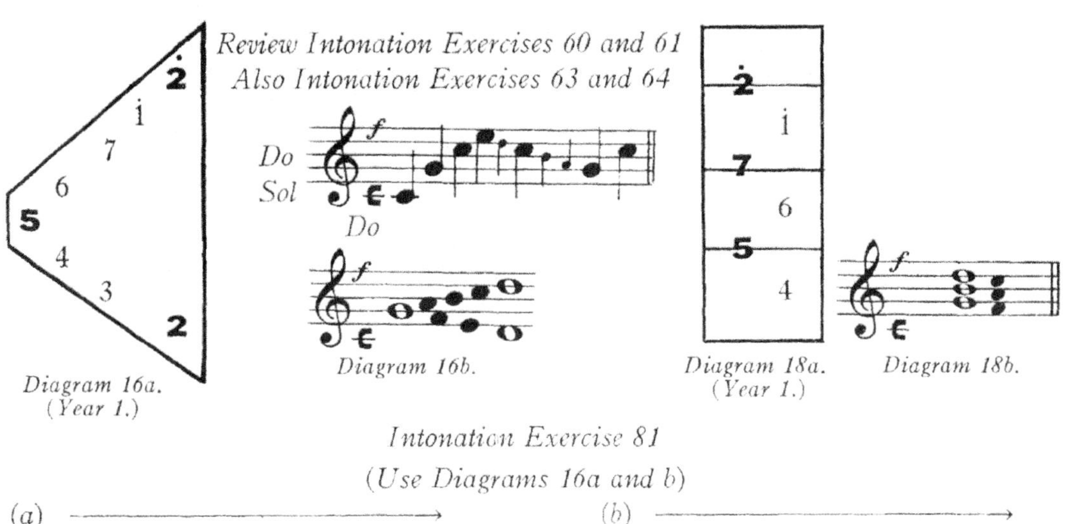

Diagram 16a. (Year 1.)

Diagram 16b.

Diagram 18a. (Year 1.)

Diagram 18b.

Intonation Exercise 81

(Use Diagrams 16a and b)

(*a*) ⟶

| 5 6 7 1̇ 2̇ 1̇ 5 6 7 1̇ 5 |
| 5 6 7 1̇ 2̇ 1̇ 6 7 5 |
| 5 6 7 1̇ 2̇ 1̇ 6 7 5 |
| 5 7 2̇ 1̇ 6 7 5 |
| 5 7 1̇ 6 5 |
| 5 7 6 1̇ 1̇ 2̇ 7 1̇ 6 5 |

(*b*) ⟶

| 5 6 1̇ 2̇ | 1̇ 5 6 1̇ 5 |
| 5 6 1̇ 7 | 1̇ 6 7 1̇ 5 |

(*c*) ⟶

| 5 4 3 2 2 3 4 5 5 6 5 |
| 5 4 3 2 2 3 4 5 5 6 5 |
| 5 2 5 6 5 |
| 5 4 3 2 5 6 5 |
| 5 4 5 6 5 |

Intonation Exercise 82

(Use Diagrams 18a and b)

(*a*) | 5 1̇ 7 1̇ 2̇ 1̇ 5 6 5 4 |
| 5 1̇ 7 1̇ 2̇ 1̇ 5 6 5 4 | 5

(*b*) | 2̇ 1̇ 7 1̇ 5 4 5 6 5 1̇ |
| 2̇ 1̇ 7 1̇ 5 4 5 6 5 1̇ | 5

Using Diagrams 18a and b, bring out the following intervals:

|| 6–4 with 5. 6–1̇ with 7–5 6–1̇ with 6–5 4 5–7 with 6–1̇
|| 4–6 with 5. 1̇–6 with 7–5 6–1̇ with 6–4 5 5 6 with 1̇2̇ and 1̇7
|| 1̇–6 with 1̇ 7–5 5 6 with 45 and 465

Go up one column of the diagram and down the other, always ending on *Sol*. The intervals listed above, however, are those which are most likely to occur in melodies of the *Eighth Mode*. They should be embodied in ear tests, observation work, and rhythmic phrases. A few typical examples follow:

Melody and Rhythm—Modes VII and VIII

	1̇ 6	7 6	5 6	5 .
4 6	1̇ 1̇	7 6	1̇ 2̇	2̇ .
2̇ 4̇	3̇ 4̇	2̇ .	1̇ .
6 4	6 6	5 .	. .	

|| 6 | 5 4 | 5 6 | 5 . | .
6 | 6 1̇ | 6 5 | 4 .
4 | 5 6 | 5 . | 5 . | . ||

|| 1̇ | 75 | 71̇ | 65 | 65 | 4. | 61̇ | 75 | 71̇ | 66 | 76 | 5. | 5. | . ||

|| 2̇ . | 5 6 | 5 6 | 4 . |
| 6 1̇ | 6 7 | 6 . | 5 . ||

	5 6	4 5	5 .
6 1̇	7 1̇	6 .	× 5
6 7	6 5	6'4	5 6	5 .	5 .	

Words and Melody

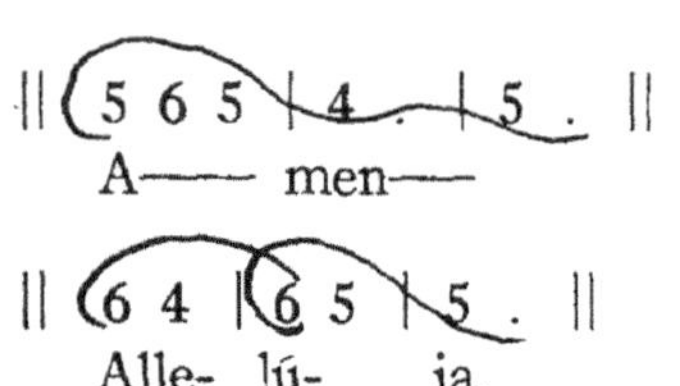

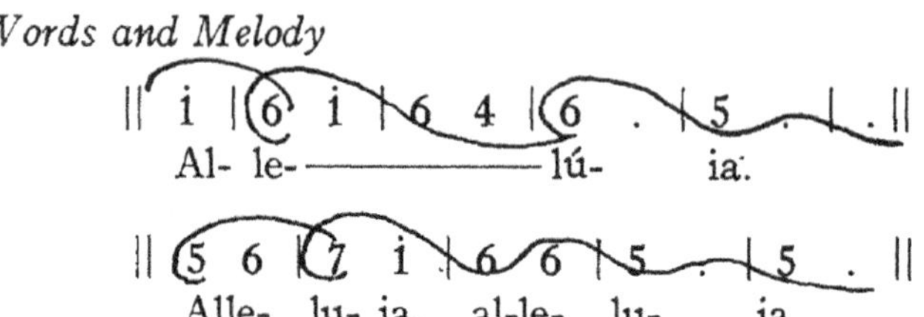

Melody 105

|| 5 | 6 5 | 6 7 | 1̇ 6 | 7
7 | 7 1̇ | 6 5 | 6 1̇ | 7 1̇ | 2̇ 1̇ | 7 . | ×
6 | 7 1̇ | 2̇ 7 | 1̇ 1̇ | 7
6 | 7 1̇ | 7 6 | 7 6 | 5 . | . ||

Melody 106

|| 5 | 7 6 | 1̇ 1̇ | 1̇ 7 | 6
6 | 1̇ 1̇ | 1̇ 5 | 6 5 | 4 . | ×
6 | 6 5 | 1̇ 7 | 6 5 | 6 7 | 6 .
6 | 6 5 | 4 5 | 6 5 | 5 . | . ||

Rhythm (Alternate groups of two and three pulses)

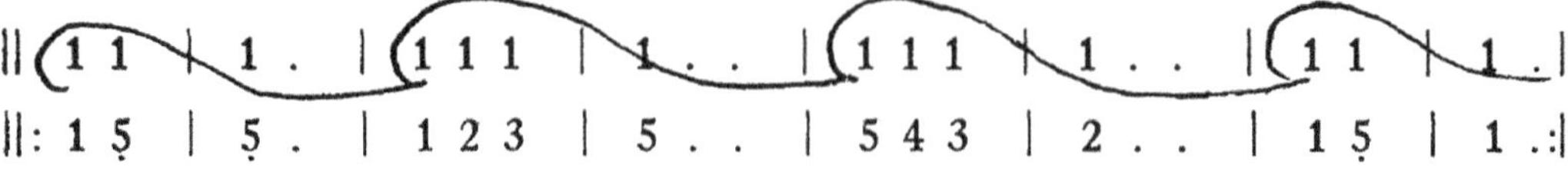

When a group contains *three* pulses, the curve (arsic or thetic) must be larger than that which represents a group of *two* pulses.

The teacher should make gestures in silence: the pupils deciding which curves represent a duplex group and which, a triplex one. The children, themselves, should then present the same problem to the class. Thus, attention having been drawn to this important point, the study of the phrases, Rhythm and Melody should be resumed.

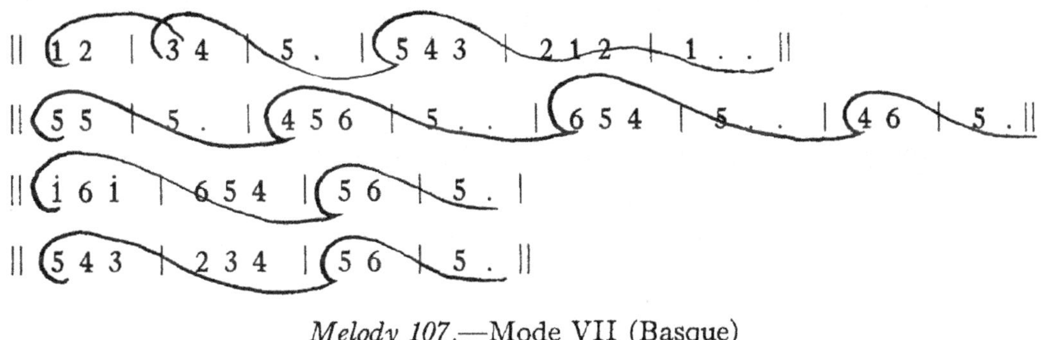

Melody 107.—Mode VII (Basque)

||: 5 5 | 7 2 | 5 . | 5 4 | 3 43 | 2 . |
| 7 1 | 2 7 | 2 . | 7 6 | 5 . | . ✕ || *Fine*
| 7 1 | 2 3 | 4 . | 5 4 | 3 43 | 2 . |
| 7 1 | 2 3 | 4 . | 4 3 | 2 . | . ✕ :|| *D. C.*

Melody 108.—Mode VII

|| 7 | 2 2 | i i | 7 . | 5' 7 | 2 2 | 3 i | 2 . | ✕
7 | 2 2 | i i | 7 . | 5' 6 | 7 i | 5 4 | 5 . | ✕
23 | 4 4 | 2 3 | i . | i' i | 2 3 | 4 4 | 2 . | ✕
7 | 2 2 | i i | 7 . | 5' 6 | 7 i | 5 4 | 5 . | . ||

Study several of the following numbers in the Children's Manual:

The Creed, page 40.
Agnus Dei, page 109.
Deus Meus, page 24.
Rosa Mystica, page 25.
Lullaby of the Infant Jesus, page 26.
Why? page 30.
The Spring, page 21.

Vocal Exercises of the Second Year, Nos. 24c, 25c, 26c, and 27c. Also 28a and 29a.—These should be prepared carefully as described in the Introduction to the Vocal Exercises (page 27).

Intonation.—Review of the chords of the Tonic and Dominant in the plagal range. *Exercise 78,* which should be studied first on the diagram, then horizontally as written, develops power to find any interval of the tonic chord measured from *low sol* and from *high sol. Exercise 79* develops the same power as regards the dominant chord. The last line of *Exercises 78 and 79* are identical in so far as we consider the notes that are to be *sung;* but they are quite different as regards the notes to be *thought.* In order to assure *honest thinking* (not mere guesswork) the teacher should occasionally tap a help-note and the children will sing it, thus verifying the fact that the pupils are really thinking each tone as indicated. When this careful preliminary drill has been carried out, the children should sing the intervals in question freely, without help-notes, from the diagram.

Intonation Exercise 80 gives practice in singing the octave $\underset{\cdot}{5}$ – 5 and from these extremities, measuring the intervening notes. After the exercise has been sung, dictation, ear tests, and observation work should be given on fragments of this exercise.

Review of Sol as Tonic.—A rapid review of *Intonation Exercises 60* and *61* (First Year) will prepare the children for *Intonation Exercise 81*. *Diagrams 16a* and *b* will serve for this work, after which the horizontal form will be studied. *Exercise 82* should be studied in like manner but from *Diagrams 18a* and *b*, after a rapid review of *Intonation Exercises 63* and *64* (First Year). The principal habit to establish at this point is that of feeling the tones: 5 7 2̇ as related to 1̇ and 1̇ 6 4 as related to 5 . While the children should be able to sing, without difficulty, up one column and down the other (Diagram 18), and any two tones of one column, supported on the intervening note of the opposite column (4–6 leaning on 5, etc.) the intervals which should be given especial care are those listed on page 79. They are characteristic of the eighth mode.

The VII and VIII Modes offer one difficulty only: the cadence *fa sol:* a whole tone cadence. The ear tests then, should bring out in bold relief this characteristic feature.

Major Cadences	1 2 1 7̣ 1	*Modes of Sol*	5 6 5 4 5 5 .
	1 2 7̣ 1		5 6 4 5 .

When we hear	1 2 34 5 6 5	and	1 3 5
It reminds us of	5 6 71̇ 2̇ 3̇ 2̇	and	5 7 2̇

We might easily become confused. But we cannot make any mistake when we hear a cadence on *do* and a cadence on *sol*

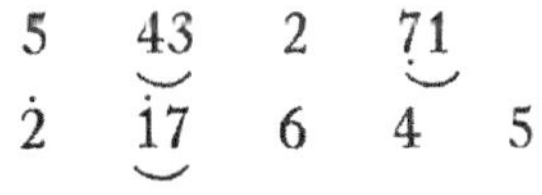

5	43	2	71	
2̇	1̇7	6	4	5

There is no mistake possible. Then insist on these endings when giving ear tests.

Rhythm.—No new rhythmic designs are presented in this chapter. Instead, the children approach the problem of combining groups containing three pulses with groups containing two pulses. Everything here depends on the gesture. A group of three must be lifted on a larger arsis or drooped on a broader thesis than a group containing two pulses only. This gesture should be practiced while counting. Then the phrases should be sung, giving *full value to each pulse* that the groups of *three* may not be reduced to the value of a modern triplet, but consist of *three full notes.* The melody helps the child to feel the rhythm.

Give silent dictation with gestures only. Problem: how many pulses in each arsis? in each thesis? The size of the curve will indicate the number of pulses. Gradually the children will learn to "guess" whether a group *is to be* duplex or triplex by the character of the curve *at its start.* Both teacher and pupils must form the habit of clear indications on this point: all must know, at the first note of a group whether a duplex or triplex group is to follow. The teacher must communicate its character by gesture and the class must grasp it. This habit is easily formed provided attention be drawn to the point. Lack of such precautions will leave the class hesitant and timid.

Study of the Creed.—The Creed is a simple *recitation,* with melodic inflexions which punctuate the text. The bar lines which appear are merely an aid to rapid visualization: they should not be interpreted as meaning that the text is measured in the sense of a composition that is primarily *musical.* The grouping of the notes will be an aid in *ensemble* recitation, particularly during the process of study. When the melody and rhythm are familiar the Creed should be sung with a certain freedom and at the tempo of quiet speech.

Material for Dictation

Major Mode. While studying *Intonation Exercise 80,* use fragments of the exercise itself, thus:

(*a*) | 1 5̣ 5 1 2 5̣ |
| 1 5̣ 5 1 2 |
| 2 5̣ 5 2 3 |
etc.

(*b*) | 1 5 5̣ 1 2 |
| 2 5 5̣ 2 3 |
etc.

(*c*) | 3 5 5̣ 1 |
| 3 5 5̣ 2 |
etc.

(*d*) | 1 2 5 5̣ 1 |
| 1 2 5 5̣ 7̣ |
etc.

While studying the Tonic chord with the dominant and dominant seventh:

(*a*) | 1 5̣ 1 3 5 |
| 1 5̣ 7̣ 2 5 |

(*b*) | 1 5 3 1 5̣ |
| 5 4 2 7̣ 5̣ |

(*c*) | 1 5 3 5 |
| 4 5 2 5 |
| 1 5 7̣ 5 1 |
etc.

(*d*) | 1 5 3 1 |
| 1 5 4 2 1 |
| 1 5 4 2 4 3 |
etc.

When dictating *a* and *b* leave Diagrams 23 and 36 before the children that the eye may aid the ear in discovering the chord.

Sol as Tonic (Keep Diagram **16** before the children.)

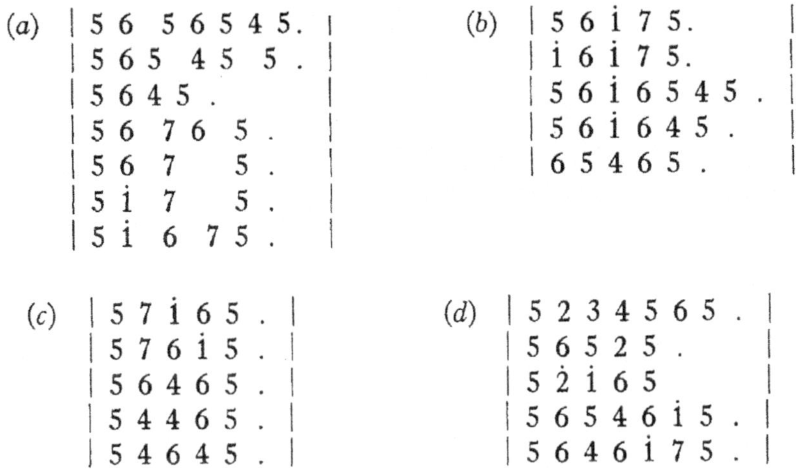

(*a*)
| 5 6 5 6 5 4 5. |
| 5 6 5 4 5 5 . |
| 5 6 4 5 . |
| 5 6 7 6 5 . |
| 5 6 7 5 . |
| 5 1̇ 7 5 . |
| 5 1̇ 6 7 5 . |

(*b*)
| 5 6 1̇ 7 5. |
| 1̇ 6 1̇ 7 5. |
| 5 6 1̇ 6 5 4 5 . |
| 5 6 1̇ 6 4 5 . |
| 6 5 4 6 5 . |

(*c*)
| 5 7 1̇ 6 5 . |
| 5 7 6 1̇ 5 . |
| 5 6 4 6 5 . |
| 5 4 4 6 5 . |
| 5 4 6 4 5 . |

(*d*)
| 5 2 3 4 5 6 5 . |
| 5 6 5 2 5 . |
| 5 2̇ 1̇ 6 5 |
| 5 6 5 4 6 1̇ 5 . |
| 5 6 4 6 1̇ 7 5 . |

Dictation with Melody and Rhythm

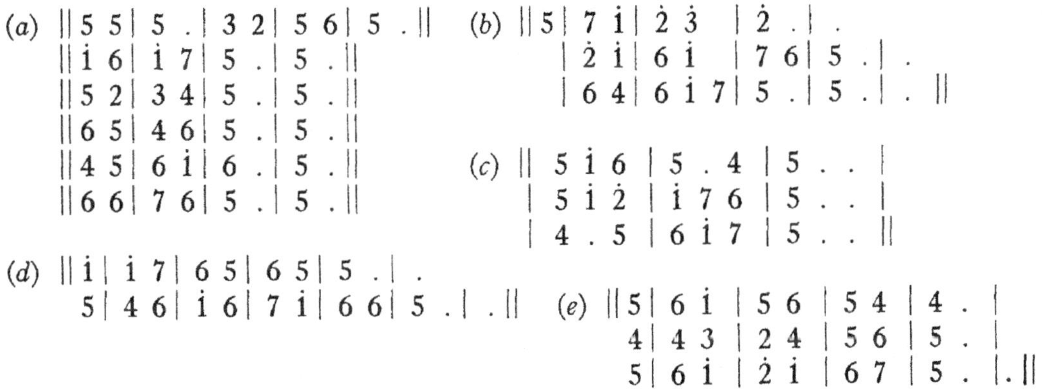

(*a*)
	5 5	5 .	3 2	5 6	5 .	
	1̇ 6	1̇ 7	5 .	5 .	
	5 2	3 4	5 .	5 .	
	6 5	4 6	5 .	5 .	
	4 5	6 1̇	6 .	5 .	
	6 6	7 6	5 .	5 .	

(*b*)
|| 5 | 7 1̇ | 2̇ 3̇ | 2̇ . | .
| 2̇ 1̇ | 6 1̇ | 7 6 | 5 . | .
| 6 4 | 6 1̇ 7 | 5 . | 5 . | . ||

(*c*)
	5 1̇ 6	5 . 4	5 . .
5 1̇ 2̇	1̇ 7 6	5 . .
4 . 5	6 1̇ 7	5 . .	

(*d*)
|| 1̇ | 1̇ 7 | 6 5 | 6 5 | 5 . | .
5 | 4 6 | 1̇ 6 | 7 1̇ | 6 6 | 5 . | . ||

(*e*)
|| 5 | 6 1̇ | 5 6 | 5 4 | 4 . |
4 | 4 3 | 2 4 | 5 6 | 5 . |
5 | 6 1̇ | 2̇ 1̇ | 6 7 | 5 . | . ||

Themes for Compositions

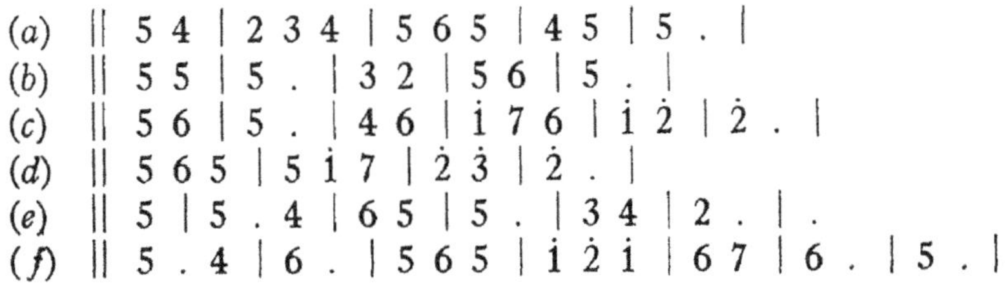

(*a*) || 5 4 | 2 3 4 | 5 6 5 | 4 5 | 5 . |
(*b*) || 5 5 | 5 . | 3 2 | 5 6 | 5 . |
(*c*) || 5 6 | 5 . | 4 6 | 1̇ 7 6 | 1̇ 2̇ | 2̇ . |
(*d*) || 5 6 5 | 5 1̇ 7 | 2̇ 3̇ | 2̇ . |
(*e*) || 5 | 5 . 4 | 6 5 | 5 . | 3 4 | 2 . | .
(*f*) || 5 . 4 | 6 . | 5 6 5 | 1̇ 2̇ 1̇ | 6 7 | 6 . | 5 . |

CHAPTER SEVEN

Vocal Exercises: As in Chapter Six.

Intonation.—Mode VII and Mode VIII.

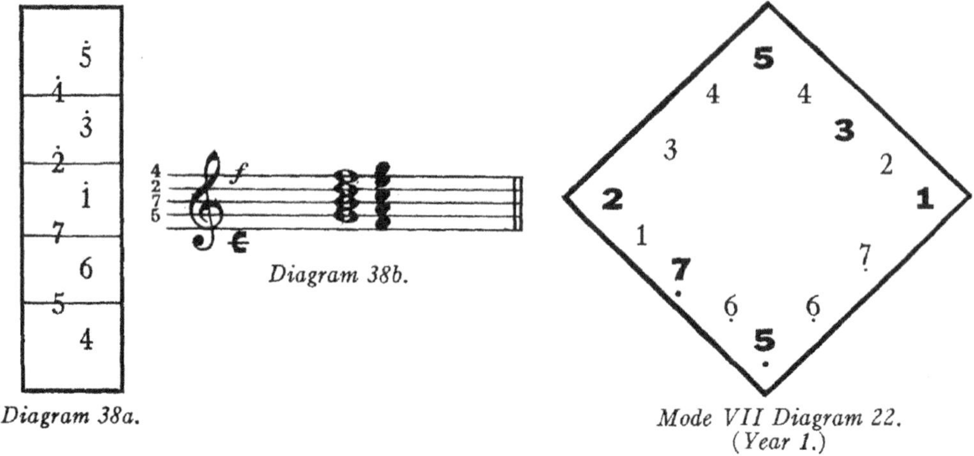

Diagram 38a.

Diagram 38b.

Mode VII Diagram 22.
(Year 1.)

Intonation Exercise 83

Mode VII (5-E flat)

| 5 1̇ 7 1̇ 2̇ 3̇ 2̇   1̇ 2̇ 4̇ 3̇ 2̇ 1̇ 2̇   2̇ 7 1̇ 6 5 |

| 5 i 7 1̇ 2̇ 3̇ 2̇   2̇ 1̇ 6 1̇ 7 6 5   7 1̇ 6 5 |

| 2̇ 7 2̇ 3̇ 4̇ 2̇ 2̇   2̇ 7 1̇ 2̇ 1̇ 6 5   6 7 6 5 |

| 5 5 7 1̇ 2̇ 3̇ 2̇   1̇ 3̇ 4̇ 3̇ 2̇   7 1̇ 2̇ 1̇ 6 5 |

Intonation Exercise 84

(*a*) | 5 7 2̇ 2̇ 1̇ 6 1̇ 7 6 5 |

| 5 ₇2̇ 2̇ 2̇ 3̇ 4̇ 2̇ 2̇ |

| 5 2̇ 2̇ 3̇ 2̇ 4̇ 3̇ 2̇ ' 7 |

| 1̇ 2̇ 1̇ 6 5 6 7 6 5 5 |

(*b*) | 5 6 1̇ 1̇ 2̇ 2̇ ' 1̇ 2̇ 3̇ 4̇ 5̇ 4̇ 3̇ 2̇ |

| 2̇ 1̇ 6 7 6 5 ' 6 5 4 5 6 5 |

| 1̇ 7 6 1̇ 2̇ 2̇ ' 2̇ 1̇ 6 7 6 5 |

| 5 2̇ 1̇ 6 7 5 ' 5 2̇ 2̇ 4̇ 2̇ 1̣̇ 6 7 5 |

Melody and Rhythm

	5	7 1̇	2̇ 2̇	1̇ 6	1̇ 1̇	7 .	1̇ 6	5 6	7 6	5 .	5 .	.	
	5 2̇	2̇ .	7 1̇	2̇ 3̇	2̇ .	2̇ 1̇	6 1̇	7 6	5 . 6	6 1̇ 7	5 .	5 .	
	5 2̇	2̇ 1̇	2̇ 3̇	2̇ .	1̇ 6	7 1̇	6 5 4	5 6 6	5 .	5 .	
	5 2̇	7 1̇	2̇ 3̇	2̇ .	2̇ 4̇ 2̇	1̇ 2̇	2̇ . ’	1̇ 6	7 6	5 .	5 .	
	5 2̇	2̇ 3̇	4̇ 2̇	2̇ .	2̇ 7	1̇ 6	5 .	4 6	5 .	5 .	
	5 2̇	1̇ 7	6 1̇	2̇ 3̇	2̇ .	7 1̇	2̇ 1̇ 6	5 .	5 .	

Melody, Rhythm and Words

|| 5 6 7 1̇ 6 6 5 5 . ||
Al- le- lú- ia, al- le- lú- ia.

|| 4 3 4 5 5 . 5 . ||
Al- le- lú- ia.

|| 6 5 6 6 1̇ 7 5 . 5 . ||
Al- le- lú- ia, al- le- lú- ia.

|| 7 1̇ | 2̇ 3̇ | 2̇ . | 2̇ 1̇ | 6 1̇ | 7 6 | 5 . ’ 6 | 6 1̇ 7 | 5 . | 5 . ||
Al-le- lú- ia. al- le- lú ia, al- le- lú- ia.

|| 5 7 | 1̇ 2̇ | 2̇ . | 2̇ 3̇ 2̇ | 1̇ 7 6 | 1̇ 7 | 5 . | 5 . ||
Al-le- lú- ia, al- le- lú- ia, al- le- lú- ia.

Rhythm 32, 3/4 Time

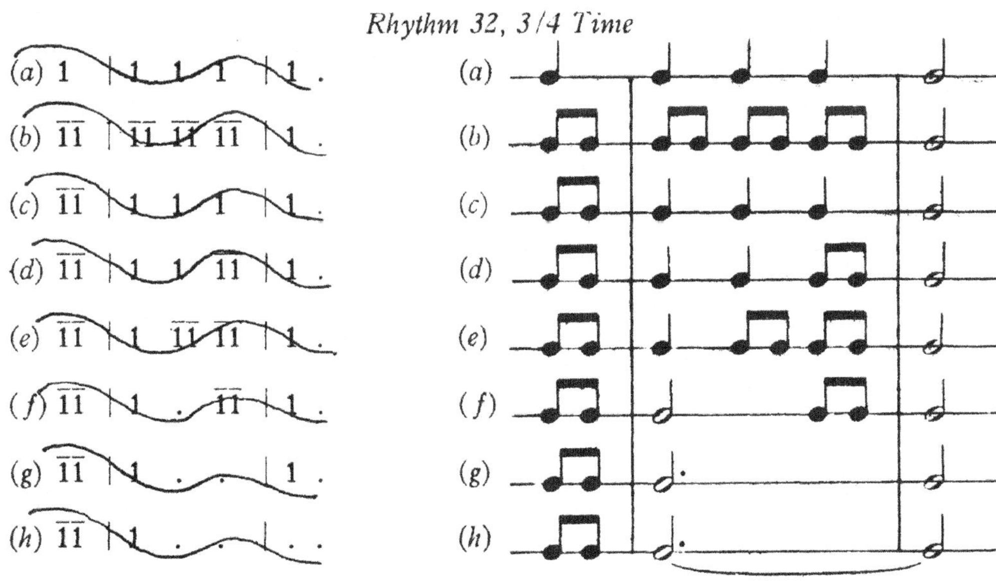

Rhythm and Melody

(*a* + *b*) || 5 | 1̇ 7 1̇ | 2̇ .

$\overline{23}$ | $\overline{\dot{2}\dot{1}}$ $\overline{76}$ $\overline{56}$ | 5 . ||

(*d* + *d*) || $\overline{56}$ | 5 2̇ $\overline{23}$ | 2̇ .

$\overline{12}$ | 1̇ 6 $\overline{76}$ | 5 . ||

(*c* + *b*) || $\overline{56}$ | 5 1̇ 6 | 5 .

$\overline{56}$ | $\overline{54}$ $\overline{32}$ $\overline{34}$ | 5 . ||

(*e* + *f*) || $\overline{56}$ | 5 $\overline{32}$ $\overline{34}$ | 5 .

$\overline{67}$ | 1̇ . $\overline{76}$ | 5 . ||

(*e* + *g*) || $\overline{56}$ | 5 1̇ 6 | 5 .

(*a* + *g*) || 5 | 6 1̇ 1̇ | 1̇ .

(*c* + *h*) $\overline{45}$ | 6 . . | 6 .

$\overline{46}$ | 1̇ 7 6 | 5 .

$\overline{56}$ | 5 . . | . . ||

(*g* + *h*) $\overline{7\dot{1}}$ | 2̇ . . | 5 .

$\overline{56}$ | 1̇ . . | 6 .

$\overline{76}$ | 5 . . | . . ||

Sing. Find four Designs

Alternating Groups of 2 and 3 Pulses

|| 1̇ 7 | 6 5 | 6 1̇ 6 | 7 . | 6 1̇ 2̇ | 1̇ 7 | 5 6 5 | 5 . ||

|| 2̇ . | 7 1̇ | 2̇ 3̇ 2̇ | 1̇ . | 1̇ 7 6 | 7 1̇ | 2̇ 1̇ 6 | 5 . | 5 . ||

Melody 110—Mode VIII (Spanish)

|| $\overline{55}$ | 1̇ 2̇ $\overline{7\dot{1}}$ | $\overline{65}$ $\overline{45}$ | 1̇ 2̇ $\overline{7\dot{1}}$ | 7 .

$\overline{55}$ | 1̇ 2̇ $\overline{7\dot{1}}$ | $\overline{65}$ $\overline{45}$ | 6 7 $\overline{56}$ | 5 . ||

Rhythm and Melody

Form a

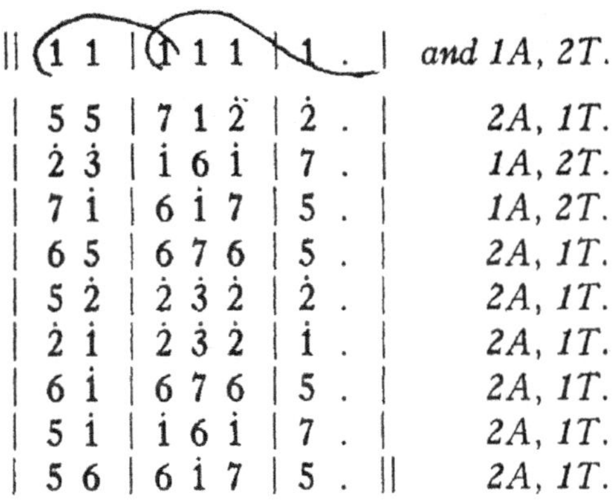

|| 1 1 | 1 1 1 | 1 . | *and 1A, 2T.*
| 5 5 | 7 1 2̈ | 2̇ . | *2A, 1T.*
| 2̇ 3̇ | 1̇ 6 1̇ | 7 . | *1A, 2T.*
| 7 1̇ | 6 1̇ 7 | 5 . | *1A, 2T.*
| 6 5 | 6 7 6 | 5 . | *2A, 1T.*
| 5 2̇ | 2̇ 3̇ 2̇ | 2̇ . | *2A, 1T.*
| 2̇ 1̇ | 2̇ 3̇ 2̇ | 1̇ . | *2A, 1T.*
| 6 1̇ | 6 7 6 | 5 . | *2A, 1T.*
| 5 1̇ | 1̇ 6 1̇ | 7 . | *2A, 1T.*
| 5 6 | 6 1̇ 7 | 5 . || *2A, 1T.*

Form b

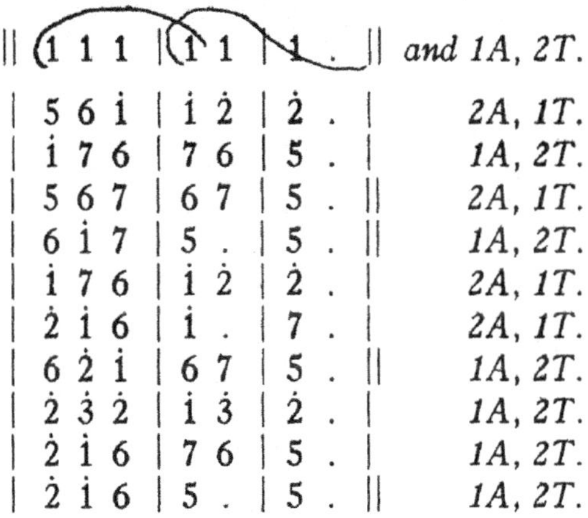

|| 1 1 1 | 1 1 | 1 . || *and 1A, 2T.*
| 5 6 1̇ | 1̇ 2̇ | 2̇ . | *2A, 1T.*
| 1̇ 7 6 | 7 6 | 5 . | *1A, 2T.*
| 5 6 7 | 6 7 | 5 . || *2A, 1T.*
| 6 1̇ 7 | 5 . | 5 . || *1A, 2T.*
| 1̇ 7 6 | 1̇ 2̇ | 2̇ . | *2A, 1T.*
| 2̇ 1̇ 6 | 1̇ . | 7 . | *2A, 1T.*
| 6 2̇ 1̇ | 6 7 | 5 . || *1A, 2T.*
| 2̇ 3̇ 2̇ | 1̇ 3̇ | 2̇ . | *1A, 2T.*
| 2̇ 1̇ 6 | 7 6 | 5 . | *1A, 2T.*
| 2̇ 1̇ 6 | 5 . | 5 . || *1A, 2T.*

Form c

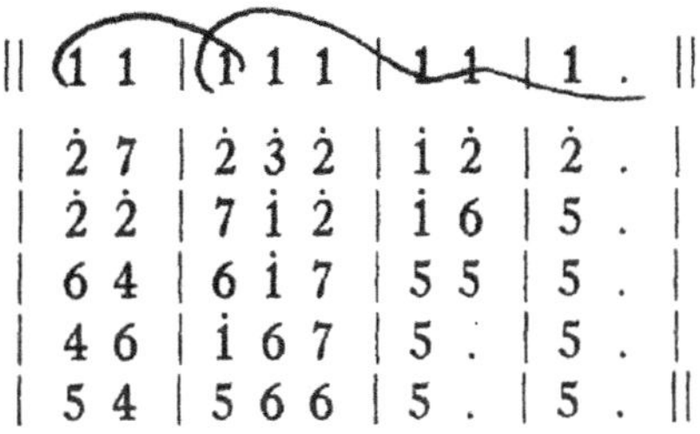

	1 1	1 1 1	1 1	1 .	
2̇ 7	2̇ 3̇ 2̇	1̇ 2̇	2̇ .
2̇ 2̇	7 1̇ 2̇	1̇ 6	5 .
6 4	6 1̇ 7	5 5	5 .
4 6	1̇ 6 7	5 .	5 .
5 4	5 6 6	5 .	5 .	

Form d

|| 1 1 1 | 1 1 | 1 1 1 | 1 . ||
| 5 4 2 | 3 4 | 5 6 6 | 5 . |
| 5 4 6 | 1̇ 7 | 1̇ 2̇ 1̇ | 6 . | *3A, 1T.*
| 6 5 6 | 7 6 | 5 6 5 | 5 . | *2A, 2T.*
| 5 4 2 | 3 4 | 5 6 6 | 5 . ||

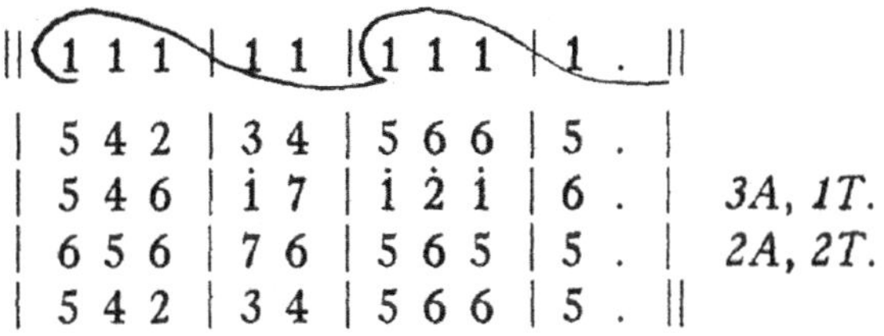

Phrases to Read at Sight

(*a*) ||: 5 6 | 5 . | 4 6 | 1̇ 5 | 6 5 | 4 6 | 1̇ 7 6 | 2̇ 3̇ | 2̇ . |
| 2̇ 1̇ | 7 5 | 6 4 | 5 . | 5 1̇ | 6 7 | 6 . | 5 . ||

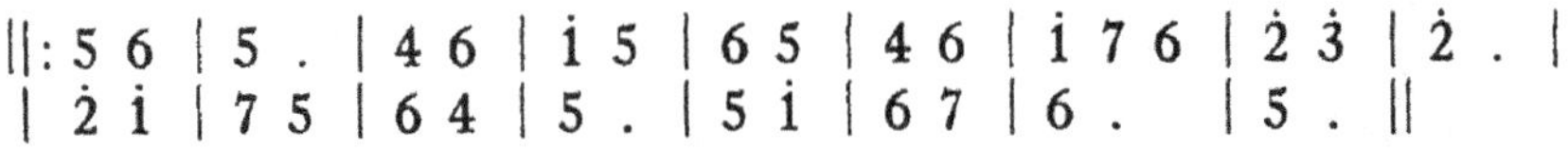

(*b*) ||: 5 6 | 5 . | 4 6 | 1̇ 7 6 | 1̇ 2̇ | 2̇ . :|| 3̇ 2̇ | 1̇ . | 7 6 | 5 . |
| 4 6 | 1̇ 7 6 | 1̇ 2̇ | 3̇ 2̇ | 1̇ . | 7 6 | 5 . 4 | 6 7 | 6 . | 5 . ||

(*c*) ||: 5 | 5 6 | 5 4 | 4 6 | 1̇ . | 2̇ 3̇ | 2̇ . :|| 1̇ 2̇ | 3̇ 1̇ | 3̇ . 2̇ | 3̇ 2̇ | 1̇ . |
| 6 1̇ | 7 5 | 6 . | 5 . | 4 6 | 1̇ . | 2̇ 3̇ 2̇ | 1̇ . | 7 6 5 | 6 . | 5 . | . ||

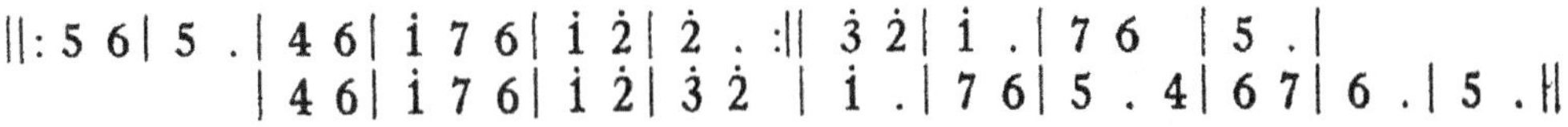

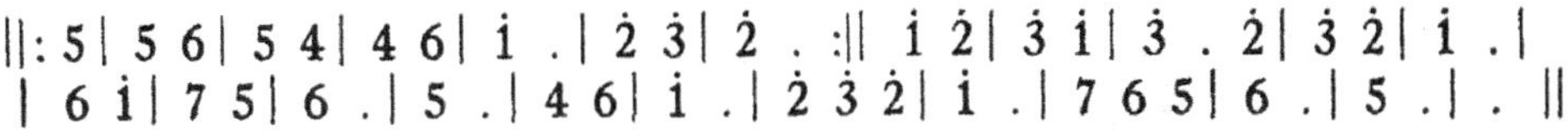

Study the following numbers from the Children's Manual:
Melodies 111, 112 and 113, page 31.
The Asperges, page 99.
The Sanctus, page 108.
The First Noel, page 28.

Vocal Exercises as in Chapter Six.

Intonation. Mode VII and Mode VIII.—The intervals of *Exercises 83* and *84*, followed by the phrases "Melody and Rhythm," give a clear impression of the melodic tendencies of these modes. When using the Diagrams of this chapter, the teacher will do well to follow these phrases in order to form the taste of the children. The two modes of *Sol* are less familiar to the teacher, as well as to the pupils, than are the Major and Minor. For this reason we have provided a good deal of melodic material in this chapter. It can be used in many ways: for interval work on the Diagrams or as given in the exercise itself; for the study of cadences; for observation and memory work; for themes on which to compose melodies; for subjects from which to build up musical conversations.

Rhythm.—(*a*) Development of the Divided beat in 3/4 Time. The designs should be used one by one; then each one repeated, then combined with others. Observation and memory work as usual in such cases. A few examples of single designs with melody are included; the children should be encouraged to use various designs in their compositions, remembering that principle of good composition which requires that there be *unity* as well as variety in a melody.

(*b*) Development of rhythm with alternating groups of two pulses and of three. In the brief phrases on Page 89 the children should make the gesture indicated while singing, but *a small gesture* with one arm only, that the singing may be extremely legato.

Staff Notation.—The C clef on leger line below staff (Key of C). This position of *Do* is particularly useful for melodies whose range is from 3 to $\dot{3}$. The children may write on the staff melodies of the First Year which have the above range. They should sing the melodies of this chapter.

Themes for Musical Compositions

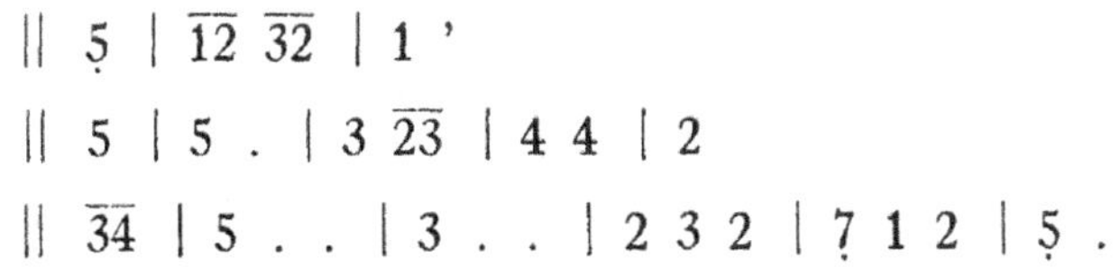

|| $\underset{\cdot}{5}$ | $\overline{12}$ $\overline{32}$ | 1 '

|| 5 | 5 . | 3 $\overline{23}$ | 4 4 | 2

|| $\overline{34}$ | 5 . . | 3 . . | 2 3 2 | $\underset{\cdot}{7}$ 1 2 | $\underset{\cdot}{5}$.

|| $\underset{\cdot}{5}$ $\underset{\cdot}{5}$ | $\underset{\cdot}{7}$ 1 | 2 3 | 2 . |

|| $\underset{\cdot}{5}$ | $\underset{\cdot}{7}$ 1 | 2 . | 2 3 | 1 2 | $\underset{\cdot}{7}$. |

|| $\underset{\cdot}{5}$ | $\underset{\cdot}{7}$ 1 | 2 1 | $\underset{\cdot}{6}$. | 1 $\underset{\cdot}{7}$ | $\underset{\cdot}{5}$ $\underset{\cdot}{5}$ | $\underset{\cdot}{5}$. | .

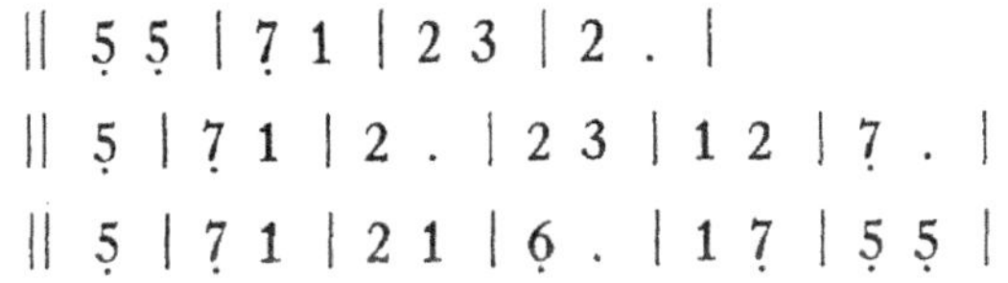

Write an answer to each of these questions. (Mode *VII* or *VIII*.)

Write a question to each of these answers

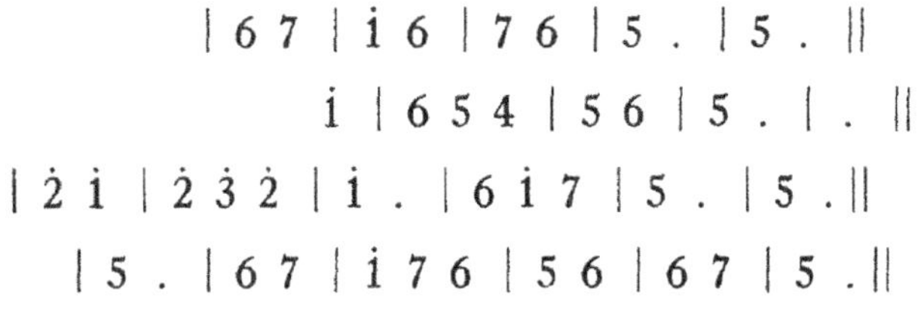

| 6 7 | $\dot{1}$ 6 | 7 6 | 5 . | 5 . ||

$\dot{1}$ | 6 5 4 | 5 6 | 5 . | . ||

| $\dot{2}$ $\dot{1}$ | $\dot{2}$ $\dot{3}$ $\dot{2}$ | $\dot{1}$. | 6 $\dot{1}$ 7 | 5 . | 5 . ||

| 5 . | 6 7 | $\dot{1}$ 7 6 | 5 6 | 6 7 | 5 . ||

Dictation

Follow the intervals of the Intonation Exercises, giving variety by repetition, particularly of *sol* and *re*. Also bringing out the cadences 5 6 5 . 6 4 5 . 4 5 5. This distinguishes the Modes of *Sol* from the Major Mode.

CHAPTER EIGHT

Vocal Exercise Nos. 25a and 26a, also 25b after study of Diagram 39.

Intonation.—The Minor Mode: Pentachord and Hexachord.

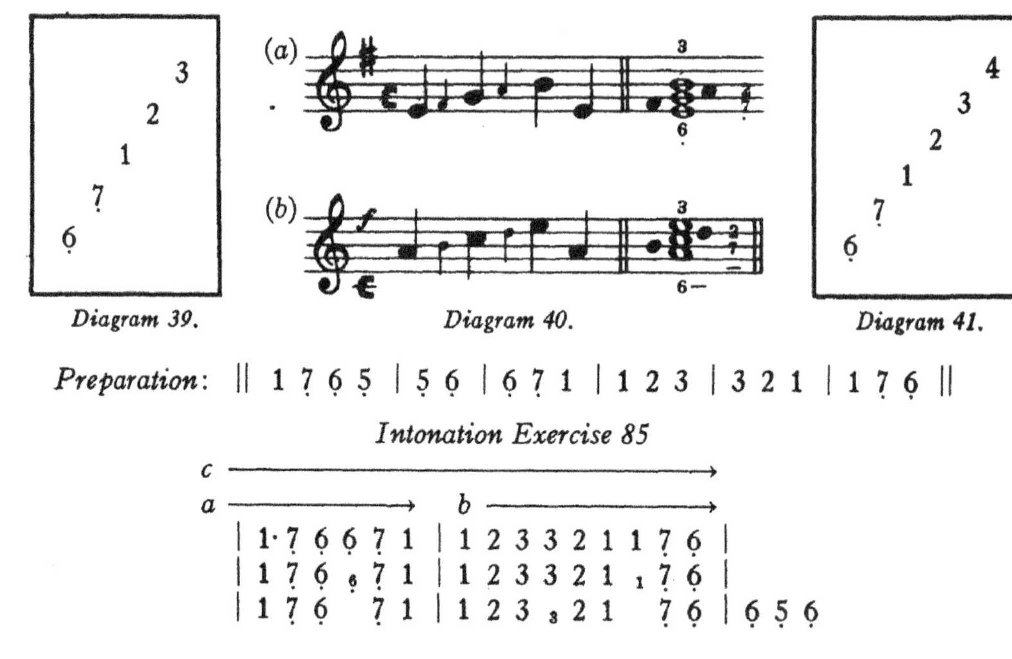

Diagram 39. *Diagram 40.* *Diagram 41.*

Preparation: || 1 7 6 5 | 5 6 | 6 7 1 | 1 2 3 | 3 2 1 | 1 7 6 ||

Intonation Exercise 85

Intonation Exercise 86

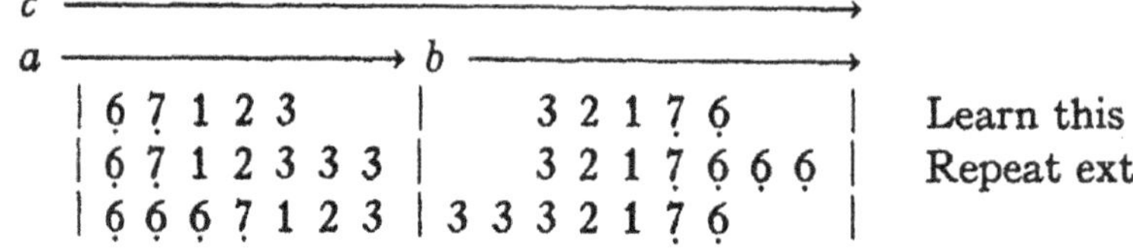

Learn this line as a melody.
Repeat extremities.

Intonation Exercise 87a

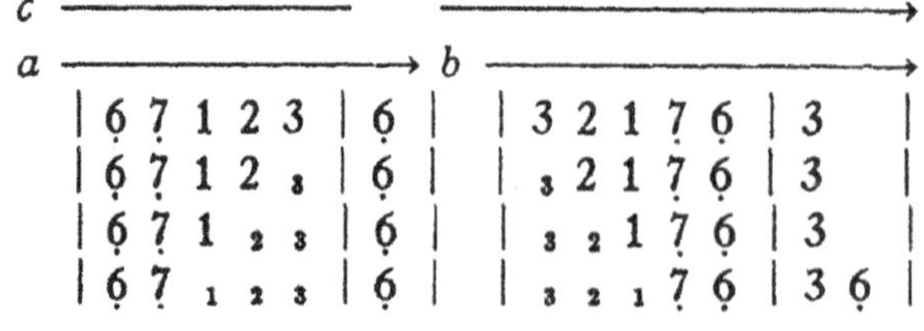

(*a b*) Stop at any point.
(*c*) Stop and turn back.

Melody and Rhythm

(*a*) || 6 | 6 . 7 | 1 . 2 | 3 3 3 | 3 .
3 | 3 . 2 | 1 . 7 | 6 . . | 6 . ||

(*b*) || 6 | 6 . 7 | 1 . 2 | 3 . . | 6 .
6 | 6 . 7 | 1 . 2 | 6 . . | . 𝄽
6 | 6 . 7 | 1 . 1 | 6 . . | 7 .
6 | 6 . 7 | 1 . 6 | 6 . . | . 𝄽 ||

Intonation Exercise 87b

c ——— ———→
a ———→ b ———→
3 2 1 7 6	3	6 7 1 2 3	6
3 2 1 7 6	3	6 7 1 2 3	6
3 2 1 7 6	3	6 7 1 2 3	6
3 2 1 7 6	3	6 7 1 2 3	6

(*c*) || 3 | 3 . 2 | 1 . 7 | 6 . . | 3 .
2 | 2 . 1 | 7 . 6 | 3 . . | . 𝄽
3 | 3 . 2 | 1 . 7 | 6 . . | 3 .
2 | 1 7 6 | 3 . 6 | 6 . . | . 𝄽 ||

Intonation Exercise 88

c ——— ———→
a ———→ b ———→
6 7 1 2 3 3 3	3 6		3 2 1 7 6 6 6	6 3
6 7 1 2 2 2 3	3 6		3 2 1 7 7 7 6	6 3
6 7 1 1 1 2 3	3 6		3 2 1 1 1 7 6	6 3
6 7 7 7 1 2 3	3 6		3 2 2 2 1 7 6	6 3 6

Stop at any point and repeat continuing in same direction.

Melody and Rhythm

|| 67 | 1 2 | 3 3 | 6 . | .
67 | 1 2 | 2 3 | 3 . | .
32 | 1 7 | 6 6 | 3 . | .
32 | 21 76 | 3 3 | 6 . | . ||

|| 67 | 1 2 | 2 3 | 3 . | .
32 | 2 1 | 7 7 | 6 . | 𝄽
67 | 1 12 | 3 32 | 3 . | .
12 | 32 17 | 6 67 | 6 . | . ||

Melody 114. (French Folk Song)

||: 6 | 6 . 7 | 1 . 2 | 3 . 3 | 2 3 2 | 1 . 7 | 6 . :||
||: 7 | 1 . 7 | 6 . :||
3 | 3 . 3 | 2 . 3 | 1 . 7 | 6 . . | . 𝄽 ||

Intonation Exercise 89a

d ———→
a ———→ b ———→ c ———→

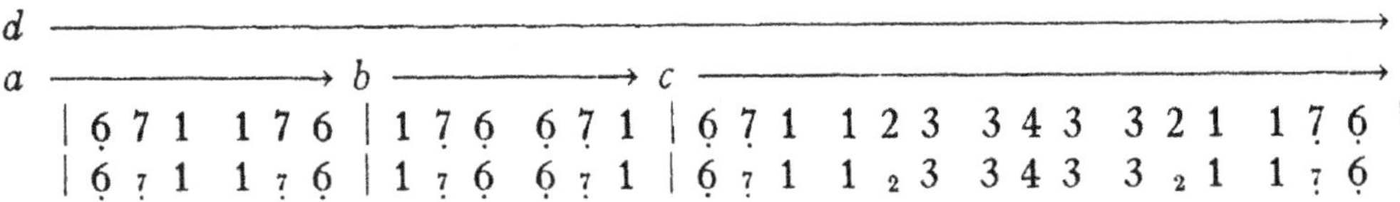

Intonation Exercise 89b

| 3 4 3 3 2 1 1 7 6 | 6 7 1 . 1 2 3 3 4 3 | 3 6 |
| 3 4 3 3 ₂ 1 1 ₇ 6 | 6 ₇ 1 1 ₂ 3 3 4 3 | 3 6 |

Melody and Rhythm

	67 12	3 3	3 4	3 .
3 1	1 7	6 1	7 .
6 3	3 4	32 12	3 .
34 32	1 7	6 .	6 .

	6 1	1 6	1 .	7 .
6 1	1 3	32 12	3 .
34 32	3 3	34 32	1 7
12 17	6 1	3 .	. ✗
34 32	1 7	6 .	. .	

Rhythm 33

(Beat Time 3/4. Then Arsis-Thesis)

Rhythm and Melody

Minor Mode

(*c*)

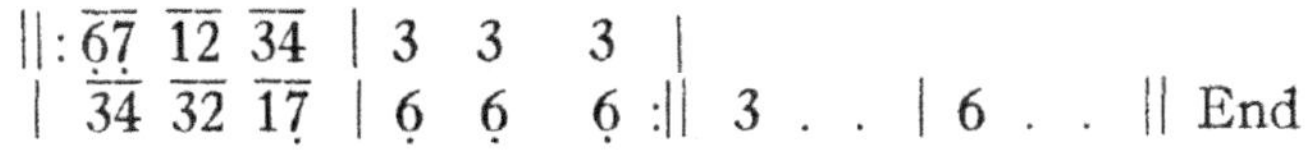

||: 67 12 34 | 3 3 3 |
| 34 32 17 | 6 6 6 :|| 3 . . | 6 . . || End

(*d*) || 6 1 2 | 34 32 12 |
| 3 3 3 | 34 32 17 :||
| 6 . . || End.

(*e*) ||: 1 6 12 | 3 3 3 |
| 3 4 32 | 1 7 6 :||
| 34 32 17 | 6 . . || End.

(*d*)

	6 1 2	34 32 17	6 . .
6 1 2	34 32 12	3 . .
3 4 3	21 71 23
4 3 2	17 67 12
3 1 2	34 32 17	6 . .	

(*a* + *f*)

	6 1 2	3 . 2
1 . 67	1 . 2	3 . .
2 . 34	3 . 2
3 6 7	1 . 7	6 . .	

(*e* + *g*)

	6 1 67	1 2 3	6 . .
6 12 34	3 2 1	7 . .
1 6 17	6 7 1	7 . .
1 23 43	2 1 7	6 . .	

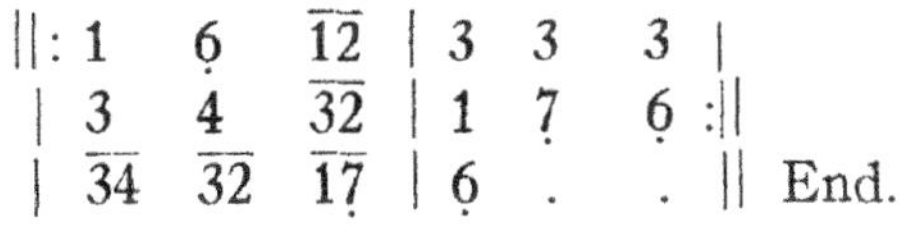

Major Mode

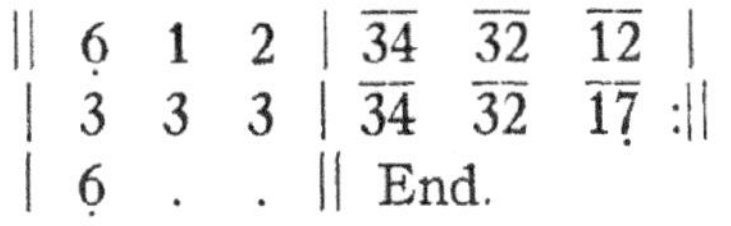

(*c* + *j*)

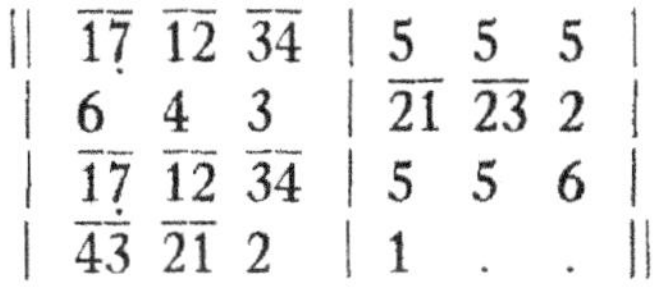

	17 12 34	5 5 5
6 4 3	21 23 2
17 12 34	5 5 6
43 21 2	1 . .	

(*j* + *i*) || 1 5 4 | 32 34 5 |
6 4 3	21 23 2
1 5 4	32 34 5
4 21 2	1 . .	

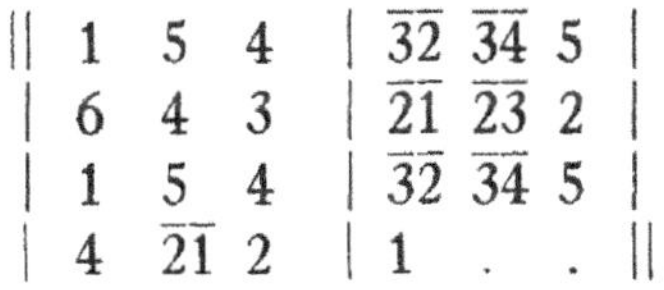

(*d*)

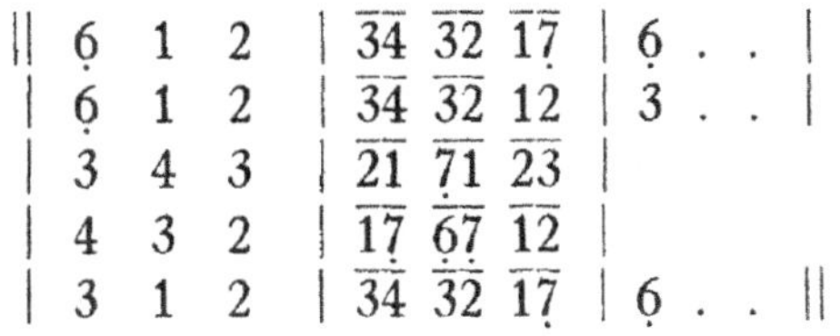

	5 5 5	56 54 32	3 . .
2 4 4	32 12 34	5 . .
5 5 5	56 54 32
3 1 2	34 32 17
6 5 ' 1	23 43 23	1 . .	

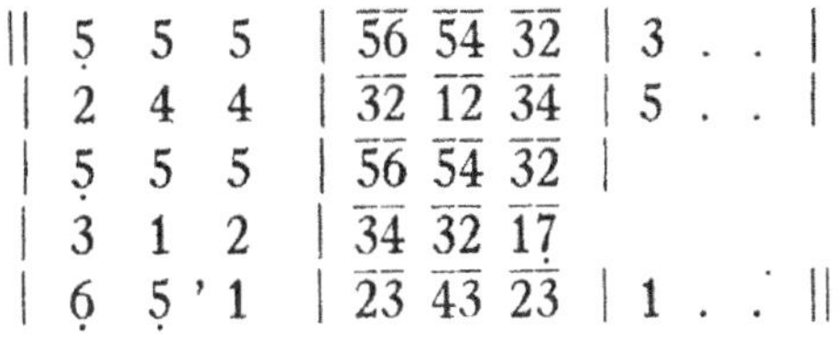

(*a* + *f*)

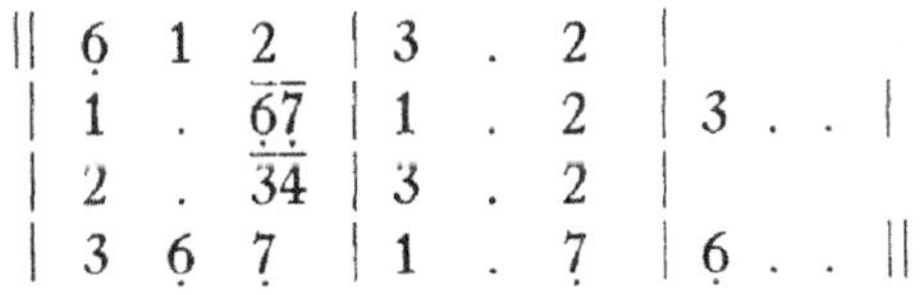

	5 3 4	3 . 2
1 . 23	4 . 3	2 . .
2 . 34	5 . 3
1 2 4	3 . 2	1 . .	

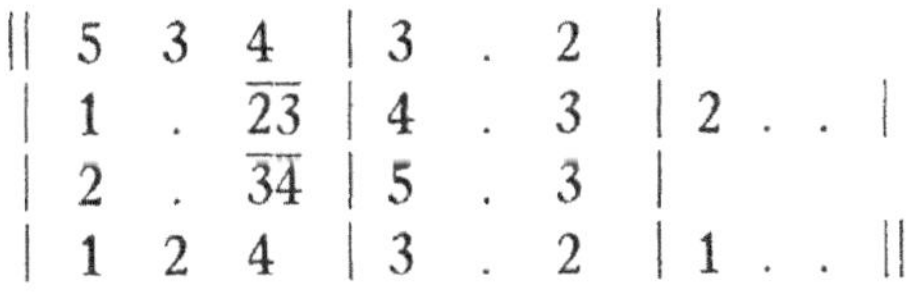

(*e* + *g*)

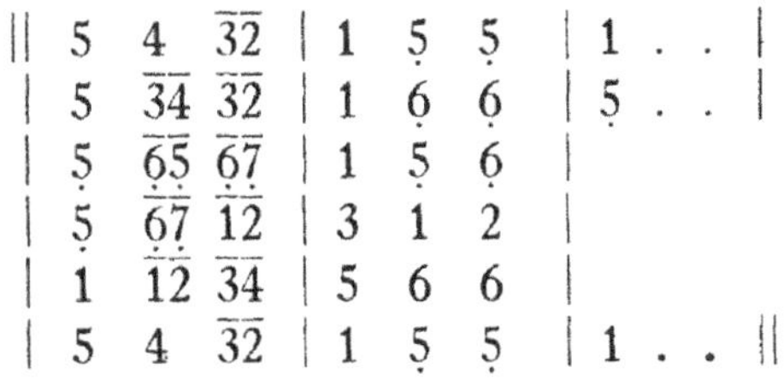

	5 4 32	1 5 5	1 . .
5 34 32	1 6 6	5 . .
5 65 67	1 5 6
5 67 12	3 1 2
1 12 34	5 6 6
5 4 32	1 5 5	1 . .	

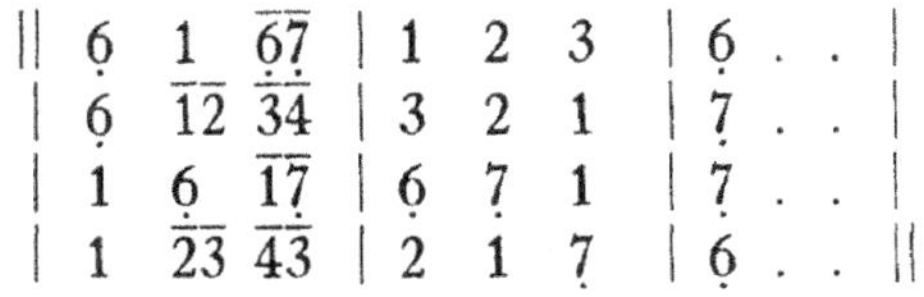

When the Minor Pentachord and Hexachord have become as it were *familiar melodies*, and have been used as indicated in the exercises of this chapter, the teacher should draw the attention of the children to the different character of the major and minor pentachords, and the reason for this difference:

The position of the half steps which occur in the Major, between the third and fourth degrees; in the Minor, between the second and third degrees.

Pentachords	1	2	34	5	(Major)	One half step (34)
	6̣	7̣1	2	3	(Minor)	One half step (7̣1)
Hexachords	1	2	34	5 6	(Major)	One half step (34)
	6̣	7̣1	2	34	(Minor)	Two half steps (7̣1 and 34)

Study Melodies 115 and 116, Children's Manual, page 32.

Vocal Exercises.—Single tones, sustained, but dictated in the order of the *Minor Pentachord*, instead of the Major.

Also *No. 25 and 26, Major*, before the Major exercises in Rhythm and Melody.

Intonation.—First presentation of the Minor Mode. The Pentachord of the Minor Mode should be studied first on *Diagrams 39 and 40*, then as written in *Intonation Exercises 85 and 86*. The Pentachord, when grasped in whole, as a melody, is then treated as the Major Pentachord in the first year. Independence is obtained through:

(*a*) Repetition of the extremities (on the diagrams, then horizontally). Also on the staff, in the two positions of *do* given in *Diagram 40*.

(*b*) *Stopping at any point*, and repeating the basic note (*la*). At first, the help-notes of the entire melody should be *thought*, as indicated in *Intonation Exercise 87a and b*.

(*c*) Stopping at any point and turning back in contrary direction, as indicated in *Intonation Exercise 87c*. The figures in the narrow columns are sung in *a* and *b*, but omitted in *c*, as indicated by the arrows. Thus:

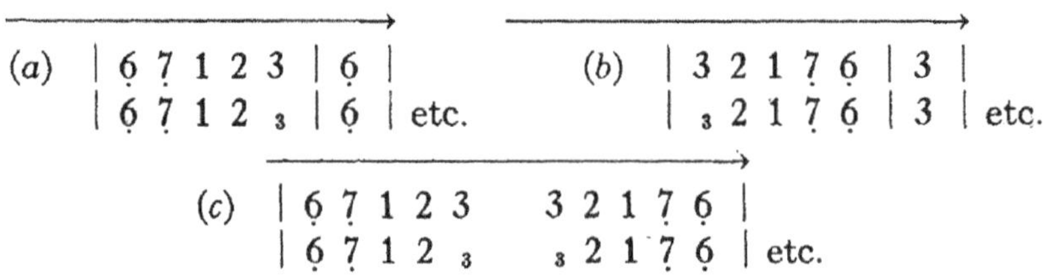

(*a*) | 6̣ 7̣ 1 2 3 | 6̣ |
| 6̣ 7̣ 1 2 ₃ | 6̣ | etc.

(*b*) | 3 2 1 7̣ 6̣ | 3 |
| ₃ 2 1 7̣ 6̣ | 3 | etc.

(*c*) | 6̣ 7̣ 1 2 3 3 2 1 7̣ 6̣ |
| 6̣ 7̣ 1 2 ₃ ₃ 2 1 7̣ 6̣ | etc.

All the exercises marked thus, with a broken arrow, are to be treated as above.

(*d*) Stopping at any point, repeating the note in question, and proceding in the same direction as before. (*Intonation Exercise 88.*)

As a rule these exercises offer little difficulty in so far as the finding of the notes is concerned. The real difficulty in the study of the *Minor Mode* is to sing the intervals *perfectly true to pitch*. The children are accustomed to sing a pentachord composed of two whole steps, one half step, and one whole step (1 2 34 5 and 5 6 7$\dot{1}$ $\dot{2}$). Now they must accustom themselves to a pentachord composed of one whole step, one half step, and two whole steps. This change of position of the half step often leads to flat singing (6 71 2 3). The difficulty of feeling *la* as *tonic* persists, also, for a time. During this time the teacher will need to verify the intervals on the harmonium, paying particular attention that the half-steps be sung in tune. The tendency of the children is to sing the interval "7–1" too large.

Although all the tones are familiar, both children and teacher will find that a tone *in a new environment* takes on a different character. The teacher will do well to bear this in mind, giving plenty of drill on the diagrams, plenty of ear training, and careful voice training in the minor mode. The exercises of this chapter may appear too simple, but in reality, they are necessary for building up a sense of relative pitch in this new mode. We also advise a conscientious use of the *help-notes* for a considerable time.

What we have said regarding the study of the *Minor Pentachord* applies also to the *Minor Hexachord.* We have a difference in the position of the half-steps in relation to the fundamental tone of the mode, which requires careful drill. *Major Hexachord:* Two whole-steps and a half-step, then two whole-steps (1 2 34 5 6). The Hexachord of the *modes of Sol* contain the same arrangement of the whole and half-steps (5 6 71 2 3). But, in the *minor mode,* our Hexachord contains *two sets of half-steps* (6 71 2 34). This difference of design, melodically, will require careful verification on the harmonium, particularly as regards *la* and *mi*.

Rhythm.—Exercise 33 is a review of 3/4 time with divided beat, and a further development of the rhythmic designs studied in the first year. The applications under *Melody and Rhythm* have been given both in *Major and Minor Modes.* The teacher will use the minor ones only after the new material has been well grasped. During the early part of the week, it is best to apply the rhythmic designs in the major mode.

Each of the designs in *Exercise 33* can be used either with or without the measure marked "*End. ad lib.*" Thus each design—up to the dotted line—can be repeated until thoroughly grasped, and then the long measure can be added; or else the entire three measures can be repeated together.

Furthermore, for economy of space, we have not given the reverse of each design. This, however, can be provided on the board for variety. Thus Lines *c* and *d* are the reverse of one another. Lines *e*, *f*, *g*, etc., have no reversed form.

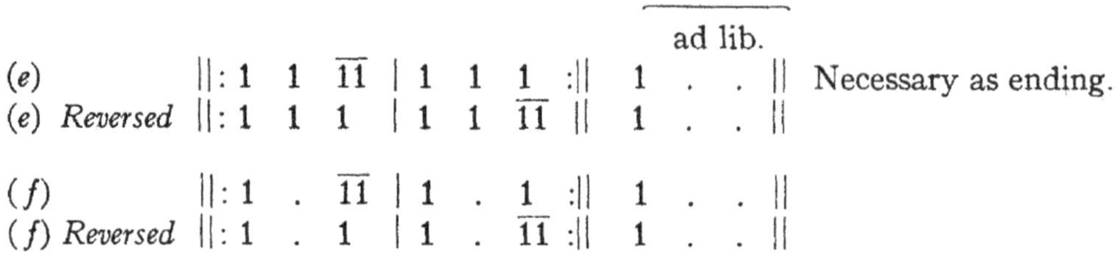

				ad lib.	
(*e*)	||: 1 1 $\overline{11}$	| 1 1 1 :||	1 . . ||		Necessary as ending.
(*e*) *Reversed*	||: 1 1 1	| 1 1 $\overline{11}$ ||	1 . . ||		
(*f*)	||: 1 . $\overline{11}$	| 1 . 1 :||	1 . . ||		
(*f*) *Reversed*	||: 1 . 1	| 1 . $\overline{11}$:||	1 . . ||		

As it is neither practical nor necessary to provide every possible form which the children will encounter in the course of their music study, we have contented ourselves with providing a number of typical rhythmic designs which will prepare them to grasp without difficulty those which they will meet with in the melodies of these chapters. We repeat, however, the general advice given in the early part of this book: wherever a melody offers a rhythmic problem which might cause hesitation in the rendering, it is best to place on the board the ***rhythmic schema*** of the melody, ***treating it as a rhythmic exercise***, before attempting to sing the melody itself.

Modal Dictation

The teacher may play certain combinations of tones on the harmonium, characteristic of the Major or of the Minor Mode, and ask the children whether they belong to the *Do Family* or the *La Family*. Phrases such as the following will be appropriate:

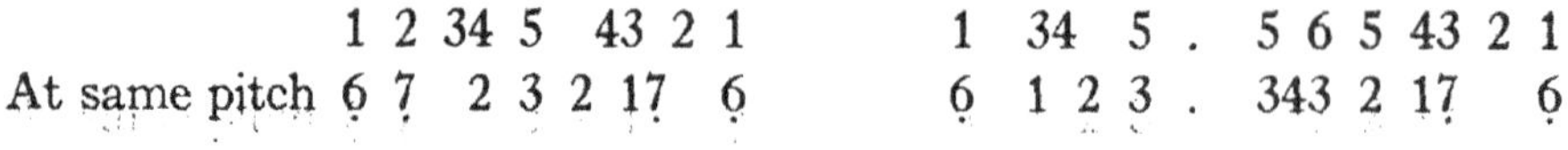

	1 2 34 5 43 2 1	1 34 5 . 5 6 5 43 2 1
At same pitch	6̣ 7̣ 2 3 2 17̣ 6̣	6̣ 1 2 3 . 343 2 17̣ 6̣

Melodic Dictation

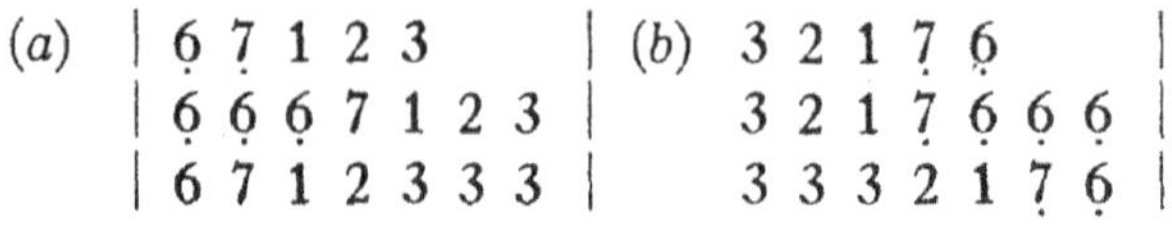

(*a*)	| 6̣ 7̣ 1 2 3 |	(*b*)	3 2 1 7̣ 6̣ |
	| 6̣ 6̣ 6̣ 7 1 2 3 |		3 2 1 7̣ 6̣ 6̣ 6̣ |
	| 6 7 1 2 3 3 3 |		3 3 3 2 1 7̣ 6̣ |

```
(c) |1 7 6 6 6|   (d) |6 7 1 7 6|   (e) |6 7 1   1 2 3|   (f) |6 7 1 2 3 4 3|
    |6 7 1 2 3|       |6 1 1 7 6|       |6 1 1 2 3    |       |3 4 3 2 1 2 3|
    |3 2 1 7 6|       |1 6 6 7 1|       |6 1 1   3    |       |3 4 3 1 1 7 6|
    |6 7 1 2 1|       |1 7 6 1 1|       |3 2 1   1 7 6|       |3 4 3   1 7 6|
    |1 2 1 7 6|       |1 6 6 1 1|       |3   1   1   6|       |3 4 3   1   6|
```

Observation

```
(a) |6 7 1 2 3    6  |   (b) |3 4 3 2 1 7 6  |   (c) |6 7 1 2 3 4 3 .|
    |6 7 1 1 2    3  |       |3 4 3 1 1 7 6  |       |6 7 1 . 3 4 3 .|
    |6 7 1   1 7 6   |       |3 4 3 . 1 7 6 .|       |6 1 1 . 3 4 3 .|
    |6 7 1   1 7 6 3 |       |3 4 3 . 1 6 6 .|       |6 1 2 1 3 4 3 .|
```

Melody and Rhythm

```
| 6 7 1 | 1 . . |    | 6  1  1  | 6 . . |    || 6 . | 1 2 | 3 . | 6 . |
| 1 7 6 | 1 . . |    | 67 17 67 | 6 . . |     | 5 6 | 7 7 | 6 . | . 𝄽 |
| 1 2 3 | 3 . . |    | 6  1  2  | 3 . . |     | 3 . | 1 2 | 1 7 | 6 . |
| 3 4 3 | 2 . . |    | 34 32 12 | 3 . . |     | 6 . | 5 . | 6 . | . 𝄽 ||
| 2 3 4 | 3 . . |    | 3  4  3  | 2 . . |
| 2 1 7 | 6 . . |    | 34 32 17 | 6 . . |
```

CHAPTER NINE

Vocal Exercises.—Single tones (6 7 1 2 3). Also, Nos. 25b and 28b.
Intonation.—The Minor Mode.

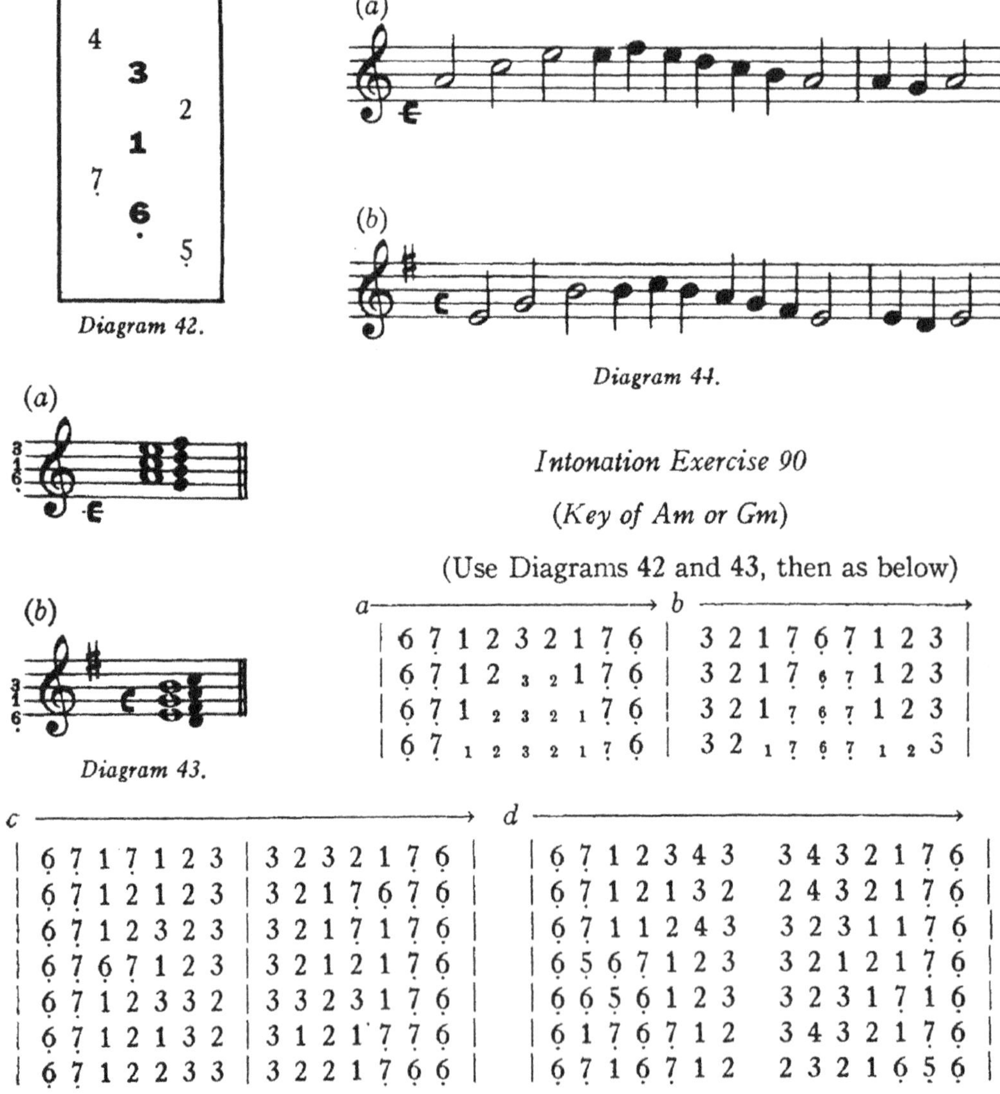

Diagram 42.

Diagram 43.

Diagram 44.

Intonation Exercise 90

(*Key of Am or Gm*)

(Use Diagrams 42 and 43, then as below)

a	b
6 7 1 2 3 2 1 7 6	3 2 1 7 6 7 1 2 3
6 7 1 2 3 2 1 7 6	3 2 1 7 6 7 1 2 3
6 7 1 2 3 2 1 7 6	3 2 1 7 6 7 1 2 3
6 7 1 2 3 2 1 7 6	3 2 1 7 6 7 1 2 3

c		d	
6 7 1 7 1 2 3	3 2 3 2 1 7 6	6 7 1 2 3 4 3	3 4 3 2 1 7 6
6 7 1 2 1 2 3	3 2 1 7 6 7 6	6 7 1 2 1 3 2	2 4 3 2 1 7 6
6 7 1 2 3 2 3	3 2 1 7 1 7 6	6 7 1 1 2 4 3	3 2 3 1 1 7 6
6 7 6 7 1 2 3	3 2 1 2 1 7 6	6 5 6 7 1 2 3	3 2 1 2 1 7 6
6 7 1 2 3 3 2	3 3 2 3 1 7 6	6 6 5 6 1 2 3	3 2 3 1 7 1 6
6 7 1 2 1 3 2	3 1 2 1 7 7 6	6 1 7 6 7 1 2	3 4 3 2 1 7 6
6 7 1 2 2 3 3	3 2 2 1 7 6 6	6 7 1 6 7 1 2	2 3 2 1 6 5 6

Intonation Exercise 91

(Use Diagrams 42 and 43)

(*Key of Am or Gm*)

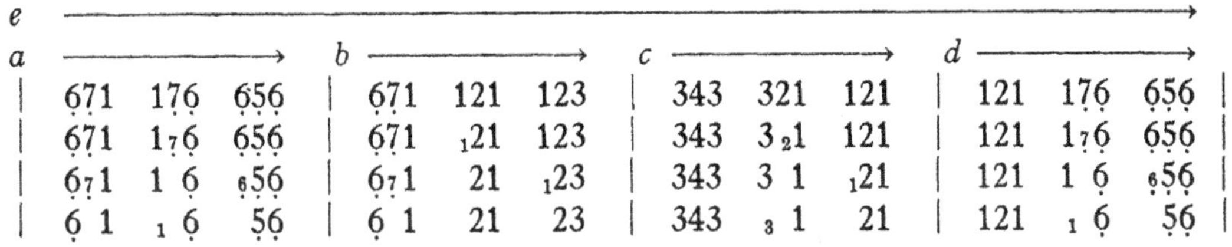

```
e  ———————————————————————————————————————————————————————→
a  ————————→     b  ————————→     c  ————————→     d  ————————→
| 671  176  656 | 671  121  123 | 343  321  121 | 121  176  656 |
| 671  176  656 | 671  121  123 | 343  321  121 | 121  176  656 |
| 671  1 6  656 | 671   21  123 | 343  3 1  121 | 121  1 6  656 |
| 6 1  1 6   56 | 6 1   21   23 | 343  3 1   21 | 121  1 6   56 |
```

Melody and Rhythm

```
|| 6 1 | 1 6 | 5 6 | 6 . | 6 1 | 2 1 | 2 3 | 3 . |
 | 3 4 | 3 1 | 2 1 | 7 . | 1 2 | 1 6 | 5 6 | 6 . ||
```

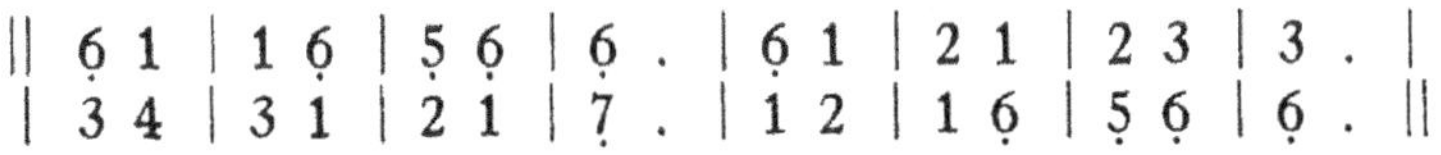

Intonation Exercise 92

(Use Diagrams 42 and 43)

(*Key of Gm*)

```
| 1 7 6  6 7 1  1 2 1  1 2 3  3 4 3 | 3 4 3  3 2 1  1 2 1  1 7 6  6 5 6 |
| 1 7 6  6 7 1  1 2 1  1 2 3  3 4 3 | 3 4 3  3 2 1  1 2 1  1 7 6    5 6 |
| 1   6  6 7 1    2 1    2 3    4 3 |   4 3    2 1    2 1  1 7 6    5 6 |
```

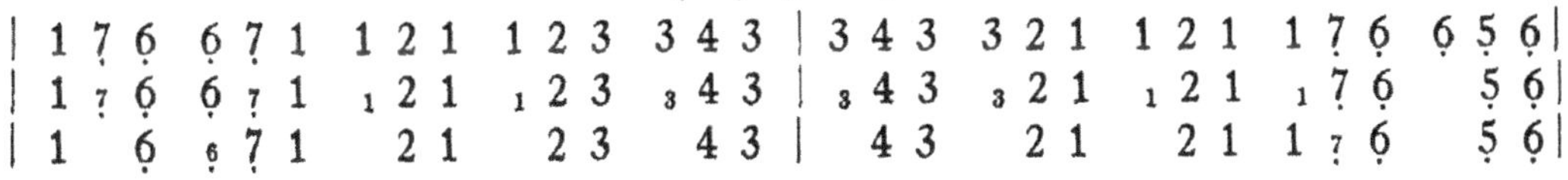

Intonation Exercise 93

(Diagrams 42 and 43)

(*Key of Gm*)

```
 (a)          (b)            (c)               (d)
| 671  176 | 6712  2176 | 67123  32176 | 6712343  3432176  6 3 6 |
| 6 1  176 | 6712  2176 | 67123   2176 | 671234     32176  6 3 6 |
| 6    176 | 6712   176 | 67123  32176 | 6712     3432176  6 3 6 |
| 671    6 | 6712   176 | 6   3  32176 | 6712     3432176  6 3 6 |
```

```
(e)                          (f)                                  (g)
| 343  321  176  3 6 | 34 32 17 6   6 3     |        | 671  6 1 2 1  6 1 2 1  |
| 343  321  176  3 6 | 34 32 17 7 7 12 3    |        | 67123  6  3            |
| 343  321  176  3 6 | 34 32 17   7  12 3   | 32176  | 3 2  321  3217  32176  |
                                                     | 34321767123  36 343 6  |
```

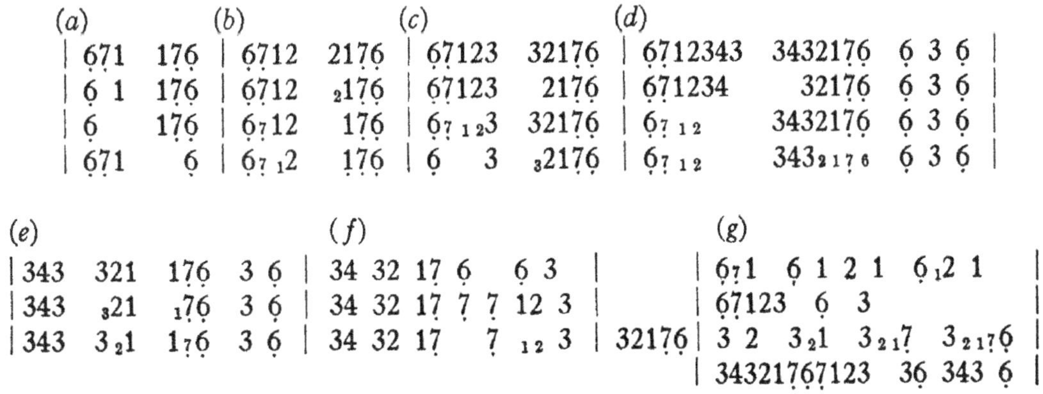

Rhythm and Melody

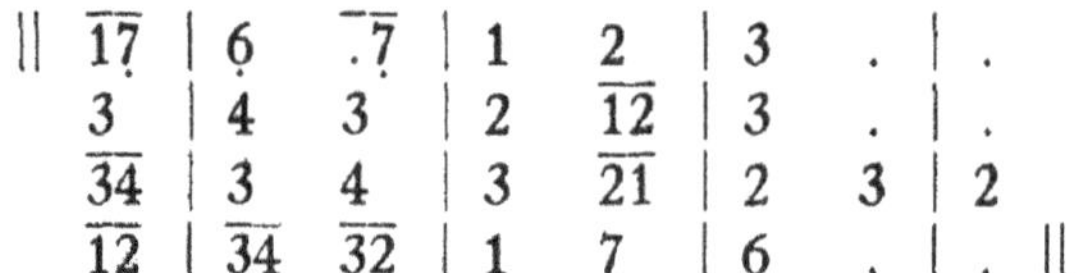

Melody 118(a) (Major Mode)

Melody 118(b)

Melody 120 (Sixteenth Century) Mode VII (5=G)

|| 2̇ | 2̇ 7 | 1̇ 2̇ | 3̇ .2̇ | 1̇' 3̇ | 2̇ 1̇ | 7 6 | 5 . | ✕
7 | 1̇ 1̇ | 6 7 | 1̇7 65 | 6' 6 | 76 71̇ | 2̇ 7 | 3̇2̇ 1̇7 | 6 6 | 5 . | . ||

Melody 121 (Sixteenth Century) Mode VII (5=E)

|| 5̣ | 2 2 | 2 4 | 3 2 | 1 . | .
1 | 1 7̣ | 6̣ 5̣ | 1 .2 | 3 . | 2 . | ✕
2 '| 5 5 | 3 4 | 5 3 | 2 . | .
2 | 5 2 | 3 1 | 2 7̣1 | 7̣6̣ 7̣1 | 2 . | ✕
2 | 3 2 | 1 .7̣ | 1 .7̣ | 6̣ 5̣ | 6̣ . | . . | 5̣ . | . ||

Vocal Exercises.—Single tones with various vowel sounds, dictated one after the other according to the line of the minor pentachord (6, 7, 1, 2, 3). *Also Vocal Exercise 25b* (Key of Gm, Am, Bm, Cm, Dm).

|| 6̣ 1 7̣ | 6̣ . . ||

Verify the pitch. If there is the slightest imperfection, prepare as follows:

|| 6̣ 1 | 1 7̣ | 6̣ . || and || 6̣ | 1 7̣ | 6̣ . | . ||

This change of rhythm which places the ictic sound on "*do*" often suffices, but when the pitch of the minor pentachord remains imperfect—whether in a vocal exercise or an intonation exercise, a mental background must be formed by returning to the major mode and linking the minor to the major, thus:

```
| 1 2 3 .  3 4  3 .  3 4  3 2  1 .      |
| 1 2 3 .  1 7̣  6̣ .  5̣ .  6̣ 5̣  6̣ 7̣  1 . |
| 5̣ 6̣      1 7̣  6̣ .  6̣ 5̣  6̣ .  1 7̣  6̣ . |
| 6̣ 7̣      1 6̣  6̣ .  1 .  1 7̣  6̣ 5̣  6̣ . |
```

This linking of the unknown to the known never fails to produce a true sense of relative pitch, and the teacher should use it without hesitation rather than attempt to obtain the desired result through dry imitation. It is better to attack the *cause* rather than seek to remedy the *effect*. The cause, in this case, is that the children do not yet feel the minor modality. To prove to them that they are singing flat by sounding the tone on the harmonium will discourage them unless we aid them practically to overcome the difficulty.

Intonation.—Exercises 90, 91, 92 and 93 should be studied, first, on *Diagram 42;* then horizontally, as written; finally, on *Staff Diagrams 43 a and b. Diagrams 44a and b* are to be used for eye training and for rapid visualization and singing. *Diagrams 42 and 43* may also be used for this purpose.

The lessons should always begin, during this week, by a return to some of the Exercises of Chapter Eight to establish the Minor Pentachord in scale progression. Emphasis should be given to the rapid thinking of the help-notes (as in Exercise 87a and b). The children should form the habit of *thinking the whole pentachord as a melody* in order to keep true to pitch. Thus, if they are to sing (see Intonation Exercise 90):

```
    6̣ 7̣ 6̣    they should think     6̣ (7̣12321) 7̣ 6̣
6̣ 7̣ 1 7̣ 6̣    they should think   6̣ 7̣ 1 (2321) 7̣ 6̣
```

until such time as the intervals are firmly established. This work of thinking help-notes can be done on the Diagrams, the teacher tapping the notes that are to be sung and pointing silently to those which are to be thought. A little time devoted to these gymnastics in pitch will amply repay the trouble of the teacher, for negligence on this point will produce uncertainties in the minor mode which will be difficult to correct when once they have become a habit. The *thinking of help-notes* is the only sure path to perfection.

Rhythm.—The dotted quarter-note. We may lay a foundation for this problem as follows:

||: 1 | 1 . | 1 1 | 1 . | . :||
Do do – do do do – –

*
||: 1 | 1 . | . 1 | 1 . | . :||
Do do – – do do – –

* There must be no pressure of the voice on the dot which commences the measure. It is a sustained sound.

The new problem presents the above in reduced form:

(*a*) ||: 1 | 1 1 1 | 1 :||
Do do do do do

(*b*) ||: 1 | 1 1 1 | 1 :||
Do do – do do

(*c*) ||: 1 | 1 . 1 | 1 :||

The *tie* in *Line b* and the *dot* on *Line c* are equivalent. Both forms should be studied since we find them in modern notation.

It is not easy for the children to sing these dotted notes with perfect accuracy and without any pressure of the voice on the dot. In order to avoid any pressure of the voice, the children may tap *Line a* with their hands while singing *Line b*. Thus:

(*a*) Tap: 1 | 1 1 1 | 1
(*b*) Sing: 1 | 1 . 1 | 1

When that first difficulty has been overcome, they may be allowed to tap (but inaudibly) with their foot on the dot of prolongation. Much dictation of this form should be given always surrounded by designs similar to that of *Line a*. The forms should be repeated until they are familiar:

	1	1 1 1	1 1	1 1 1·	1 1	1 1 1	1 1	1 .	.	
	1	1 . 1	1 1	1 . 1	1 1	1 . 1	1 1	1 .	.	
	1	1 1 1	1 1 1	1 1 1	1 1 1	1 1 1	1 1 1	1 .	.	
	1	1 . 1	1 . 1	1 . 1	1 1	1 . 1	1 . 1	1 .	.	

Comparisons from daily experience will help the children to grasp this uneven grouping of the notes. A horse trotting gives us an even rhythm; when he gallops, we have an uneven rhythm somewhat similar to the above. A lame man walks with the uneven sound of this rhythm.

When teacher or children tap one of these rhythmic designs, they must do so with scrupulous accuracy. If the school possesses a metronome, it would be well to measure the early efforts to the sound of this instrument. Where no metronome is available, the pendulum of a clock or a weight tied to a cord and allowed to swing can answer the purpose. In the early stages of the work, all melodies containing dotted quarter notes should be measured by tapping as in *Line a* while singing as in *Line b* or *Line c*.

If the form remains difficult, the analysis may be carried even further thus:

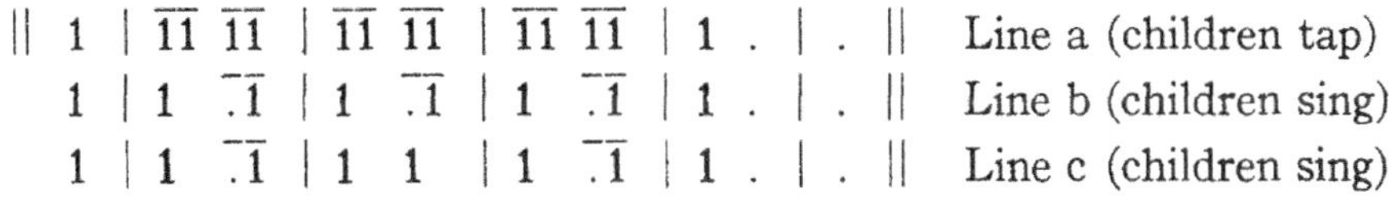

|| 1 | 11 11 | 11 11 | 11 11 | 1 . | . || Line a (children tap)
1 | 1 .1 | 1 .1 | 1 .1 | 1 . | . || Line b (children sing)
1 | 1 .1 | 1 1 | 1 .1 | 1 . | . || Line c (children sing)

This tapping is a mechanical aid, and should be discarded as soon as it has served its purpose, which is to give its precise value to the dot and to the brief note which follows it.

Melody helps in the early stages. Here are a few phrases to be used in the same manner as the above exercise: namely, to tap *Line a* while singing it and also while singing *Line b*. When this has been done repeat the two phrases without any tapping, but with the First Gesture of Music First Year. Then, *without any gesture or tapping.*

Melodies for the Assimilation of the Dotted Note

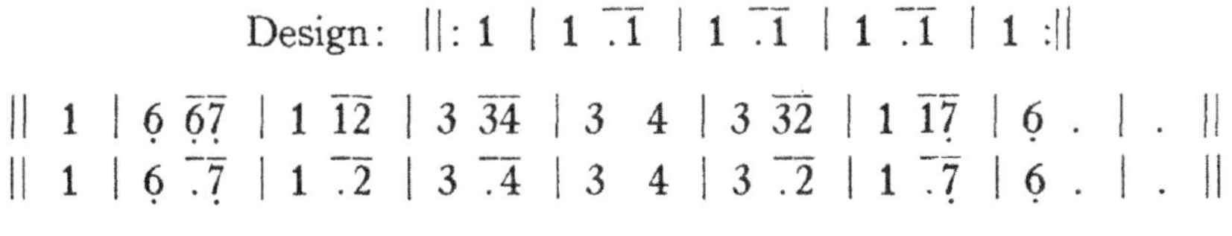

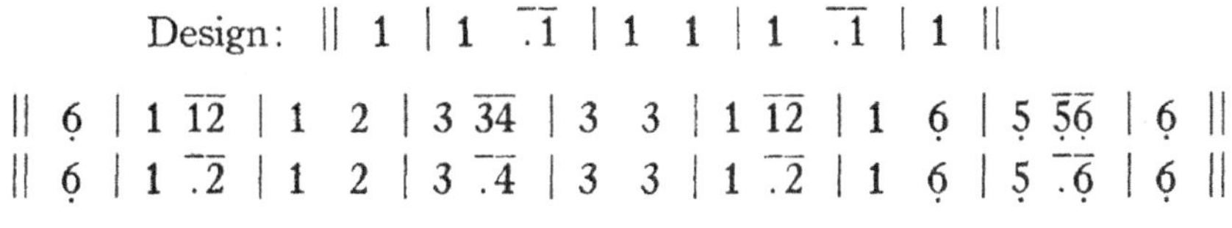

Design: ||: 1 | 1 .1 | 1 .1 | 1 .1 | 1 :||

|| 1 | 6 67 | 1 12 | 3 34 | 3 4 | 3 32 | 1 17 | 6 . | . ||
|| 1 | 6 .7 | 1 .2 | 3 .4 | 3 4 | 3 .2 | 1 .7 | 6 . | . ||

Design: || 1 | 1 .1 | 1 1 | 1 .1 | 1 ||

|| 6 | 1 12 | 1 2 | 3 34 | 3 3 | 1 12 | 1 6 | 5 56 | 6 ||
|| 6 | 1 .2 | 1 2 | 3 .4 | 3 3 | 1 .2 | 1 6 | 5 .6 | 6 ||

Dictation

→	→	→	→
676 121 343	343 121 676	676 121 676	67 12 31 6 .
676 176 343	343 123 676	121 676 121	32 17 61 3 .
676 161 6	343 131 676	676 343 676	32 13 21 7 .
676 161 3	343 123 676	121 343 676	71 23 16 6 .

Visualization

→	→	→
67 16 1.	671 6..	6 7 1 2 3 4 3 .
17 67 6.	612 3..	6 . 1 . 3 4 3 .
66 16 1.	343 2..	6 . 1 . 3 . 3 .
67 12 3.	121 6..	6 7 6 . 1 . 3 .
67 13 3.	617 6..	6 . 17 6 . 3 .
61 13 3.	567 6..	3. 1 7 6 7 6 .
61 32 1.	323 1..	3 4 3 1 6 7 6 .
61 31 3.	171 6..	3 4 3 . 1 . 6 .
61 31 6.	317 6.:	

Melody and Rhythm

	6 1	7 6	5 6	6 .
67 12	3 32	1 2	3 .
32 12	3 .2	1 2	1 .
67 12	1 .7	6 7	6 .	

	6 7	1 6	6 1	3 .
3 2	1 6	6 5	6 .
6 3	3 2	3 4	3 .
3 1	6 7	6 5	6 .	

Aural Memory

|| 6 | 6 12 | 3 2 | 12 17 | 6
6 | 7 1 | 2 3 | 2 . | .
2 | 3 12 | 3 2 | 17 67 | 1
1 | 7 6 | 5 .67 | 6 . | . ||

CHAPTER TEN

Vocal Exercises.—Single tones (dictated along minor pentachord).

Also *Nos. 25b, 26b* and *27b.* To which should be added *No. 28b* as soon as the intervals of the minor hexachord have been thoroughly mastered and can be sung perfectly true to pitch.

Intonation.—The Minor Mode, continued.

Begin the week by a review of *Intonation Exercise 94.*

Intonation Exercise 97 (Gm)

(Use Diagrams 42 and 43)

a ————————→b ————————→

| 6̣7̣6̣ 121 343 34321 7̣6̣ 6̣5̣6̣ | 343 121 6̣7̣6̣ 6̣7̣12343 |
| 6̣7̣6̣ 121 343 34321 7̣6̣ 6̣5̣6̣ | 343 121 6̣7̣6̣ 6̣7̣12343 |
| 6̣ 6̣ 1 1 3 3 34321 7̣6̣ 5̣6̣ | 3 3 1 1 6̣ 6̣ 6̣7̣12343 | 3 6̣

Intonation Exercise 98

Intonation Exercise 99

Preparation: || 12 32 17̣ 6̣ . || (for both exercises).

Exercise 98:

c ————————→

a ————→b ————→

6̣ 1 3 3 3	3 1 6̣ 6̣ 6̣
6̣ 6̣ 6̣ 1 3	3 3 3 1 6̣
6̣ 1 1 1 3	3 1 1 1 6̣
6̣ 1	3 1
6̣ 1 1	3 1 1
6̣ 1 1 3	3 1 1 6̣

Exercise 99:

c ————————→

a ————→b ————→

| 6̣ 1 3 3 1 6̣ | 3 1 6̣ 6̣ 1 3 |
| 6̣ 1 3 3 1 6̣ | 3 1 6̣ 6̣ 1 3 |
| 6̣ 1 3 1 6̣ | 3 1 6̣ 1 3 | 3 6̣

Intonation Exercise 100

Preparation: 6̣7̣ 1. 6̣7̣ 12 3.

| 6̣ 1 6̣ 1 3 | 3 1 3 1 6̣ |
| 6̣ 1 6̣ 1 3 | 3 1 3 1 6̣ | 6̣ 5̣ 6̣

Melody and Rhythm

|| 6̣ | 6̣ 6̣ | 1 6̣ | 1 2 | 3 . | 3 . | 2 . | 3 . | 𝄎
3 | 34 32 | 1 2 | 3 . | .
3 | 34 32 | 1 6̣ | 6̣ . | 𝄎
6̣ | 6̣ 6̣ | 1 6̣ | 1 2 | 3 . | 2 . | 1 6̣ | 1 . | 𝄎:
3 | 21 7̣6̣ | 7̣ 1 | 2 . | .
3 | 21 7̣6̣ | 1 2 | 3 . | .
3 | 3 3 | 1 3 | 1 7̣ | 6̣ . | 6̣ . | 1 7̣ | 6̣ . | . ||

Rapid Visualization on Staff

When *Do* is on a *line, la* and *mi* are also on lines. When *Do* is in a *space, la* and *mi* are also in spaces.

(*Key of A Minor*)

(*Key of E Minor*)

Vocal Exercises.—Single tones, dictated along the minor pentachord, using various syllables. Then add *25b, 26b,* or *27b,* alternating the use of these exercises.

Number 28b should be used regularly as soon as the intervals of the minor hexachord can be sung perfectly true to pitch.

The Minor Hexachord is more freely used in this chapter. The *tonic chord* and the third form of the *Compass Exercise* are introduced, and should be studied in the same manner as the Major chord and Compass Exercise in the first year. All the intonation exercises of this chapter should be sung from *Diagram 42,* then as written, horizontally; finally from the staff-diagrams 43a and b. In using these diagrams, a certain variety can be brought into the work. The intervals can be presented with more freedom, provided the help-notes be suggested (and even sung) to avoid errors.

The *Rhythmic Exercises* present the dotted quarter-note in measures which begin on the down-beat. The same precautions must be taken as regards precision as for the exercises of the last chapter which presented the dotted quarter-note in measures beginning on the up-beat. The rhythmic designs should be used for rapid observation and for dictation.

Dictation

```
| 6̣ 7̣ 1 2 3 | 3 2 1 7̣ 6̣ | 6̣ 1 3  3 4 3̇ | 3 1 6̣  6̣ 7̣ 6̣     |
| 6̣ 6̣ 6̣ 1 3 | 3 3 3 1 6̣ | 6̣ 1 3  3 2 1 | 3 1 6̣  5̣ 6̣ 6̣     |
| 6̣ 1 3 3 3 | 3 1 6̣ 6̣ 6̣ | 6̣ 1 3  1 2 1 | 3 1 6̣  1 2 1     |
| 6̣ 6̣ 1 1 3 | 3 1 1 6̣ 6̣ | 6̣ 1 3  6̣ 7̣ 6̣ | 3 1 6̣  3 4 3  6̣ |
```

```
| 6̣ 6̣ 1 1 3 | 3 3 1 1 6̣ |
| 6̣ 1 6̣ 6̣ 1 | 3 1 3 1 6̣ |
| 6̣ 1 6̣ 1 3 | 3 1 6̣ 1 6̣ |
| 6̣ 1 6̣   3 | 3 1 3   6̣ |
| 6̣ 3 6̣   3 | 3 6̣ 3   6̣ |
```

With Rhythm

```
|| 6̣  1  | 3  3̅4̅ | 3  . | 3  . |
|  3  2̅1̅ | 2  1̅7̣̅ | 6̣  . | .  . |
|  6̣  1̅7̣̅ | 6̣  1̅2̅ | 3  . | 2  . |
|  3  4̅3̅ | 2  1̅2̅ | 3  . | .  . |
|  3  1̅2̅ | 1  7̣  | 6̣  . | .  . ||
```

CHAPTER ELEVEN

Vocal Exercises 25b, 26b, 27b and 28b.
Intonation.—The Minor Mode.

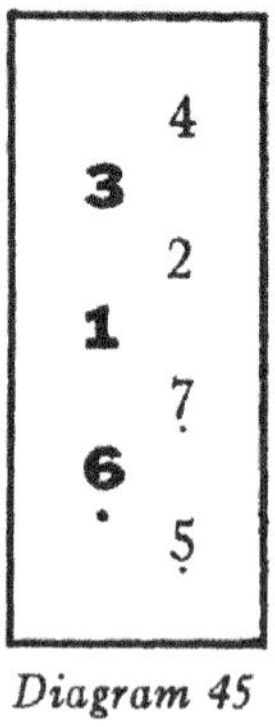

4
3
2
1
7
6
5

Diagram 45

Intonation Exercise 102 (Gm)

(Use Diagrams 45 and 43)

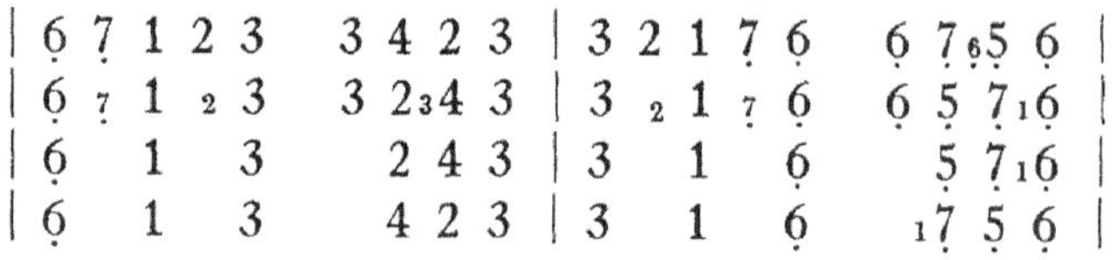

| 6 7 1 2 3   3 4 2 3 | 3 2 1 7 6   6 7 6 5 6 |

| 6 7 1 2 3   3 2 3 4 3 | 3 2 1 7 6   6 5 7 1 6 |

| 6   1   3   2 4 3 | 3   1   6   5 7 1 6 |

| 6   1   3   4 2 3 | 3   1   6   1 7 5 6 |

Intonation Exercise 103 (Am)

(Use Diagrams 45 and 43)

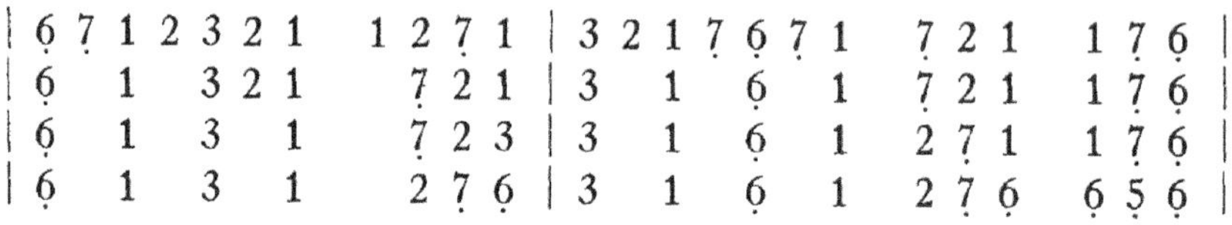

| 6 7 1 2 3 2 1   1 2 7 1 | 3 2 1 7 6 7 1   7 2 1   1 7 6 |

| 6   1   3 2 1   7 2 1 | 3   1   6   1   7 2 1   1 7 6 |

| 6   1   3   1   7 2 3 | 3   1   6   1   2 7 1   1 7 6 |

| 6   1   3   1   2 7 6 | 3   1   6   1   2 7 6   6 5 6 |

Melody and Rhythm (Gm)

|| 67 17 | 67 17 | 6 1 | 3 . | 23 43 | 2 12 | 3 . | 3 . |

| 67 17 | 67 17 | 6 3 | 2 . | 24 32 | 17 65 | 6 . | 6 . ||

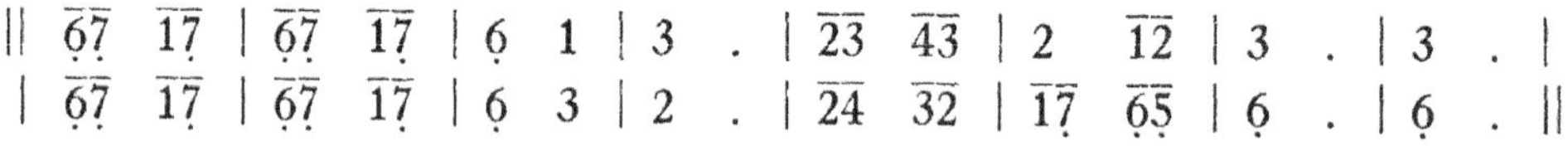

Study Melodies 127, 128 and 129, Children's Manual, page 36.
Begin study of Puer natus in Bethlehem, Children's Manual, page 35.
Study Hymn: O Salutaris Hostia (Melody 1), Children's Manual, page 120.

Intonation Exercise 104 (Gm)

(Use Diagrams 45 and 43)

a ⟶ *b* ⟶ *c* ⟶

| 6 1   765   6 6 | 6 1   2 7   1 6 | 6 1   3 1   2 7 |

| 6 1   7 5   6 6 | 6 1   7 2   1 6 | 6 1   3 1   7 2 |

| 1 6   567   6 6 | 1 6   7 2   1 6 | 7 2   3 1   6 1 |

| 1 6   5 7   6 6 | 1 6   2 7   1 6 | 2 7   1 6   5 6 |

| 1 6   7 5   6 6 | 1 3   2 7   1 6 | 6 1   3 4   2 3 |

| 3 4   2 3   1 6 |

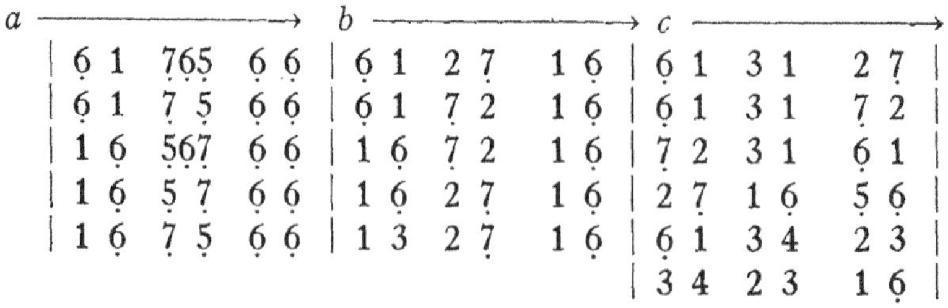

Melody and Rhythm — *Rhythm and Melody*

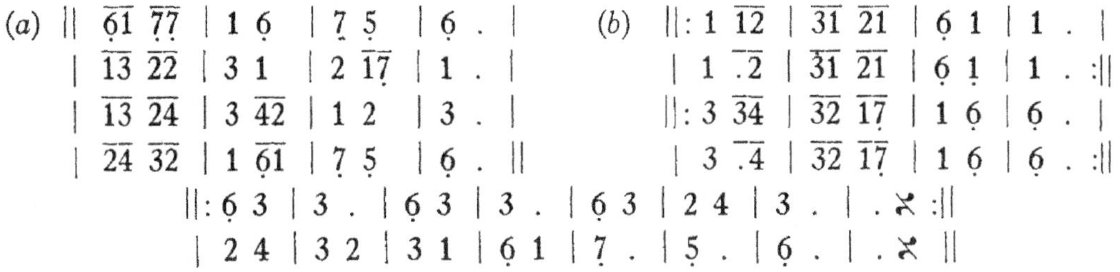

(*a*) || 61 77 | 1 6 | 7 5 | 6 . |
13 22	3 1	2 17	1 .
13 24	3 42	1 2	3 .
24 32	1 61	7 5	6 .	

(*b*) ||: 1 12 | 31 21 | 6 1 | 1 . |
1 .2	31 21	6 1	1 . :	
	: 3 34	32 17	1 6	6 .
3 .4	32 17	1 6	6 . :	

||: 6 3 | 3 . | 6 3 | 3 . | 6 3 | 2 4 | 3 . | . X :||
| 2 4 | 3 2 | 3 1 | 6 1 | 7 . | 5 . | 6 . | . X ||

Vocal Exercises 25b, 26b, 27b and 28b. Pay great attention to correct pitch, to legato phrasing, to clear vowel sounds.

The *Intonation Exercises* of this chapter bring the tonic chord into relation with the surrounding intervals. We have suggested the more important intervals in Exercises 102, 103 and 104. These exercises should be studied first on *Diagram 45* of this chapter, then on *Diagrams 43a and b.* The children should be able to sing any two intervals of the left column in relation to the intermediate interval of the right column and vice versa. The diagrams should also be used for rapid visualization, always along the lines suggested in the exercises. The melodic dictation should use this material. We add a few suggestions which the teacher can build upon according to need.

Dictation

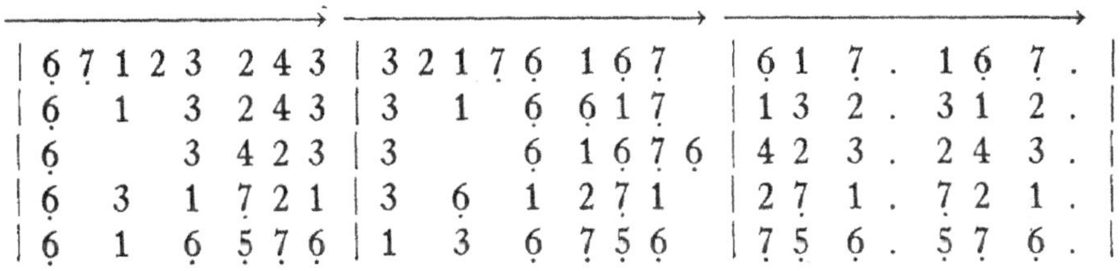

6 7 1 2 3 2 4 3	3 2 1 7 6 1 6 7	6 1 7 . 1 6 7 .
6 1 3 2 4 3	3 1 6 6 1 7	1 3 2 . 3 1 2 .
6 3 4 2 3	3 6 1 6 7 6	4 2 3 . 2 4 3 .
6 3 1 7 2 1	3 6 1 2 7 1	2 7 1 . 7 2 1 .
6 1 6 5 7 6	1 3 6 7 5 6	7 5 6 . 5 7 6 .

Any of these forms can be varied by repetition, thus:

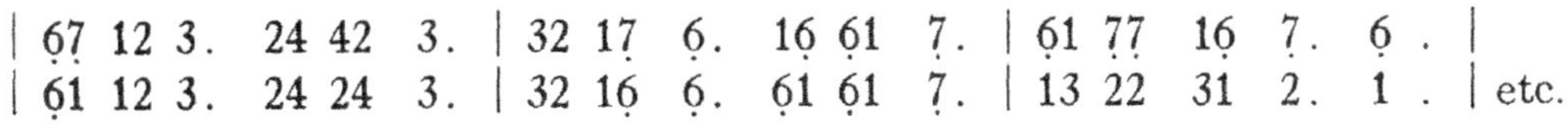

| 67 12 3. 24 42 3. | 32 17 6. 16 61 7. | 61 77 16 7. 6 . |
| 61 12 3. 24 24 3. | 32 16 6. 61 61 7. | 13 22 31 2. 1 . | etc.

In this way the teacher can vary the exercises and adapt them to the capacity of the class.

The teacher may begin simple dictation on the staff in the minor mode, using the Key of A minor and also the Key of E minor (and E flat minor). Such dictation should be confined to the intervals of the tonic chord and scale-progression.

CHAPTER TWELVE

Vocal Exercises 27b and 28b. Add *Special Exercise* after the study of *Diagram 46.*

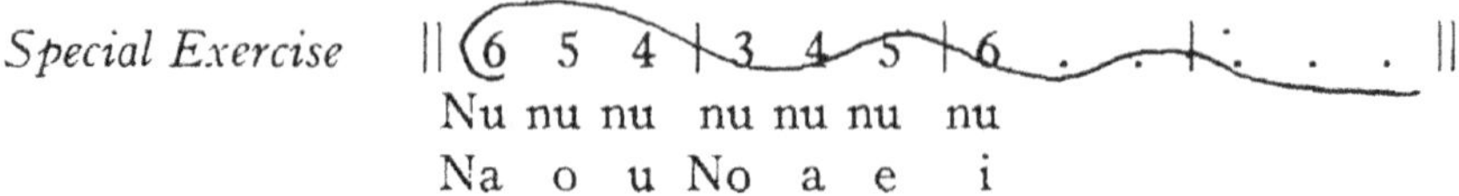

Intonation.—The Upper Tetrachord of the Minor Mode (diatonic).

6
5
4
3

Diagram 46.

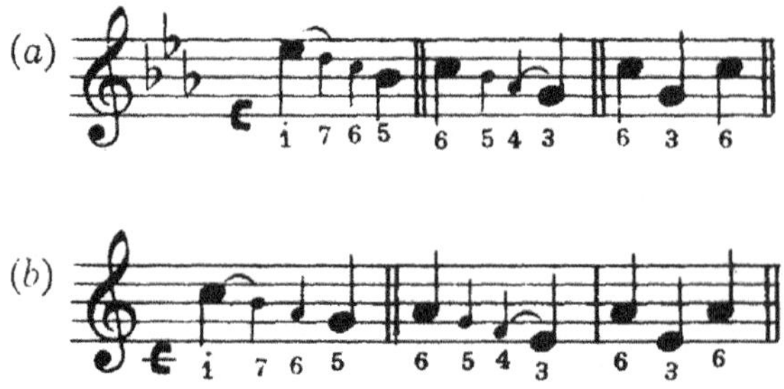

(a) 1̇ 7 6 5 | 6 5 4 3 | 6 3 6

(b) 1̇ 7 6 5 | 6 5 4 3 | 6 3 6

Diagram 47.

7
6
5
4
3
2

Diagram 48a.

Intonation Exercise 105 (Cm)

c ————————————→
a ————————→ b ————→

1̇76	656	6543	343	343	3456	656		
	656	6$_{54}$3	343	343	3$_{45}$6	656	671̇76
	656	6 3	343	343	3 6	656	671̇66

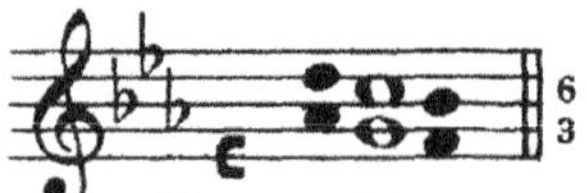

6
3

Diagram 48b

Intonation Exercise 106 (Cm)

c ————————————→
a ————————→ b ————→

343	3456	671̇76	671̇76	6543	343	323	
343	3$_{45}$6	671̇76	671̇76	6$_{54}$3	343	323	
343	3 6	67 6	67 6	6 3	343	23	36

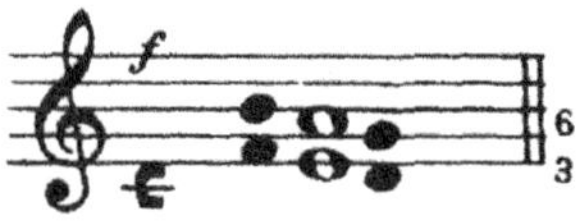

6
3

Diagram 48c.

Intonation Exercise 107 (Cm)

————————————→

1̇76	65676	6543	34323	34323	3456	65676	
	65676	6$_{54}$3	34323	34323	3$_{45}$6	65676	
	65676	6 3	34323	34323	3 6	65676	671̇76

Intonation Exercise 108a (Cm)

i̇ 6 | 6 5 4 3 3 3 3 4 3 | 3 4 3 3 4 5 6 6 6 |
| 6 6 6 5 4 3 3 4 3 | 3 4 3 3 3 3 4 5 6 | 6 7 i̇ 7 6

Intonation Exercise 108b (Cm)

i̇ 6 | 6 5 4 3 3 4 5 6 | 3 6 | 3 4 5 6 6 5 4 3 | 6 3 6 |
| 6 5 4 3 3 4 5 6 | 3 6 | 3 4 5 6 6 5 4 3 | 6 3 6 |
| 6 5 3 5 6 | 3 6 | 3 5 6 5 3 | 6 3 6 |

Intonation Exercise 109 (Cm)

i̇ 6 | 6 5 6 3 4 3 3 4 3 6 5 6 |
| 6 5 6 3 4 3 3 4 3 6 5 6 |
| 6 3 3 6 | 6 5 4 3 4 5 6

Intonation Exercise 110 (Cm)

i̇ 6 | 67656 6 3 34323 3 6 65676 6 3 6 |
| 67656 6 3 34323 3 6 65676 6 3 6 |

Melody and Rhythm

	6 . 5	6 . .	5 6 5	3 . .
3 2 3	5 . 3	5 . .	6 . .
6 . 5	6 . .	5 4 3	3 . .
3 5 6	5 6 7	6 . .	6 . .	

Melody and Rhythm

	6 6	5 5	6 .	3 .
6 6	5 5	6 .	3 .
3 3	3 2	3 5	6 .
6 6	5 6	3 .	6 .	

|| 6 6 | 5 6 | 7 . 6 | 6 . |
| 6 6 | 5 6 | 5 . 3 | 3 . ||

Intonation Exercise 111 (Cm)

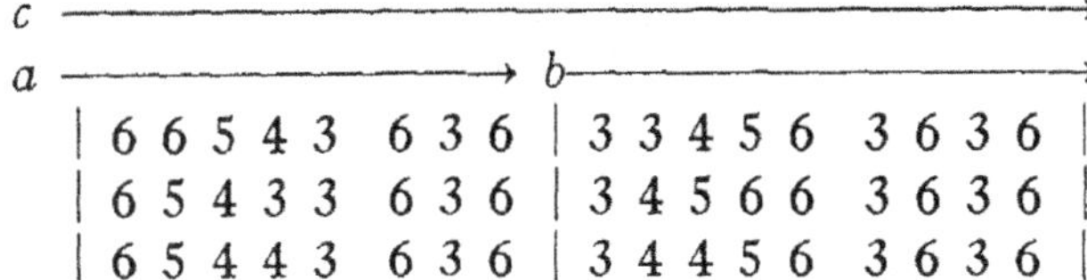

Intonation Exercise 112
(Cm)

6 5 4 3 $_4$ $_5$ 6	6 $_5$ $_4$ 3 4 5 6
6 5 4 $_3$ $_4$ $_5$ 6	6 $_5$ $_4$ $_3$ 4 5 6
6 5 $_4$ $_3$ $_4$ $_5$ 6	6 $_5$ $_4$ $_3$ $_4$ 5 6

Melody and Rhythm

	6 .	5 4	3 .	3 .
6 5	6 7	6 .	. 𝄽
6 .	5 4	3 .	2 .
3 2	3 5	6 .	. 𝄽

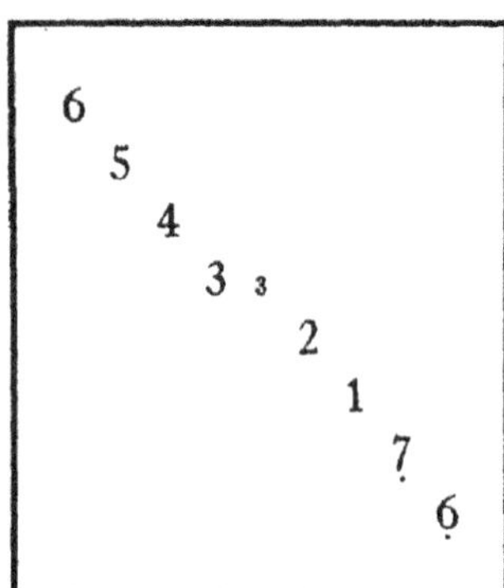

Diagram 49.

Diagram 50.

Intonation Exercise 113

The Minor Scale (diatonic) Em

(Use Diagrams 49 and 50)

| 6 5 4 3 3 2 1 7 6 6 7 1 2 3 3 4 5 6 |
| 6 5 4 3 $_3$ 2 1 7 6 6 7 1 2 3 $_3$ 4 5 6 |

Rhythm 37—The dotted quarter-note in 3/4 time. (Up-beat)

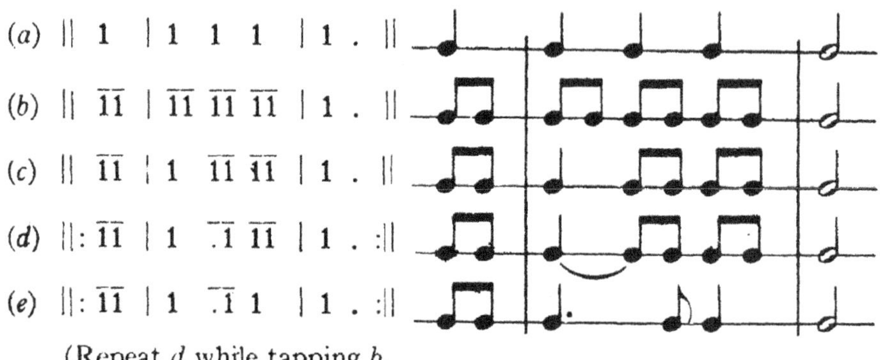

(Repeat *d* while tapping *b*.
Repeat *e* while tapping *b*.)

Melody 130

Recite rhythmically before attempting to sing.

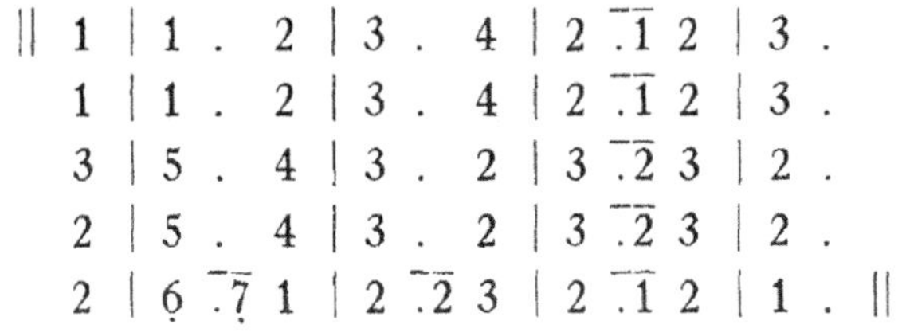

|| 1 | 1 . 2 | 3 . 4 | 2 .1 2 | 3 .
1 | 1 . 2 | 3 . 4 | 2 .1 2 | 3 .
3 | 5 . 4 | 3 . 2 | 3 .2 3 | 2 .
2 | 5 . 4 | 3 . 2 | 3 .2 3 | 2 .
2 | 6 .7 1 | 2 .2 3 | 2 .1 2 | 1 . ||

Study the following numbers from the Children's Manual:
Prayers: Our Father (Melody 1), page 37.
Hail Mary, page 39.
Christus Vincit, page 127.

Vocal Exercises 27b and 28b.—A special exercise using the intervals of *Diagram 46* should be added as soon as the intervals themselves have been studied.

Intonation.—The upper tetrachord of the *Minor* (diatonic) *Mode.* At this point, our study of the minor mode is at variance with the ordinary procedure. We have found by experience that the children obtain a better sense of pitch by studying the diatonic intervals before facing the accidental sharps which raise the seventh, or the sixth and seventh degrees of the modern minor mode. The upper tetrachord as presented in this chapter prepares the children for the third and fourth Gregorian Modes. The *Intonation Exercises* should be sung from the diagrams in numbers and on the staff, as well as form the horizontal form printed on the Chart. There are a good many exercises in this chapter because the children need variety rather than repetition. Their difficulty will not be one of *finding the intervals*—for this offers no difficulty—but of singing them with perfection. All the notes are familiar. The environment, alone, is unfamiliar. The work of this week is to make these tones and their environment seem familiar. In order to accomplish this result, these tones should be attached, as it were, to *do* (as in Exercises 105 and 107). In giving ear tests and finger dictation, we should begin always by attaching this tetrachord to the "*do*" above. When the children can sing these intervals with assurance and in tune, the teacher may pass to Diagrams 49 and 50 presenting the whole extent of the scale in minor mode.

Rhythm.—The dotted quarter-note in 3/4 time. This study should be undertaken only after the dotted quarter-note in 2/4 time has been thoroughly grasped.

In case the former problem still gives difficulty, the present exercise should be postponed. The same applies to *Melody 130*.

Material for Dictation

| 1̇ 7 6 5 6 |
| 6 5 4 3 3 |
| 6 5 6 5 3 |
| 6 5 3 5 6 |
| 6 3 3 5 6 |
| 6 3 5 6 6 |
| 6 5 6 7 6 |
| 6 6 5 4 3 |

| 1̇ 7 6 5 4 3 |
| 3 4 5 6 |
| 3 3 5 6 6 |
| 3 5 6 6 6 |
| 3 5 6 7 6 |
| 3 6 5 4 3 |
| 3 6 5 6 6 |
| 5 6 7 6 6 |

|| 6 6 | 5 6 | 5 4 | 3 . |
| 6 6 | 5 6 | 5 . | 3 . |
| 3 4 | 3 2 | 3 6 | 3 2 |
| 3 6 | 5 6 | 7 . | 6 . ||

|| 3 $\overline{55}$ | 6 6 | 5 6 | 3 . |
| 3 $\overline{55}$ | 6 6 | 7 . | 6 . |
| 6 $\overline{65}$ | 6 6 | 5 4 | 3 . |
| 6 $\overline{65}$ | 6 7 | 6 . | 6 . ||

Themes for Composition

|| 3 5 | 6 6 | 5 6 | 5 . | 3 . |
|| 3 5 | 6 5 | 6 7 | 6 . |
|| 6 . 5 | 3 . 2 | 3 . 5 | 6 . . |
|| $\overline{66}$ $\overline{55}$ | 6 3 | 6 . | . 𝄾 |
|| 6 6 | 6 $\overline{.6}$ | $\overline{56}$ $\overline{54}$ | 3 . |

Dictation and Visualization

| 6 5 4 3 3 2 1 7̣ 6̣ |
| 6̣ 7̣ 1 2 3 3 4 5 6 |
| 6 6 5 4 3 3 3 |
| 6 5 4 3 2 3 3 |
| 6 5 4 3 4 3 2 3 |
| 6 3 6 5 4 3 |
| 3 6 3 2 1 7̣ 6̣ |
| 6̣ 7̣ 1 2 3 4 3 3 6 6 |
| 6̣ 7̣ 1 2 3 4 3 3 6 5 4 3 |
| 3 3 6 6 5 4 3 3 2 1 7̣ 6̣ |

CHAPTER THIRTEEN

Vocal Exercises.—Nos. 27b and 28b. Also the *Special Exercise* of this chapter, after the study of the whole Minor range.

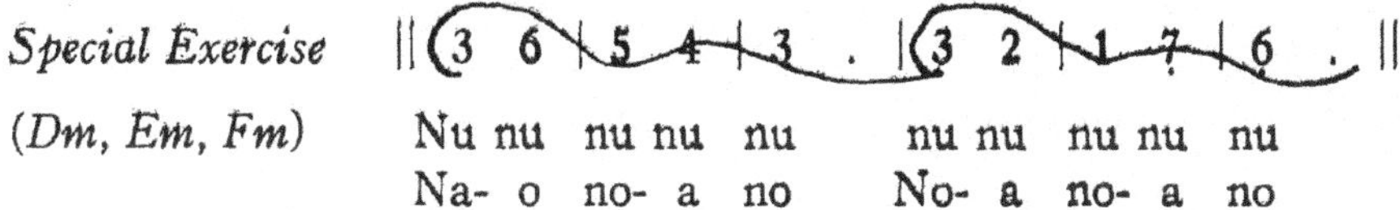

Intonation. The Minor Mode.—The entire scale from *La* to *La*.

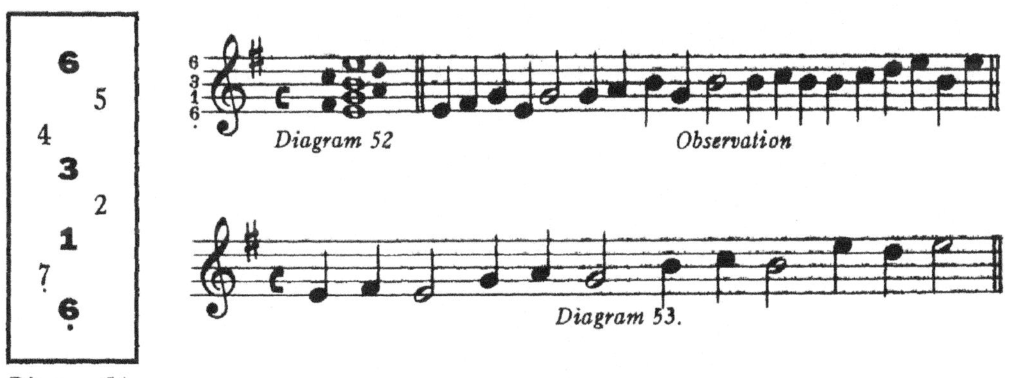

Diagram 51. *Diagram 52* *Diagram 53.*

Intonation Exercise 114—Compass Exercise Minor Mode (Em)

(*a*)	6 7 6	6 7 1	1 2 1	1 2 3	3 4 3	3 4 5 6	6 5 6	
	6 7 6	6 7 1	1 2 1	1 2 3	3 4 3	3 4 5 6	6 5 6	
	6 7 6		1 2 1		3 4 3		6 5 6	
(*b*)	6 5 6	6 5 4 3	3 4 3	3 2 1	1 2 1	1 7 6	6 7 6	6 5 6
	6 5 6	6 5 4 3	3 4 3	3 2 1	1 2 1	1 7 6	6 7 6	6 5 6
	6 5 6		3 4 3		1 2 1		6 7 6	6 5 6

Memorize the last line of *a* and *b*. Use Diagrams 51, 52 and 53 as well as the form written above.

Melody and Rhythm (Key of Em)

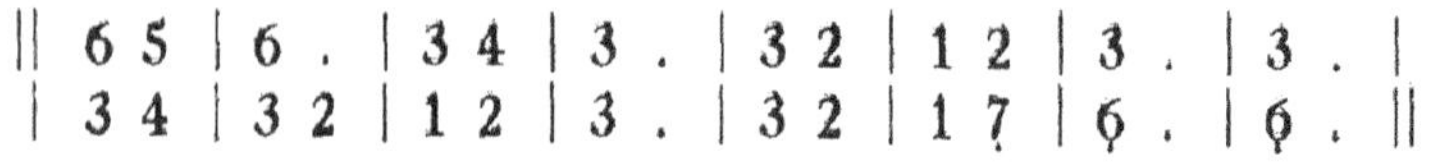

|| 6 5 | 6 . | 3 4 | 3 . | 3 2 | 1 2 | 3 . | 3 . |
| 3 4 | 3 2 | 1 2 | 3 . | 3 2 | 1 7 | 6 . | 6 . ||

|| 67 | 6 12 | 1 7 | 6 . | .
67 | 6 12 | 3 4 | 3 . | .
34 | 3 65 | 6 6 | 5 4 | 3
34 | 3 12 | 1 7 | 6 . | . ||

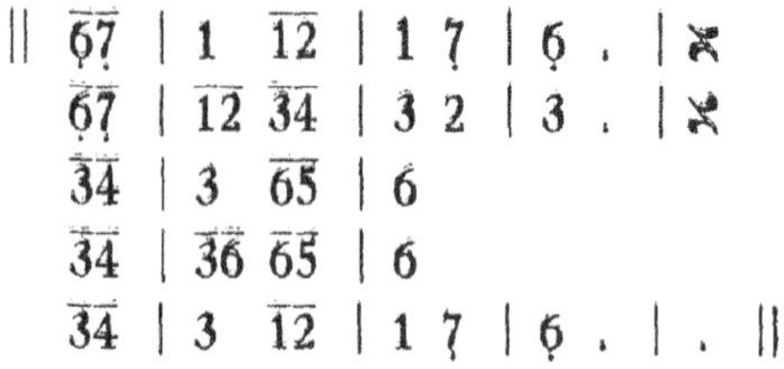

|| 67 | 1 12 | 1 7 | 6 . | ✕
67 | 12 34 | 3 2 | 3 . | ✕
34 | 3 65 | 6
34 | 36 65 | 6
34 | 3 12 | 1 7 | 6 . | . ||

Alternate groups of two and of three pulses

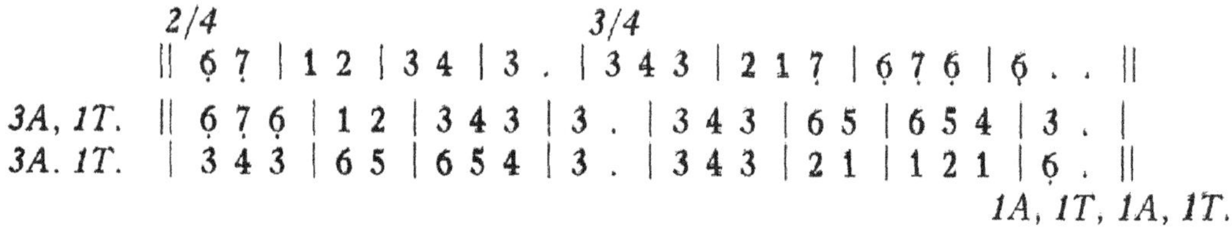

2/4 3/4
|| 6 7 | 1 2 | 3 4 | 3 . | 3 4 3 | 2 1 7 | 6 7 6 | 6 . . ||

3A, 1T. || 6 7 6 | 1 2 | 3 4 3 | 3 . | 3 4 3 | 6 5 | 6 5 4 | 3 . |
3A. 1T. | 3 4 3 | 6 5 | 6 5 4 | 3 . | 3 4 3 | 2 1 | 1 2 1 | 6 . ||
1A, 1T, 1A, 1T.

Intonation Exercise 115 (Em or Dm)

Groups of the Compass Exercise used freely

(Use Diagrams 51 and 52)

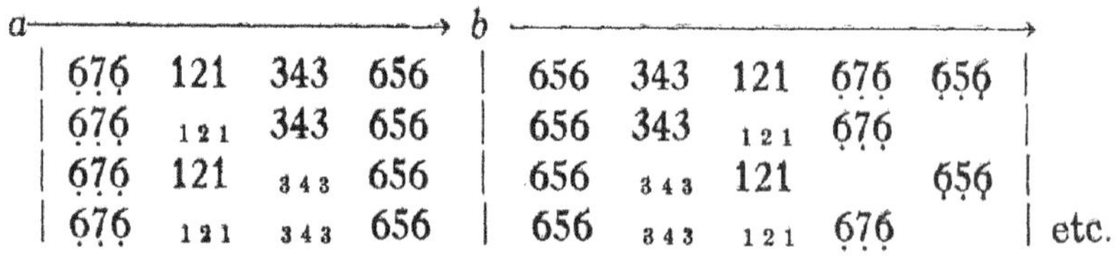

a ⟶ b ⟶

676 121 343 656	656 343 121 676 656
676 121 343 656	656 343 121 676
676 121 343 656	656 343 121 656
676 121 343 656	656 343 121 676	etc.

(Use the intermediary groups as help-notes)

Intonation Exercise 116

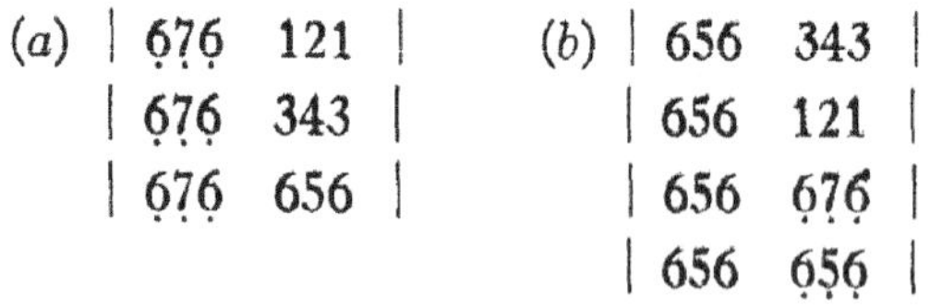

(a) | 676 121 |
| 676 343 |
| 676 656 |

(b) | 656 343 |
| 656 121 |
| 656 676 |
| 656 656 |

(Without help-notes)

Melody and Rhythm

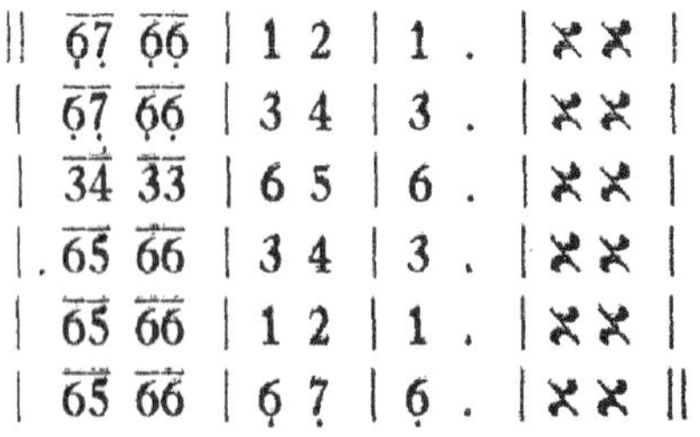

	67 66	1 2	1 .	✕✕
67 66	3 4	3 .	✕✕
34 33	6 5	6 .	✕✕
. 65 66	3 4	3 .	✕✕
65 66	1 2	1 .	✕✕
65 66	6 7	6 .	✕✕	

Intonation Exercise 117 (Em or Dm)

The Compass Exercise with Scale progression

676 121 12176		656 343 34566
676 343 34323		656 121 123456
676 656 65433		656 676 67656

Study Melodies 131, 132, 133, 134 and *135*, Children's Manual, page 44.
Study Song: To Egypt, Children's Manual, page 42.

Rhythm 38

The dotted quarter-note, 3/4 time (Down-beat)

(*a*) | 11 11 11 | 1 1 1 | (*f*) | 1 1 1 | 11 11 11 |
(*b*) | 1 11 11 | 1 1 1 | (*g*) | 1 1 1 | 1 11 11 |
(*c*) | 1 .1 11 | 1 1 1 | (*h*) | 1 1 1 | 1 .1 11 |
(*d*) | 1 .1 11 | 1 . 1 | (*i*) | 1 1 1 | 1 .1 1 |
(*e*) | 1 .1 11 | 1 . . | (*j*) | 1 . 1 | 1 .1 1 |

Each of the above designs, after being repeated, should end with a design suitable for a cadence, such as | 1 1 1 | 1 . . || or
| 1 .1 1 | 1 . . ||

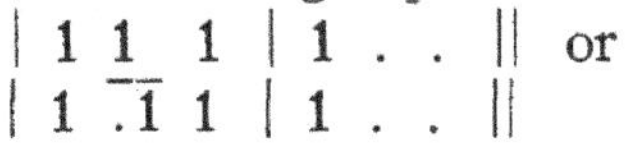

Rhythm and Melody

(*a* + *d* + *e*)
	17 67 12	3 3 3	3 .4 32	1 . 2	1 .2 17	6 . .
1 .2 17	6 . 3
3 .4 32	3 . .
34 32 17	1 2 3	6 .5 43	2 . 3	1 .2 17	6 . .	

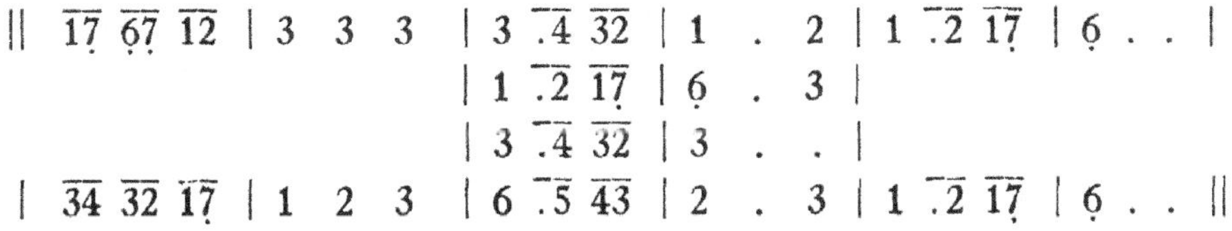

(*c* + *d*)
|| 6 .7 12 | 3 3 3 | 4 .3 23 | 4 . 2 | 3 . . | . . ✕ |
| 3 .2 17 | 6 1 2 | 3 .4 32 | 1 . 7 | 6 . . | . . ✕ ||

(*f* + *i* + *h* and *f* + *i* + *j*)
|| 6 1 2 | 34 32 12 | 3 6 5 | 4 .3 2 | 3 1 2 | 3 .2 17 | 6 . . | . . ✕ |
| 6 1 2 | 34 32 12 | 3 6 3 | 2 .1 7 | 1 6 1 | 2 .1 7 | 6 . . | . . ✕ ||

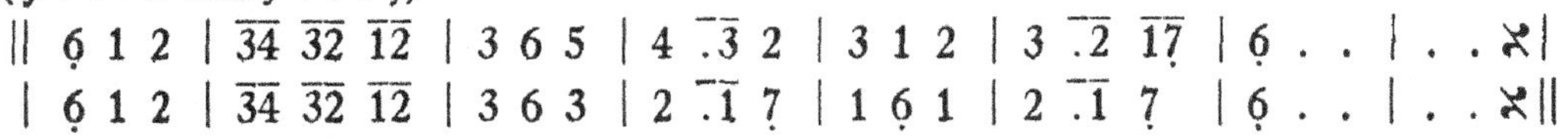

Vocal Exercises Nos. 27b and 28b, also the Special Exercise of this chapter. In singing this exercise, great attention should be given to the half tone "4 3." Should there be a tendency to sing out of tune, the exercise should be prepared as follows:

3 6 3 4 3 . Then 3 6 6 5 4 3 4 3 . Then, as written.

Intonation.—The Compass Exercise having been prepared during the study of the minor hexachord and again during the study of the upper tetrachord, should offer little difficulty when applied to the whole range of the minor scale. It should be studied on the diagram in numbers (*Diagram 51*) and also on the staff (*Diagrams 52 and 53*). As soon as the intervals have been covered in this way, the various groups should be sung more independently as in *Exercise 115*. The intermediary groups of the Compass Exercise should serve as help-notes until the children can sing the various groups freely, as in *Intonation Exercise 116*.

Intonation Exercise 117 combines the groups of the Compass Exercise with the notes sung according to the scale progression. This exercise gives an example of how to organize the work, but the teacher may vary the figures, both on the diagrams and when giving finger dictation, visualization exercises, and ear tests.

In the composition of melodies, it is not well to follow the intervals of the chord only, but the scale progression should always alternate with the larger intervals. For examples, we refer the teacher to the melodies given in this book.

The children should continue to practice the dotted quarter-note with and without gestures.

Dictation

→		
6̣ 7̣ 6̣	1 2 1	3 4 3
6̣ 7̣ 6̣	1 2 1	6 5 6
6̣ 7̣ 6̣	3 4 3	6 5 6
6̣ 7̣ 6̣	6 5 6	3 4 3

→		
6 5 6	3 4 3	1 2 1
6 5 6	3 4 3	6̣ 7̣ 6̣
6 5 6	6̣ 7̣ 6̣	1 2 1
1 2 1	3 4 3	6 5 6

Visualization

→	
6̣ 7̣ 6̣	1 7̣ 6̣
6̣ 7̣ 1	3 4 3
3 4 3	1 2 3
6 5 6	5 4 3
3 4 3	3 5 6

→	
6̣ 7̣ 1 2 3	3 4 3
3 4 3 2 1	6̣ 7̣ 6̣
3 4 3 3 6	5 4 3
6 5 6 6 3	3 4 3
3 2 1 7̣ 6̣	6̣ 5̣ 6̣

→	
6̣ 7̣ 6̣	3 4 3 2 1
1 2 1	3 6 5 4 3
3 4 3	1 2 1 7̣ 6̣
3 4 3	6 5 4 3 3
3 2 1	6̣ 7̣ 6̣ 5̣ 6̣

Melody and Rhythm

	6̣ 7̣	6̣ 7̣	1 .	1 .
1 2	1 2	3 4	3 .
3 4	3 6	6 .	3 .
1 2	1 7̣	6̣ .	. .	

	6̣ 7̣ 6̣	1 . 2	3 . .
3 4 3	6 . 3	6 . .
6 5 4	3 . 4	3 . .
3 6̣ 7̣	6̣ . 5̣	6̣ . .	

	6̣ 7̣	6̣̅7̣̅ 1̅2̅	3 4	3 .
3 2	1̅2̅ 3̅2̅	1 7̣	6̣ .
6 5	6̅5̅ 4̅3̅	3 4	3 .
3 4	3̅2̅ 1̅7̣̅	6̣ 5̣	6 .	

CHAPTER FOURTEEN

Vocal Exercises 27b, 28b and Special Exercise of Chapter 13.
Intonation.—The Minor Mode. Tonic Chord.

Intonation Exercise 118 (Em or Dm)

Compass Exercise Form 2. The Tonic Chord

(Use Diagrams 51 and 52)

| 6̣7̣6̣ 121 343 656 | 656 343 121 6̣7̣6̣ | 6̣5̣6̣
| 6̣$_{76}$ 1$_{21}$ 3$_{43}$ 6$_{56}$ | 6$_{56}$ 3$_{43}$ 1$_{21}$ 6̣$_{76}$ |
| 6̣ 1 3 6 | 6 3 1 6̣ | Memorize the last line.

Intonation Exercise 119 (Em or Dm)

6̣ 6̣ 6̣ 1 3 3 3 3 3 6 6 6	6 6 6 3 3 1 1 1 1 6̣ 6̣ 6̣
6̣ 6̣ 6̣ 1 1 3 3 3 3 6 3 6	6 6 3 3 3 6 3 3 1 6̣ 7̣ 6̣
6̣ 1 1 1 2 3 3 3 2 3 6 3	6 3 3 2 3 6 3 3 2 1 7̣ 6̣

Intonation Exercise 120 (Em or Dm)

6̣ 1 3 3 4 3 2 1 7̣ 6̣		3 1 6̣ 6̣ 5̣ 6̣ 7̣ 1 2 3
6̣ 1 3 2 3 2 1 7̣ 7̣ 6̣		3 1 6̣ 7̣ 6̣ 5̣ 6̣ 7̣ 1 2 3 3
6̣ 1 3 6 6 5 4 3 4 5 6		3 6 6 6 5 4 3 2 3 3 3 1 6̣ 5̣ 6̣

Intonation Exercise 121

Melody and Rhythm (Em or Dm)

	6̣7̣ 12	3 3	6 .	3 .
24 32	1 2	3 .	. 𝄽
24 32	1 7̣	1̇ .	6̣ .
7̣2 17̣	6̣ 5̣	6̣ .	. 𝄽	

	6 6	6 3	6 .	6 .
6 54	3 2	3 .	. 𝄽
2 34	5 6	5 .	6 .
6 32	1 7̣	6̣ .	. 𝄽	

Intonation Exercise 122 (Em or Dm)

Preparation: 6 7 1 2 3 6

| 6 1 3 1 6 6 1 3 3 6 6 3 3 1 6 |
| 6 1 3 1 6 6 1 3 3 6 6 3 3 1 6 |
| 6 1 6 3 3 6 6 3 3 6 |

7
6
5
4
3
2
1
7
6
5

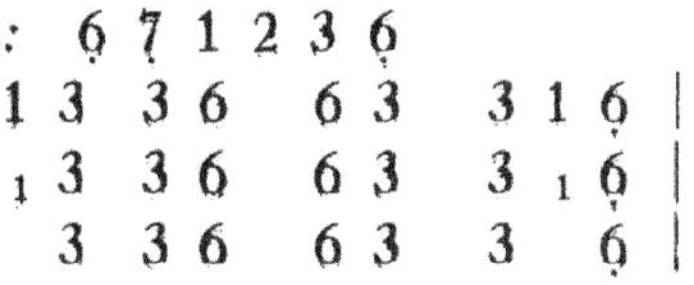

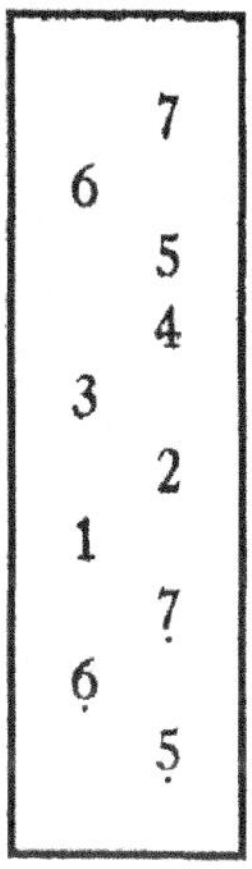

Diagram 54.

Intonation Exercise 123 (Em or Dm)

Tonic chord with scale progression.

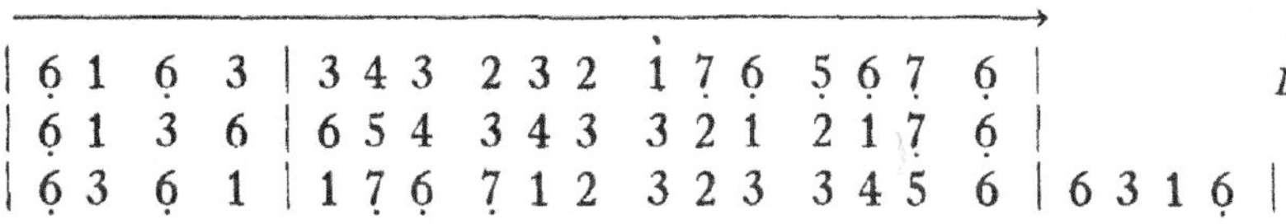

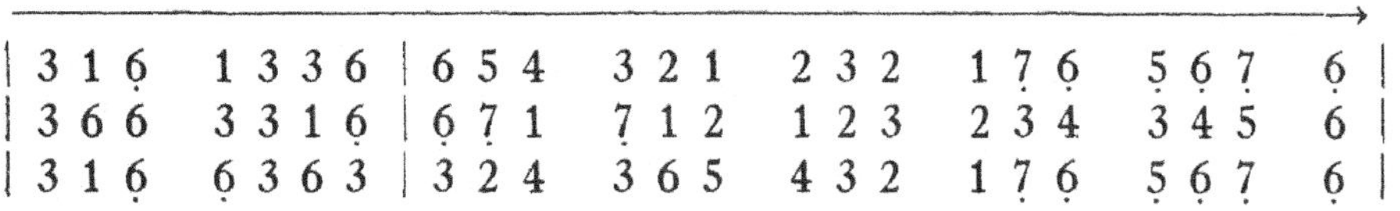

6 1 6 3	3 4 3 2 3 2 1 7 6 5 6 7 6
6 1 3 6	6 5 4 3 4 3 3 2 1 2 1 7 6
6 3 6 1	1 7 6 7 1 2 3 2 3 3 4 5 6	6 3 1 6

3 1 6 1 3 3 6	6 5 4 3 2 1 2 3 2 1 7 6 5 6 7 6
3 6 6 3 3 1 6	6 7 1 7 1 2 1 2 3 2 3 4 3 4 5 6
3 1 6 6 3 6 3	3 2 4 3 6 5 4 3 2 1 7 6 5 6 7 6

Intonation Exercise 124 (Em or Dm)

Tonic Chord with surrounding tones. Use Diagram 54.

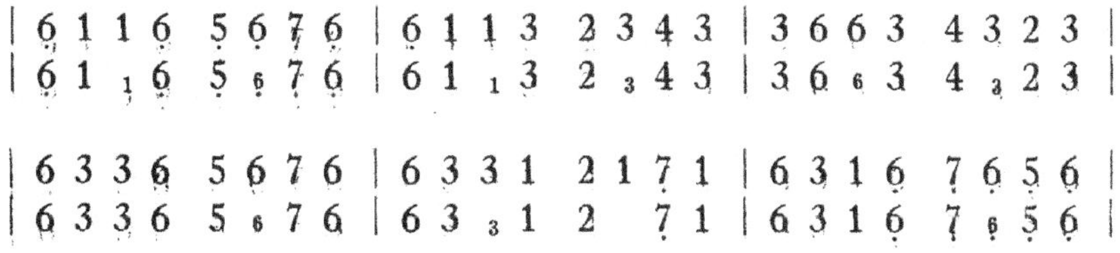

| 6 1 1 6 5 6 7 6 | 6 1 1 3 2 3 4 3 | 3 6 6 3 4 3 2 3 |
| 6 1 1 6 5 6 7 6 | 6 1 1 3 2 3 4 3 | 3 6 6 3 4 3 2 3 |

| 6 3 3 6 5 6 7 6 | 6 3 3 1 2 1 7 1 | 6 3 1 6 7 6 5 6 |
| 6 3 3 6 5 6 7 6 | 6 3 3 1 2 7 1 | 6 3 1 6 7 6 5 6 |

Melody and Rhythm

|| 67 | 6 6 | 1 2 | 3 . | 2
32 | 1 6 | 6 5 | 6 . | .
12 | 3 6 | 6 5 | 6 . | 3
32 | 1 6 | 7 5 | 6 . | . ||

	6 6	6 3	6 .	6 .
3 32	4 2	3 .	. ✗
4 2	3 4	5 .	6 .
3 6	5 7	6 .	. ✗	

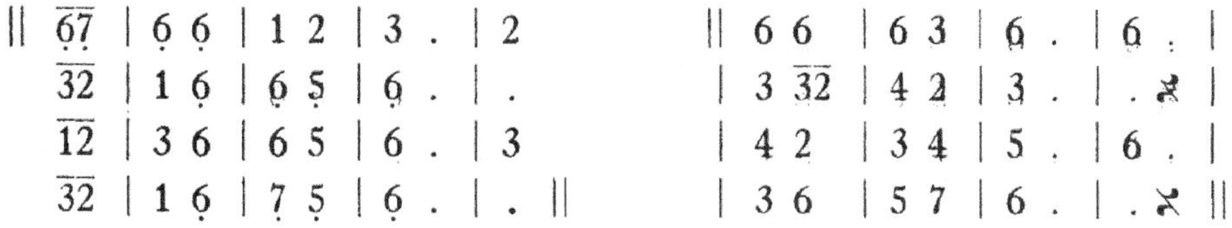

Melody 136. Italian. (Em or Dm)

||: 17 | 6 .7 12 | 3 3 4 | 3 .2 17 | 6 6 :||
3 | 6 6 34 | 5 5
3 | 6 6 34 | 5 5
2 | 4 4 12 | 3 3 4 | 3 .2 17 | 6 6 ||

Rhythm: Continue to study the designs of *Chapter 13.*

Study Melodies 137, 138, 139 and 140, Children's Manual, page 45.

Study Song: The Stream, Children's Manual, page 46.

Vocal Exercises 27b, 28b, and the *Special Exercise* of *Chapter 13.*

Intonation.—Study of the *Tonic chord, minor mode,* in the range: 6–6. The tonic chord has already been studied in the range: 6–3 and in the range: 6–3. The drill this week should be directed toward uniting the tones below *mi* with those above it. The *Diagrams* should be used to give variety to the work. The *Intonation Exercises* will serve as a general indication to the teacher as to the method of approach to each problem: the tonic chord itself (*Intonation Exercise 118*), the tones repeated (No. 119), the tonic chord combined with the intervals in scale progression (No. 120), the tonic chord, scale and Compass Exercise, in their full range on the staff (No. 121), the intervals of the tonic chord sung with more freedom (No. 122), and combined with phrases in scale progression (No. 123), the intervals of the tonic chord with the tones that surround them (No. 124).

Each of these exercises can be varied greatly: can be rendered more simple by the use of help-notes or more difficult by their omission. Each should be a starting point for rapid observation, for silent visualization and for aural memory.

There is no new rhythmic problem in this chapter, but an application of the rhythmic designs of *Chapter 13* embodied in melodies. We repeat the advice given elsewhere, that the melodies containing metrical problems (such as Nos. 136, 139 and 140) should be studied *as rhythmic exercises:* the rhythmic designs being placed on the board and recited with and without gestures; after which the melody should be sung slowly, and repeated at the proper tempo. The other melodies (Ncs. 137 and 138) offer no rhythmic or metrical problem and should be sung at sight. If there should be any hesitation, allow the children to *name the notes in time* before singing the melody.

Dictation

6̣ 7̣ 1 2 3	6 6 5 4 3	6̣ 1 3 4 3 2 3	6̣ 1 3 6 3
6̣ 6̣ 1 2 3	6 5 4 3 3	6̣ 1 3 4 2 3	6 3 3 1 6̣
6̣ 1 3 3 3	6 6 3 4 3	6 3 6 5 6 7 6	6̣ 1 6̣ 1 3
6̣ 1 3 3 6	6 3 4 3 6	6 3 6 5 7 6	3 6 6 5 6
6̣ 6̣ 1 3 6	6 3 3 2 1	6 3 1 2 1 7̣ 1	6 3 4 3 3
6̣ 1 3 6 6	6 3 1 2 1	6 3 1 2 7̣ 1	3 4 3 1 6̣
6̣ 1 6̣ 3 6	6 3 1 7̣ 6̣	1 3 6̣ 5̣ 7̣ 6̣	6̣ 1 7̣ 5̣ 6̣

Visualization

| 6̣ 6̣ 1 2 3 . 3 . |
| 3 6 3 6 3 . . . |
| 6 3 3 2 1 . 6̣ . |
| 6̣ 1 6̣ 7̣ 6̣ . . . |

→

| 6̣ 1 3 . 2 4 3 2 1 . |
| 3 1 6̣ . 1 7̣ 6̣ 5̣ 6̣ . |
| 6̣ 1 3 . 3 6 5 4 3 . |
| 3 4 3 . 3 1 6̣ 7̣ 6̣ . |

Aural Memory

	6̣ 1	3 .	. 4	2 4	3 .	. .
3 6	3 .	. 2	1 7̣	6̣ .	. .
6̣ 1	3 .	. 6	5 4	3 .	. .
6 3	2 .	. 3	1 7̣	6̣ .	. .	

	6̣ 1 3	6 . .	5 4 3	3 . .
3 2 3	4 . 2	3 . .	3 . .
6̣ 1 3	6 . .	3 4 3	2 . .
3 1 6̣	1 . 7̣	6̣ . .	. . .	

Themes for Compositions

1. || 3 .4 5 | 6 . 5 | 1̇ .5 6 | 5 . 3 | (Schubert.)
2. || 3 .2 3 | 1 .7̣ 1 | 5 .6 5 | 5 .4 3 | (Charbonnieres.)
3. || 5̣ 5̣ 5̣ | 5̣ .6̣ 7̣ | 1 1 1 | 1 .2 3 | (Purcell.)
4. || 3 .4 3 | 3 . 6 | 6 . . | 6 5 4 | 3 . . | (Mozart.)

6
3
1
6

Intonation Exercise 128

6 1 3 3 6	6 3 3 1 6
6 1 3 3 6	6 3 3 1 6
6 3 3 6	6 3 3 6

6 1	6 3
6 1 3	6 3 1
6 1 3 6	6 3 1 6

Study *Melodies 141 and 142*, Children's Manual, page 48.
Study Hymn: *Ave Maris Stella*, Children's Manual, page 49.

Vocal Exercises Nos. 25b, 26b, 27b and 28b. These should be used as preparation for the *Special Exercise* of this chapter. This exercise should be sung at first giving each note a separate syllable (*Nu* or *No*), then with the syllables indicated in the exercise itself.

Intonation.—Study of *Compass Exercise, Form 3,* for the direct attack of the dependant tones in the minor mode. When *Exercise 125* has been studied with the help-notes, both on the diagrams and as written horizontally, the last line should be memorized. After this exercise has been thoroughly grasped and can be sung without difficulty, then the intervals (as suggested in Exercise 126) can be taken more freely, using the intermediary *groups* as help-notes. This process should not be hurried.

Intonation Exercise 127 provides a convenient review of the three forms of the *Compass Exercise* in the *Minor Mode.* When the three forms have been sung correctly as indicated in the exercise, the teacher should pass from one form of the *Compass Exercise* to another so that the children may form the habit of changing from the use of one to another, passing from a *tonic chord group* to a group in scale progression or to a group attacking the dependant tones directly. All this work takes a good deal of time if it be done thoroughly, and it can well be carried over into the following weeks.

Intonation Exercise 128 is a review of the tonic chord and an exercise for the free use of its intervals. It should be studied on the diagrams in numbers and on the staff.

Melodies 141 and 142 should be used as *rhythmic exercises,* then as intonation exercises, and finally should be sung as written.

The Hymn: *Ave Maris Stella* should be studied in the same manner: first the groups should be sung with rhythmic gestures for the alternation of groups of two and three pulses:

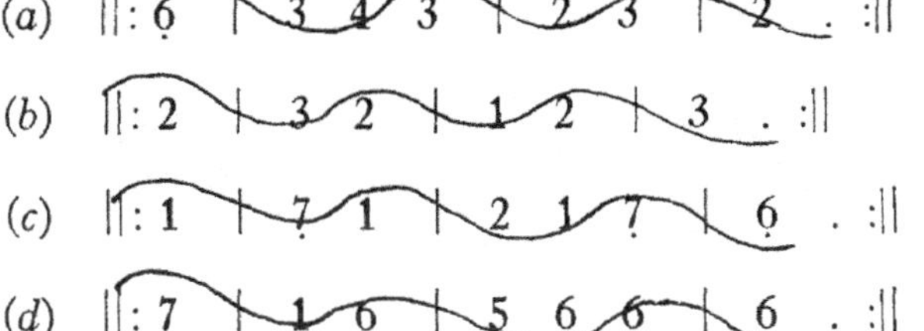

Repeat each line; then repeat $a + b$, then $e + c$, then the whole melody.

The preliminary work should include a study of the dynamics of this melody. The first note of each measure should be sung lightly, *pianissimo,*—as a butterfly would alight on a flower. Thus:

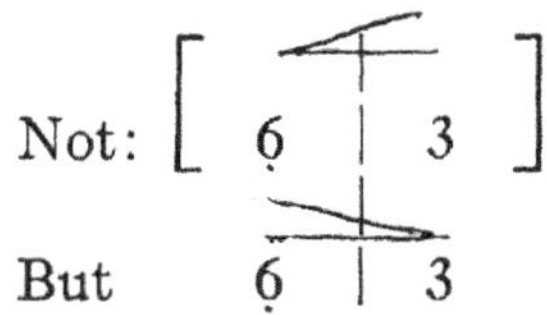

Thus rule applies to all the groups in this melody.

On the other hand, the individual notes must not be given undue stress. In each phrase, we will select a point for the summit of a delicate phraseological crescendo. A slight *ritardando* should be given the last two groups of the melody:

Rit.. . . . .
| 5 6 6 | 6 . ||

The whole melody should be sung *legato* and *calmly*.

Dictation

6 1 3 2 1 7 6	6 1 6 6 1 3	6 1 3 2 1 4 3
6 1 6 2 1 4 3	3 6 3 3 4 3	6 3 6 5 6 4 3
3 4 3 1 6 7 6	3 6 3 4 3 6	6 6 6 6 5 4 3
6 7 6 1 3 4 3	6 3 3 2 1 3	6 6 6 2 1 7 6
3 1 6 7 6 5 6	3 6 3 3 1 6	6 6 3 3 6 5 6

Visualization

```
| 6̣ 1 3 6     | 6̣ 3 6 4 3 2 1 7̣ 6̣ |
| 343 121 6̣   | 6̣ 3 6 5 6 5 4 3 3 |
| 6̣ 1 3 6 6̣   | 3 6 3 4 3 2 1 2 3 |
| 6 6̣ 1 2 3   | 3 6 5 4 3 1 6̣ 7̣ 6̣ |
| 3 6 6̣ 7̣ 6̣   | 6̣ 2 1 4 3 2 1 7̣ 6̣ |
```

Aural Memory

```
|| 6̣ . 1 | 3 . 4 | 3 . . | 2 . . |
|  2 . 1 | 3 . 6 | 3 . . | . . 𝄽 |
|  6̣ . 1 | 3 . 6 | 5 . . | 6 . . |
|  6 . 6̣ | 1 . 7̣ | 6̣ . . | . . 𝄽 |
```

Sing once, repeat by memory: One line at a time; then two lines at a time; then whole melody.

Dictation

Melody and Rhythm

```
|| 32 12 | 3 3 | 12 17̣  | 6̣ . |
|  34 32 | 3 6 | 32 12  | 3 . |
|  66 65 | 6 6 | 34 32  | 3 . |
|  32 12 | 3 6 | 6̣7̣ 17̣ | 6̣ . ||
```

Dictation on the Staff

(Key of Em.)

```
| 6̣ 3 | 3 . | 4 . | 3 . |
| 6̣ 3 | 4 . | 3 . | 6 . |
| 6 6 | 5 4 | 3 2 | 1 2 |
| 3 . | 3 . | 6̣ . | . 𝄽 ||
```

```
|| 3 .2 | 3 3 | 1 .7̣ | 6̣ . |
|  3 .4 | 3 6 | 3 .2 | 3 . |
|  6 .5 | 6 6 | 3 .2 | 1 . |
|  1 .2 | 1 6̣ | 5̣ .6̣ | 6̣ . ||
```

(Key of Am.)

```
|| 6̣ .6̣ 6̣ | 6̣ 7̣ 1   | 2 .1 7̣ | 6̣ . . |
|  6̣ .6̣ 6̣ | 1 7̣ 6̣   | 1 .2 3 | 3 . . |
|  3 .4 3  | 2 .3 2   | 1 .7̣ 6̣ | 3 . . |
|  3 .4 3  | 1 6̣ 1   | 2 .1 7̣ | 6̣ . . |
```

The suggestions given above should be used as a guide to the type of dictation required, but should be used freely in order to adapt this part of the training to the capacity of the various groups in the class, as was explained fully in the First Year.

CHAPTER SIXTEEN

Vocal Exercises 28b, 29b and 30b.

Intonation.—The Minor Mode in Plagal Range.

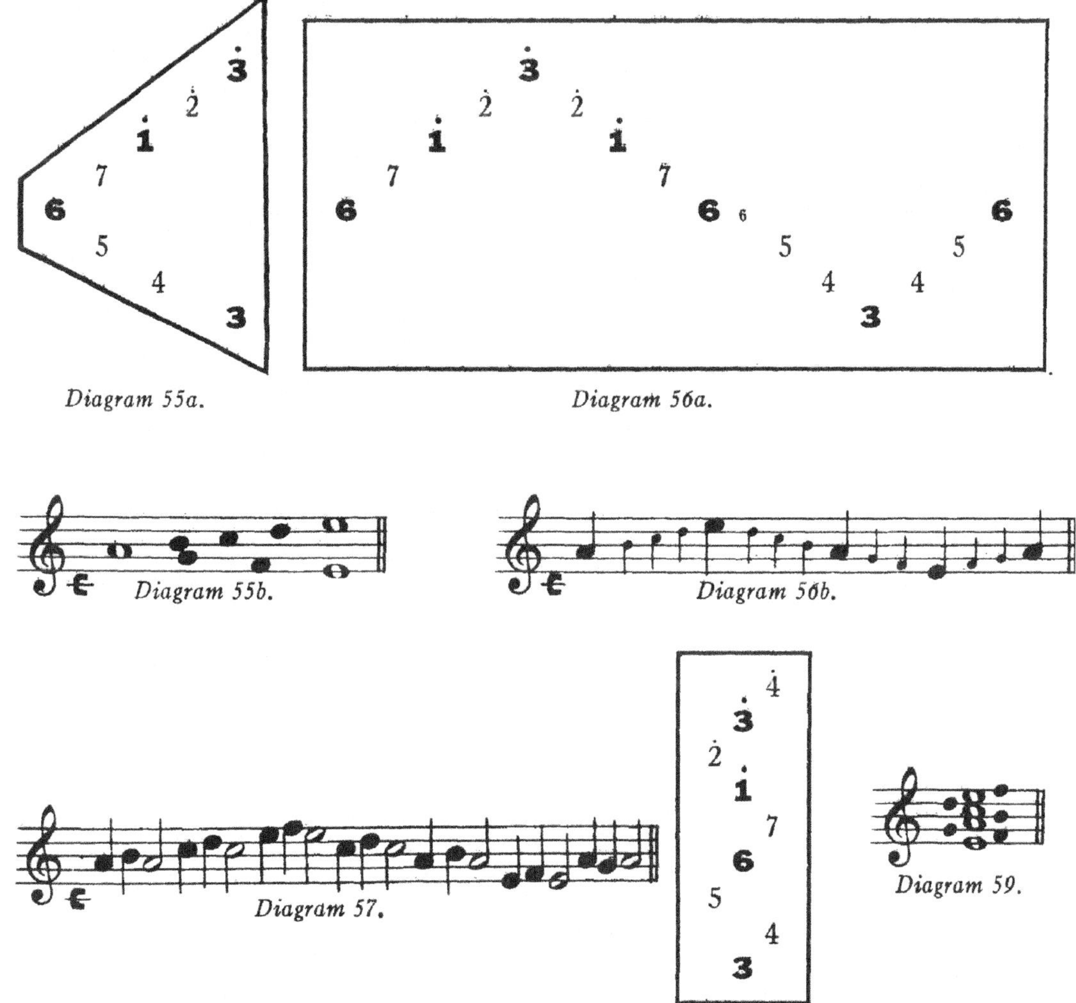

Diagram 55a.

Diagram 56a.

Diagram 55b.

Diagram 56b.

Diagram 57.

Diagram 58.

Diagram 59.

Intonation Exercise 129

(Key of Am)

a →

```
| 6 7 1̇ 2̇ 3̇   3̇ 2̇ 1̇ 7 6   6 5 4 3   3 4 5 6   6 5 6 |
| 6 7 1̇ 2̇ 3̇   3̇ 2̇ 1̇ 7 6   6 5 4 3   3 4 5 6   6 5 6 |
```

b →

```
| 6 5 4 3   3 4 5 6   6 7 1̇ 2̇ 3̇   3̇ 2̇ 1̇ 7 6   6 3̇ 6 |
| 6 5 4 3   3 4 5 6   6 7 1̇ 2̇ 3̇   3̇ 2̇ 1̇ 7 6   6 3̇ 6 |
```

Intonation Exercise 130 (Gm)

Compass Exercise, Form 1, Plagal Range

a →

```
| 676  1̇2̇1̇  3̇4̇3̇  3̇4̇3̇  1̇2̇1̇  676  656  6543  343  343  676  656 |
| 676  1̇2̇1̇  3̇4̇3̇  3̇4̇3̇  1̇2̇1̇  676  656  6543  343  343  676  656 |
| 676  1̇2̇1̇  3̇43   3̇4̇3̇  1̇2̇1̇  676  656        343  343  676  656 |
```

Intonation Exercise 131 (Am)

a →

```
| 6 7 1̇ 2̇ 3̇   3̇         6 | 6 5 4 3   3         6 |
| 6         3̇   3̇ 2̇ 1̇ 7 6 | 6       3   3 4 5 6 |
```

b →

```
| 6 5 4 3   3         6 | 6 7 1̇ 2̇ 3̇   3̇         6 |
| 6       3   3 4 5 6 | 6         3̇   3̇ 2̇ 1̇ 7 6 |
```

Intonation Exercise 132a (Gm)

Compass Exercise, Form 2, Plagal Range

Preparation: 671̇2̇3̇2̇1̇76 6543 3456

```
| 676  1̇2̇1̇  3̇4̇3̇  3̇4̇3̇  1̇2̇1̇  676 | 656  343  343  656 |
| 676  1̇2̇1̇  3̇4̇3̇  3̇4̇3̇  1̇2̇1̇  676 | 656  343  343  656 |
| 6    1̇    3̇    3̇    1̇    6   | 6    3    3    6   |
| 6    1̇    3̇    3̇    1̇    6   | 6    3    3    6   |
```

Control: 671̇2̇3̇2̇1̇76 6543 3456

Intonation Exercise 132b (Gm)

Preparation: 6543 3456 671̇2̇3̇2̇1̇76

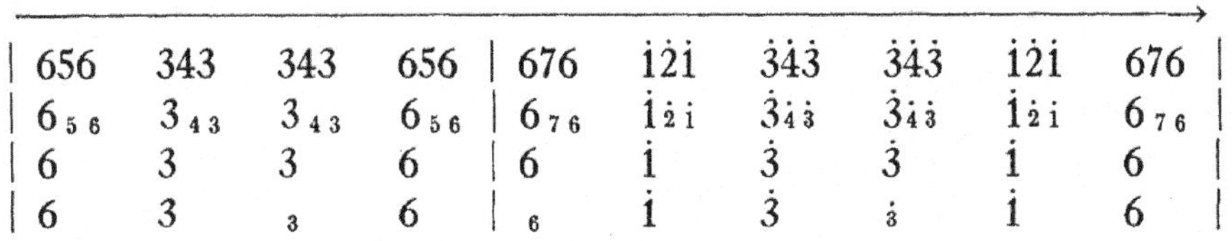

656	343	343	656	676	1̇2̇1̇	3̇4̇3̇	3̇4̇3̇	1̇2̇1̇	676
6_{56}	3_{43}	3_{43}	6_{56}	6_{76}	$\dot{1}_{\dot{2}\dot{1}}$	$\dot{3}_{\dot{4}\dot{3}}$	$\dot{3}_{\dot{4}\dot{3}}$	$\dot{1}_{\dot{2}\dot{1}}$	6_{76}
6	3	3	6	6	1̇	3̇	3̇	1̇	6
6	3	3	6	6	1̇	3̇	3̇	1̇	6

Control: 6543 3456 671̇2̇3̇2̇1̇76

Melody and Rhythm

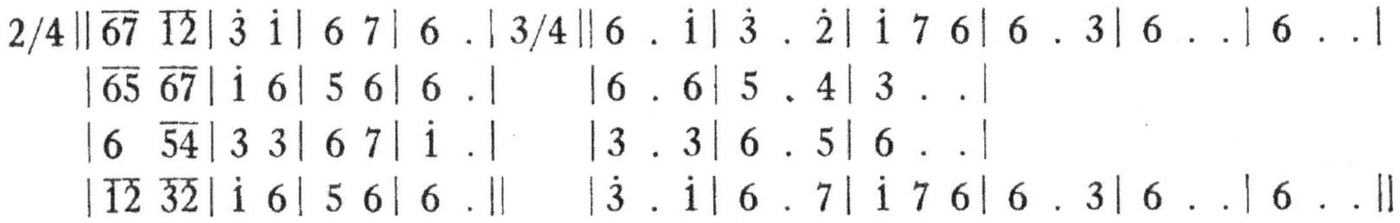

2/4 ‖ $\overline{67}$ $\overline{\dot{1}2}$ | 3̇ 1̇ | 6 7 | 6 . | 3/4 ‖ 6 . 1̇ | 3̇ . 2̇ | 1̇ 7 6 | 6 . 3 | 6 . . | 6 . . |

| $\overline{65}$ $\overline{67}$ | 1̇ 6 | 5 6 | 6 . | | 6 . 6 | 5 . 4 | 3 . . |

| 6 $\overline{54}$ | 3 3 | 6 7 | 1̇ . | | 3 . 3 | 6 . 5 | 6 . . |

| $\overline{\dot{1}\dot{2}}$ $\overline{\dot{3}\dot{2}}$ | 1̇ 6 | 5 6 | 6 . ‖ | 3̇ . 1̇ | 6 . 7 | 1̇ 7 6 | 6 . 3 | 6 . . | 6 . . ‖

Melody 143 (Spanish)

(Key of Am)

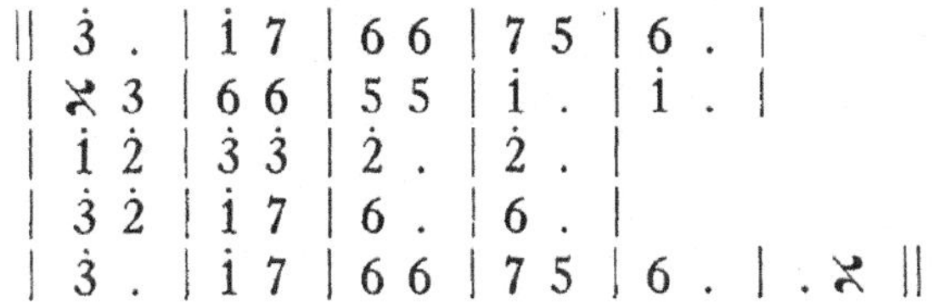

‖ 3̇ . | 1̇ 7 | 6 6 | 7 5 | 6 . |

| 𝄎 3 | 6 6 | 5 5 | 1̇ . | 1̇ . |

| 1̇ 2̇ | 3̇ 3̇ | 2̇ . | 2̇ . |

| 3̇ 2̇ | 1̇ 7 | 6 . | 6 . |

| 3̇ . | 1̇ 7 | 6 6 | 7 5 | 6 . | . 𝄎 ‖

Melody 144 (Catalan)

(Key of Am)

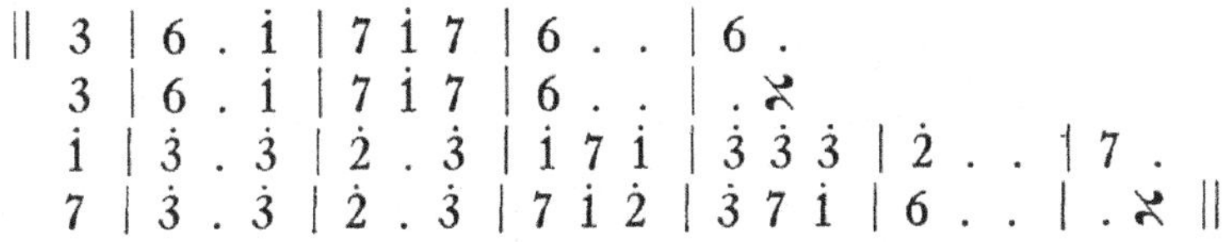

‖ 3 | 6 . 1̇ | 7 1̇ 7 | 6 . . | 6 .

3 | 6 . 1̇ | 7 1̇ 7 | 6 . . | . 𝄎

1̇ | 3̇ . 3̇ | 2̇ . 3̇ | 1̇ 7 1̇ | 3̇ 3̇ 3̇ | 2̇ . . | 7 .

7 | 3̇ . 3̇ | 2̇ . 3̇ | 7 1̇ 2̇ | 3̇ 7 1̇ | 6 . . | . 𝄎 ‖

Study Melodies 145, page 48; *146 and 147*, page 50, Children's Manual..

Vocal Exercise 28b.—After the study of *Diagrams 55, 56, and 57*, add *Vocal Exercises 29b and 30b.*

Intonation.—Study of the Minor Mode in Plagal Range. The upper tetrachord (34 5 6) is placed *below* the pentachord (6 71̇ 2̇ 3̇). Instead of having our scale bounded at each end by a *la*, we have *la* (tonic of the mode) in the center, and a *mi* at each extremity. The children will have little difficulty in finding the desired tones, but the problem is to sing the tones *perfectly true to pitch.* We advise the teacher to use help-notes faithfully, and *never to omit them in beginning a lesson,* until such time as the minor mode in plagal range has become thoroughly familiar. This will require several weeks. The grading of the Intonation Exercises follows the usual process which is now familiar to the teacher. The children should use the number diagrams and the staff diagrams alternately that each form may become familiar.

Begin to study the *Kyrie,* page 98, and the *Gloria,* page 99, Children's Manual.

Dictation

```
(a) | 6 7 1̇ 2̇ 3̇ 6 |      (b) | 6 3̇ 2̇ 1̇ 7 6 |        (c) | 6 3̇ 2̇ 1̇ 7 6 6 3 |
    | 6 5 4 3   6 |          | 6 3 4 5 6   |            | 3 6 7 1̇ 2̇ 3̇ 3̇ 6 |
    | 676 1̇2̇1̇ 3̇ 6 |          | 6 3̇4̇3̇ 1̇2̇1̇ 6 |            | 6 1̇ 3̇ 1̇ 6 6 3   |
    | 656 343   6 |          | 6 343 656 6 |            | 6 3 6 1̇ 3̇ 1̇ 6   |

(d) | 6 7 1̇ 2̇ 3̇  6 5 6   |      (e) | 3̇ 2̇ 1̇ 7 6  3 6     |
    | 6   1̇   3̇  6 3 6   |          | 3̇   1̇   6  7 6 5 6 |
    | 3̇   1̇   6  6 5 4 3 |          | 3̇   1̇   6  7 6 3 6 |
    | 3   6   1̇ 2̇ 1̇ 7 6  |          | 3̇   1̇ 7 6  6 3 4 3 |
    | 6   3   6 7 1̇ 2̇ 3̇  |          | 3̇   1̇ 7 6  3 4 3 6 |
```

Melody and Rhythm

```
|| 6̅7̅ | 6 1̇̅2̇̅ | 3̇ 3̇  | 3 . | .
   3̇̅2̇̅ | 1̇ 1̇̅7̅ | 6 5̅4̅ | 3 . | .
   3̅4̅ | 3 6  | 6 6̅7̅ | 6 . | .
   6̅7̅ | 6 1̇̅2̇̅ | 3̇ 1̇̅7̅ | 6 . | . ||
```

CHAPTER SEVENTEEN

Vocal Exercises 29b, 30b and 31b.

Intonation.—The Minor Mode in Plagal Range.

Intonation Exercise 133 (Am)

(Use Diagrams 58 and 59)

(*a*) ⟶ (*b*) ⟶

(a)	(b)
6 7 1̇ 2̇ 3̇ 1̇ 6 6 7 6 5 6	3̇ 2̇ 1̇ 7 6 6 5 4 3 4 5 6 6 5 6 7 6
6 1̇ 3̇ 1̇ 6 7 5 6	3̇ 1̇ 6 3 6 5 7 6
6 7 1̇ 7 6 6 5 4 3 3 4 3 2 3	6 5 4 3 3 4 5 6 6 7 1̇ 1̇ 7 1̇ 2̇ 1̇
6 1̇ 6 6 3 4 2 3	6 3 6 6 1̇ 7 2̇ 1̇
3 4 5 6 6 7 1̇ 7 6 6 7 6 5 6	1̇ 7 6 5 4 3 3 6 6 1̇ 1̇ 2̇ 1̇ 7 1̇
3 6 6 1̇ 6 7 5 6	1̇ 6 3 3 6 1̇ 2̇ 7 1̇
6 5 4 3 4 5 6 6 7 1̇ 2̇ 3̇ 2̇ 3̇	1̇ 3̇ 1̇ 6 6 5 4 3 3 4 3 2 3
6 3 6 6 1̇ 3̇ 2̇ 3̇	1̇ 3̇ 1̇ 6 6 3 4 2 3

Melody and Rhythm (Am)

	6 1̇	3̇ .	$\overline{23}$ $\overline{12}$	3̇ .
3̇ 1̇	6 .	$\overline{76}$ $\overline{57}$	6 .
1̇ 6	3 .	$\overline{43}$ $\overline{24}$	3 .
3 6	1̇ .	$\overline{72}$ $\overline{17}$	6 .
6 3	6 .	$\overline{56}$ $\overline{77}$	6 .
1̇ 6	3 .	$\overline{35}$ $\overline{67}$	6 .	

	6 3	3 .	$\overline{67}$ $\overline{12}$	3̇ .
$\overline{32}$ $\overline{17}$	6 3	6 .	6 .
6 3	6 .	$\overline{17}$ $\overline{67}$	1̇ .
$\overline{12}$ $\overline{32}$	1̇ 7	6 .	6 .
6 1̇	6 .	$\overline{56}$ $\overline{54}$	3 .
3 6	$\overline{17}$ $\overline{65}$	6 .	6 .	

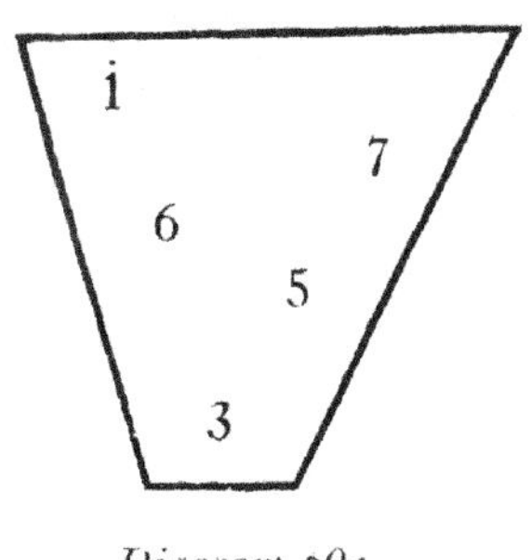

Diagram 60a.

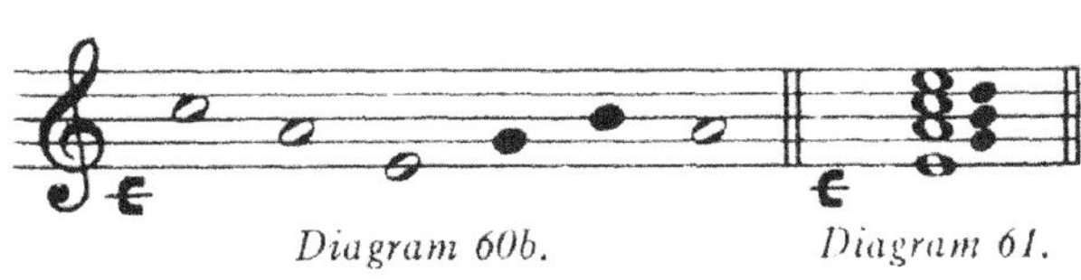

Diagram 60b. *Diagram 61.*

Intonation Exercise 134 (*Bm*)

(Use Diagrams 60 *a* and *b*)

a →									*b* →							
$\dot{1}$	6	3	3	6	5	7	6		3	6	$\dot{1}$	7	5	6	$\dot{1}$	6
$\dot{1}$	6	3	3	6	7	5	6		3	6	$\dot{1}$	7	5	6	3	6
$\dot{1}$	6	3	5	3	3	5	6		3	6	$\dot{1}$	7	5	3	5	3
$\dot{1}$	6	3	3	5	6	7	6		3	6	$\dot{1}$	7	5	3	5	6
$\dot{1}$	6	3	5	3	6	$\dot{1}$	6		3	6	$\dot{1}$	6	7	6	5	6
$\dot{1}$	6	3	5	3	5	7	6		3	6	$\dot{1}$	6	7	5	3	3
$\dot{1}$	6	3	5	3	6	3	6		3	6	$\dot{1}$	6	7	5	3	6

Intonation Exercise 135 (*Bm*)

(*a*)	$\dot{1}$ 6 3 3 5 3 6		(*b*)	$\dot{1}$ 6 3 6 5 7 5 6
	$\dot{1}$ 6 3 5 3 5 6			$\dot{1}$ 6 3 6 7 5 7 6

Melody and Rhythm

Study Melodies 148, 149, 150, page 50; *151, 152, 153, 154,* page 53, Children's Manual.

Study Song: The Son of Man, Children's Manual, page 52.

Vocal Exercises 29b, 30b, and 31b.—No. 29 must be thoroughly mastered before attempting Nos. 30 and 31, since the former provides a separate syllable for each tone, while the latter assumes that *several tones* can be sung to each syllable. Evidently, *Nos. 30 and 31* can be prepared by singing each tone to a syllable (*nu* or *no*) until the exercise is rendered perfectly in tune, after which the syllables should be distributed as written. In *No. 31*, the children should be able to sing the phrase on any one of the vowel sounds, and the teacher should use those vowels which are less perfect approaching them in the sequence of "*Nu-o-a-e-i.*" That is to say, the exercises should be sung on the syllable *nu*, then on *no*, etc.

Intonation Exercise 133 should be studied on *Diagrams 58* and *59*. This exercise prepares the use of the dependant tones in relation to the tones of the tonic chord: 7–5 in relation to 6; 4–2 in relation to 3, etc.

Intonation Exercise 134 (*with Diagrams 60 and 61*) serve a similar purpose. The tonic chord in the second inversion, is presented to the eye and ear. While this drill is provided by way of exercise, the children should not be encouraged to use the two chords (1̇ 6 3 and 3 5 7) in their compositions. If one chord is used, the other should be broken up, or it should be followed by notes in scale-progression (See Melodies 148, 149, 150, 151).

We advise the teacher to continue the use of help-notes throughout the week, especially when beginning a lesson.

Dictation

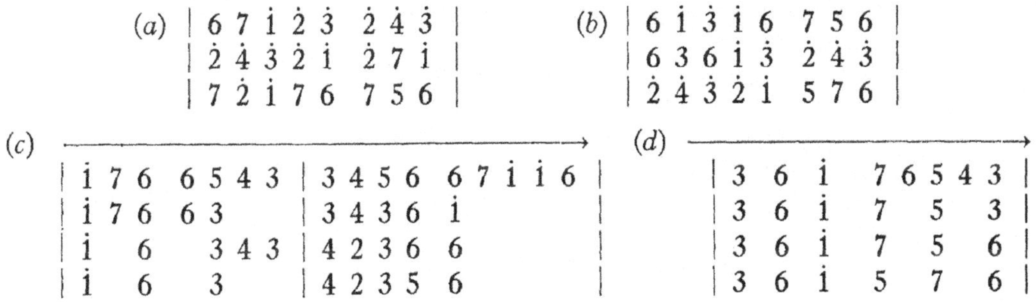

(*a*) | 6 7 1̇ 2̇ 3̇ 2̇ 4̇ 3̇ |
| 2̇ 4̇ 3̇ 2̇ 1̇ 2̇ 7 1̇ |
| 7 2̇ 1̇ 7 6 7 5 6 |

(*b*) | 6 1̇ 3̇ 1̇ 6 7 5 6 |
| 6 3 6 1̇ 3̇ 2̇ 4̇ 3̇ |
| 2̇ 4̇ 3̇ 2̇ 1̇ 5 7 6 |

(*c*) ⟶
1̇ 7 6 6 5 4 3	3 4 5 6 6 7 1̇ 1̇ 6
1̇ 7 6 6 3	3 4 3 6 1̇
1̇ 6 3 4 3	4 2 3 6 6
1̇ 6 3	4 2 3 5 6

(*d*) ⟶
| 3 6 1̇ 7 6 5 4 3 |
| 3 6 1̇ 7 5 3 |
| 3 6 1̇ 7 5 6 |
| 3 6 1̇ 5 7 6 |

Melody and Rhythm (*Bm*)

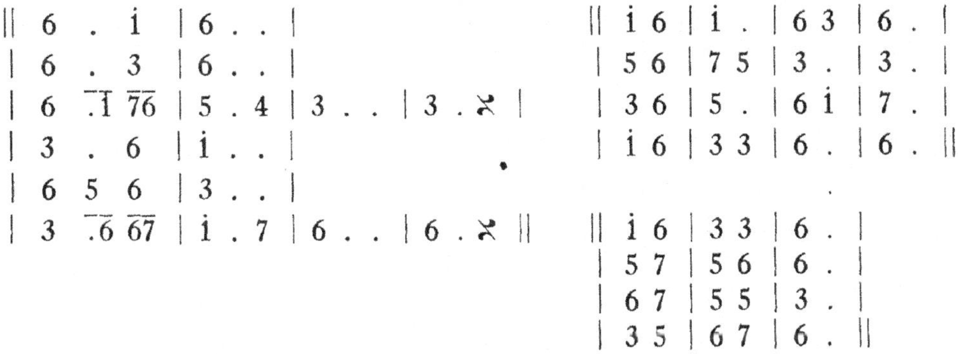

	6 . 1̇	6 . .
6 . 3	6 . .
6 $\overline{.1̇}$ $\overline{76}$	5 . 4	3 . .	3 . 𝄽
3 . 6	1̇ . .
6 5 6	3 . .
3 $\overline{.6}$ $\overline{67}$	1̇ . 7	6 . .	6 . 𝄽	

	1̇ 6	1̇ .	6 3	6 .
5 6	7 5	3 .	3 .
3 6	5 .	6 1̇	7 .
1̇ 6	3 3	6 .	6 .	

	1̇ 6	3 3	6 .
5 7	5 6	6 .
6 7	5 5	3 .
3 5	6 7	6 .	

Visualization (*Bm*)

(*a*) | 1̇ 7 6 . 6 5 3 . |
| 1̇ 6 6 . 3 6 6 . |
| 6 1̇ 6 . 1̇ 6 3 . |
| 3 6 3 . 3 5 6 . |
| 6 1̇ 1̇ . 6 3 3 . |
| 3 6 1̇ . 7 5 6 . |
| 6 1̇ 7 5 6 . 6 . |

(*b*) || $\overline{1̇1̇}$ $\overline{1̇6}$ | 1̇ 1̇ ||
$\overline{61̇}$ $\overline{65}$	6 .
$\overline{66}$ $\overline{63}$	6 6
$\overline{56}$ $\overline{54}$	3 .
$\overline{33}$ $\overline{36}$	1̇ 7
$\overline{67}$ $\overline{65}$	6 .	

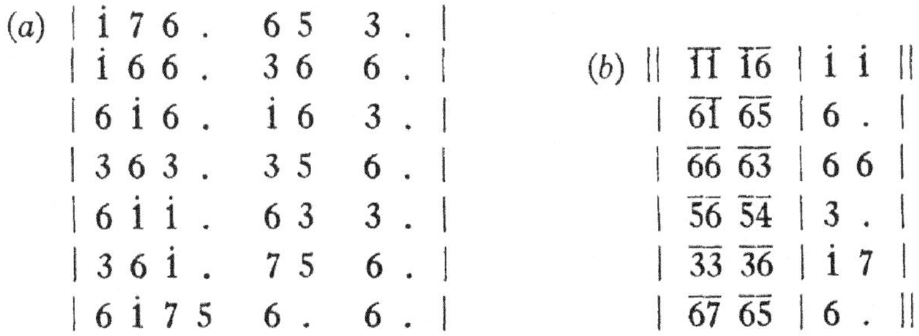

CHAPTER EIGHTEEN

Vocal Exercises 29b, 30b and 31b.

Intonation.—The Minor Mode in Plagal Range.

Intonation Exercise 136 (Gm)

Minor Compass Exercise, Form 3, Plagal Range

(Use Diagrams 58 and 59)

a ⟶
| 676 1̇2̇1̇ 3̇4̇3̇ 3̇4̇3̇ 1̇2̇1̇ 676 | 656 343 343 656 |
| $_6$76 $_{\dot{1}}$2̇1̇ $_{\dot{3}}$4̇3̇ $_{\dot{3}}$4̇3̇ $_{\dot{1}}$2̇1̇ $_6$76 | $_6$56 $_3$43 $_3$43 $_6$56 |
| 76 2̇1̇ 4̇3̇ 4̇3̇ 2̇1̇ 76 | 56 43 43 56 |
Memorize the last line.

b ⟶
| 656 343 656 676 1̇2̇1̇ 3̇4̇3̇ 3̇4̇3̇ 1̇2̇1̇ 676 |
| $_6$56 $_3$43 $_6$56 $_6$76 $_{\dot{1}}$2̇1̇ $_{\dot{3}}$4̇3̇ $_{\dot{3}}$4̇3̇ $_{\dot{1}}$2̇1̇ $_6$76 |
| 56 43 56 76 2̇1̇ 4̇3̇ 4̇3̇ 2̇1̇ 76 |
Memorize the last line.

Intonation Exercise 137 (Gm)

c ⟶
a ⟶ *b* ⟶
| 676 1̇2̇1̇ 3̇4̇3̇ 1̇2̇1̇ 676 6 1̇ 3̇ 1̇ 6 | 656 343 656 6 3 6 |
| 76 2̇1̇ 4̇3̇ 2̇1̇ 76 6 1̇ 3̇ 1̇ 6 | 56 43 56 6 3 6 |

Intonation Exercise 138 (Bm or Am)

(*a*) | 6 5 4 3 6 6 3 6 6 1̇ 56 43 56 76 2̇1̇ | 1̇2̇1̇76543 6
| 6 5 4 3 6 6 3 6 1̇ 2̇1̇ 76 56 43 56 |
| 6 7 1̇ 1̇ 6 3 3 6 2̇1̇ 76 43 43 56 |
| 6 7 1̇ 1̇ 6 3 6 1̇ 2̇1̇ 76 43 56 2̇1̇ | 1̇2̇1̇76543 6

b ⟶
| 1̇ 7 6 6 5 4 3 | 3 6 1̇ 6 3 | 43 56 2̇1̇ 76 43 | 36
| 1̇ 7 6 6 5 4 3 | 3 6 1̇ 6 1̇ | 43 56 2̇1̇ 76 2̇1̇ |
| 3 4 5 6 6 7 1̇ | 1̇ 6 1̇ 3 | 2̇1̇ 76 2̇1̇ 43 |
| 3 4 5 6 6 7 1̇ | 3 6 3 6 1̇ | 43 56 43 76 2̇1̇ | 1̇76543 6

Melody and Rhythm (Bm or Am)

|| 6 1̇ | 6 6 | 5 4 | 3 . |
| 6 7 | 6 2̇ | 1̇ 7 | 6 . |
| 6 3 | 4 3 | 6 1̇ | 7 . |
| 2̇ 1̇ | 7 6 | 5 . | 6 . ||

|| 3 | 6 1̇ | 7 6 | 2̇ 1̇ | 6 7 | 6 . | 𝄽
7 | 6 2̇ | 1̇ 7 | 6 7 | 6 . | 6 . | 𝄽
5 | 6 7 | 6 4 | 3 2 | 3 4 | 3 . | 𝄽
3 | 6 2̇ | 1̇ 7 | 6 5 | 6 . | 6 . | . ||

Intonation Exercise 139 (Am or Gm)

a ⟶

| 6 5 4 3 6 | 6 7 1̇ 2̇ 3̇ 6 |
| 6 5 4 6 | 6 7 1̇ 2̇ 6 |
| 6 5 6 | 6 7 1̇ 6 |
| 6 5 | 6 7 6 |

b ⟶

| 6 7 1̇ 2̇ 3̇ 6 | 6 5 4 3 6 |
| 6 7 1̇ 2̇ 6 | 6 5 4 6 |
| 6 7 1̇ 6 | 6 5 6 |
| 6 7 | 6 5 6 |

(*c*) | 6 3 4 5 6 6 3̇ 2̇ 1̇ 7 6 |
| 6 4 5 6 6 2̇ 1̇ 7 6 |
| 6 5 6 6 1̇ 7 6 |
| 6 5 6 7 6 |

(*d*) | 6 3̇ 2̇ 1̇ 7 6 6 3 4 5 6 |
| 6 2̇ 1̇ 7 6 6 4 5 6 |
| 6 1̇ 7 6 6 5 6 |
| 6 7 6 5 6 |

Melody 155 (Gregorian) (Am)

|| 6 | 5 6 | 1̇ 2̇ | 1̇ 7 | 6
2̇ | 2̇ 1̇ | 2̇ 3̇ | 1̇ 7 | 6
6 | 6 7 | 5 3 | 5 6 | 6
6 | 5 6 | 1̇ 2̇ | 1̇ 7 | 6 . | . ||

Melody 156 (Gregorian) (Am)

|| 6 5 6 | 1̇ 7 1̇ | 6 7 | 6 5 | 6 . |
| 1̇ 7 | 1̇ 2̇ | 2̇ 1̇ | 6 1̇ | 6 7 6 | 5 .
5 | 6 7 | 1̇ 7 6 | 7 1̇ | 2̇ . |
| 5 6 | 1̇ 2̇ 7 | 1̇ 7 6 | 7 6 5 | 6 . ||

Staff Notation
Do on the Third Line
Major Mode. Plagal Range

Diagram 62. *Diagram 63.* *Diagram 64.*

Diagram 65.

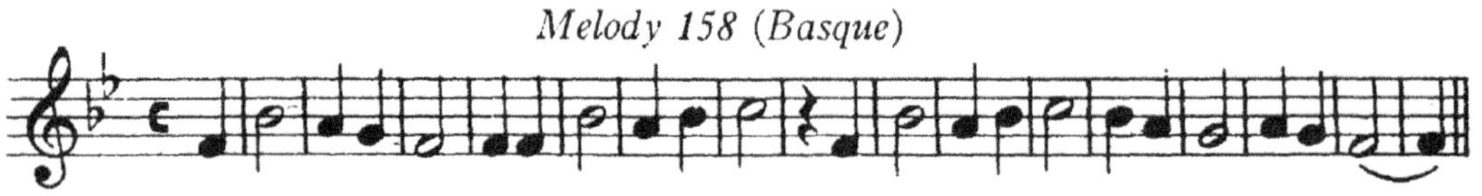

Study the following numbers from the Children's Manual:

Melodies 159, 160 and 161, page 56.
The Visible Creation, page 54.
Adam and Eve, page 58.

Rhythmic Exercise

The Linking of Simple and Composite Time by Gesture

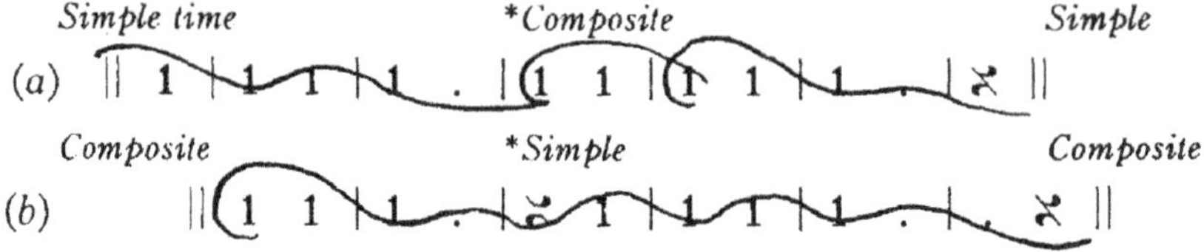

The change from one movement to the other is extremely easy when once the fundamental gestures have been grasped.

Rule: A thesis always joins simple time to composite time.

Rule: The end must correspond to the beginning.

The change of gesture does not abolish the rule for proper cadences which we have learned: a full measure at the beginning requires a full measure at the end of the phrase. A fraction of a measure at the beginning requires the other fraction to complete it at the end of the phrase.

Rhythmic Exercise

Preparation for

Composite Time Where a Measure Begins on a Rest

Beginning in Simple Time.

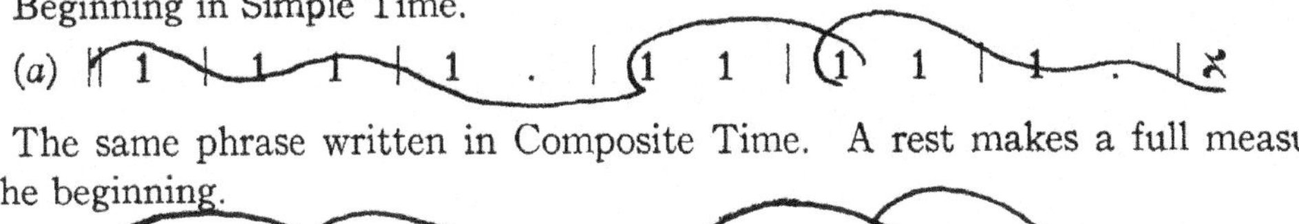

The same phrase written in Composite Time. A rest makes a full measure at the beginning.

(b) || 𝄽 1 | 1 1 | 1 . | 1 1 | 1 1 | 1 . ||

These two phrases (*a* and *b*) are, in reality, identical. One is written in simple time and the other in composite time. What is the difference?

1. A difference to the eye. The *rest* on the first pulse of (*b*) cannot be *heard.*

2. A difference of *gesture.* (In some melodies, composite time is indicated from the beginning and this rest should be used.)

3. A difference of *cadence.* Since we begin with an entire measure, we will end by an entire measure.

Whenever a melody begins with a rest, as in example (*b*) given above, the teacher would do well to reduce the phrase to simple rhythm (*a*) as a preparation: returning to the composite form later.

Vocal Exercises 29b, 30b and 31b.

Intonation.—The Minor Compass Exercise, Form 3. The study of the dependant notes sung directly, first by means of help-notes, then without help-notes, in the plagal range. Use *Diagrams 58* and *59*, studying the exercise as written, then when the exercise can be sung in its original form, using the groups more freely: 76 43 $\dot{2}$1 56 43, etc., using the intermediary *groups* as *help-notes* until such time as the intervals can be sung with precision without such aid.

Intonation Exercise 137 uses the third form of the *Compass Exercise* combined with the intervals of the *tonic chord.* This exercise is important and should be sung, first, as it is written; then the intervals should be used more freely (as described above for the compass exercise itself).

Intonation Exercise 138 combines the intervals sung in scale progression with those of the tonic chord and those of the third compass exercise. This is an important exercise since each one of these progressions tends to control the other: at the end of each line the pitch should be verified on the harmonium.

Intonation Exercise 139 measures each tone (in plagal range) from the central *la*. This work should be done on the diagrams and also from the exercise written horizontally. Much rapid observation and visualization should be given, using the material of all three exercises as a starting point.

The *Gregorian Melody 156* should be used as a *rhythmic exercise* before being sung. Each line should be taken separately. Finish each line with a diminuendo, save the third line which finishes *forte*, though without any stress. When the melody has been sung as a whole, it may be repeated as a vocal exercise, each measure being sung to a syllable, thus:

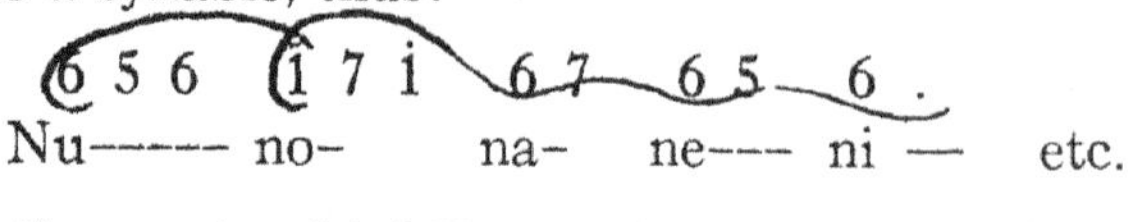

6 5 6 1̇ 7 1̇ 6 7 6 5 6 .
Nu------ no- na- ne--- ni — etc.

Staff Notation.—Do on the *third line*. This corresponds in modern notation to the *Key of B flat major* (two flats) or *B major* (five sharps). *Diagrams 62, 63* and *64* should be used for eye training: that is, for rapid *naming* of the notes. *Diagram 64* represents the range in which this position will be used, namely *mi-mi*. When the eye training has accustomed the children to this new position of *do* they should be asked to sing from the diagrams.

Melodies 157 and *158* should then be sung at sight from the Chart. Also *No. 159* from the *Children's Manual*.

As soon as the major mode in this new position has become familiar, the teacher will introduce the *Minor mode* with *do on the third line*. This corresponds in modern notation to the *Key of G minor* (two flats) or *G sharp minor* (five sharps). See *Daigram 65*. All these diagrams should be used for rapid observation, as described above, then for singing. *Melodies 160 and 161* should be sung at sight.

Dictation

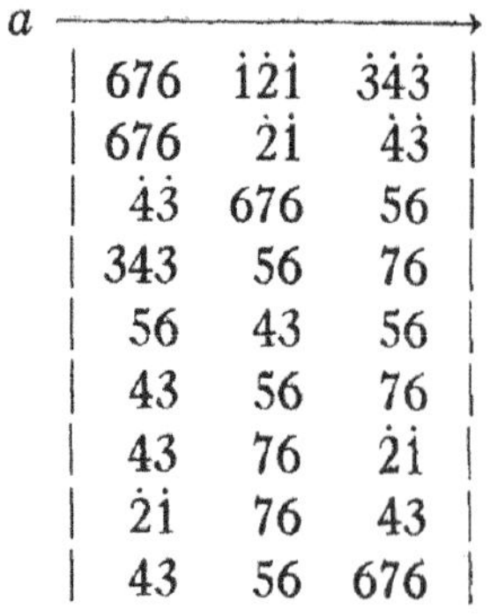

a →

676	1̇2̇1̇	3̇4̇3̇
676	2̇1̇	4̇3̇
4̇3̇	676	56
343	56	76
56	43	56
43	56	76
43	76	2̇1̇
2̇1̇	76	43
43	56	676

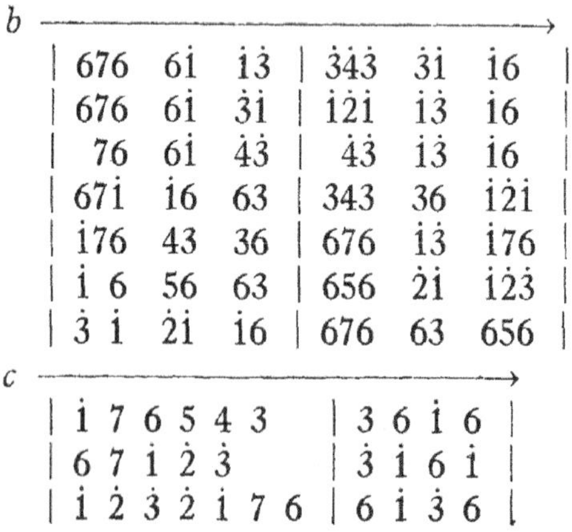

b →

676	61̇	1̇3̇	3̇4̇3̇	3̇1̇	1̇6
676	61̇	3̇1̇	1̇2̇1̇	1̇3̇	1̇6
76	61̇	4̇3̇	4̇3̇	1̇3̇	1̇6
671̇	1̇6	63	343	36	1̇2̇1̇
1̇76	43	36	676	1̇3̇	1̇76
1̇ 6	56	63	656	2̇1̇	1̇2̇3̇
3̇ 1̇	2̇1̇	1̇6	676	63	656

c →

1̇ 7 6 5 4 3	3 6 1̇ 6
6 7 1̇ 2̇ 3̇	3̇ 1̇ 6 1̇
1̇ 2̇ 3̇ 2̇ 1̇ 7 6	6 1̇ 3̇ 6

Visualization

| 6 5 4 3   6 7 1̇ 2̇ 3̇ |
| 6 5 4   6 7 1̇ 2̇ 3̇ |
| 6 5   6 7 1̇ 2̇ 3̇ 6 |
| 6 5 6̇   1̇ 6 7 1̇ 6 |
| 6 5 6   1̇ 7 6 3 6 |

| 3̇ 2̇ 1̇ 7 6   3 4 5 6 |
| 2̇ 1̇ 7 6   3 4 5 6 |
| 1̇ 7 6   3 4 5 6   3 |
| 3̇ 2̇ 1̇ 7 6   3 4 3 6 |
| 2̇ 1̇ 7 6   3 4 3 6 |

| 6 3 4 5 6 7 1̇ 2̇ 3̇ |
| 6 3 4 5 6 2̇ 1̇ 7 6 |
| 6 3 6 5 6 1̇ 7 6 |
| 6 3 6 1̇ 7 6 3 6 |

| 6 3̇ 2̇ 1̇ 7 6 5 4 3 |
| 6 2̇ 1̇ 7 6 5 4 3 |
| 6 1̇ 7 6 4 5 6̇ |
| 6 1̇ 7 6 5 6 7 6 |

Melody and Rhythm

	6 5	4 3	6 7	1̇ .
2̇ 1̇	7 6	5 4	3 .
3 6	1̇ 2̇	1̇ 7	6 .
6 1̇	2̇ 1̇	6 7	6 .

|| 6 | $\overline{32}$ $\overline{17}$ | 6 7 | 6 . | .
6 | 7 1̇ | 2̇ 6 | 2̇ . | .
2̇ | $\overline{32}$ $\overline{17}$ | 6 5 | 3 . | .
3 | 6 1̇ | 6 5 | 6 . | . ||

CHAPTER NINETEEN

Vocal Exercises 29b, 30b and *31b.*
Intonation.—The Minor Mode, Plagal Range.

Intonation Exercise 140 (Gm)

| 676 1̇2̇1̇ 3̇4̇3̇ 1̇2̇1̇ 676 656 343 656 |
| 6 1̇ 3̇ 1̇ 6 6 3 6 |
| 76 2̇1̇ 4̇3̇ 2̇1̇ 76 56 43 56 |

Use the groups freely, moving from one form of the Compass Exercise to the other.

Rhythm and Melody

	6 7 6	1̇ . 3̇	2̇ 1̇ 4̇	3̇ . 4̇
3̇ . 1̇	6 . 3	6 . .	6 . 𝄽
3 4 3	6 . 1̇	7 6 2̇	1̇ . 7
6 . 5	6 . 3	6 . .	6 . 𝄽	

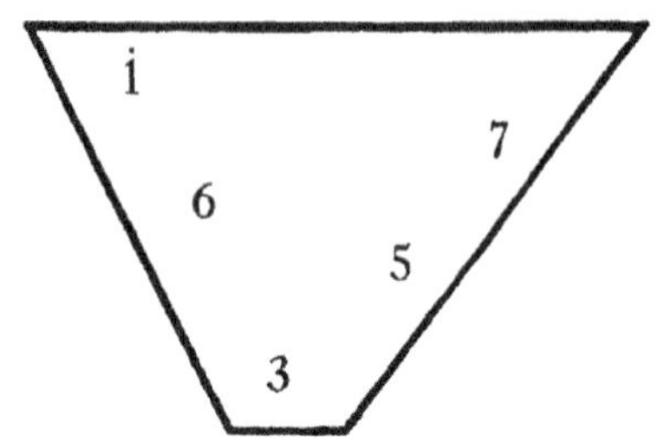

Diagram 60a.
(As in Chapter 17.)

Preparation
1̇76543 345676 6 *Intonation Exercise 141 (Bm or Am)*

1̇ 6 3 6	56 7 5 3	3 6
1̇ 6 3 6	5 7 5 3	3 6
1̇ 6 3 6	3 567 6	3 6
1̇ 6 3 6	3 5 7 6	3 6

3 6 1̇ 6	7654 3 3 6
3 6 1̇ 6	7 5 3 3 6
3 6 1̇ 6	567 65 43 6
3 6 1̇ 6	5 7 5 3 6

Diagram 60b.
(As in Chapter 17.)

Diagram 66.

Melody and Rhythm (Bm or Am)

|| 1̇ | 7 6 | 5 4 | 3 . | .
3 | 5 6 | 7 7 | 6 . | .
6 | 1̇ 6 | 5 3 | 5 . | .
3 | 6 1̇ | 7 5 | 6 . | . ||

	3 6	1̇ .	$\overline{65}$ $\overline{67}$	6 .
6 1̇	6 .	$\overline{76}$ $\overline{54}$	3 .
3 6	6 .	$\overline{76}$ $\overline{57}$	6 .
6 3	3 .	$\overline{53}$ $\overline{35}$	6 .	

Study Melodies 162, 163 and 164, Children's Manual, page 57.

Staff Exercise for Changing the Position of the Clef

(Key of E♭)

(Key of G)

Name the notes, then sing. (The help-note before the change of clef indicates the note as it would have appeared with the previous clef.) The help-note to the left of the bar equals the first note to the right of the bar. As soon as the children can read easily, the help-note should be omitted.

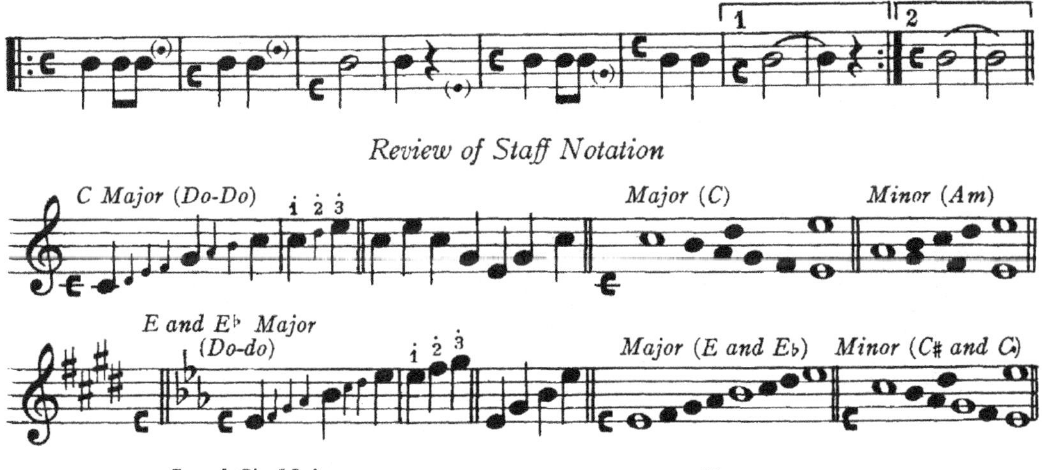

Study Melodies 165, 166, page 57; *167, 168, 169, 170*, page 62, Children's Manual. *Prepare each melody on the diagram corresponding to its tonality.* Then sing the melody at sight

Study Song: The Tailor and the Mouse, page 60.

Vocal Exercises 29b, 30b and 31b. To which should be added *Nos. 29a, 30a and 31a* during the *Review of the Major Mode* on the *Staff Diagrams* of this chapter, and as preparation, also, for the singing of the melodies in *Major Mode*.

Intonation.—The Minor Mode in Plagal Range.

Intonation Exercise 140 gives the three forms of the *Compass Exercise* all three of which are familiar taken separately. During this week, the teacher should combine them freely, passing from one column to the other, thus: 676 $\dot{1}\dot{2}\dot{1}$ $\dot{3}$ $\dot{3}\dot{1}$676 $\dot{2}\dot{1}$ $\dot{1}$6 63 43 56 76 etc. These exercises should be carried out using the exercise in numbers as written, and also on *Diagrams 58* and *59*, (page 135).

Intonation Exercise 141 continues the drill on the tonic chord in the second inversion combined with intervals of the minor dominant chord. The latter should rarely be used as a whole. Two of its intervals, combined with those of the tonic chord and depending upon the latter, are what should be brought out during the drill, which should be given on *Diagrams 60a* and *b*, and also on *Diagram 66*, (page 148).

Review of Staff Notation.—The children have studied already four positions of *do* on the staff: *do* on the leger line below the staff, *do* on the first line, *do* on the second line, and *do* on the third line. In order to read easily from the staff, it is important to cultivate the habit of reading *from the clef* and not from the lines and spaces. The latter habit develops slow readers, or those who can only read in one or two tonalities. The lines and spaces, in themselves, mean nothing. Everything depends on the *clef*. Our children, then, should form the habit of *reading by the clef*. In order to form this habit, the teacher should change frequently from one tonality to another, that the pupils may not become rigid in this matter. We have included in this chapter an exercise in *rapid change of clef* where the melody is written on a single line, the change of pitch being indicated by the movement of the clef only. This is a gymnastic the object of which is to form the habit of *reading by clef* and not by lines and spaces.

At this point, the teacher may determine whether or not to explain to the children *how to place the C clef* when they see a melody in modern notation with sharps or flats at the key signature. This will depend on the age of the children who are studying Music Second Year. It is not absolutely necessary that they should know the secret, but, if the children are quick and intelligent, they will enjoy finding for themselves the proper place for the C clef.

When we see the clef: 𝄞 with no sharp or flat, we put the C clef on the leger line below the staff. (See Key of C Major and Key of A Minor.)

When we see one or more *sharps* at the clef, the *last sharp* is like a "7." The note above the last sharp will be *Do.* Look at the diagrams and verify this fact. Thus we *place our C clef a half tone above the last sharp.* When the last sharp is *on a line* the *C clef* would be in *a space* were we to place it above. To avoid this difficulty we *count down an octave.* Example:

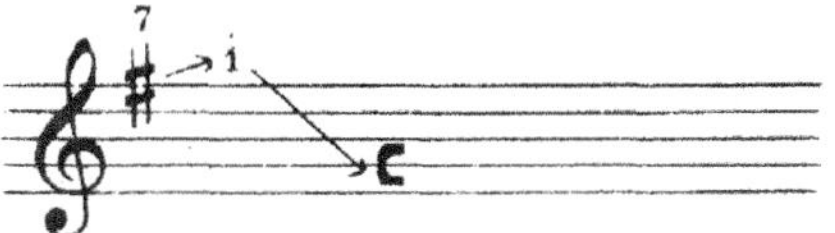

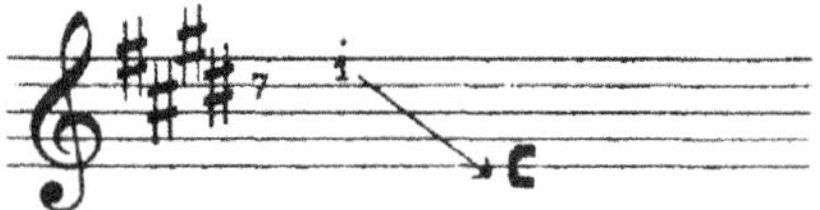

Thus we place our C clef *on a line*, not in a space.

When we see one or more *flats* in the key signature, the *last flat* is like a *Fa.* To find *do* we count *down* a tetrachord (43 2 1) or *up* a pentachord (4 5 6 7 1̇). (See Diagrams, Key of E flat, B flat, G flat.) When there is *more than one flat* at the clef, the *next to last* flat will be "*Do.*" We always *put the clef on a line* and not in a space even if it be necessary to *count down an octave* from the next to last flat, as described above in the case of the sharps. Example:

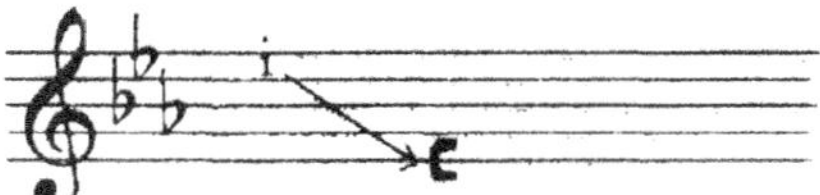

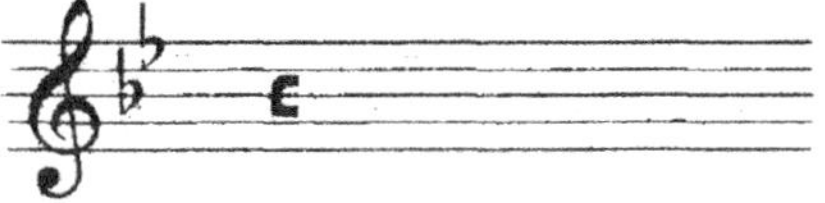

Thus we place our C clef on a line and not in a space.

The teacher can give a certain amount of drill on the board on this point, as follows:

(*a*) The teacher places the clef 𝄞 and the key signature. The children place the C clef where it belongs.

(*b*) The teacher places the C clef: the children write in the sharps or flats that are required. This latter form is a more difficult exercise since it requires that the children should know *the order in which these sharps and flats appear.* At the present time, this could be learned only through memorizing the order.[1] During the third year, the children will discover *the reason for this order*, while studying *modulation*. For young children, therefore, it is advisable to use the drill under (*a*) and await the third year for the drill under (*b*). With older children, the two forms of drill can be given.

Using each tonality placed under the Review Diagrams, the forms with black notes are intended for eye training. The notes should be *named rapidly*. The diagrams with the hollow notes are intended for *singing*, as they follow the *normal range to be used in each tonality*.

In the review, the children should be familiar with the *minor mode* as well as the *major*. The minor tonic (*la*) should be counted down from *do* (1̇76). A melody on the staff is provided in each tonality under review. These should be prepared on the diagram and then sung at sight from the Children's Manual.

Dictation

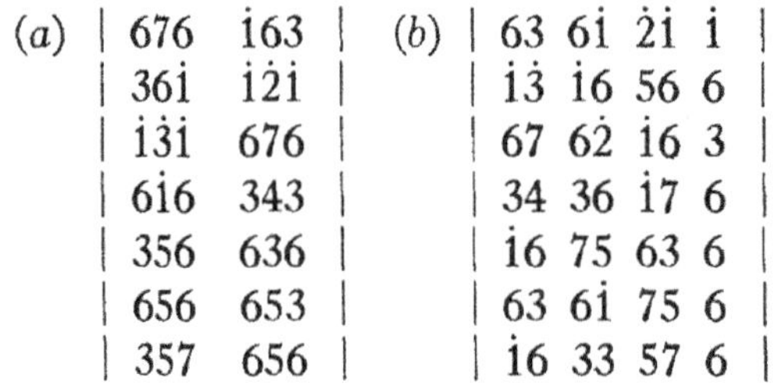

(*a*)
| 676 1̇63 |
| 361̇ 1̇2̇1̇ |
| 1̇3̇1̇ 676 |
| 61̇6 343 |
| 356 636 |
| 656 653 |
| 357 656 |

(*b*)
| 63 61̇ 2̇1̇ 1̇ |
| 1̇3̇ 1̇6 56 6 |
| 67 62̇ 1̇6 3 |
| 34 36 1̇7 6 |
| 1̇6 75 63 6 |
| 63 61̇ 75 6 |
| 1̇6 33 57 6 |

(*c*) →
1̇7636	35653	3561̇6
1̇6356	63576	75336
61̇6756	636576	1̇63576

Melody and Rhythm

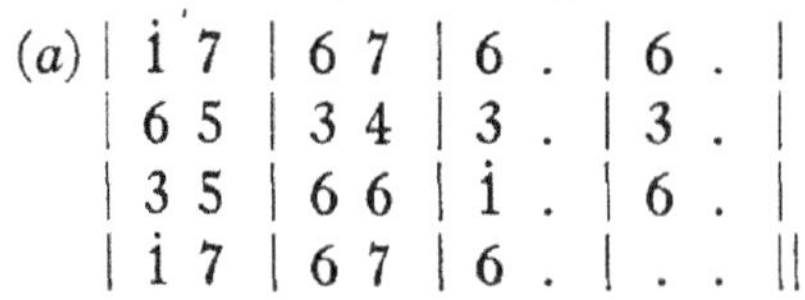

(*a*)
1̇ 7	6 7	6 .	6 .
6 5	3 4	3 .	3 .
3 5	6 6	1̇ .	6 .
1̇ 7	6 7	6 .	. .	

Melody and Rhythm

(*b*)
|| 6 | 3 6 | 1̇ . | .
1̇ | 7 6 | 5 6 | 3 . | .
1̇ | 7 6 | 6 5 | 6 . | .
6 | 3 6 | 1̇ . | .
7 | 6 5 | 6 . | .
3 | 6 1̇ | 7 6 | 6 . | .
3 | 6 1̇ | 5 7 | 6 . | . ||

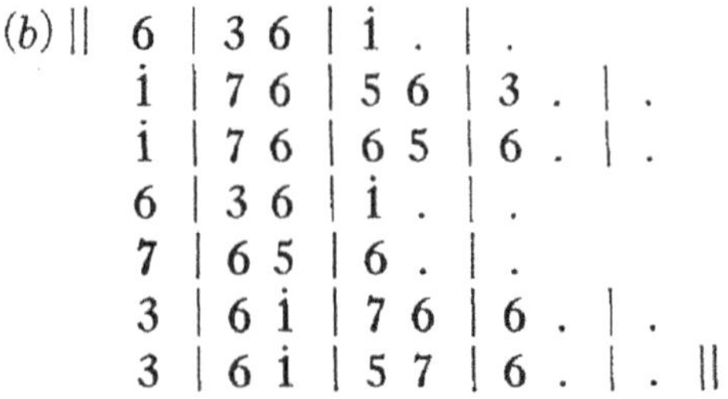

[1] *Order of Sharps: F, C, G, D, A, E, B.*
Order of Flats: B, E, A, D, G, C, F.

Dictation on Staff
Do on the Third Line

$\dot{1}$. | 5 $\dot{1}$ | $\dot{2}$ $\dot{2}$ | $\dot{3}$ $\dot{2}$ | $\dot{1}$. | 5 $\dot{1}$ | $\dot{2}$ $\dot{3}$ | $\dot{1}$. ||

Do on the Second Line

|| 15 | 32 | 34 | 32 | 15 | 31 | 2$\underset{\cdot}{5}$ | 1. ||

Do on the First Line

|| $\dot{1}$.5 | 3.1 | 567 | $\dot{1}$.. | $\dot{1}$76 | 565 | 432 | 3.1 |
| $\dot{1}$.5 | 3.1 | 567 | $\dot{1}$.. | $\dot{1}$76 | 565 | 432 | 1.. ||

Write on the staff the following phrase, placing the notes on the central line and moving the clefs to produce the melody:

|| $\dot{1}$ $\overline{66}$ | $\dot{3}$. | $\dot{3}$. | $\dot{1}$ $\overline{\dot{3}\dot{3}}$ | 6 . | . . ||

CHAPTER TWENTY

Vocal Exercises 29b, 30b and 31b.
Intonation.—Minor Mode, Plagal Range.

Intonation Exercise 142

(Key of Bm)

(Use Diagram 60*a* and *b*)

(*a*) ⟶ (*b*) ⟶

1̇ 6 3 3 4 5 6 7 6 5 4 3 6	3 6 1̇ 7 6 5 4 3 4 5 6 7 6
1̇ 6 3 3 ₄ 5 ₆ 7 ₅ 3 6	3 6 1̇ 7 ₆ 5 ₄ 3 ₅ 7 6
1̇ 6 3 3 ₅ 7 3 6	3 6 1̇ 7 ₅ 3 7 6

Study Melodies 171, 172 and 173, Children's Manual, page 63.

Intonation Exercise 143

(Key of Gm or Am)

(*a*) | 6 3 6 7 3 7 1̇ 3 1̇ 2̇ 3 2̇ 1̇ 3 1̇ 7 3 7 6 . 3 . 6 7 6 . |
| 6 3 ₆ 7 3 ₇ 1̇ 3 ₁̇ 2̇ 3 ₂̇ 1̇ 3 ₁̇ 7 3 ₇ 6 . 3 . 6 7 6 . |
| 6 3   7 3   1̇ 3   2̇ 3   1̇ 3   7 3   6 . 3 . 6 7 6 . |

(*b*) | 6 3̇ 6 7 3̇ 7 1̇ 3̇ 1̇ 2̇ 3̇ 2̇ 1̇ 3̇ 1̇ 7 3̇ 7 6 . 3̇ . 6 5 6 . |
| 6 3̇ ₆ 7 3̇ ₇ 1̇ 3̇ ₁̇ 2̇ 3̇ ₂̇ 1̇ 3̇ ₁̇ 7 3̇ ₇ 6 . 3̇ . 6 5 6 . |
| 6 3̇   7 3̇   1̇ 3̇   2̇ 3̇   1̇ 3̇   7 3̇   6 . 3̇ . 6 5 6 . |

Study Melodies 174 and 175, Children's Manual, page 63.

Rhythm 39.—4/4 Time

We can begin on the Up-pulse or on the Down-pulse

Up-pulse

(*a*) 1 | 1   1 : 1
(*b*) 1 | 1   . : 1
(*c*) 1 | 1   . : .

Down-pulse

(*a*) | 1   1 : 1   1 |
(*b*) | 1   . : 1   1 |
(*c*) | 1   . : 1   . |
(*d*) | 1   . : .   . |

Combine several short designs to form one long one.

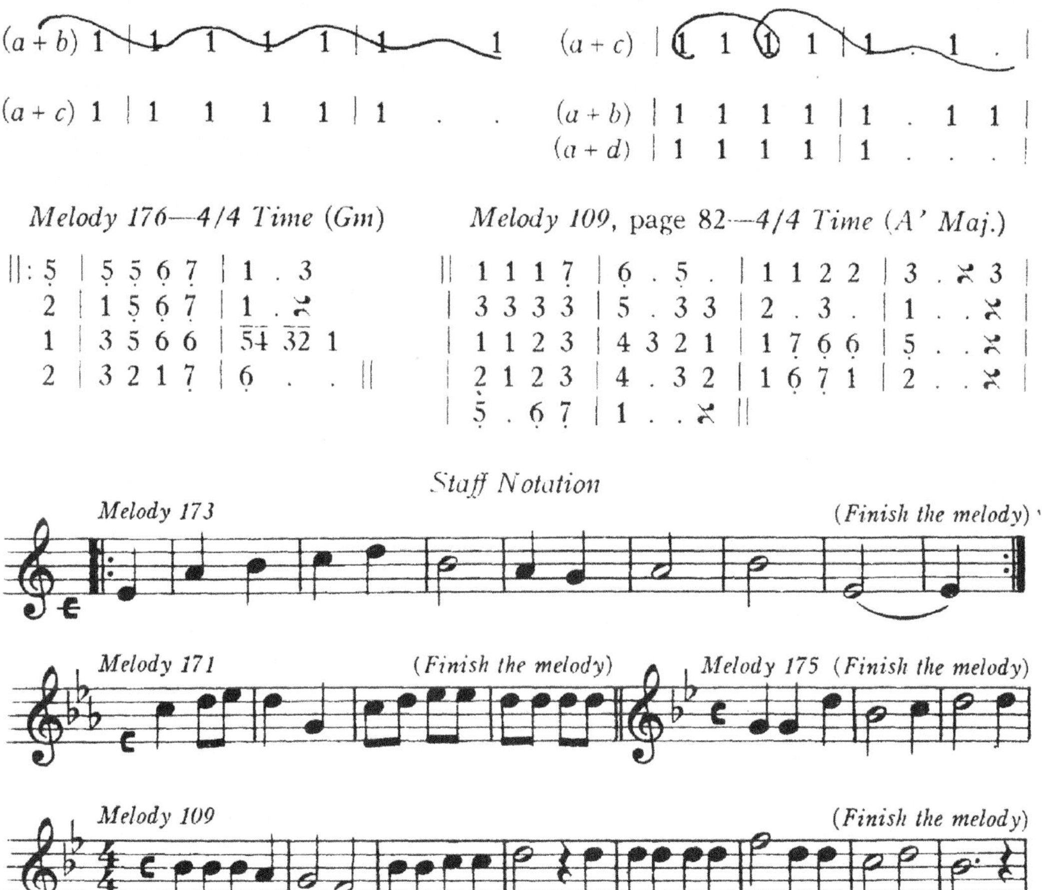

Study Melodies 177, 178, 179 and 180, Children's Manual, page 68.

Staff Notation

Continue the Review of the Staff as in Chapter 19.
Melodies 178, 179 and *180* should be read at sight.
Melody 173 should be copied on the staff in the Key of *A minor*.
Melody 171 copied in the Key of *C minor*.
Melody 175 should be copied in the Key of *G minor*.
Melody 109 should be copied in the Key of *B major*.

All this work should be prepared by rapid observation exercises on the Staff Diagrams of Chapter 19.

A staff should be made of the hand, using the fingers as lines. The clef can be indicated by placing a ring or a thimble on the finger which represents "*do*." If the "staff" is on the right hand, the index of the left hand will be used as a pointer. The children should use their own hand to represent the staff—the lines and the spaces.

The major mode offers less difficulty than the minor. The latter, then, requires more attention, because it is relatively new.

When *high do* is on a *line*, where will we find *la?*

When *high do* is in a *space*, where will we find *la?*

Before beginning a minor melody, the teacher will be careful to establish the relation between the major and the minor, at least until such time as the minor is as familiar as the major mode. Thus: 123 321 $1\underset{\cdot}{7}\underset{\cdot}{6}$.

Study Hymn: Vexilla Regis, Children's Manual, page 64.

Study Sequence: Stabat Mater, Children's Manual, page 66.

Vocal Exercises 29, 30 and 31, using *form b* when preparing the exercises and melodies in the minor mode, and using *form a* when preparing to sing a melody in the major mode.

Intonation Exercise 142 prepares the intervals 3 5 7 and 3 7 in relation to the minor chord (second inversion) $\dot{1}$ 6 3. These intervals should be used as drill rather than as a basis for musical composition, for while they are found, occasionally, in ancient melodies such as Numbers 171, 172 and 173, these intervals are harsh unless used with taste and discretion.

Intonation Exercise 143a and b measures each tone in the minor scale from 3 and from 3 respectively. This exercise provides for the minor mode exactly the same drill as No. 77 (see Chapter Five) provides for the major mode. In the major mode, each tone was measured from *low sol* and then from *high sol* (*sol* being the dominant of the major mode). Now we measure each tone from *low mi*, then from *high mi* (*mi* being the dominant of the minor mode). The importance of controlling the pitch carefully on the harmonium (if need be after each group) during the first approach to the exercise, can scarcely be over-emphasized. If the exercise be not sung perfectly true to pitch, it will not accomplish its purpose. It should be studied on the staff and number diagrams, and as it is written.

Rhythm.—The study of 4/4 time will offer no difficulty to the children if it be approached simply. We should merely remove the bar line between two groups of notes in 2/4 time. (See example below.) In 4/4 time, as in 2/4 time, the rhythmic unit may begin (*a*) on the up-pulse or (*b*) on the down-pulse:

(*a*) 1 | 1 1 ⋮ 1 (*b*) | 1 1 ⋮ 1 1 |

When we have *Form a* the rhythmic movement will be similar to that which we have been using for measures in 2/4 time beginning on the up-pulse. When we have *Form b*, the movement will be similar to that which we have used for measures in 2/4 composite time for groups beginning on the down-pulse. This presentation on the board, followed by the singing of *Melody 176* and *109* in 4/4 time, will at once give confidence to the children. In singing *Melody 176*, they will use Rhythmic Movement 1 or 2, and proceed exactly as though the melody were written thus:

|| 5 | 5 5 ⋮ 6 7 | 1 . ⋮ 3 2 | 1 5 ⋮ 6 7 | 1 . ⋮ 𝄽

In *Melody 109* they will use arses and theses as though the melody were written thus:

|| 1 1 ⋮ 1 7 | 6 . ⋮ 5 . | 1 1 ⋮ 2 2 | 3 . ⋮ 𝄽 3 | etc.

Then the children will study the Designs for the up-pulse (*a*, *b*, *c*) and those for the down-pulse (*a*, *b*, *c* and *d*). They will combine several short designs to form longer ones. All this work should precede the gesture by which we distinguish 4/4 time from 2/4—a distinction which, often, is an arbitrary one corresponding to no musical reality. The beating of time may be useful, however, in the study of the details of the subdivision of measures during the later years. It is well, therefore, that the children should be able to execute this gesture and recognize it should a conductor make use of it. It is less used by conductors of our day, however, than it was some fifty years ago, the more rhythmic motions having come into their own. We give the formula, however, for this "beating" of 4/4 time. The children stand at attention. If the design begins on the "downbeat" of the measure (*form b*) the formula is:

Design	↓	←	→	↑	
| 1 1 1 1 |	*One* Down	*Two* Left	*Three* Right	*Four* Up	4 (top), 2 (left), 3 (right), 1 (bottom)

If the design begins on the "up-beat" of the measure, the formula is:

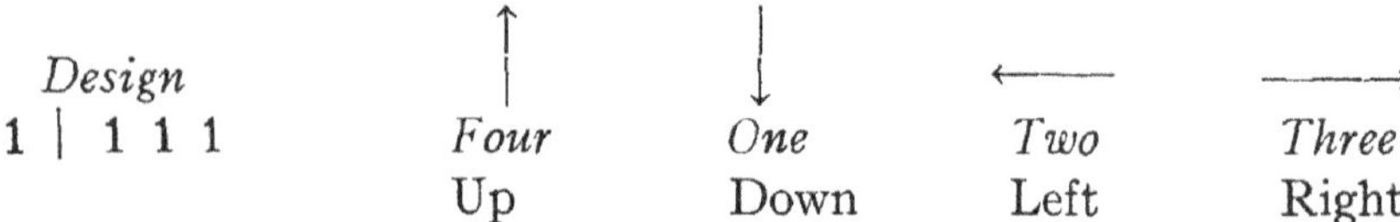

The children can execute this gesture either standing or sitting. When standing, the right arm should be extended horizontally forward, palm downward (position for the first beat of the measure). "Two" brings the arm to the left, across the body; "Three," the arm extended to the right; "Four," the arm extended upward, above the head. These gestures should be carried out slowly, until familiar. Then the children should carry out the same general movements, while seated, moving the arm from the elbow only, to obtain greater exactitude. On the "down-beat," the right hand should touch the back of the left hand, at "two" the right hand touches the left shoulder, at three it moves outward to the right, at "four" it is in position against the right shoulder.

Under no circumstances should the children be encouraged to use this gesture (standing or sitting) while singing a melody. Its use should be confined strictly to the analysis of a complicated passage, such as, for instance, passages containing dotted notes, or phrases containing some feature that is not easily fitted into the more rhythmic gesture. As soon as the passage has been studied with the 4/4 time gesture and has been mastered, it should be *sung with the rhythmic gesture* or without any external movement. The reason for this is that the 4/4 time gesture is extremely difficult to execute without carrying over into the voice something of its own angularity and a sort of staccato quality, which is not an aid to good phrasing. Only where the melody requires such an angular rendering—as for military music—is this gesture desirable.

In 4/4 time, as in 2/4 or 3/4 time, we must always finish our phrase with a design containing *length*. Moreover, our melody should end on a "down-beat" of the measure.

All the rules which we have applied in 2/4 and in 3/4 time regarding the relation between the beginning and the end of a phrase apply to 4/4 time. If our melody begins with a full measure, it will end with a full measure (see *Form b*). If it begins with a fraction of a measure, the last phrase will contain the other fragment which is required to complete the measure (see *Form a*).

Form a

	Melody begins:		*Melody will end:*	
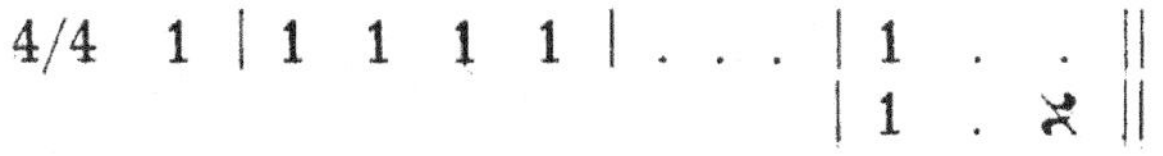 4/4	1 | 1 1 1 1 | . . .		| 1 . . ||	*One pulse* (out of four) at the beginning: we must find the other *three pulses* at the end of the melody, thus completing that measure.
			| 1 . ꭗ ||	

Form b

Melody begins:	*Melody will end:*	
|| 1 1 1 1 | . . .	| 1 . . . ||	The measure is complete (four pulses) at the beginning: the last measure will also be complete. We will find four pulses consisting of notes, dots, or rests.
	| 1 . 1 . ||	

Thus all the rules which the children have learned and applied in the study of 2/4 and 3/4 time apply with equal force to the study of 4/4 time.

Staff Notation.—Continue review. Note:

When *low do* is on a line, *high do* will be on a space.

When *low do* is on a line, where will we find *mi* and *sol?* On lines or on spaces?

When *high do* is on a line, where will we find *sol* and *mi?* On lines or spaces?

The teacher will not expect memorized answers to these questions, nor will this matter be imposed as a dry memory load. These questions should be used to stimulate the children's attention to such details, that they may form the habit of orientating themselves at once in each tonality, by finding the notes of the tonic chord *in relation to the clef* whether they are using the C clef or the G clef with signature of sharps or flats. The child should be given *time* to make, as it were, a mental map of the tonality as expressed on the staff. This quiet moment, in which the child *looks at the melody* in relation to the *clef* before being asked to sing it, is necessary if we are ever to teach children to read music from the staff notation. The number notation becomes a transparency through which the tone appears without any obscurity whatever. The child sees the number and the corresponding tone rings in his inner ear. He hears it through the eye. But with the staff notation and the constant changes of position the child receives a less direct impression. He has to recognize a known fact but represented to his eyes by an unfamiliar symbol. It is therefore important to give the child due time for self-direction in the matter. A teacher who is impatient for quick results would do better to leave aside the reading by means of staff notation and keep to the number notation. If the capacity to read from the staff is desired, then the children should be given sufficient time to look over the ground, as it were, before they are asked to sing a melody. The melody should also be prepared on the Staff Diagram which gives the picture of the scale in the tonality in question, and on the *finger staff*.

After placing the *C clef* on the third line, the letter *f* can be placed on the first line. The *f* represents "fa" to the children. It gives them an additional point of security in reading. It also prepares their mind to depend on the *F clef* as well as the *C clef* and *G clef*, a habit which will be useful in later years, both for the Gregorian notation where the *clef* of *do* and of *fa* are of equal importance, and for the study of instrumental music where the *F clef* is a necessity.

Dictation

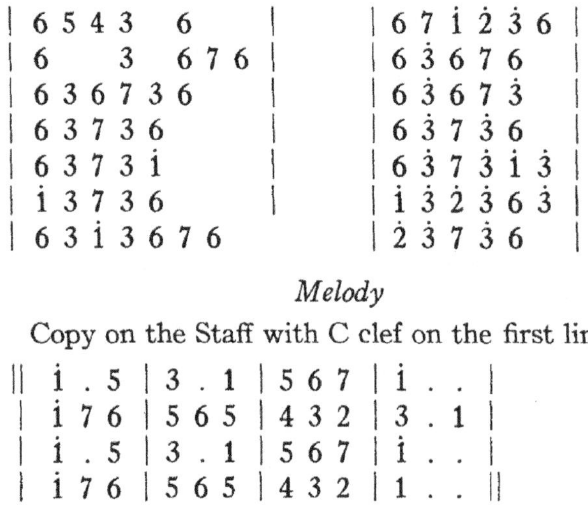

```
| 6 5 4 3   6       |     | 6 7 1̇ 2̇ 3̇ 6 |
| 6     3   6 7 6   |     | 6 3̇ 6 7 6   |
| 6 3 6 7 3 6       |     | 6 3̇ 6 7 3̇   |
| 6 3 7 3 6         |     | 6 3̇ 7 3̇ 6   |
| 6 3 7 3 1̇         |     | 6 3̇ 7 3̇ 1 3̇ |
| 1̇ 3 7 3 6         |     | 1̇ 3̇ 2̇ 3̇ 6 3̇ |
| 6 3 1̇ 3 6 7 6           | 2̇ 3̇ 7 3̇ 6   |
```

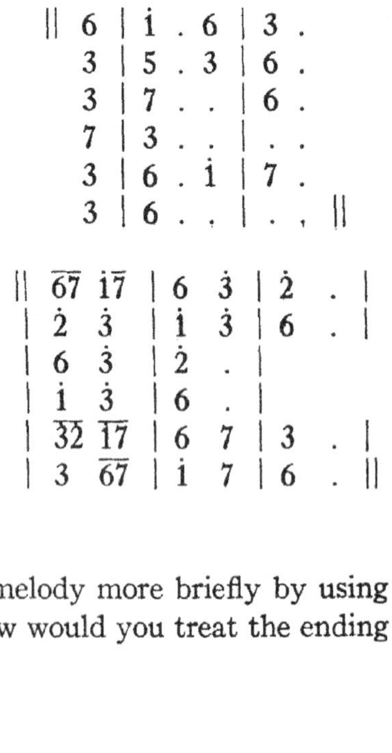

Melody

Copy on the Staff with C clef on the first line.

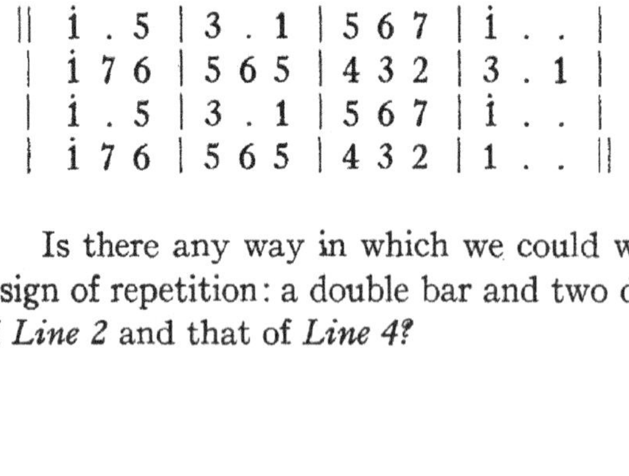

```
|| 1̇ . 5 | 3 . 1 | 5 6 7 | 1̇ . . |
 | 1̇ 7 6 | 5 6 5 | 4 3 2 | 3 . 1 |
 | 1̇ . 5 | 3 . 1 | 5 6 7 | 1̇ . . |
 | 1̇ 7 6 | 5 6 5 | 4 3 2 | 1 . . ||
```

Melody and Rhythm

```
|| 6 | 1̇ . 6 | 3 .
   3 | 5 . 3 | 6 .
   3 | 7 . . | 6 .
   7 | 3 . . | . .
   3 | 6 . 1̇ | 7 .
   3 | 6 . . | . .  ||
```

```
|| 6̅7̅ 1̇̅7̅ | 6 3̇ | 2̇ . |
 | 2̇ 3̇   | 1̇ 3̇ | 6 . |
 | 6 3̇   | 2̇ . |
 | 1̇ 3̇   | 6 . |
 | 3̇̅2̅ 1̇̅7̅ | 6 7 | 3 . |
 | 3 6̅7̅  | 1̇ 7 | 6 . ||
```

Is there any way in which we could write this melody more briefly by using a sign of repetition: a double bar and two dots? How would you treat the ending of *Line 2* and that of *Line 4?*

CHAPTER TWENTY-ONE

Vocal Exercises 29, 30 and 31. Both forms (a and b).

Intonation.—The Minor Mode, Plagal Range.

Diagram 55b.
(As in Chapter 16.)

Diagram 65.
(As in Chapter 18.)

Intonation Exercise 144

(Key of Am or Gm)

Preparation: 6 5 4 3 6 6 7 1̇ 2̇ 3̇ 6

(*a*)

| 6 3 3̇ 6 7 3 3̇ 7 1̇ 3 3̇ 1̇ 2̇ 3 3̇ 2̇ 1̇ 3 3̇ 1̇ 7 3 3̇ 7 6 3 3̇ . | $\overline{\dot{3}\dot{2}}$ $\overline{\dot{1}7}$ | 6 5 | 6 . |

| 6 3 3̇ $_{6}$ 7 3 3̇ $_{7}$ 1̇ 3 3̇ $_{\dot{1}}$ 2̇ 3 3̇ $_{\dot{2}}$ 1̇ 3 3̇ $_{\dot{1}}$ 7 3 3̇ $_{7}$ 6 3 3̇ . | $\overline{\dot{3}\dot{2}}$ $\overline{\dot{1}7}$ | 6 5 | 6 . |

| 6 3 3̇ 7 3 3̇ 1̇ 3 3̇ 2̇ 3 3̇ 1̇ 3 3̇ 7 3 3̇ 6 3 3̇ . | $\overline{\dot{3}\dot{2}}$ $\overline{\dot{1}7}$ | 6 5 | 6 . |

(*b*)

| 6 3̇ 3 6 7 3̇ 3 7 1̇ 3̇ 3 1̇ 2̇ 3̇ 3 2̇ 1̇ 3̇ 3 1̇ 7 3̇ 3 7 6 3̇ 3 6 | 5 . | 6 7 | 6 . | . ||

| 6 3̇ 3 $_{6}$ 7 3̇ 3 $_{7}$ 1̇ 3̇ 3 $_{\dot{1}}$ 2̇ 3̇ 3 $_{\dot{2}}$ 1̇ 3̇ 3 $_{\dot{1}}$ 7 3̇ 3 $_{7}$ 6 3̇ 3 6 | 5 . | 6 7 | 6 . | . ||

| 6 3̇ 3 7 3̇ 3 1̇ 3̇ 3 2̇ 3̇ 3 1̇ 3̇ 3 7 3̇ 3 6 3̇ 3 6 | 5 . | 6 7 | 6 . | . ||

Melody and Rhythm (Am or Gm)

4/4 || 6 | 3̇ 3 6 7 | 6 . .
3 | $\overline{67}$ $\overline{\dot{1}\dot{2}}$ 3̇ 3 | $\overline{67}$ $\overline{\dot{1}\dot{2}}$ 3̇
3 | 3̇ 3̇ 1̇ 6 | 7 . .
3 | 3̇ 3̇ 1̇ 6 | $\overline{56}$ $\overline{75}$ 6
3 | 3̇ $\overline{67}$ 1̇ 7 | 6 . . ||

4/4 || 6 3 3̇ . | $\overline{67}$ $\overline{\dot{1}\dot{2}}$ 3̇ . |
2̇ 3̇ 3 7	6 . 3 .
3̇ 3 6 .	3̇ 6 7 .
$\overline{\dot{3}\dot{2}}$ $\overline{\dot{3}\dot{1}}$ $\overline{67}$ $\overline{\dot{1}7}$	6 . 6 .	

Study the following pieces from the Children's Manual:

Melodics 181 and 182, page 72.

Garden and Cradle, page 80.

Regina caeli lactare, page 69.

Christ Our Lord hath Risen, page 70.

O Filii et Filiae, page 74.

Rhythmic Exercise 40

Designs in 4/4 Time

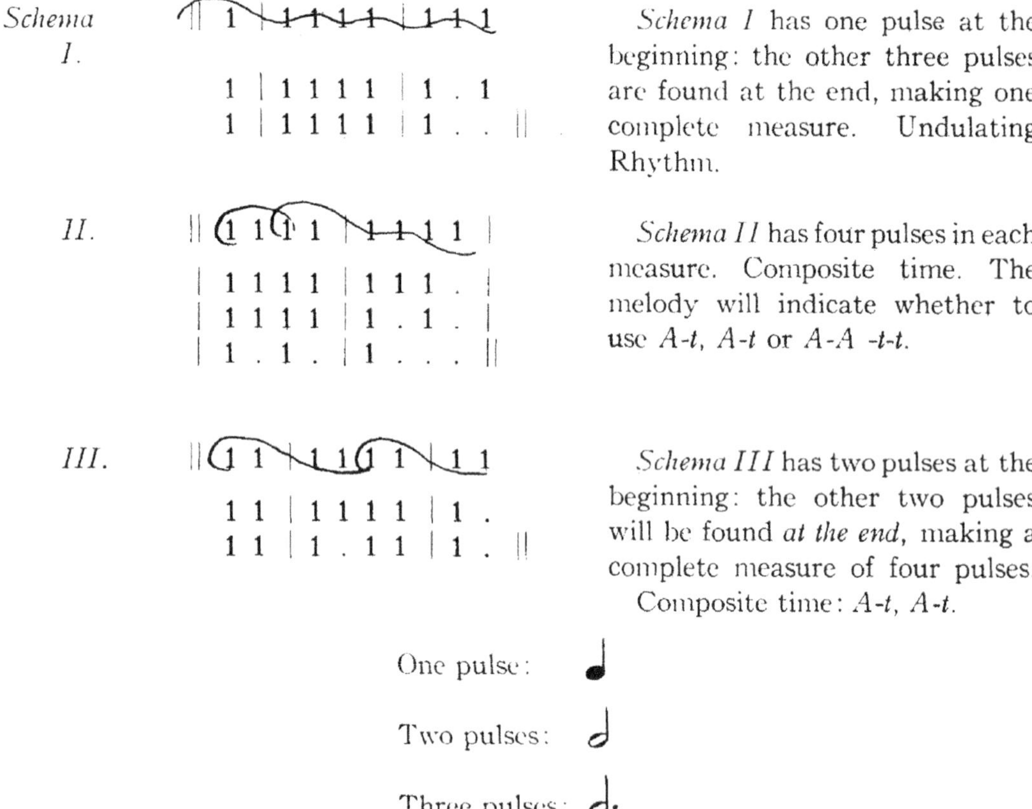

Schema I has one pulse at the beginning: the other three pulses are found at the end, making one complete measure. Undulating Rhythm.

Schema II has four pulses in each measure. Composite time. The melody will indicate whether to use *A-t*, *A-t* or *A-A -t-t*.

Schema III has two pulses at the beginning: the other two pulses will be found *at the end*, making a complete measure of four pulses.

Composite time: *A-t*, *A-t*.

One pulse: ♩

Two pulses: 𝅗𝅥

Three pulses: 𝅗𝅥.

Four pulses: 𝅝

Staff Diagram 4/4 Time

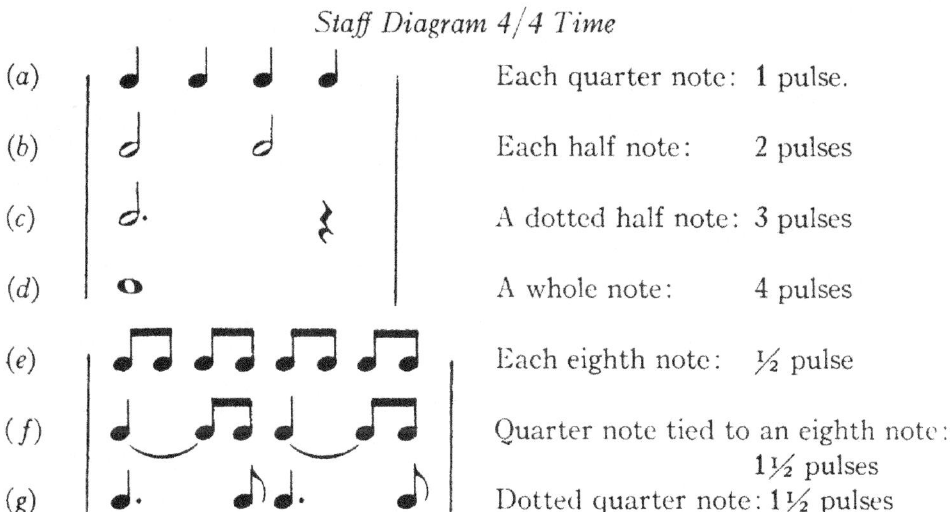

Figure *f* and figure *g* are identical in value. They are two ways of writing the same thing.

An example of each schema follows:

Melody 183. Bach Chorale. (Em)

Schema I. || 6 | 6 7 1 2 | 3 3 3
3 | 3 2 1 2 | 7 . 7
7 | 1 2 3 3 | 2 . 3
3 | 1 2 3 3 | 2 . 1
3 | 5 3 3 3 | 2 . 2
2 | 3 2 1 2 | 7 . 6 ||

Melody 184. Bach Chorale. (Em)

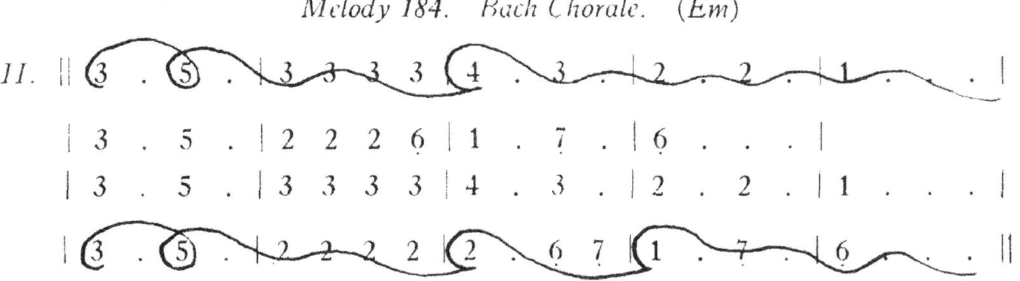

Melody 185. French Noel. (Gm)

III. ||: 3 6 | 5 3 6 7 | i . 5 6 | 3 .
i . | 2 . 3 . | 4 3 2 . | i . :||
||: i 3 | 2 i 7 6 | 2 . 7 6 | 7 .
3 . | 6 . 5 i | 7 6 5 . | 6 . :||

Rhythm 41 (Schema 1)

		1.	2.
(a) 1	1 1 1 1	1 1 1	1 . .
(b) 11	1 1 1 11	1 . 1	1 . .
(c) 11	1 11 1 11	1 . 1	1 . .
(d) 11	11 11 1 11	1 . 1	1 . .
(e) 11	11 11 11 11	1 . 1	1 . .
(f) 11	11 11 1 1	1 . 1	1 . .

Render each line following the upper arrow, then the lower arrow. Then combine more than one of these designs to form longer phrases and compose melodies based upon these designs.

Example.—How to read each single design.

Line a: || 1 | 1 1 1 1 | 1 1 1' 1 | 1 1 1 1 | 1 . . ||

Example of the combination of several designs.

(a + c) || 3 | 1 2 3 5 | 4 3 2' 23 | 4 32 3 32 | 1 . . ||

Themes for Composition in 4/4 Time

(a) || 67 | 1 7 6 3 | 2 1 7 Write a melody in the minor mode.
(b) || 1 | 17 67 12 3 | 2 2 1 Write a melody in the major mode.
(c) || 5 | 1 2 3 6 | 5 .4 3 Write a melody in the major mode.

Study Melodies 186 and 187, Children's Manual, page 72.

Melody 182

Exercises in the Changing of Clefs (C and F)

Diagrams of Minor Tonalities

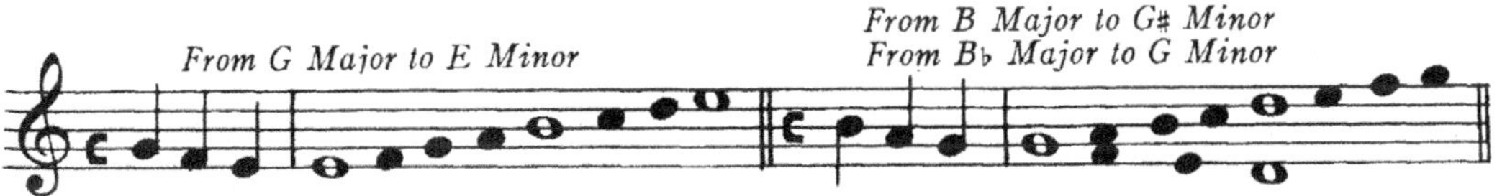

Vocal Exercises 29, 30 and 31 should be used both in their major and minor forms: the former, before singing a melody in the major mode; the latter, before singing exercises or melodies in the minor mode.

Intonation Exercise 144 is a development of *Exercise 143* studied in *Chapter 20.* All the tones of the minor mode are measured both from *high mi and from low mi.* This drill in the minor modality corresponds to a similar drill in the major modality embodied in *Intonation Exercise 80* (*Chapter Six.*) This exercise should be practised on the staff diagrams (*55b* and *65*) as well as from the number notation. As in all such exercises, the material should be broken up after the exercise has been studied as a whole and applied for creative work, etc. Thus:

|| 6 3 3̇ 6 | 7 1̇2̇ 1̇ 6 | (Theme for a composition)

|| 6 3̇ 3 | 7 3̇ 3 | 6 . . || (Visualization)
|| 6 3̇ 3 | 6 . . || Ear tests, etc.
|| 3̇ 3 6 | 7 . . ||

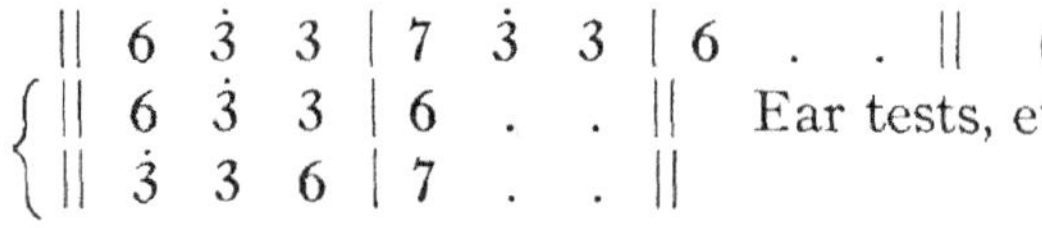

All this prevents rigidity and mere memory work, where what is needed is a personal vital application of each problem to a musical object. If an exercise remains in its original form as something *simply learned*, it will not accomplish its purpose, which is to stimulate the child to an ever greater self-activity.

Rhythmic Exercise 40 presents the three possible schemas which we find in measures of 4/4 time. They can begin on the up-beat with a single note (as in Schema I); they can begin on the down-beat, first note of the measure (as in Schema II); they can begin on the second half of the measure on the arsis or thesis according to the melodic design (as in Schema III). In all these forms, the notes can be subdivided, just as in 2/4 and 3/4 time. For the convenience of the teacher we have placed the value of these notes in staff notation close to the rhythmic schemas. All are familiar save the *whole note* (four pulses). The children should write in staff notation each of the schemas given in 4/4 time in *Rhythmic Exercise 41*. They should be asked to decide to which of the three rhythmic schemas belongs: *Melody 184? Melody 185? Melody 187?*

Rhythmic Exercise 41 develops Schema I in various designs, all of which are more or less familiar since they have been studied in measures of 2/4 time.

How to Read the Designs of Exercise 41

1. Follow the arrow above the exercise.
2. Repeat the same line following the lower arrow.

Each line is sung twice, the first time using the measure marked "1," the second time using the measure marked "2" and omitting the measure marked "1."

Staff Notation.—Review of the Minor Mode in the four positions already presented. Always count down from "do." Then use each diagram as follows:

(*a*) Naming the notes rapidly.
(*b*) Singing the notes slowly and evenly in response to the teacher's pointer.

(*c*) Visualizing a group of notes to which the teacher points, and singing them from the memory picture after the teacher has ceased to point.

(*d*) Using certain notes of the diagram as help-notes to pass to more difficult intervals. The *Compass Exercise* (minor mode) is always the basis of such help-notes, and it is the best means of fixing a new tonality on the staff in the minds of the children.

Questions: When *high la* is on a *line*, where will we find *low la?* When *low la* is in a *space*, where will we find *do* and *mi?* When *low la* is on a *line*, where will we find *do* and *mi?*

Exercises in the Changing of Clefs.—These exercises being devised for the sole purpose of cultivating in the children the habit of calculating a tone from its relation to a clef, and not according to the position of that note on a line or a space, it is not necessary that such exercises be a matter of constant practice, since the children will not meet with such rapid changes of clef in ordinary music. The object is to *build up a habit* which will be extremely useful. When that object has been attained, these exercises will have served their purpose.

Dictation

a ⟶

$\mid 6\ 7\ \dot{1}\ \dot{2}\ \dot{3}\ \ 3\ \ 6 \mid$
$\mid \dot{3}\ 3\ 6\ 6\ 7\ \ 6 \mid$
$\mid 6\ \dot{3}\ 3\ 6\ 7\ \ 6 \mid$
$\mid 6\ \dot{3}\ 3\ \dot{1}\ 7\ \ 6 \mid$
$\mid \dot{3}\ 3\ \dot{1}\ 7\ 6 \mid$
$\mid 6\ \dot{3}\ \dot{2}\ \dot{3}\ 3\ 6 \mid$
$\mid 6\ \dot{3}\ 3\ 7\ \dot{3}\ 3\ 6 \mid$

b ⟶

$\mid 6\ 3\ \dot{3}\ \ \dot{2}\ \dot{3}\ 3\ \ 6 \mid$
$\mid 6\ 3\ \dot{3}\ \ \dot{1}\ \dot{3}\ 3\ \ 6 \mid$
$\mid 6\ 7\ 6\ \ \dot{3}\ 3\ 7\ \ 6 \mid$
$\mid 6\ 7\ 6\ \ 3\ \dot{3}\ \dot{1}\ \ 6 \mid$
$\mid 6\ \dot{3}\ \dot{2}\ \ \dot{3}\ 3\ 5\ \ 6 \mid$
$\mid 6\ 3\ \dot{3}\ \ \dot{1}\ 7\ \dot{3}\ \ 6 \mid$

c ⟶

$\Vert\ 6\ \dot{3} \mid \overline{\dot{3}\dot{2}}\ \overline{\dot{1}7} \mid 6\ . \mid$
$\mid \dot{3}\ 3 \mid \overline{67}\ \overline{\dot{1}\dot{2}} \mid \dot{3}\ . \mid$
$\mid \dot{3}\ \dot{2} \mid \overline{\dot{3}\dot{2}}\ \overline{\dot{1}7} \mid 6\ . \mid$
$\mid 3\ \dot{3} \mid \overline{\dot{2}\dot{3}}\ \overline{\dot{1}\dot{2}} \mid \dot{3}\ . \mid$
$\mid \dot{3}\ 3 \mid \overline{6\dot{1}}\ \overline{7\dot{1}} \mid 6\ .\ \Vert$

Visualization

⟶

$\mid 6\ \dot{3}\ 3 \mid 7\ \dot{3}\ 3 \mid 6\ .\ . \mid$
$\mid \dot{1}\ \dot{3}\ 3 \mid \dot{2}\ \dot{3}\ 3 \mid 6\ .\ . \mid$ etc.

⟶

$\mid \overline{67}\ \overline{\dot{1}\dot{2}} \mid \dot{3}\ 3 \mid \dot{3}\ . \mid$
$\mid \overline{\dot{2}\dot{3}}\ \overline{\dot{2}\dot{1}} \mid 7\ \dot{3} \mid 6\ . \mid$ etc.

Aural Memory

$\Vert\ \overline{67}\ \overline{\dot{1}\dot{2}}\ \ \dot{3}\ \ 3 \mid 6\ .\ .\ \text{𝄽} \mid$
$\mid \overline{\dot{3}\dot{2}}\ \overline{\dot{1}7}\ \ 6\ \ \dot{3} \mid 3\ .\ .\ \text{𝄽} \mid$
$\mid 3\ \ .\ \ \overline{\dot{3}\dot{2}}\ \overline{\dot{1}7} \mid \dot{3}\ 3\ \dot{3}\ \ . \mid$
$\mid \overline{\dot{2}\dot{3}}\ \overline{\dot{1}\dot{2}}\ \ \dot{3}\ \ 3 \mid 6\ .\ .\ \text{𝄽}\ \Vert$

$\Vert\ 6 \mid \dot{3}\ \ \dot{3}\ \ \overline{\dot{2}\dot{3}}\ \overline{\dot{2}\dot{1}} \mid 7\ \ \dot{3}\ \ 6$
$6 \mid 7\ 3\ \ \overline{\dot{1}7}\ \overline{67} \mid \dot{1}\ \ \dot{2}\ \ \dot{3}$
$\dot{3} \mid \dot{2}\ \dot{3}\ \ \dot{3}\ \ 3 \mid 6\ \ \dot{1}\ \ 7$
$\dot{3} \mid \overline{\dot{2}\dot{3}}\ \overline{\dot{2}\dot{1}}\ 7\ \ \dot{3} \mid \dot{1}\ \ 6\ \ 6\ \Vert$

CHAPTER TWENTY-TWO

Vocal Exercise

(Key of Am and Bm)

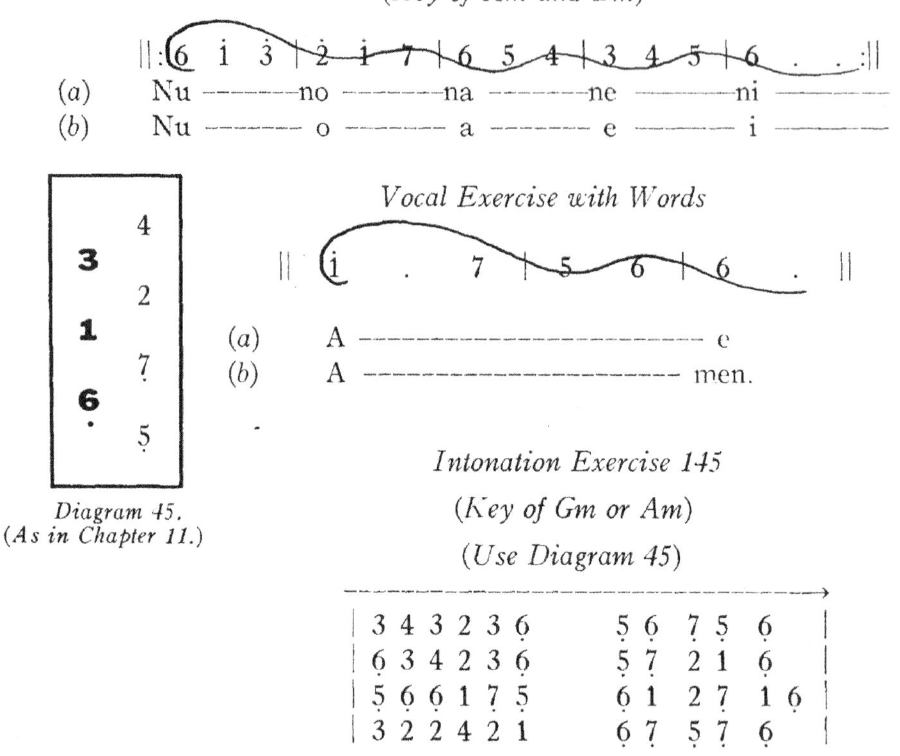

Rhythm, Melody and Words

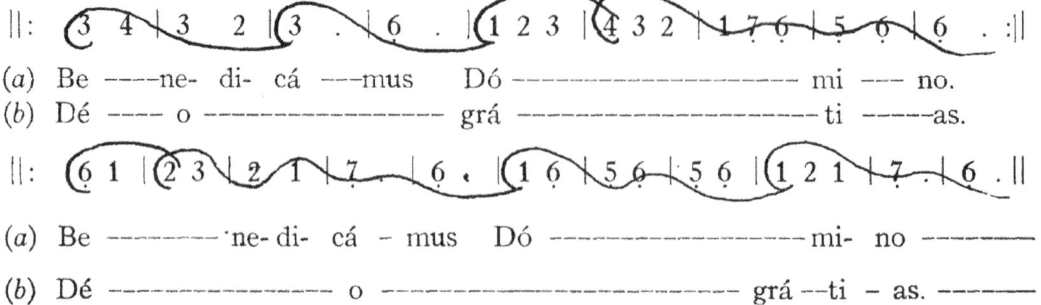

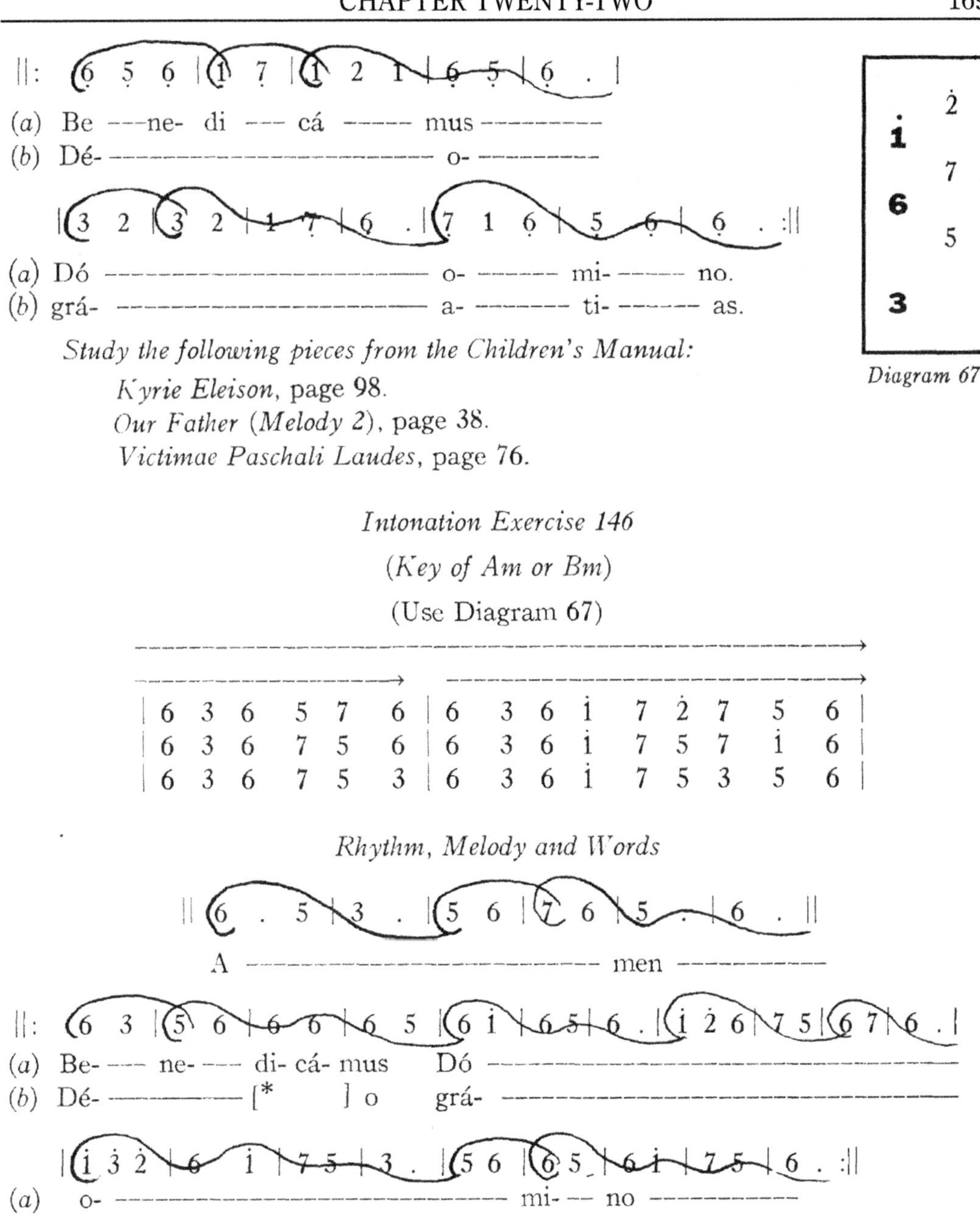

Study the following pieces from the Children's Manual:

Kyrie Eleison, page 98.

Our Father (*Melody 2*), page 38.

Victimae Paschali Laudes, page 76.

Intonation Exercise 146

(*Key of Am or Bm*)

(Use Diagram 67)

Rhythm, Melody and Words

* Omit the notes in parenthesis when singing the *Deo gratias*.

Melody 188 (Cm.)

4/4 ||: 3 | 3 3 5 5 | 6 . 3 . | 𝄽 1̇ 1̇ 1̇ | 7 6 5 6 | 3 . 𝄽 :||

and 5 | 5 5 6 1̇ | 1̇ 7 1̇ . | 𝄽 1̇ 1̇ 1̇ | 2̇ .1̇ 7 1̇ | 6 . | 5 . | 𝄽

2/4 . 5 | 1̇ .7 6 5 | 6 2̇ 1̇ . | 𝄽 1̇ 1̇ 7 | 6 1̇ 7 6 | 7 . | 6 . | 𝄽 ||

Melody 189 (Am.)

3/4 ||: 3 | 6 . 1̇ | 7 . 2̇ | 1̇ . . | 6 . 1̇ | 7 . 6 | 5 . 7 | 6 . . | . 𝄽 :||

6 | 3̇ . 3̇ | 7 . 1̇ | 2̇ . . | 1̇ . 7 | 1̇ . 7 | 6 . 6 | 1̇ . . | 7 .

||: 5 | 6 . 6 | 5 . 5 | 3 . . | 1̇ . . | 3̇ . 2̇ | 1̇ . 7 | 6 . . | . 𝄽 :||

Rhythm 42

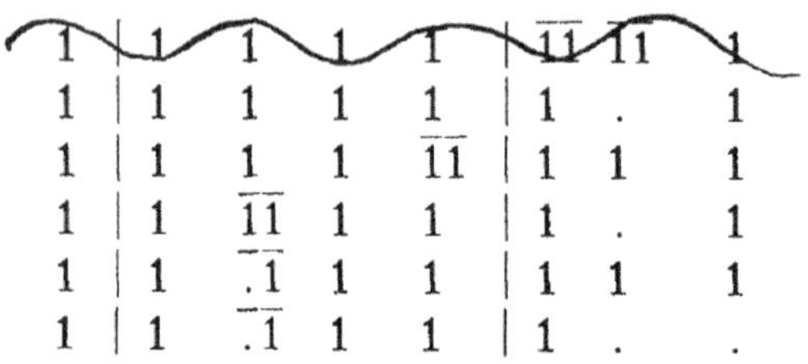

1 | 1 1 1 1 | 11 11 1

1 | 1 1 1 1 | 1 . 1

1 | 1 1 1 11 | 1 1 1

1 | 1 11 1 1 | 1 . 1

1 | 1 .1 1 1 | 1 1 1

1 | 1 .1 1 1 | 1 . .

Find these designs in the various melodies of this chapter.

Study Melodies 190, 191 and 192, Children's Manual, page 73.

Vocal Exercise.—Special Exercise for this chapter. Also Vocal Exercises with the word "Amen." The latter should be sung, first, to the vowel sounds "a–e," then with the consonants.

The longer phrases under "Rhythm, Melody and Words" may also be used as vocal exercises and approached in the same manner.

Intonation Exercises 145 and 146 contain no matter which has not been prepared in previous chapters. They are mere suggestions for the use of *Diagrams 45 and 67* by means of which the children are prepared for the melodies that appear in this chapter. Such preparation, even though it be brief, helps the children to sing in tune. The three phrases with words (*Benedicámus Dómino* and *Déo grátias*) are among these which are used at the end of Vespers. The children may sing them as a brief prayer at the ending of the school day: *line a* being rendered by a small group of cantors, *line b* being rendered by the entire class.

Rhythm 42 continues the development of 4/4 time in Schema I. The melodies themselves, however, provide the most practical experience and there will be little need of the exercise, save for rapid observation and for guidance in melody writing. Any of the melodies in 4/4 time can be used as a rhythmic exercise should such preliminary practice be necessary.

Dictation

Key of Gm		*Key of Am*	
6̣ 3 4 3 2 3 6̣ .	6̣ 7̣ 5̣ 6̣ 7̣ 6̣ .	6 3 6 1̇ 7 6	6 5 3 5 6 .
6̣ 3 4 2 3 1 6̣ .	6̣ 1 2 7̣ 1 6̣ .	6 3 6 7 5 3	3 5 6 1̇ 7 6 .
6̣ 2 1 2 3 1 6̣ .	5̣ 6̣ 1 7̣ 5̣ 6̣ .	6 3 6 1̇ 6 7	5 3 6 7 5 6 .

For Visualization, use Diagrams 45 and 67.

CHAPTER TWENTY-THREE

Vocal Exercises 29, 30 and 31 (Forms a and b).

Special Vocal Exercise

Key of Gm, of G♯m, of Am, B♭m and Bm (ad lib.)

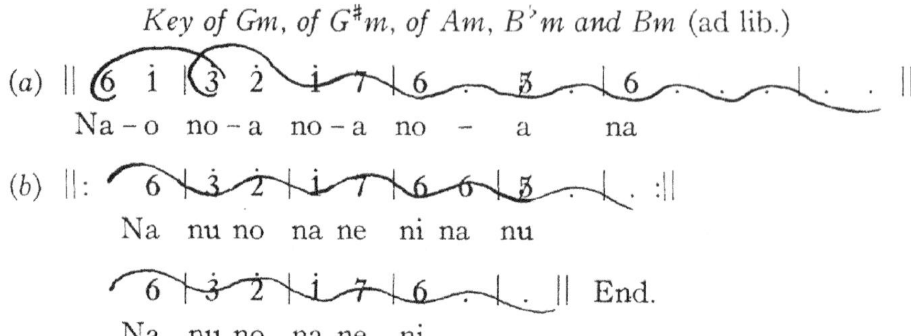

Intonation.—The accidental: *Sol* sharp, called *Seh*, and written: 5̸.

Sing:	
1̇ 7 1̇	At the same pitch, sing the same melody:
Do si do	The melody of "do si do" is equivalent to the melody
6 5̸ 6	of "la *seh* la." When this equivalence has been estab-
La *seh* la	lished and the intervals have been sung, then place

the interval "la seh la" where it belongs in the minor scale, thus:

Intonation Exercise 147

(Key of Am)

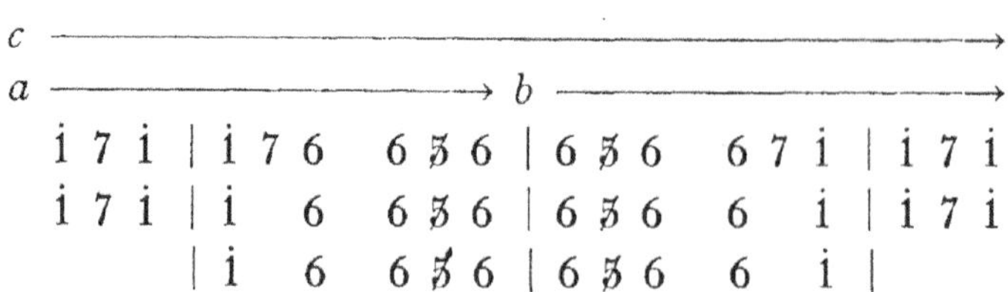

(Use great care that the melody "6 5̸ 6" be exactly like the melody of "1̇ 7 1̇." It must be a *small interval.*

Intonation Exercise 148

(Key of Am or Gm)

c ⟶

a ⟶ b ⟶

| 1̇ 2̇ 3̇ 3̇ 2̇ 1̇ 1̇ 7 6 6 5̸ 6 | 6 5̸ 6 6 7 1̇ 1̇ 2̇ 3̇ 3̇ 6 |

| 1̇ 3̇ 3̇ 1̇ 1̇ 6 6 5̸ 6 | 6 5̸ 6 6 1̇ 1̇ 3̇ 3̇ 6 |

Control: 6 7 1̇ 2̇ 3̇ 2̇ 1̇ 7 6

Intonation Exercise 149

(Key of Cm)

c ⟶

a ⟶ b ⟶

| 1̇ 7 6 6 5̸ 6 6 5 4 3 3 4 3 | 3 4 3 3 4 5 6 6 5̸ 6 6 7 1̇ 1̇ 6 |

| 1̇ 6 6 5̸ 6 6 3 3 4 3 | 3 4 3 3 6 6 5̸ 6 6 1̇ 1̇ 6 |

(*Cm*) *Melody and Rhythm*

4/4 || 1̇ 1̇7 6 6 | 6 65̸ 6 6 | 3 34 3 3 | 6 65̸ 6 . |

| 1̇ .7 6 6 | 6 .5̸ 6 6 | 3 .4 3 3 | 6 .5̸ 6 . ||

(*Am*)

3/4 || 6 3̇ 3̇ | 3̇ 3̇2̇ 1̇ | 7 71̇ 2̇ | 1̇ 1̇7 6 | 6 65̸ 6 | 3 6 1̇ | 7 . . | 6 . . |

| 6 3̇ 3̇ | 3̇ .2̇ 1̇ | 7 .1̇ 2̇ | 1̇ .7 6 | 6 .5̸ 6 | 3 6 5̸ | 6 . . | 6 . . ||

Staff Notation: ♯ *Sharp:* raises the tone.
♮ *Natural:* cancels the sharp.

Diagram 68.

Diagram 69. *Diagram 70.*

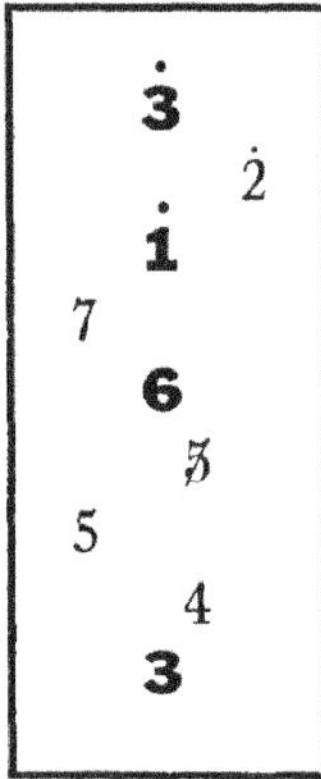

Diagram 71.

Number Notation.—The sharp is always expressed by a diagonal line running through the number and slanting from right to left: 5̸.

The sharp is cancelled on subsequent notes by the mere fact of omitting the diagonal line: 5.

Staff Notation.—The sharp is expressed by placing the following sign: ♯ *before* the note affected.

The sharp is cancelled in two ways:

(*a*) By the *bar line* which indicates a new measure. (See Diagram 68.)

(*b*) By a natural ♮ placed before the note itself when the cancellation takes place inside the limits of a measure. (See Diagram 69).

Thus, in the number notation, any figure which does not carry a diagonal line should be sung as a *normal* tone, and any figure that bears the diagonal line should be sung as a *raised* tone, regardless of its position in relation to any given measure. In the staff notation, however, a sharp, having once been used within the limits of a measure, that same tone will be sharp each time it is used without the need of repeating the symbol before the note. In the following measure, the tone will be *natural unless* the sharp sign precedes the note in question. Thus, it is only *within the limits of a measure* that the natural sign is used to cancel the sharp.

Rhythm and Melody

(Key of Cm)

Slowly

	6 . 5 4	3 . 3 .	6 . 6 .	5̸ . . 4̸
6 . 6 7	1̇ . 6 .	5̸ . . .	6 . . 4̸
3 . 3 4	3 . 6 .	6 . 7 .	1̇ . 6 .
1̇ . 7 6	5 . 4 .	3 . 6 .	5̸ . 6 .	7 . . .	6 . . .	

Melody 193 (Key of Am)

Slowly

|| $\overline{66}$ $\overline{67}$ | 1̇ $\overline{76}$ | 1̇ 7 | $\overline{66}$ $\overline{67}$ | 1̇ 6 | 7 . |
| $\overline{71̇}$ $\overline{2̇7}$ | 3̇ $\overline{.7}$ | 1̇ 6 | $\overline{71̇}$ $\overline{2̇7}$ | 6 $\overline{.5̸}$ | 6 . ||

Melody 194 (*Key of Am*)

Fine

||: 6 ‾7 6 | 1̇ . 1̇ | 3̇ . . | 1̇ . ⨯ | 2̇ 3̇ 2̇ | 1̇ . 7 | 6 . . | . . ⨯ :||
| 7 1̇ 2̇ | 1̇ . 7 | 6 . . | 5̸ . ⨯ | 6 5̸ 6 | 7 . 1̇ | 1̇ . . | 7 . . :||

D. C.

Melody 195—French Folk Song (*Key of Am*)

Briskly

|| 6 | 1̇ 7 | 5 . | 6 . | 5 4 | 3 4 | 5 6 | 5 . | 6 . | 5 4 | 3
6 | 6 7 | 1̇ 7 | 1̇ 6 | 1̇ ‾71̇ | 2̇ ‾1̇2̇ | 3̇
6 | 6 7 | 1̇ 7 | 6 . | 5̸ 5̸ | 6 . | . ||

Rhythm 43 (*4/4 Time.*) *Schema 2 Developed*

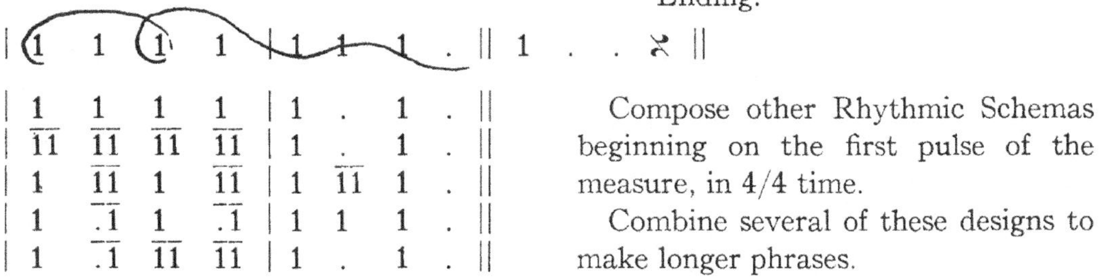

Compose other Rhythmic Schemas beginning on the first pulse of the measure, in 4/4 time.

Combine several of these designs to make longer phrases.

Compose melodies based on such designs.

Study Melodies 196, page 75; *197*, page 77; *198*, *199*, page 78, Children's Manual.

Study Song: Joseph and Jesus, Children's Manual, page 79.

Vocal Exercises 29, 30 and 31.—Use the major form as a preparation for melodies in the major mode, and the minor form as preparation for those in the minor mode. After the study of *Intonation Exercises 147, 148 and 149*, the special exercises *a* and *b* of this chapter should be used. They should be sung slowly and with great care as regards the new interval 6 5̸ 6.

Intonation.—Introduction of the accidental: *seh*. Hitherto we have studied the ancient form of the mode based on *la*. During the centuries where melody was all important, this form was used exclusively and it remains in all its austere beauty in the folk-lore of the various countries of Europe. With the development of the art of harmony, musicians turned away from the ancient melodic system and limited themselves to a single mode: the major mode with its *related* minor form. For the purposes of harmony, the seventh degree of the minor mode was raised. Thus, instead of a whole tone between *sol* and *la*, the *sol* was raised until there was only a half-tone between the seventh and eighth degrees of the mode. It is necessary that the children should be able to sing this interval when they meet it in compositions written in the modern minor mode.

That they may not confuse the two sounds, a different name will be used for the raised seventh degree. Instead of *sol*, it will be called *seh*. In the number notation it will be represented by running a diagonal line through the number 5, thus: $\not{5}$. On the staff, a sharp: $^{\#}$, will be placed before the note thus raised. (This is not the only way in which a raised interval is represented on the staff, but it will suffice for the moment.)

To link the unknown to the known, the children will sing the melody: $\dot{1}$ 7 $\dot{1}$. At the same pitch, they will sing the same melody to the words: *La seh la.* The model $\dot{1}$ 7 $\dot{1}$ becomes the model for this accidental sharp, as it will later become the model for all other chromatic intervals raised in like manner.

When the children have sung $\dot{1}$ 7 $\dot{1}$ and 6 $\not{5}$ 6 at the same pitch, as one would sing two verses to the same melody, then they should place 6 $\not{5}$ 6 where it belongs in the minor mode, and in its relation to $\dot{1}$ 7 $\dot{1}$. They will sing *Intonation Exercises 147 and 148*, remembering to keep the melody of 6 $\not{5}$ 6 (*la seh la*) similar to that of $\dot{1}$ 7 $\dot{1}$ and different from that of 6 5 6 (*la sol la*).

Intonation Exercise 149 contains the two forms of the seventh degree (*sé* and *sol*). The children should sing $\dot{1}$ 7 6   6 $\not{5}$ 6; pause, and *think the whole group of notes that is to come:* 6 5 4 3 before singing it. During this work, the teacher should not hesitate to verify the intervals on the harmonium, and may even play them several times to help the children to form a mental picture of this new interval. The important point is that this half-tone be sung perfectly true to pitch from the beginning, and that there be no confusion between the sound of "sol" and the sound of "*seh.*" *Seh must depend on la* just as *ti depends on do.* Thus whenever "*seh*" is to be sung the children must form the habit of *thinking* 6 $\not{5}$ 6. Otherwise the *seh* will not be sung perfectly true to pitch.

Diagram 71 can be used to vary the work. The teacher will bear in mind, however, that the sound "$\not{5}$" must not yet be approached from a distance. It must always be approached from the sound 6 and return to the same sound. The other intervals of the diagram may be used with freedom. Thus:

| 6 7 1̇ 2̇ 3̇ 2̇ 1̇ 7 6 6 5̸ 5̸ 6 |
| 6 1̇ 3̇ 2̇ 1̇ 7 6 5̸ 6 |
| 6 3̇ 1̇ 6 7 6 5̸ 6 |
| 6 5 4 3 3 6 5̸ 6 |
| 6 3 6 6 7 1̇ 6 6 5̸ 6 |
| 6 1̇ 6 5̸ 6 6 3 6 |
| 6 5 4 3 3 6 6 5̸ 6 |

That the children may become used to the sharp on the staff, use *Diagram 70* (Key of A minor). The same diagram can be used in the Key of *G minor*. In this case the sharp will come on a space instead of on a line.

By means of these little variations the necessary drill on the new interval can be carried out without loss of interest on the part of the children.

Their attention should be drawn to the cancellation of the sharp by means of the *natural sign*, as explained on page 174, or by the bar line of a new measure.

The melodies of this chapter employ the 5̸ depending on 6, and several employ both the 5̸ and the 5 in the course of the melody.

Rhythmic Exercise 43 develops *Schema II* in 4/4 time. These designs have been fully covered in the study of 2/4 time and should be employed principally for observation, for combination into longer designs and for ideas as regards the composition of melodies.

Dictation

| 6 7 1̇ 7 6 5̸ 6 |
| 6 5̸ 6 7 1̇ 2̇ 3̇ |
| 3̇ 1̇ 6 5̸ 6 . 6 |
| 6 5 4 3 6 5̸ 6 |
| 6 5̸ 6 3 6 . 6 | etc.

| 6 5̸ 6 3 4 3 6 |
| 3 4 3 6 6 5̸ 6 |
| 6 1̇ 7 6 5̸ 6 6 |
| 6 5̸ 6 3 4 3 6 |
| 6 5̸ 6 1̇ 7 . 6 | etc.

| 6 5̸ 6 6 5 4 3 |
| 3 6 5̸ 6 5 4 3 |
| 3 6 6 1̇ 7 6 5̸ 6 |
| 3 6 6 1̇ 7 6 5 6 |
| 1̇ 7 6 5 3 6 5̸ 6 | etc.

Aural Memory

	6 $\overline{67}$	1̇ 7	6 5̸	6 .
6 $\overline{\dot{1}7}$	6 $\overline{54}$	3 .	3 .
3 $\overline{67}$	1̇ $\overline{76}$	5 4	3 .
3 $\overline{67}$	$\overline{\dot{1}7}$ $\overline{6\not{5}}$	6 .	6 .	

Visualization

| 6 7 1̇ 2̇ 3̇ 1̇ 6 |
| 6 7 1̇ 6 6 5̸ 6 |
| 6 5̸ 6 7 1̇ 2̇ 3̇ |
| 3̇ 2̇ 1̇ 7 6 5 6 |
| 6 6 5 4 3 6 6 |
| 6 7 6 5̸ 6 . 6 . |

CHAPTER TWENTY-FOUR

Vocal Exercises.—The *Special Exercise of Chapter 23.* Also the following:

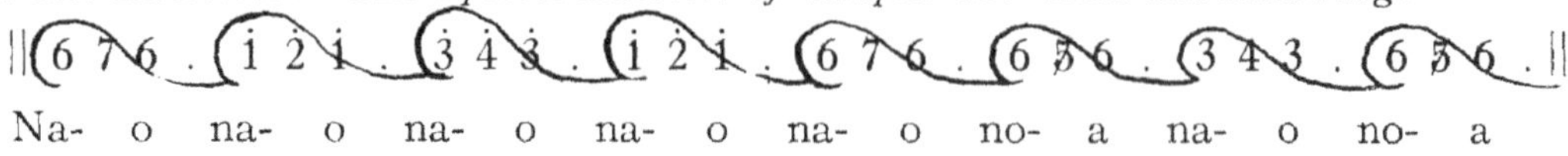

Na- o na- o na- o na- o na- o no- a na- o no- a

After singing the exercise with the syllables indicated, repeat the exercise using words of two syllables in English.

Intonation.—The Modern Minor Mode.

6
5̸
4 **3** 2
1
7̣
6̣
5̸̣

Diagram 72.

Intonation Exercise 150

(Key of Em)

(Use Diagram 72)

Compass Exercise, 3 forms, Authentic Range

6̣7̣6̣	121	343	65̸6	65̸6	343	121	6̣7̣6̣	6̣5̸̣6̣
6̣	1	3	6	6	3	1	6̣	
$_6$7̣6̣	$_1$21	$_3$43	$_6$5̸6	$_6$5̸6	$_3$43	$_1$21	$_6$7̣6̣	$_6$5̸̣6̣

In studying this exercise, use *seh* until this tone is well established, then use sometimes *sol*, sometimes *seh*, to bring out the contrast. *(See Diagram 73.)*

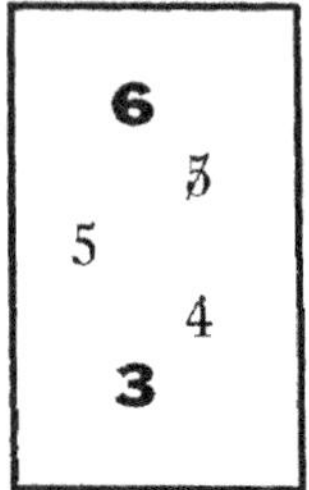

Diagram 73.

Melody and Rhythm

‖ 6 .	5 4	3 6	6 5̸	6 .	. ✕
6 .	6 7	1̇ .	6 .	5̸ .	6 .
1̇ .	7 6	5 .	3 .	6 6	5̸ .
6 .	3 4	3 .	6 .	5̸ .	6 . ‖

Intonation Exercise 151

(Key of Am, or Gm)

Compass Exercise, 3 Forms, Plagal Range (Diagram 71)

6̣76	1̇2̇1̇	3̇4̇3̇	1̇2̇1̇	676	65̸6	343	65̸6
6	1̇	3̇	1̇	6	6	3	6
$_6$76	1̇2̇1̇	$_3$4̇3̇	1̇2̇1̇	$_6$76	$_6$5̸6	$_3$43	$_6$5̸6

Rule: Before singing *seh*, always think "*la*" (65̸6).

Melody and Rhythm (Gm)

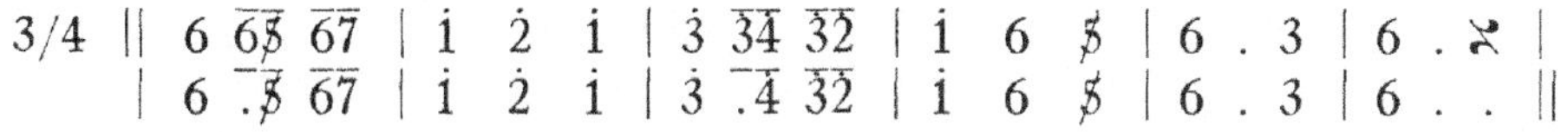

3/4 || 6 65 67 | 1 2 1 | 3 34 32 | 1 6 5 | 6 . 3 | 6 . ≈ |
| 6 .5 67 | 1 2 1 | 3 .4 32 | 1 6 5 | 6 . 3 | 6 . . ||

Melody 200. Basque. (Gm)

	67 17 67 17	67 17 6 17	6 1 3 .
6 17 6 .	1 2 3 .
34 42 17 65	6 1 7 .
6 1 7 3	6 . . .	

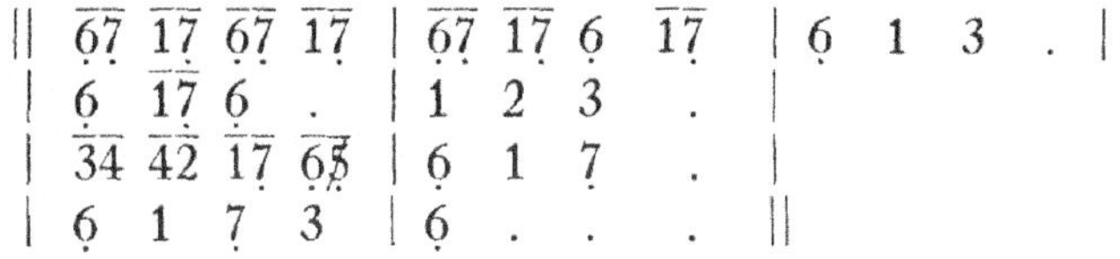

Melody 201. Sixteenth Century German. (Am)

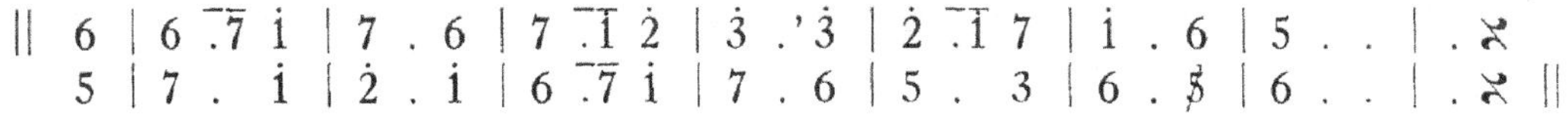

|| 6 | 6 .7 1 | 7 . 6 | 7 .1 2 | 3 .'3 | 2 .1 7 | 1 . 6 | 5 . . | . ≈
5 | 7 . 1 | 2 . 1 | 6 .7 1 | 7 . 6 | 5 . 3 | 6 . 5 | 6 . . | . ≈ ||

Melody 202. French Folk Song. (Bm)

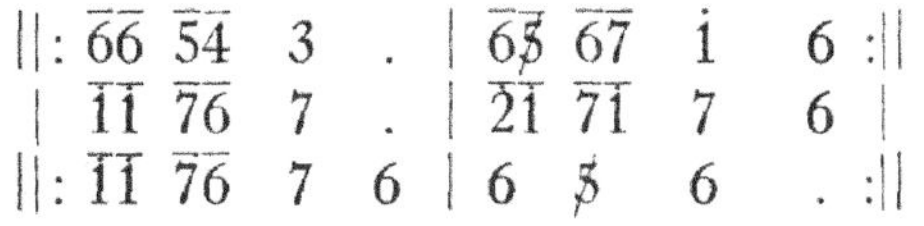

	: 66 54 3 .	65 67 1 6 :	
11 76 7 .	21 71 7 6
	: 11 76 7 6	6 5 6 . :	

Melody 203. Flemish, 1609. (Am)

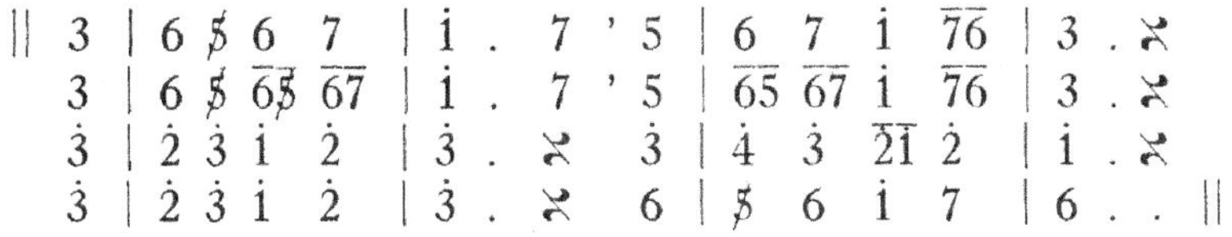

|| 3 | 6 5 6 7 | 1 . 7 ' 5 | 6 7 1 76 | 3 . ≈
3 | 6 5 65 67 | 1 . 7 ' 5 | 65 67 1 76 | 3 . ≈
3 | 2 3 1 2 | 3 . ≈ 3 | 4 3 21 2 | 1 . ≈
3 | 2 3 1 2 | 3 . ≈ 6 | 5 6 1 7 | 6 . . ||

Rhythm 44 (4/4 Time, Schema 3)

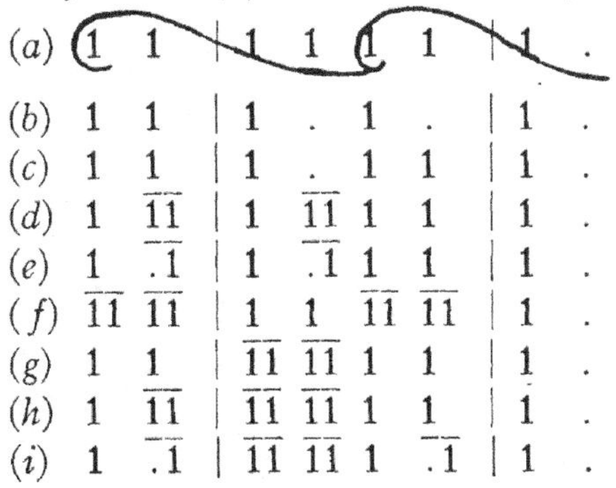

(a) 1 1 | 1 1 1 1 | 1 .
(b) 1 1 | 1 . 1 . | 1 .
(c) 1 1 | 1 . 1 1 | 1 .
(d) 1 11 | 1 11 1 1 | 1 .
(e) 1 .1 | 1 .1 1 1 | 1 .
(f) 11 11 | 1 1 11 11 | 1 .
(g) 1 1 | 11 11 1 1 | 1 .
(h) 1 11 | 11 11 1 1 | 1 .
(i) 1 .1 | 11 11 1 .1 | 1 .

Rhythm and Melody

|| 6 5 | 6 . 3 . | 6 .
3 4 | 3 6 5 6 | 7 .
1 12 | 1 7 6 4 | 3 .
3 .4 | 3 3 6 5 | 6 .
67 17 | 6 6 56 54 | 3 .
6 1 | 32 17 6 6 | 6 .
6 .1 | 7 6 5 .4 | 3 .
3 6 | 17 65 6 6 | 6 . ||

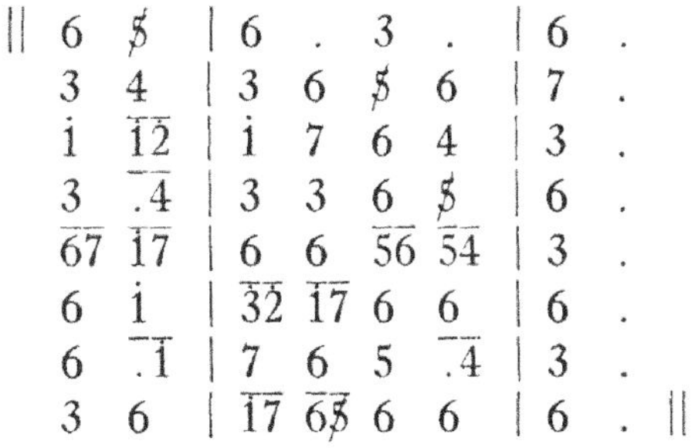

(Which models are used?)

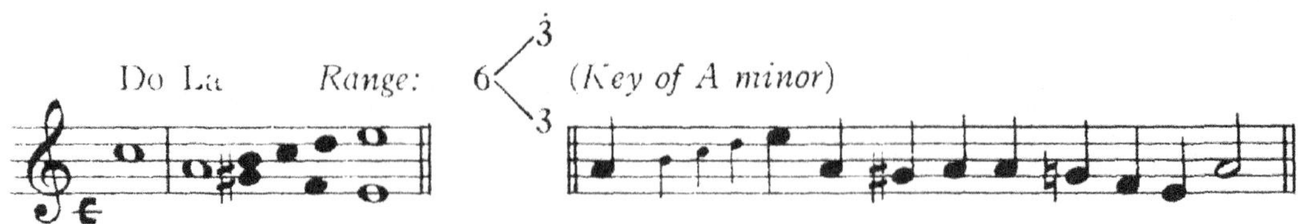

Study Melodies 204, page 78; *205, 206 and 207*, page 82, Children's Manual.

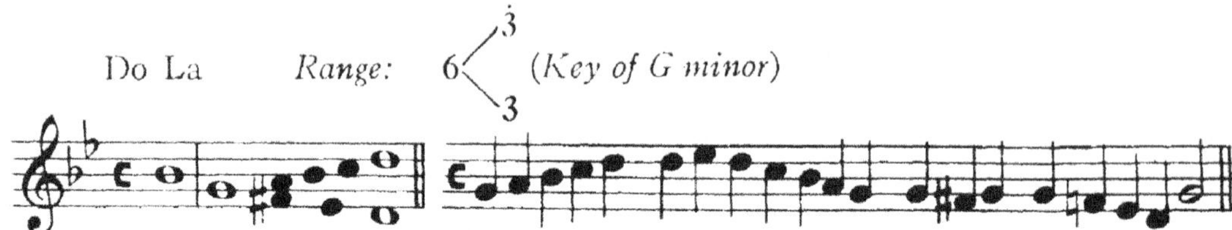

Study the following pieces from the Children's Manual:

Melody 208, page 82.

The Fairy Ship, page 83, or *The Cat and the Pigeon*, page 84.

Begin Study of the Gloria, page 111, *and the Sanctus*, page 114.

Vocal Exercises of Chapter 23. Also the special exercise of this chapter. Each group should be sung *legato* and *diminuendo*, which does not mean that the first note of each group should be stressed, but that there should be a *slight shade* of diminution of the normal force for the other tones. This must not be carried to the point of making the group jerky. Above all, there must be no contraction of the throat. The children must render this diminuendo only in so far as they can do so without effort, and without losing the placing of the tone and full command of its volume.

Words of two syllables should then be substituted for the vocalize sounds. The words chosen should be prepared before singing them, by a clear and crisp pronunciation of the consonants. Such words as the following could be used:

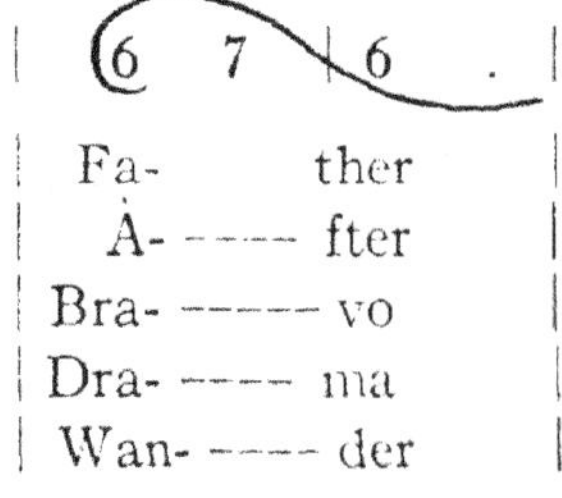

The first vowel must be kept perfectly pure, when a word is sung, until the time for the next syllable. A consonant, in singing, belongs to the *syllable ahead*.

Example

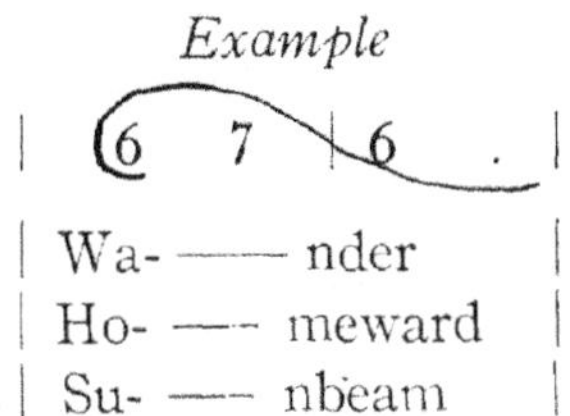

Where there are several consecutive consonants (as in such words as *homeward, sunbeam*, etc.), these require a rapid, crisp articulation. In singing, this rule must be observed strictly; otherwise the proper timbre of the vowel of the first syllable will be altered and produce a muddy effect which is ugly in itself and makes the words hard to understand.

Intonation.—The three forms of the *Compass Exercise* in the minor mode with the accidental, 5̸. These exercises should be studied on the diagrams as well as horizontally. The teacher should also move freely from one form to the other, (see *Intonation Exercises 150 and 151*).

While studying *Seh*, it is well to return to *Sol* occasionally, especially in *descending passages.* Draw the attention of the children to *Diagram 73:* 5̸ is very close to *la*, just as *fa* is close to *mi*. Sing *la seh la*. Then sing *la sol la*. This *difference* should be brought out in the work of these chapters, by ear tests, by visualization and aural memory, etc. Using Diagram 73, point rapidly to 6 5̸ 6 3 6, then 6 5 3 5 6, 6 5 4 3 6 5̸ 6. Draw attention to the use of *sol* and *seh* in *Melodies 201, 202, 203, 204, 205*. Also in the melodies of *Chapter 23*. Very often a melody will use *sol* throughout and turn to *seh* for the final cadence only.

Rhythm.—Study of 4/4 time according to *Schema 3*. In this form we begin on the second half of the measure (4/4 time); we have thus *a half measure* at the beginning of our rhythmic design, and must find a *half measure* at the end of the design. This correlation between the beginning and end is a point that we should insist upon with the children, in spite of the fact that we sometimes find the rule enforced rather loosely by certain composers who replace this proper rhythmic balance by a *pause*, thus: 𝄐 Such a sign is too vague for use by children, and we prefer to give the exact value of each cadence expressed by dots of prolongation or by rests.

Composition—Forms

The simplest form in music is the form A B A.

‖: A ———————————— :‖	(The first statement of a musical idea.)
B ————————————	(Something new.)
A ———————————— ‖	(Repetition of the first statement.)

Example (*Melody 101*, *Ch. 5*)

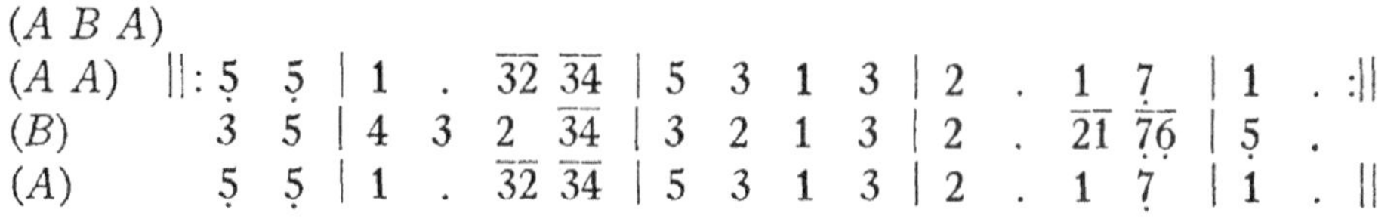

(*A B A*)
(*A A*) ||: $\underset{.}{5}$ $\underset{.}{5}$ | 1 . $\overline{32}$ $\overline{34}$ | 5 3 1 3 | 2 . 1 $\underset{.}{7}$ | 1 . :||
(*B*) 3 5 | 4 3 2 $\overline{34}$ | 3 2 1 3 | 2 . $\overline{21}$ $\overline{7\underset{.}{6}}$ | $\underset{.}{5}$.
(*A*) $\underset{.}{5}$ $\underset{.}{5}$ | 1 . $\overline{32}$ $\overline{34}$ | 5 3 1 3 | 2 . 1 $\underset{.}{7}$ | 1 . ||

In this form, the first statement is usually repeated (as above) giving us *AA* + *B* + *A*. When the first statement is repeated exactly (as in the melody given above) the final repetition of phrase *A* is usually represented by the sign: D.C.

||: A ———— :|| Fine
|| B ———— || D.C.

For other melodies of this form, see Numbers **116**, **172**, **179**, **182**, **194**, etc.

Themes for Composition in the Form AABA

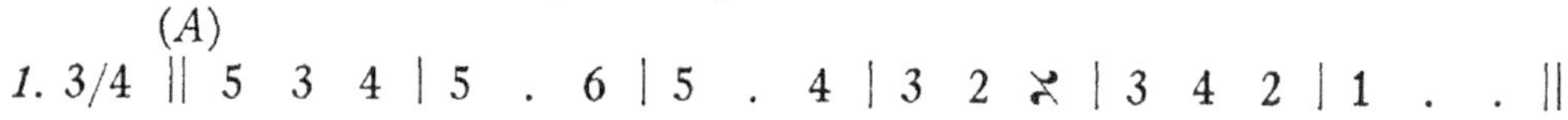

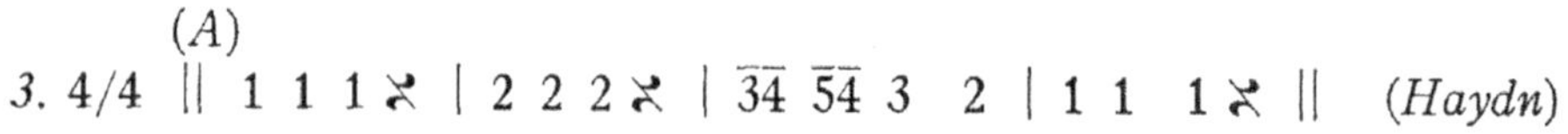

(*A*)
1. 3/4 || 5 3 4 | 5 . 6 | 5 . 4 | 3 2 𝄽 | 3 4 2 | 1 . . ||

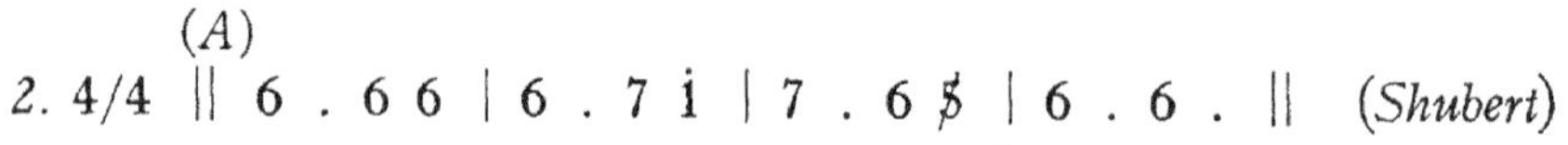

(*A*)
2. 4/4 || 6 . 6 6 | 6 . 7 $\dot{1}$ | 7 . 6 $\not{5}$ | 6 . 6 . || (*Shubert*)

(*A*)
3. 4/4 || 1 1 1 𝄽 | 2 2 2 𝄽 | $\overline{34}$ $\overline{54}$ 3 2 | 1 1 1 𝄽 || (*Haydn*)

Write a melody using each one of these themes in turn for the opening phrase (*A*). Compose a contrasting phrase (*B*) and return by the sign D.C. to the original phrase.

In the *Form A B A*, we do not always find the theme repeated in exactly its original form; sometimes there are slight variations.

Suppose we have a first statement which ends on some tone that is not the tonic of the mode: can we end our melody with an exact repetition? No; we must either change our original statement slightly to make a good ending or we must choose another form than *A B A* for our melody.

Example: $\overline{35}$ | $\overline{43}$ $\overline{21}$ $\overline{\underset{.}{7}\underset{.}{5}}$ $\overline{1\underset{.}{5}}$ | $\overline{1\underset{.}{5}}$ $\overline{12}$ 3

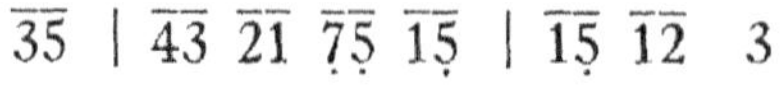

There are two things that we could do with such a theme:

1. Our *Aa* could be a repetition that was not exactly the same for the *A1* and the *a2*, thus:

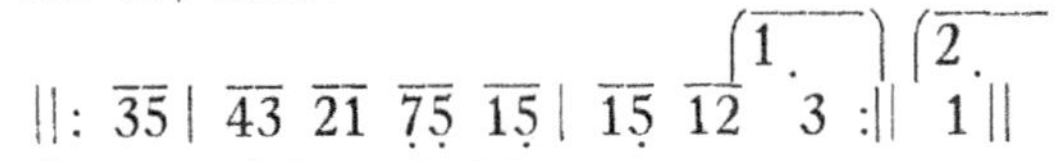

||: 35 | 43 21 75 15 | 15 12 3 :|| 1 || After which would come a phrase *B* and a repetition of *A2*.

2. Or we could select another form more in keeping with the theme.

A B + C + A B

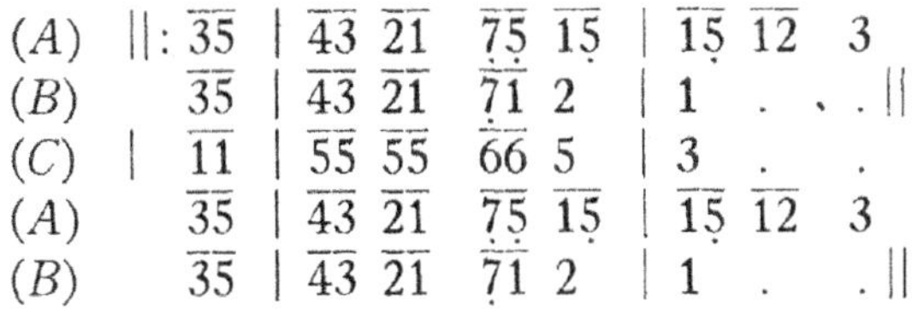

(*A*)	||: 35	43 21	75 15	15 12	3		
(*B*)	35	43 21	71 2	1	. . . ||		
(*C*)	| 11	55 55	66 5	3	. .		
(*A*)	35	43 21	75 15	15 12	3		These two lines are often represented
(*B*)	35	43 21	71 2	1	. . ||	by the sign: D.C. and *Fine* at the end of line *B*.

Themes for Composition of a Melody in the Form A B C A B

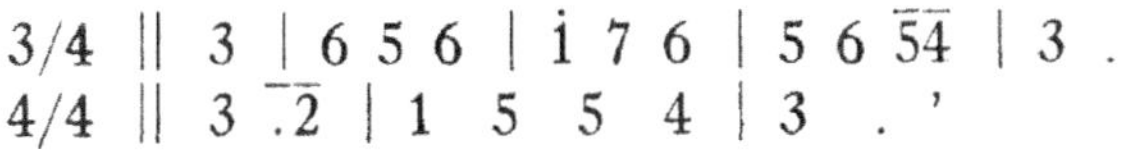

3/4 || 3 | 6 5 6 | i 7 6 | 5 6 54 | 3 . (End in the minor mode.)
4/4 || 3 .2 | 1 5 5 4 | 3 . ' (End in the major mode.)

In teaching the children to look for certain characteristic forms (as we shall do during these chapters) and in teaching them to make use of such forms for their own compositions, the teacher should not give the children the impression that *all melodies* must follow one or the other of these forms. Many of the most beautiful melodies are conceived in a form that is free. The work we are undertaking at present is one which will open the children's eyes to certain types of beauty and quicken their powers of observation.

Dictation

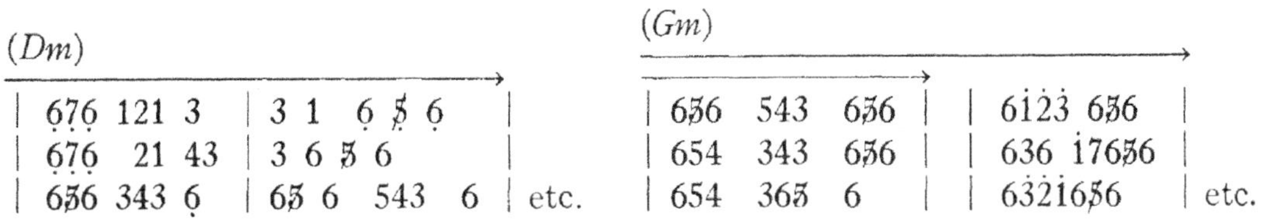

(*Dm*) (*Gm*)

| 676 121 3 | 3 1 6 ♯5 6 | | 6♯56 543 6♯56 | 6i2̇3 6♯56 |
| 676 21 43 | 3 6 ♯5 6 | | 654 343 6♯56 | 636 i76♯56 |
| 6♯56 343 6 | 6♯5 6 543 6 | etc. | 654 36♯5 6 | 63̇2̇i6♯56 | etc.

CHAPTER TWENTY-FIVE

Vocal Exercises.—The special exercises of Chapters 23 and 24.

Intonation.—Study of Seh.

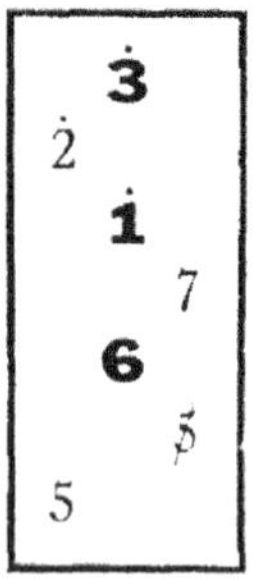

3̇
2̇
1̇
7
6
5̸
5

Diagram 74.

1̇
7
6
5̸
5
4
3

Diagram 75.

3̇
2̇
1̇
7
6
5̸
5
4
3

Diagram 76.

Intonation Exercise 152 (Gm)

c ⟶
a ⟶ b ⟶

6 3̇ 3̇ 2̇ 1̇ 7 6 6 5̸ 5̸ 6 6 7 7 6	6 7 1̇ 7 6 5̸ 6
6 3̇ 3̇ 2̇ 1̇ 7 6 6 5̸ 5̸ 6 6 7 7 6	6 1̇ 7 6 5̸ 6
6 3̇ 3̇ 2̇ 1̇ 7 6 5̸ 6 7 6	6 1̇ 7 6 5̸ 6 7 1̇ 6

Intonation Exercise 153 (Bm)

c ⟶
a ⟶ b ⟶

| 6 7 1̇ 7 6 5 4 3 3 6 5̸ 6 | 3 4 3 6 5̸ 6 |
| 6 1̇ 7 6 5 4 3 3 6 5̸ 6 | 3 4 3 6 5̸ 6 |

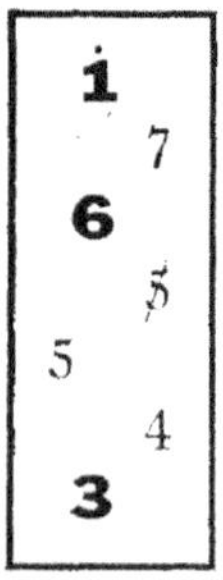

Intonation Exercise 154 (Gm or Am)

c ⟶
a ⟶ b ⟶

6 7 1̇ 2̇ 3̇ 1̇ 2̇ 7 1̇ 6 5̸ 6 7 6	6 3 4 3 6 5̸ 6
6 1̇ 3̇ 1̇ 2̇ 7 1̇ 6 5̸ 7 6	6 3 6 5̸ 6
6 1̇ 3̇ 1̇ 2̇ 7 1̇ 6 7 5̸ 6	6 3 4 3 6 5̸ 6

Melody 209. Basque. (Gm)

||: 1̇ 3̇ | 7 7 6 76 | 3 3
1̇ 3̇ | 7 7 6 .5̸ | 6 . :|| Fine
1̇ 2̇ | 33 3 34 3 | 2̇ 2̇
3̇2̇ 7 | 6 5 1̇ 2̇ | 3̇ . :|| D.C.

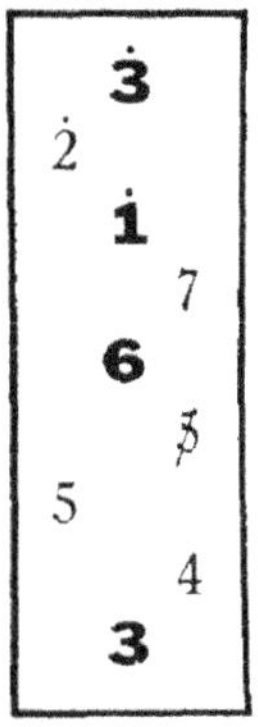

Melody and Rhythm

|| 67 1̇2̇ | 3̇ 1̇ 2̇ . | 2̇1̇ 72̇ 1̇ 6 | 5̸ 7 6 . | 3̇ .
67 1̇2̇ | 3̇ 1̇ 2̇ . | 72̇ 1̇7 6 1̇ | 7 5̸ 7 . | 6 . ||

|| 6 1̇ | 7 6 5̸ 7 | 6 . 6 6 | 3 4 3 . | 6 .
6 4 | 3 6 5̸ 7 | 6 . 6 7 | 5̸ 7 6 . | 6 . ||

Staff Notation—The Major and the Minor Mode

When we have placed "high do" on the staff, how do we find "la"?

We sing the melody "1̇7 6" and count downward, on the staff, as we sing it: "1̇7" a small interval: "7 6" a large interval.

1. Place "la" where it belongs in each of the following examples.

Note.—When *high do* is on a line, *la* will be on a line. When *high do* is in a space, *la* will be in a space.

2. Write: 6 5̸ 6 . 6 5 6 . | in each example given above.

Question: when do we express "5̸" by a sharp? and when, by a natural?

Study Melodies 210, page 84; *211, 212 and 213*, page 85, Children's Manual.

Study Song: Jesus Tender Shepherd, Children's Manual, page 86.

Vocal Exercises.—Continue the study of words applied to the vocal exercise of Chapter 24. In this work, the teacher should begin by placing the tone carefully by means of the syllable *Nu, no*, etc., and then use the words. These should be pronounced clearly and crisply before singing, that the consonants be given their true value. Only after the two elements are thus prepared separately, should they be combined.

Intonation Exercise 152 prepares the intervals: 5̸ 7 and 7 5̸. *Intonation Exercise 153* prepares 3 5̸ and 4 5̸. In both cases the help-note *6* must be used. Indeed the habit must be formed and retained always of sustaining mentally the sound 5̸ on the help-note 6. Otherwise it will not be sung perfectly true to pitch.

The children will not take the trouble to think "la" unless the teacher insists upon this point. At first they should think "6 5̸ 6"; later, after they have had a good deal of experience, it is sufficient to think "5̸ 6." The child should think of the accidental sharp (5̸) only while actually singing it. His mind must return promptly to the tone on which it is supported (6), failing which he will lose his sense of modality. The reason for this is that the accidental sharp does not form part of the modality itself. It is artificial. The child must keep in mind *the structural tones of the mode itself*. If the rule given above be scrupulously applied the children will sing perfectly true to pitch even when dealing with accidentals. It is well to insist upon this point at once, since the same rule must be applied in subsequent volumes for the introduction of all other accidental sharps. A sharp must always be sustained—at least mentally—on the degree of the scale which is a half-tone above it. To form this habit among the pupils, the teacher may use the diagrams of this chapter as follows·

Teacher points and pupils sing the large notes. One child sings the help notes. : 6 5̸ 6 7 6 5̸ 6 $\dot{1}$ 6 5̸ 6 $\dot{2}$ 6 $\dot{3}$ 6 $\dot{3}$ 6

Staff Notation.—From the clef giving the position of "do," find "la" and write 6 5̸ 6, 6 5 6, in each tonality studied.

Seh is indicated by a *sharp placed before the note* except in the case where the note is *already altered* (by a sharp or a flat) at the key-signature. The only case of this nature in the Second Year is E flat major with its relative, C minor.

When we want to raise a *normal note* we place a *sharp* before it.
When we want to raise a *flattened* note we place a *natural* before it.

Where the children are to use modern staff notation, it is necessary for them to know these things and to be able to use them without hesitation.

In classes where the children are very young or where the music periods are relatively brief, it would be wise to postpone all this theoretical study until the third year. In that case the work would be confined to the *number notation*, and these same problems as expressed on the staff would be presented during the following year. It is essential to cover the intervals of the minor mode, with and without the accidental sharp; to build up a true modal feeling and a sense of the difference between the major and minor modes. The manner in which these musical facts are expressed on the staff is useful knowledge but knowledge which may be postponed until later without destroying the essential musical content of the Second Year course.

Staff Notation

The Minor with its accidental in the tonalities studied

In these tonalities, 5̸ is expressed by the sharp in all but one case. In *example d*, it is expressed by the natural.

To restore a note to normal: *the sharp is cancelled by the natural.*
the natural is cancelled by the flat.

Both are cancelled by the bar line marking a new measure.

It is evident that the number notation is far more simple for pedagogical purposes; in the question of the raised seventh of the modern minor mode, this phenomenon is *always expressed in the same manner.* The same is true of the *cancellation of the accidental:* there is but *one way* of expressing cancellation. The childen sing with far more assurance from the number notation than from the staff because of this fact, among others. We advise, therefore, that the teacher who finds that a class of children cannot cover all the matter included in this book, should concentrate upon the tonal and rhythmic matter which is more important to the ultimate progress of the children than would be the application to the staff of a lesser amount of real *musical* knowledge. Familiarity with the modern system of notation can be built up rapidly with older children, provided there be a solid foundation of musical experience upon which to build.

Composition—Forms

We studied Form *ABA* or more exactly *AABA* in the last chapter. This week we will study Form *ABAC*.

Example 1

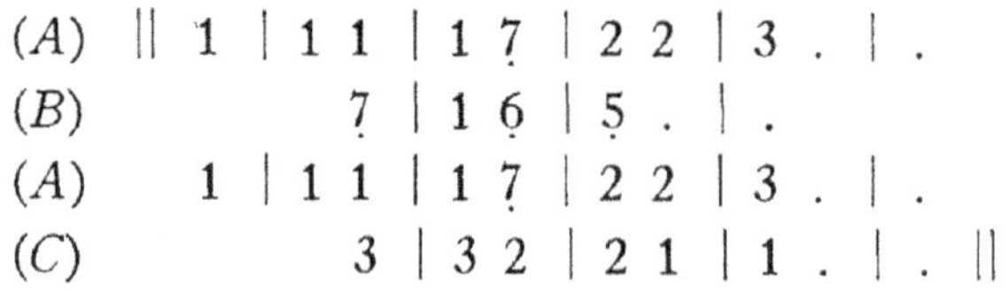

(*A*)	‖ 1 | 1 1 | 1 7̣ | 2 2 | 3 . | .	*A* is the theme.
(*B*)	7 | 1 6̣ | 5̣ . | .	*B*, something new.
(*A*)	1 | 1 1 | 1 7̣ | 2 2 | 3 . | .	*A* repeats the theme.
(*C*)	3 | 3 2 | 2 1 | 1 . | . ‖	*C*, something new.

Example 2

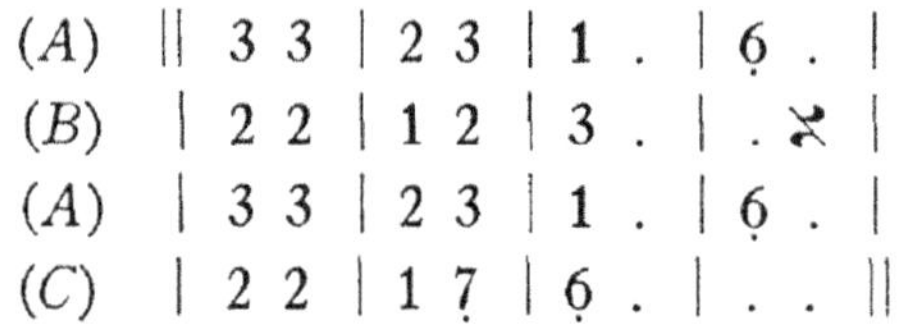

(*A*)	‖ 3 3 | 2 3 | 1 . | 6̣ . |
(*B*)	| 2 2 | 1 2 | 3 . | . 𝄎 |
(*A*)	| 3 3 | 2 3 | 1 . | 6̣ . |
(*C*)	| 2 2 | 1 7̣ | 6̣ . | . . ‖

See also Melodies **110**, **124**, **125**, **128**, **141**, **146**, **147**, **155**, **166**, **178**.

Themes for Composition in the Form ABAC

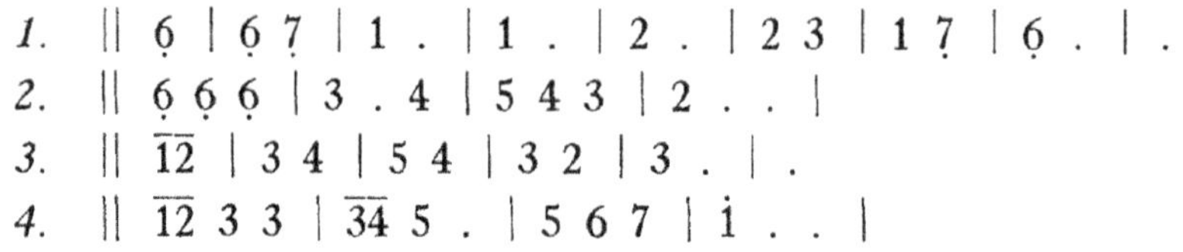

1.	‖ 6̣ | 6̣ 7̣ | 1 . | 1 . | 2 . | 2 3 | 1 7̣ | 6̣ . | .	Minor mode.
2.	‖ 6̣ 6̣ 6̣ | 3 . 4 | 5 4 3 | 2 . . |	Minor mode.
3.	‖ $\overline{12}$ | 3 4 | 5 4 | 3 2 | 3 . | .	Major mode.
4.	‖ $\overline{12}$ 3 3 | $\overline{34}$ 5 . | 5 6 7 | 1̇ . . |	Major mode.

Melodies by Children—Form ABAC

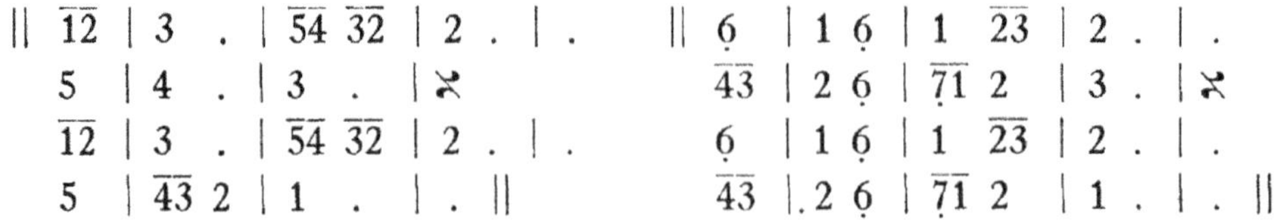

‖ $\overline{12}$ \| 3 . \| $\overline{54}$ $\overline{32}$ \| 2 . \| .
5 \| 4 . \| 3 . \| 𝄎
$\overline{12}$ \| 3 . \| $\overline{54}$ $\overline{32}$ \| 2 . \| .
5 \| $\overline{43}$ 2 \| 1 . \| . ‖

(*Maria Santini*)

‖ 6̣ \| 1 6̣ \| 1 $\overline{23}$ \| 2 . \| .
$\overline{43}$ \| 2 6̣ \| $\overline{7̣1}$ 2 \| 3 . \| 𝄎
6̣ \| 1 6̣ \| 1 $\overline{23}$ \| 2 . \| .
$\overline{43}$ \| .2 6̣ \| $\overline{7̣1}$ 2 \| 1 . \| . ‖

(*Maria Giuseppina*)

Dictation

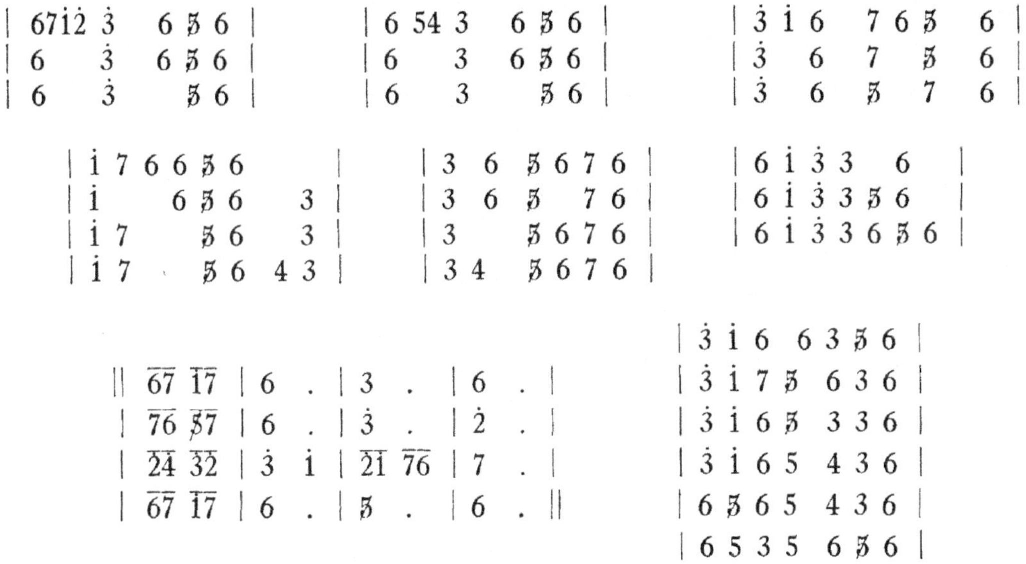

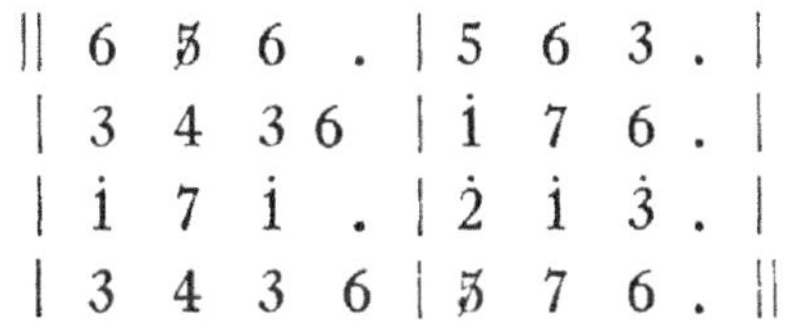

| 671̇2̇ 3̇ 6 5̸ 6 |
| 6 3̇ 6 5̸ 6 |
| 6 3̇ 5̸ 6 |

| 6 54 3 6 5̸ 6 |
| 6 3 6 5̸ 6 |
| 6 3 5̸ 6 |

| 3̇ 1̇ 6 7 6 5̸ 6 |
| 3̇ 6 7 5̸ 6 |
| 3̇ 6 5̸ 7 6 |

| 1̇ 7 6 6 5̸ 6 |
| 1̇ 6 5̸ 6 3 |
| 1̇ 7 5̸ 6 3 |
| 1̇ 7 5̸ 6 4 3 |

| 3 6 5̸ 6 7 6 |
| 3 6 5̸ 7 6 |
| 3 5̸ 6 7 6 |
| 3 4 5̸ 6 7 6 |

| 6 1̇ 3̇ 3 6 |
| 6 1̇ 3̇ 3 5̸ 6 |
| 6 1̇ 3̇ 3 6 5̸ 6 |

	67 1̇7	6 .	3 .	6 .
76 5̸7	6 .	3̇ .	2̇ .
2̇4̇ 3̇2̇	3̇ 1̇	2̇1̇ 76	7 .
67 1̇7	6 .	5̸ .	6 .	

| 3̇ 1̇ 6 6 3 5̸ 6 |
| 3̇ 1̇ 7 5̸ 6 3 6 |
| 3̇ 1̇ 6 5̸ 3 3 6 |
| 3̇ 1̇ 6 5 4 3 6 |
| 6 5̸ 6 5 4 3 6 |
| 6 5 3 5 6 5̸ 6 |

	6 5̸ 6 .	5 6 3 .
3 4 3 6	1̇ 7 6 .
1̇ 7 1̇ .	2̇ 1̇ 3̇ .
3 4 3 6	5̸ 7 6 .	

Visualization

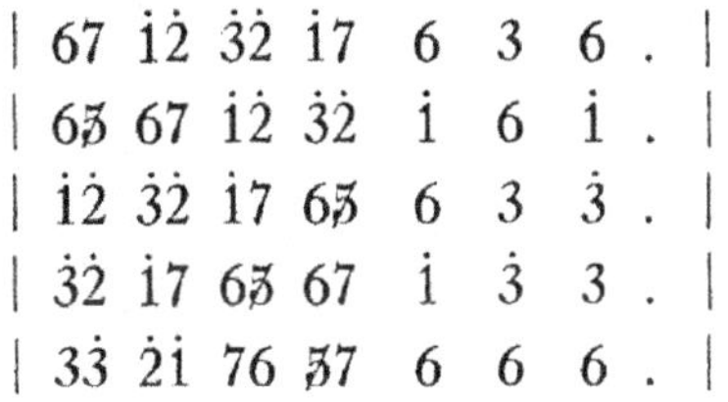

| 67 1̇2̇ 3̇2̇ 1̇7 6 3 6 . |
| 65̸ 67 1̇2̇ 3̇2̇ 1̇ 6 1̇ . |
| 1̇2̇ 3̇2̇ 1̇7 65̸ 6 3 3̇ . |
| 3̇2̇ 1̇7 65̸ 67 1̇ 3̇ 3 . |
| 3̇3̇ 2̇1̇ 76 5̸7 6 6 6 . |

Aural Memory

3̇ .1̇	6 .	7 .	1̇ .2̇	3̇ .	. 𝄽
2̇ .1̇	7 2̇	1̇ 7	6 .7	1̇ .	6̣ 𝄽
3̇ .1̇	6 .	7 .	1̇ .2̇	3̇ .	. 𝄽
2̇ .1̇	7 2̇	1̇ 6	5̸ .7	6 .	. 𝄽

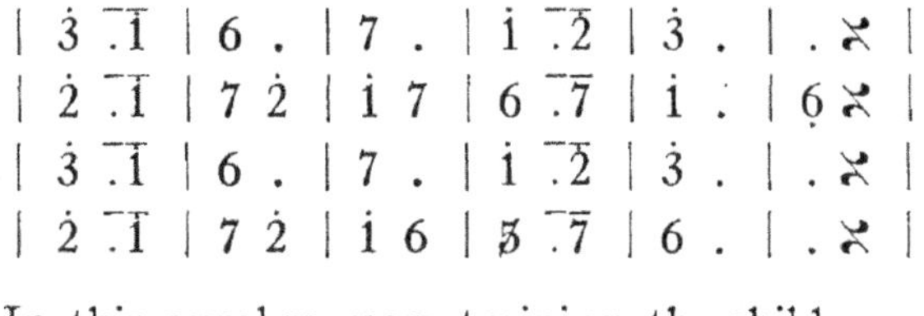

Memorize (*a*) 1 line at a time.
(*b*) 2 lines together.
(*c*) 4 lines.

In this aural memory training, the children will be helped by their study of forms.

After singing the melody through one line at a time, then two lines at a time, they will notice that the form is *ABAC*—in itself a help to the memory.

CHAPTER TWENTY-SIX

Vocal Exercises.—Comparison between the Major and Minor Modes.

Study alternately and at the same pitch, *Form a* and *b* of each vocal exercise, and continue this practice until the end of the year. Thus:

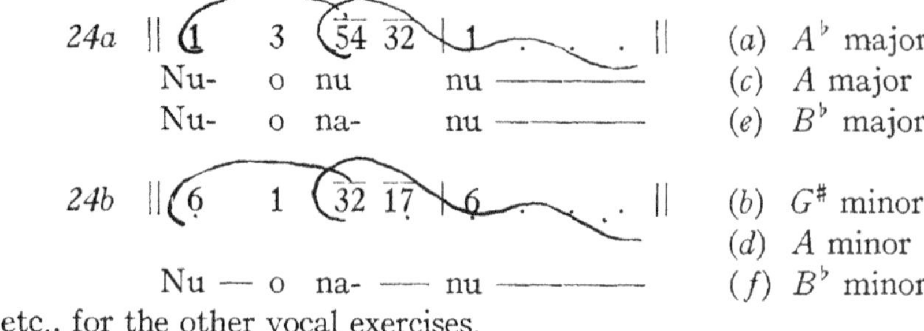

etc., for the other vocal exercises.

Intonation.—The two families: *Do* and *La*.

Structural notes of the *Do family:* 1 3 5 8
Structural notes of the *La family:* 6̣ 1 3 6

The same notes are contained in the two families, but their importance is quite different.

In the *Do* family: 1 5 8 are the strongest; next to these, 3.

In the *La* family: 6̣ 3 6 are the strongest; next to these, 1.

There is one note contained in the modern minor, that does not exist in the major. It is characteristic of the *La* family only: $\not{5}$.

We should realize, almost at once, to which family a melody belongs by the following signs:

1. Does a phrase run along the structural notes of the *Do family?* or those of the *La family?*
2. Do the cadences at the end of the phrases follow the design of the *Compass Exercise* of the *Do family* or that of the *La family?*
   (If necessary, review these forms.)
3. Does the melody *end* on *Do?* or on *La?*
4. Do we find a $\not{5}$ in the melody?

We do not need to find *all* these indications combined: one or the other will give us the necessary clue.

Intonation Exercise 155

Children will guess the modality and answer each phrase in the proper family.

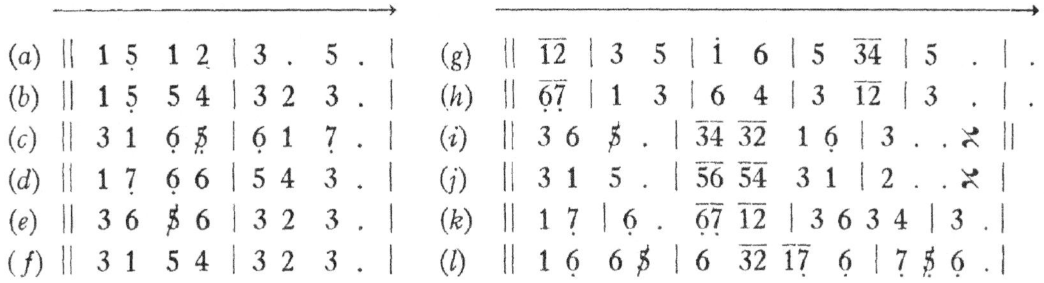

(*a*)	‖ 1 5 1 2 | 3 . 5 . |	(*g*)	‖ 12 | 3 5 | i 6 | 5 34 | 5 . | .
(*b*)	‖ 1 5 5 4 | 3 2 3 . |	(*h*)	‖ 67 | 1 3 | 6 4 | 3 12 | 3 . | .
(*c*)	‖ 3 1 6 ♯5 | 6 1 7 . |	(*i*)	‖ 3 6 ♯5 . | 34 32 1 6 | 3 . . 𝄽 ‖
(*d*)	‖ 1 7 6 6 | 5 4 3 . |	(*j*)	‖ 3 1 5 . | 56 54 3 1 | 2 . . 𝄽 |
(*e*)	‖ 3 6 ♯5 6 | 3 2 3 . |	(*k*)	‖ 1 7 | 6 . 67 12 | 3 6 3 4 | 3 . |
(*f*)	‖ 3 1 5 4 | 3 2 3 . |	(*l*)	‖ 1 6 6 ♯5 | 6 32 17 6 | 7 ♯5 6 . |

We see by the phrases of Exercise 155 that we do not need to wait for the *end of a melody* to know its modality. When the first note of each measure (or of a sufficient number of measures) rests on *do* or *sol;* or if the melody follows the chord-line: 1 3 5, or the scale line 12 34 5 ., we feel immediately that we are in the *Do family*.

On the contrary, when the first note of each measure rests on *la* or *mi*, or on *do in relation to la;* or when we see the note ♯5: or if the melody follows along the minor chord-line: 6 1 3 or the scale line 67 12 3, we feel immediately that we are in the *La family*.

These examples will not be difficult for the children. The utility of drawing their attention to these facts is precisely in order to lead them to a full understanding of *what to do* in order to bring out the *character of a mode* in their own compositions. This vivid exercise in observation will help them more than the memorizing of rigid rules.

From now on, the children should decide in what mode they are going to compose: whether major, minor, or in the modes of *Sol*. This applies to improvisations, musical conversations, etc.

Composition—Forms

We have studied the forms: *AABA* and *ABA C*.

This week we will study Forms: *ABCA* and *ABBC*.

Example 1

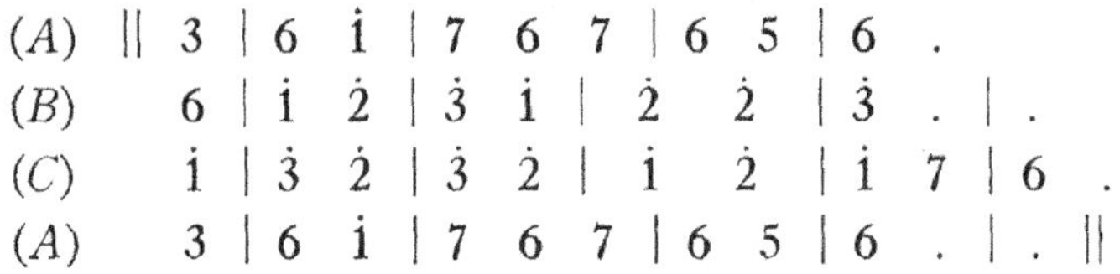

(*A*) || 3 | 6 i | 7 6 7 | 6 5 | 6 .
(*B*) 6 | i 2̇ | 3̇ i | 2̇ 2̇ | 3̇ . | .
(*C*) i | 3̇ 2̇ | 3̇ 2̇ | i 2̇ | i 7 | 6 .
(*A*) 3 | 6 i | 7 6 7 | 6 5 | 6 . | . ||

The original theme appears in the first phrase and in the last. The variety takes place in the center of the melody.

Example 2

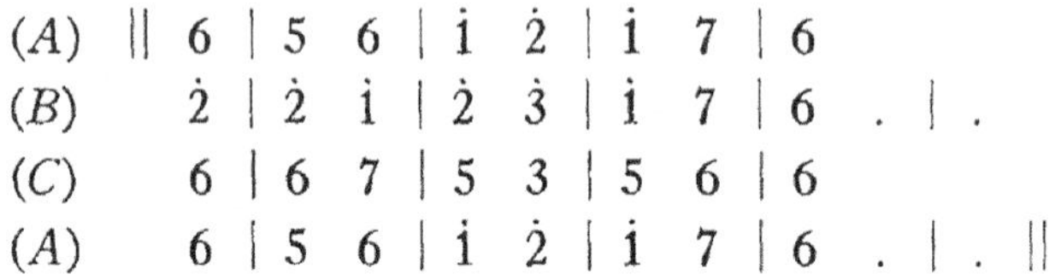

(*A*) || 6 | 5 6 | i 2̇ | i 7 | 6
(*B*) 2̇ | 2̇ i | 2̇ 3̇ | i 7 | 6 . | .
(*C*) 6 | 6 7 | 5 3 | 5 6 | 6
(*A*) 6 | 5 6 | i 2̇ | i 7 | 6 . | . ||

In this melody, the contrast is purely *melodic*.

Contrasts may be:

(*a*) Melodic.

(*b*) Rhythmic.

(*c*) Melodic and rhythmic.

Only a theme that ends on the tonic of the mode can be used for this form.

Themes to Develop in the Form ABCA

Themes in the Major Mode

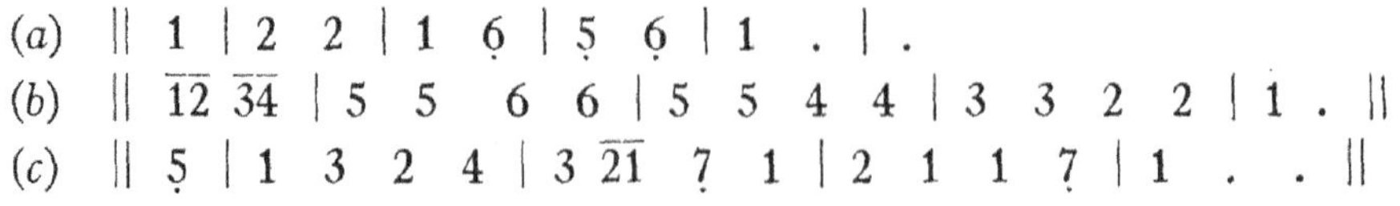

(*a*) || 1 | 2 2 | 1 6̣ | 5̣ 6̣ | 1 . | .
(*b*) || $\overline{12}$ $\overline{34}$ | 5 5 6 6 | 5 5 4 4 | 3 3 2 2 | 1 . ||
(*c*) || 5̣ | 1 3 2 4 | 3 $\overline{21}$ 7̣ 1 | 2 1 1 7̣ | 1 . . ||

Themes in the Minor Mode

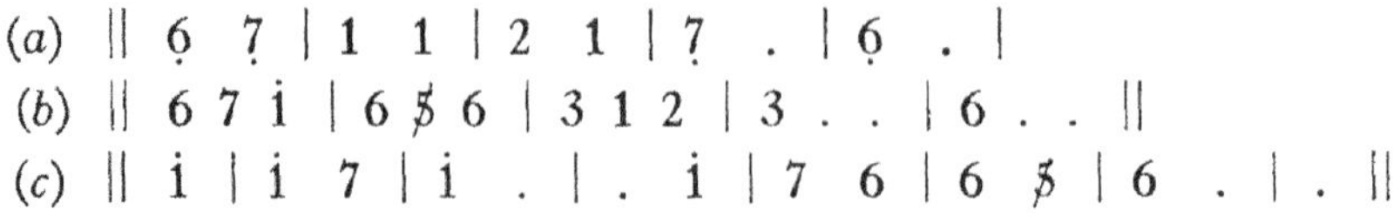

(*a*) || 6̣ 7̣ | 1 1 | 2 1 | 7̣ . | 6̣ . |
(*b*) || 6 7 i | 6 5̸ 6 | 3 1 2 | 3 . . | 6 . . ||
(*c*) || i | i 7 | i . | . i | 7 6 | 6 5̸ | 6 . | . ||

Example of Form ABBC

(*A*) || 5 | $\dot{1}$. | 7 6 | 5 . | 5
(*B*) 5 | $\dot{1}$. | 7 $\dot{1}$ | $\dot{2}$. | x
(*B*) 5 | $\dot{1}$. | 7 $\dot{1}$ | $\dot{2}$. | $\dot{1}$
(*C*) 7 | 6 . | 7 6 | 5 . | . ||

In this form the central part of the melody is repeated (*BB*).

Composition

1. 4/4 || $\underset{\cdot}{5}$ | 1 . 2 . | 3 3 2 1 | 5 . . *Family: Do or La?*
2. 2/4 || $\overline{5\dot{1}}$ $\overline{56}$ 5 3 | $\overline{56}$ $\overline{34}$ $\overline{55}$ 5 | Finish the melody.
3. 2/4 || $\underset{\cdot}{6}$ $\overline{\underset{\cdot}{6}\underset{\cdot}{7}}$ 1 $\underset{\cdot}{6}$ | 3 3 3 . |
4. 3/4 || $\underset{\cdot}{6}$. 3 | 1 . 2 | 3 . 3 | 3 . . |
5. 2/4 || 1 $\overline{34}$ | 5 5 | 6 . | 5 . | $\dot{1}$. | 7 5 | 6 . | 5 |
6. 3/4 || 5 3 4 | 5 . 6 | 5 . 4 | 3 2x | 3 4 2 | 1 . . |
7. 3/4 || 6 6 $\overline{.7}$ | $\not{5}$ . . | 6 6 $\overline{.6}$ | 7 . . |

Review of Staff Notation and of Modes

Study Melodies 214, 215, 216, 217, page 87; *218*, page 89, Children's Manual. In each case the children should state the Mode and Form of the melody.

Begin study of the following pieces from the Children's Manual:

O Salutaris Hostia (2), page 121.
Tantum Ergo Sacramentum, page 121.
Responses at Benediction, page 123.

CHAPTER TWENTY-SEVEN

Vocal Exercise: || 6 | 3 2 | 1 7 | 6 . | . || *Gm, Am, Bm.*
Na nu no ne ni na

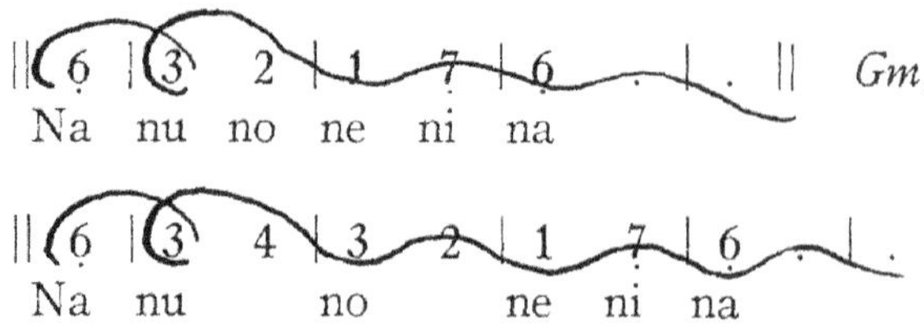

|| 6 | 3 4 | 3 2 | 1 7 | 6 . | . || *Gm, Am.*
Na nu no ne ni na

Intonation.—Study of Ti flat, called teu and written 7̸.

Model for all accidental flats: 3 4 3

Sing the melody: | 3 4 3 |
| mi fa mi |

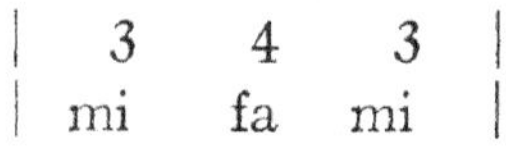

Sing at the same pitch: | 6 7̸ 6 |
| la teu la |

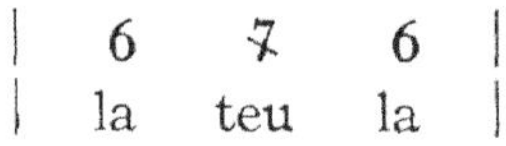

As soon as the equivalence between these two melodies has been established, place 6 7̸ 6 in its proper place in relation to the other tones of the scale.

Intonation Exercise 156 (Dm)

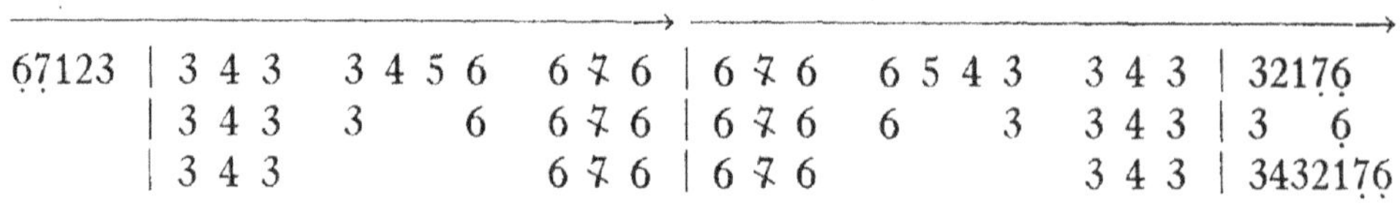

67123 | 3 4 3 3 4 5 6 6 7̸ 6 | 6 7̸ 6 6 5 4 3 3 4 3 | 32176
| 3 4 3 3 6 6 7̸ 6 | 6 7̸ 6 6 3 3 4 3 | 3 6
| 3 4 3 6 7̸ 6 | 6 7̸ 6 3 4 3 | 3432176

Melody and Rhythm

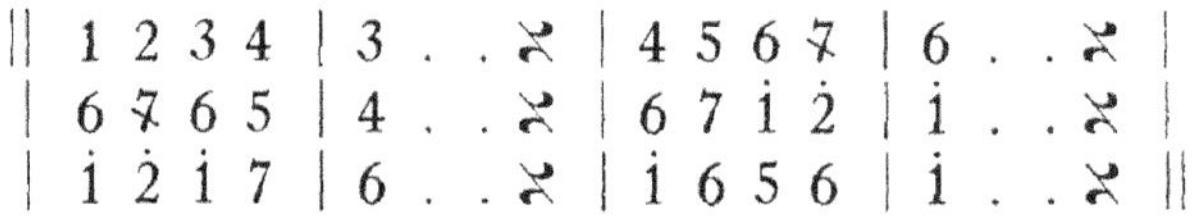

	1 2 3 4	3 . . 𝄽	4 5 6 7̸	6 . . 𝄽
6 7̸ 6 5	4 . . 𝄽	6 7 1̇ 2̇	1̇ . . 𝄽
1̇ 2̇ 1̇ 7	6 . . 𝄽	1̇ 6 5 6	1̇ . . 𝄽	

Melody and Rhythm

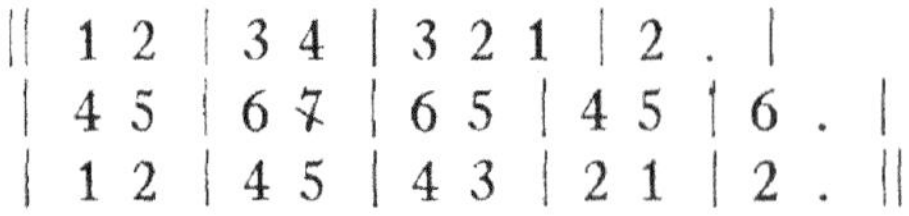

	1 2	3 4	3 2 1	2 .
4 5	6 7̸	6 5	4 5	6 .
1 2	4 5	4 3	2 1	2 .	

Melody 219. Noel Poitevin. (Key of G)

	1 . 1 5	5 4 5 6	5 . . 4	3 . ' 2 $\overline{12}$	3 3 2 $\overline{12}$	3 . . 𝄽
5 . 1 1	4 3 2 1	5 . . 𝄽
1 . 1 5	5 4 5 6	7̸ . . 6	5 . ' 4 $\overline{34}$	5 5 4 $\overline{34}$	5 . . 𝄽
5 5 1 4	3 2 1 5	1 . . 𝄽	

Staff Notation

Teu on the Staff

★ Flat cancelled by a new measure.
+ Flat cancelled by a natural.

In the *number notation*, each flat is represented by a diagonal line which runs through the figure from *left to right*. (7̸).

The flat is cancelled by the mere *absence* of the diagonal line.

In staff notation the lowered note has a *flat placed before it*.

This flat is cancelled in two ways:

(*a*) by a bar line indicating the beginning of a new measure.
(*b*) by a natural placed before the note in question.

(*a*)	(*b*)
4	7̸
3	6
2	5
1	4

Diagram 77.

Sing: | 1 2   3 4   3 . | (Then, at the same pitch:)
| 4 5   6 7̸   6 . |

Sing: | 3 4   3 2   3 .   6̣ . |
Then: | 6 7̸   6 5   6 .   2 . |

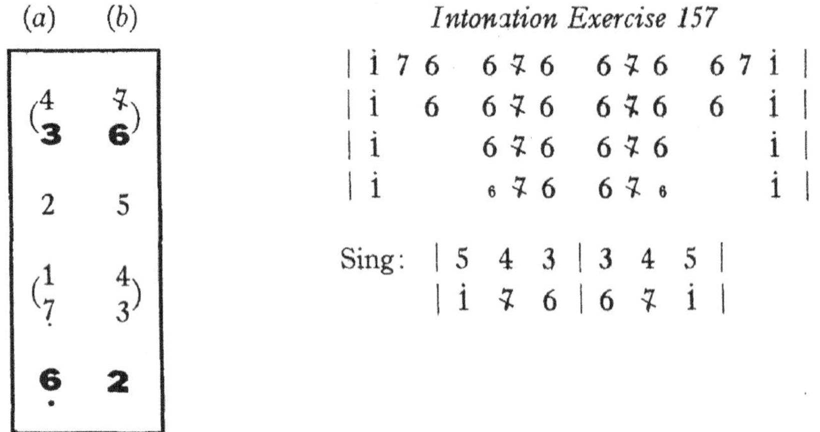

Diagram 78.

Teu sounds like a *fa*.
Teu with La sounds like *fa with mi*.

Using the *Diagrams 77 and 78*, work with the left hand column which represents the intervals that are familiar. Then work with the right hand column which represents the unfamiliar material.

Use Diagram 77

(a) | 1 2 3 4 3 3 4 3 2 1 1 3 4 3 2 1 1 2 1 1 2 3 4 3 2 1 |
(b) | **4 5 6 7 6 6 7 6 5 4 4 6 7 6 5 4 4 5 4 4 5 6 7 6 5 4** |

Use Diagram 78

(a) 6 7 1 2 3 4 3 3 4 3 2 1 7 6 6 1 3 4 3 3 4 3 2 1 2 1 1 2 1 7 6 |
(b) **2 3 4 5 6 7 6 6 7 6 5 4 3 2 2 4 6 7 6 6 7 6 5 4 5 4 4 5 4 3 2** |

Use these diagrams for rapid visualization, moving sometimes along one column and sometimes along the other.

Melody 220 (French), Mode I (2=F)

3/4 || 2 | 6 . . | 5 6 7 | 6 . . | 5 .
5 | 5 . . | 5 4 5 | 6 . . | 7 i 7 | 6 . . | 5 4 5 | 6 . . | X X
2 | 6 . . | 5 6 7 | 6 . . | 5 .
5 | 6 . 5 | 4 . 3 | 2 . 3 | 4 . 5 | 6 . 4 | 5 . . | 6 . . | X X
5 | 6 . 5 | 4 . 3 | 2 . . | . . ||

Composition Forms—Form AA BB

When the first phrase of a melody does not end on the tonic of the mode (*Do* in the major; *La* in the minor) we cannot use the forms *AaBA*, or *ABCA*. We can use the form *ABBC* or the following form: *Aa Bb*.

Example 1

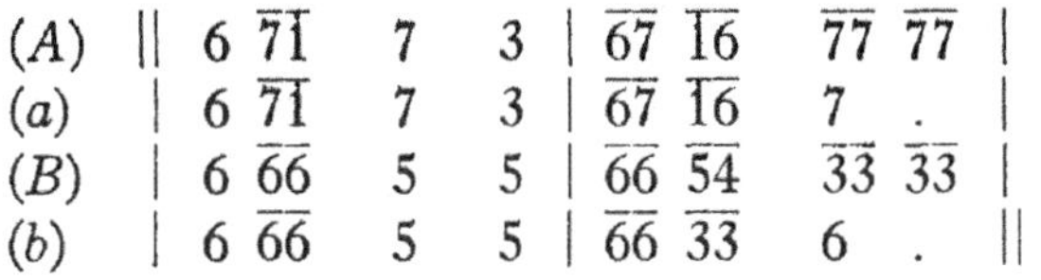

(*A*) ‖ 6 $\overline{7\dot{1}}$ 7 3 | $\overline{67}$ $\overline{\dot{1}6}$ $\overline{77}$ $\overline{77}$ |
(*a*) | 6 $\overline{7\dot{1}}$ 7 3 | $\overline{67}$ $\overline{\dot{1}6}$ 7 . |
(*B*) | 6 $\overline{66}$ 5 5 | $\overline{66}$ $\overline{54}$ $\overline{33}$ $\overline{33}$ |
(*b*) | 6 $\overline{66}$ 5 5 | $\overline{66}$ $\overline{33}$ 6 . ‖

Is the contrast melodic or rhythmic between *A* and *B*?

What likeness is there between *A* and *B*? Between *a* and *b*?

What difference is there between *A* and *a*? *B* and *b*?

Example 2

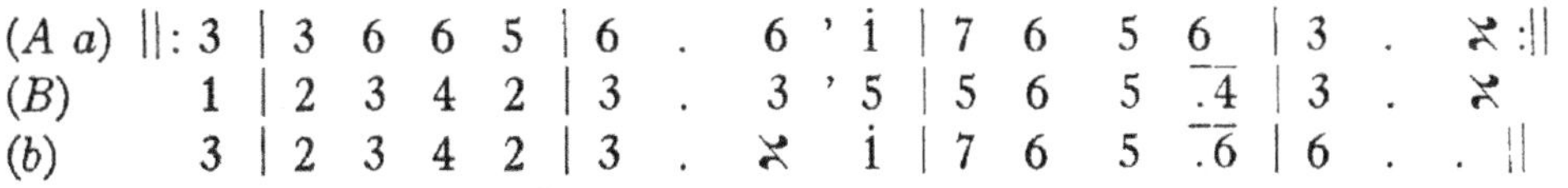

(*A a*) ‖: 3 | 3 6 6 5 | 6 . 6 ' $\dot{1}$ | 7 6 5 $\overline{6}$ | 3 . 𝄽 :‖
(*B*) 1 | 2 3 4 2 | 3 . 3 ' 5 | 5 6 5 $\overline{.4}$ | 3 . 𝄽
(*b*) 3 | 2 3 4 2 | 3 . 𝄽 $\dot{1}$ | 7 6 5 $\overline{.6}$ | 6 . . ‖

Are *B* and *b* exactly alike? Where is the difference? Why did the composer make this change?

Themes to be developed in the Form Aa Bb

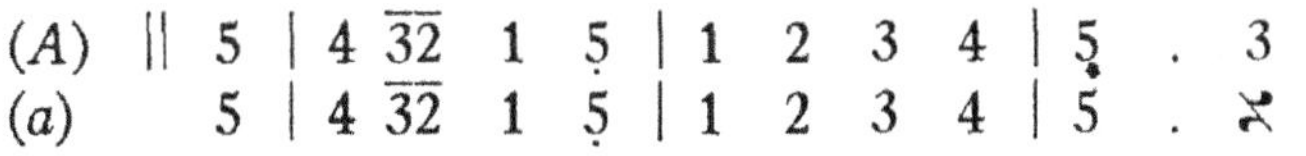

(*A*) ‖ 5 | 4 $\overline{32}$ 1 $\underset{.}{5}$ | 1 2 3 4 | $\underset{.}{5}$. 3
(*a*) 5 | 4 $\overline{32}$ 1 $\underset{.}{5}$ | 1 2 3 4 | $\underset{.}{5}$. 𝄽 (Finish the melody with *B b*)

(*A a*) ‖: $\underset{.}{6}$ $\overline{\underset{.}{6}\underset{.}{7}}$ | 1 $\underset{.}{6}$ | 3 3 | 3 . | 6 3 | $\overline{32}$ $\overline{12}$ | 3 . | . 𝄽 :‖

(Finish the melody with *B b*)

Find several melodies in the Form *AaBb* among those which have been studied in the course of this book.

Little Melodies by Children in the Forms Studied

(Mark the form of each by letters)

Melody 221

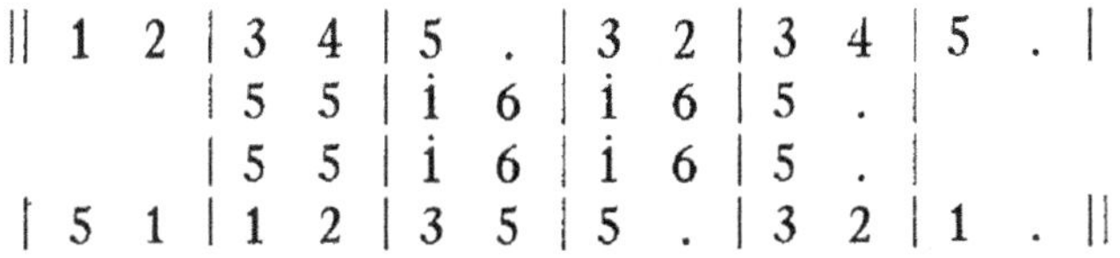

‖ 1 2 | 3 4 | 5 . | 3 2 | 3 4 | 5 . |
| 5 5 | $\dot{1}$ 6 | $\dot{1}$ 6 | 5 . |
| 5 5 | $\dot{1}$ 6 | $\dot{1}$ 6 | 5 . |
| 5 1 | 1 2 | 3 5 | 5 . | 3 2 | 1 . ‖

(Anna Falzoni)

Melody 222

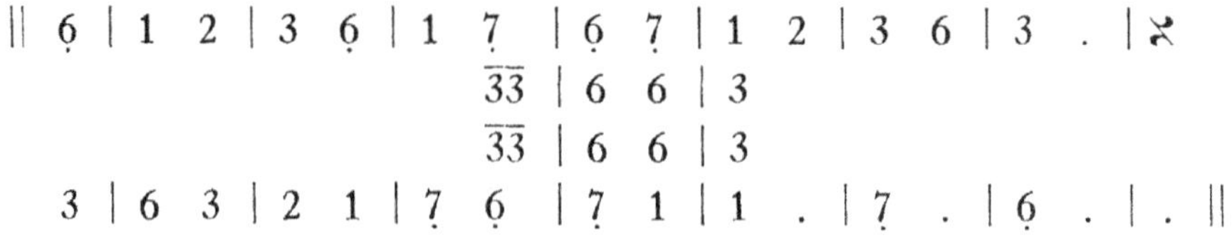

|| 6̣ | 1 2 | 3 6̣ | 1 7̣ | 6̣ 7̣ | 1 2 | 3 6 | 3 . | 𝄽

$\overline{33}$ | 6 6 | 3

$\overline{33}$ | 6 6 | 3

3 | 6 3 | 2 1 | 7̣ 6̣ | 7̣ 1 | 1 . | 7̣ . | 6̣ . | . ||

(Eva Sanaldi)

Melody 223

|| $\overline{17}$ | 6 3 | 6 5 | 4 3 | 3 . | 𝄽

3̇ | 3̇ $\overline{.2}$ | 1̇ 2̇ | 3̇ . | 𝄽

3̇ | 3̇ $\overline{.2}$ | 1̇ 2̇ | 3̇ . | 𝄽

$\overline{34}$ | $\overline{32}$ $\overline{12}$ | 3̇ 6 | 7 . | 6 . | . ||

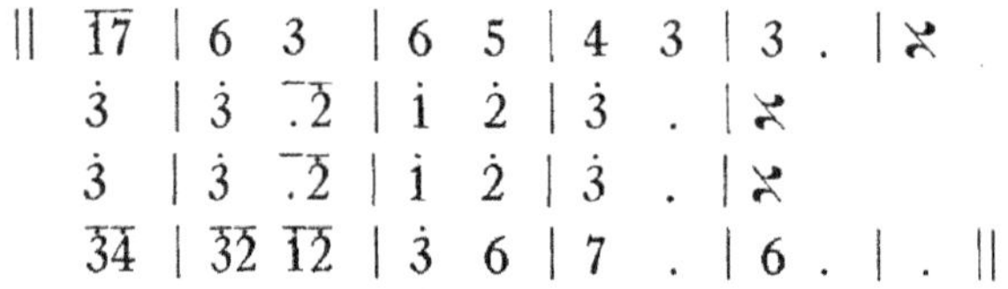

(Elda Traiaglio)

Melody 224

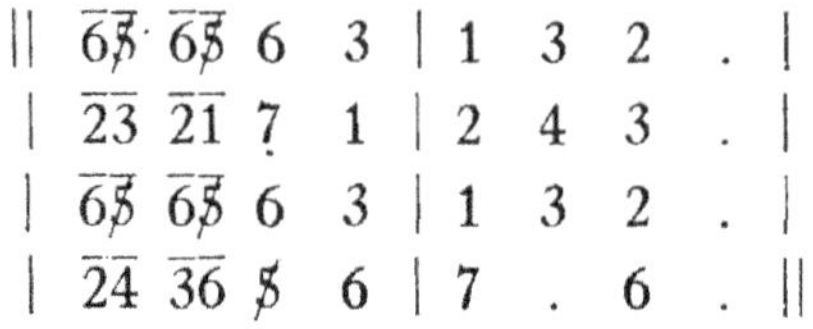

|| $\overline{6\not{5}}$· $\overline{6\not{5}}$ 6 3 | 1 3 2 . |

| $\overline{23}$ $\overline{21}$ 7̣ 1 | 2 4 3 . |

| $\overline{6\not{5}}$ $\overline{6\not{5}}$ 6 3 | 1 3 2 . |

| $\overline{24}$ $\overline{36}$ $\not{5}$ 6 | 7 . 6 . ||

(Angela Propezzi, 7 Years)

Melody 225

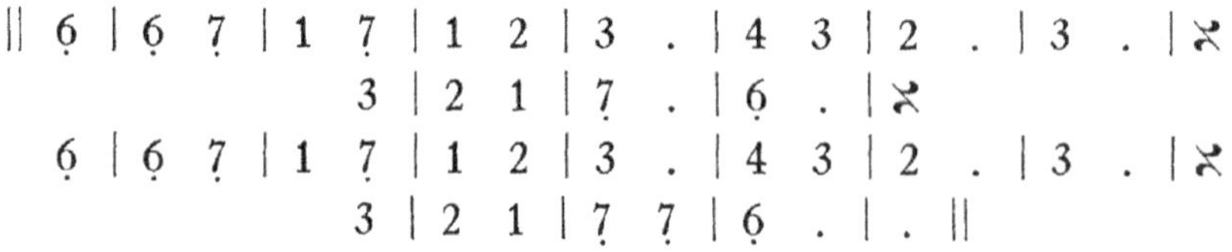

|| 6̣ | 6̣ 7̣ | 1 7̣ | 1 2 | 3 . | 4 3 | 2 . | 3 . | 𝄽

3 | 2 1 | 7̣ . | 6̣ . | 𝄽

6̣ | 6̣ 7̣ | 1 7̣ | 1 2 | 3 . | 4 3 | 2 . | 3 . | 𝄽

3 | 2 1 | 7̣ 7̣ | 6̣ . | . ||

(Giovanna Ferrari)

Melody 226

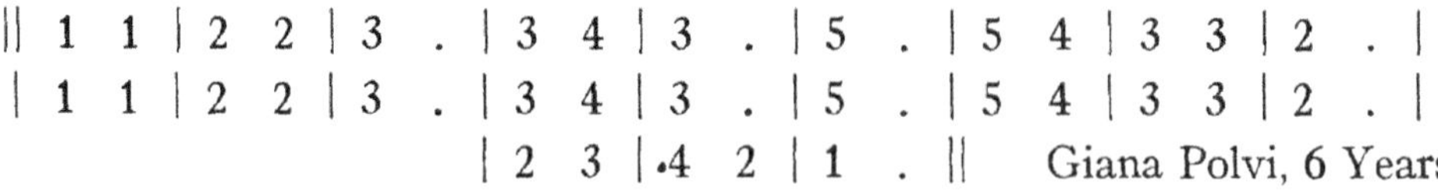

|| 1 1 | 2 2 | 3 . | 3 4 | 3 . | 5 . | 5 4 | 3 3 | 2 . |

| 1 1 | 2 2 | 3 . | 3 4 | 3 . | 5 . | 5 4 | 3 3 | 2 . |

| 2 3 | •4 2 | 1 . || Giana Polvi, 6 Years)

Study Melodies 227 and 228, Children's Manual, page 89.

Begin Study of the Credo, Children's Manual, page 102.

Intonation Exercise 158

Vocal Exercises.—The special exercises (page 194) should be written on the board and sung. After study and comparison has been made between 3 4 3 and 6 7̶ 6 the exercise may be written as follows:

|| 2 | 6 5 | 4 3 | 2 . | . ||

|| 2 | 6 7̶ | 6 5 | 4 3 | 2 . | . ||

Intonation. The Accidental Flat.—The rule for singing the accidental flat correctly is to make it lean upon the note below: as *fa* depends upon *mi*, so 7̶ must depend upon 6. This is a rule for singing true to pitch. We must either *sing* or *think la* after 7̶. This habit which the children form in regard to the one flat presented in the Second Book will apply to all flats to be studied later.

The introduction of *Teu* at this point is merely a foundation laid for the more detailed use to be made of this note in the third year: on the one hand, as an element of modulation; on the other hand, as necessary to the study of the First Mode in Gregorian Chant. As used in this chapter, the likeness between 343 and 67̶6 is the point stressed. This will be sufficient as a preliminary notion.

In this way, the children will discover that there is another "family"—the

Family of Re. In many ways it resembles the *La Family.* In the *Re Family,* we use sometimes 7̸ and at other times 7. (See Melody 220, page 196.)

Continue the study of Form.

Mark the form of each melody used in this chapter.

Staff Notation.—Teu on the staff is indicated by a flat placed before the note (see page 195). Exception to this rule: when the tone in question is already sharpened at the key signature, in which case the lowering of the tone is indicated by a natural. (See Intonation Exercise 158, page 199.)

Dictation

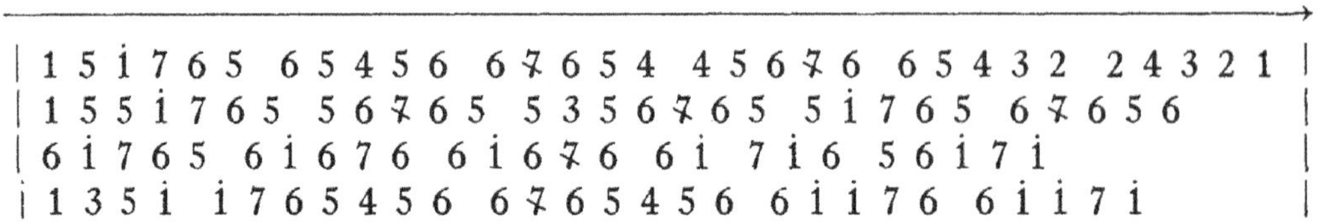

| 1 5 1̇ 7 6 5 6 5 4 5 6 6 7̸ 6 5 4 4 5 6 7̸ 6 6 5 4 3 2 2 4 3 2 1 |
| 1 5 5 1̇ 7 6 5 5 6 7̸ 6 5 5 3 5 6 7̸ 6 5 5 1̇ 7 6 5 6 7̸ 6 5 6 |
| 6 1̇ 7 6 5 6 1̇ 6 7 6 6 1̇ 6 7̸ 6 6 1̇ 7 1̇ 6 5 6 1̇ 7 1̇ |
| 1 3 5 1̇ 1̇ 7 6 5 4 5 6 6 7̸ 6 5 4 5 6 6 1̇ 1̇ 7 6 6 1̇ 1̇ 7 1̇ |

Melody and Rhythm

‖ 1 2 | 3 4 | 3 . |
| 4 5 | 6 7̸ | 6 . |
| 6 5 | 4 5 | 6 . |
| 6 1̇ | 6 5 | 4 . |
| 6 5 | 4 3 | 2 . ‖

‖ 1 5̣ 5 4 | 3 4 5 . |
| 5 6 7̸ 6 | 5 . 5 . |
| 5 1̇ 1̇ 7 | 1̇ 6 5 . |
| 5 6 7̸ 6 | 5 . 4 . |
| 4 6 1̇ 7 | 1̇ 6 5 . |
| 5 1 4 3 | 2 . 1 . ‖

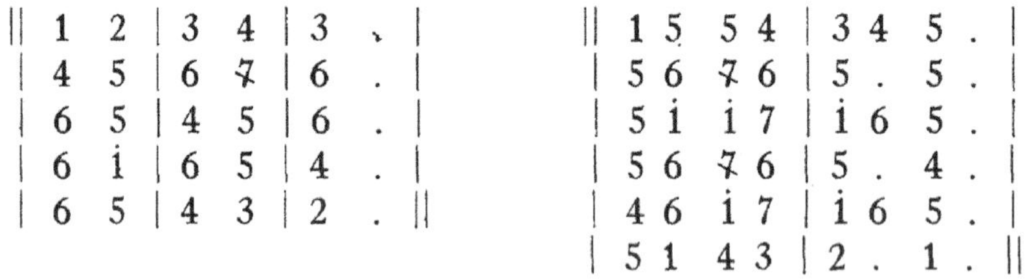

The teacher should also give some exercises on the models:

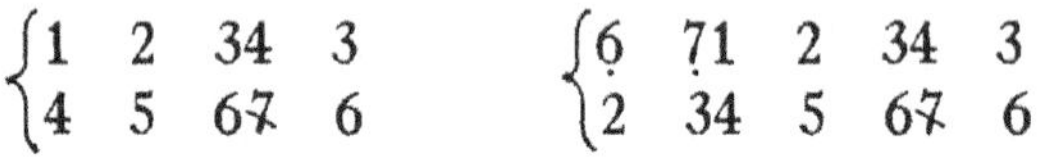

{ 1 2 34 3
{ 4 5 67̸ 6

{ 6̣ 7̣1 2 34 3
{ 2 34 5 67̸ 6

in the sense that, hearing one of these models, melodically, the children should be able to give *both solutions* (the upper or lower form). When they hear the *Tetrachord,* they know that it can be one of *two things,* and should be able to give *both answers.* The same is true for the *Hexachord* given above. For the moment, the teacher will be wise to give these models exactly in their original form, without varying the order in which the tones are dictated.

CHAPTER TWENTY-EIGHT

Vocal Exercise: || 6 7 6 . i 7 6 5 | 6 . . 7 ||
Na- o Nu no na.

Begin on A flat, A, B flat, C, C sharp, D.

Intonation.—The First Mode.

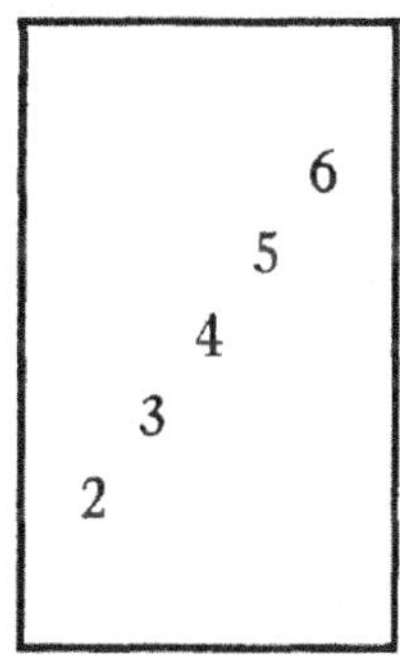

Diagram 79a.

Model: 6 7i 2 3
2 34 5 6

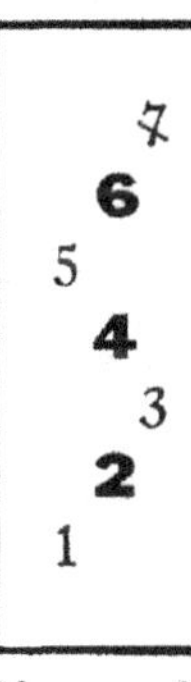

Diagram 80.

This part of the *Re family* is similar to the *La family*.

Melody and Rhythm

a || 2 1 | 4 5 | 4 6 | 6 . | 6 5 | 3 4 | 5 6 | 4 3 | 2 . | 2 . ||
b || 6 5 | 1 2 | 1 3 | 3 . | 3 2 | 7 1 | 2 3 | 1 7 | 6 . | 6 . ||

(Use Diagram 79) *Intonation Exercise 159 (2=A or G)* (Use Diagram 80)

2 3 4 5 6 6 6	6 5 4 3 2 2 2	6 2		2 3 4 4 5 6	6 5 4 4 3 2	1 2 2
2 2 2 3 4 5 6	6 6 6 5 4 3 2	6 2		2 4 4 6	6 4 4 2	1 2 2
2 3 4 4 5 6	6 5 4 4 3 2	6 2		2 4 6	6 4 2	1 2 2

Melody and Rhythm

|| 2 . | 1 2 | 3 4 | 5 . | 4 3 | 2 . | 1 . |
| 4 5 | 6 5 | 4 5 | 4 . | 4 5 | 3 4 | 2 . | 2 . ||

|| 2 4 | 2 1 | 4 5 | 4 6 | 6 . | 6 5 | 3 4 | 5 6 | 4 3 | 2 . | 2 . ||
| 4 2 | 4 5 | 6 5 | 4 5 | 4 . | 4 5 | 3 4 | 2 . | 2 . |

The *Re family* resembles the *La family* in the Pentachord: 2 34 5 6
6̣ 7̣1 2 3

It also resembles the *La family* in the Hexachord: 2 34 5 67̸ (6)
6̣ 7̣1 2 34 (3)

But, that the resemblance be perfect, we must use 7̸ and not 7.
The *Re family differs* from the *La family* when we use the note 7.

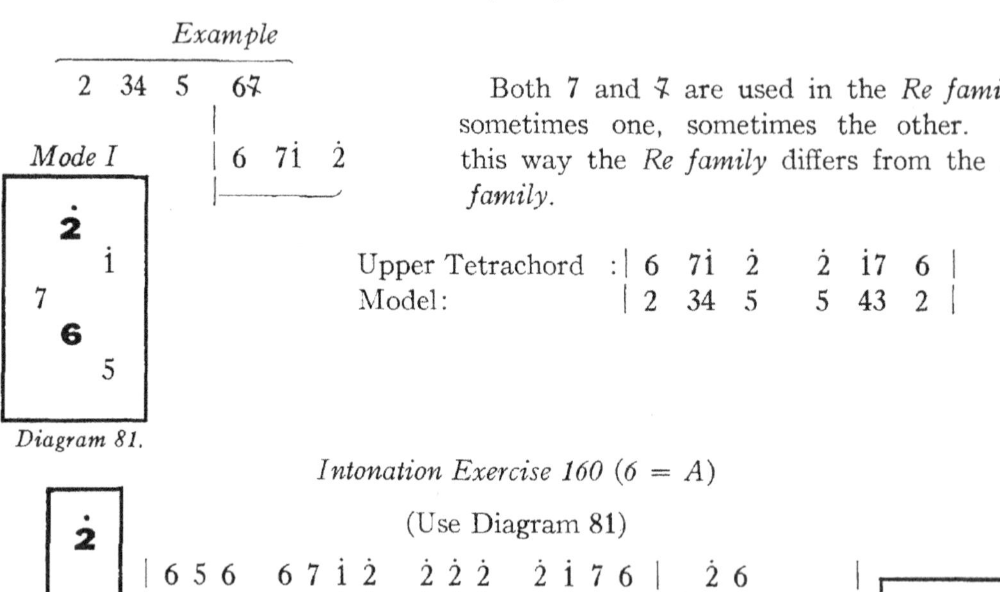

Diagram 81.

Both 7 and 7̸ are used in the *Re family;* sometimes one, sometimes the other. In this way the *Re family* differs from the *La family.*

Upper Tetrachord :| 6 71̇ 2̇ 2̇ 1̇7 6 |
Model: | 2 34 5 5 43 2 |

Intonation Exercise 160 (*6* = *A*)

(Use Diagram 81)

| 6 5 6 6 7 1̇ 2̇ 2̇ 2̇ 2̇ 2̇ 1̇ 7 6 | 2̇ 6 |
| 6 5 6 6 1̇ 2̇ 2̇ 1̇ 2̇ 2̇ 1̇ 7 6 | 1̇ 2̇ 6 5 6 |

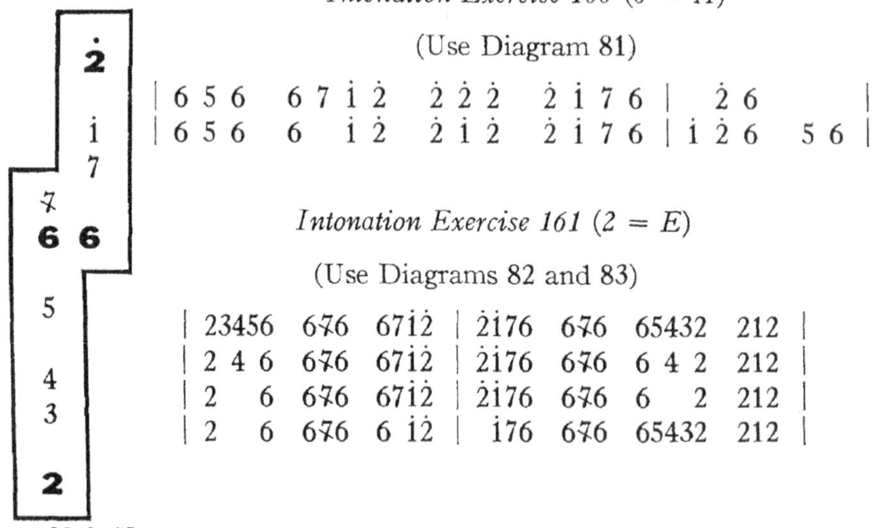

Mode 2I
Diagram 8a.

Intonation Exercise 161 (*2* = *E*)

(Use Diagrams 82 and 83)

23456 67̸6 671̇2̇	2̇1̇76 67̸6 65432 212
2 4 6 67̸6 671̇2̇	2̇1̇76 67̸6 6 4 2 212
2 6 67̸6 671̇2̇	2̇1̇76 67̸6 6 2 212
2 6 67̸6 6 1̇2̇	1̇76 67̸6 65432 212

2̇
1̇
7
7̸
6
5
4
3
2
1

Mode I
Diagram 83.

Melody and Rhythm

```
|| 21 | 45 | 46 | 6. | 65 | 34 | 56 | 43 | 2. | 2. ||
|| 21 | 45 | 46 | 6. | 61̇ | 66 | 56 | 54 | 45 | 5. | 345 | 43 | 2. | 2. ||
|| 21 | 45 | 46 | 6. | 61̇ | 71̇ | 65 | 45 | 5. | 53 | 43 | 2. | 2. ||
|| 21 | 45 | 46 | 6. | 67 | 1̇7 | 1̇2̇1̇ | 676 | 6. | 65 | 65 | 4. | 345 | 43 | 2. | 2. ||
|| 21 | 45 | 46 | 6. | 67 | 6. | 65 | 61̇ | 1̇2̇ | 1̇7 | 5. | .6 | 54 | 345 | 43 | 2. ||
```

```
|| 2 4 2 1 | 4 5 6 . |
 | 6 1̇ 6 5 | 5 6 6 . |
 | 6 1̇ 2̇ 1̇ | 1̇ 7 6 . |
 | 6 7̸ 6 5 | 4 5 4 . |
 | 4 5 3 4 | 2 . 2 . ||
```

```
|| 21 23 45 67̸ 65 6. 43 21 2. ||
|| 21 26 67̸ 65 6. 43 21 2. ||
|| 21 26 61̇ 65 67̸ 6. 65 43 2. ||
 | 21 26 67 1̇6 67̸ 6. 61̇ 2̇1̇ 76 6. 65 43 21 2. ||
```

Melody, Rhythm and Words

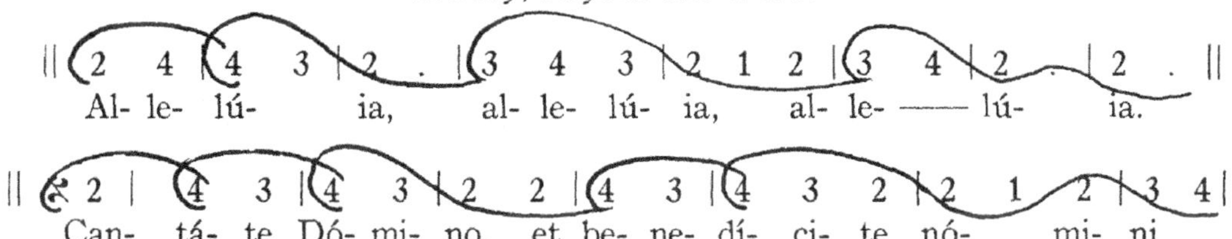

| 2 . | 2 . ||
é- jus.

Study Laudemus Dómino, Children's Manual, page 124.

Diagram 79b Diagram 79c Diagram 79d

Diagram 82b Diagram 82c

Study Melodies 229, 230, 231, page 90; *232, 233, 234,* page 91, Children's Manual.

Dictation (Mode I)

(Teacher announces "Re")

(*a*)
| 2 3 4 5 6 |
| 6 5 4 3 2 |
| 2 3 2 1 2 |
| 2 3 4 3 2 |
| 2 3 4 3 2 1 2 |
| 2 4 4 3 2 1 2 |
| 2 1 2 4 3 2 |

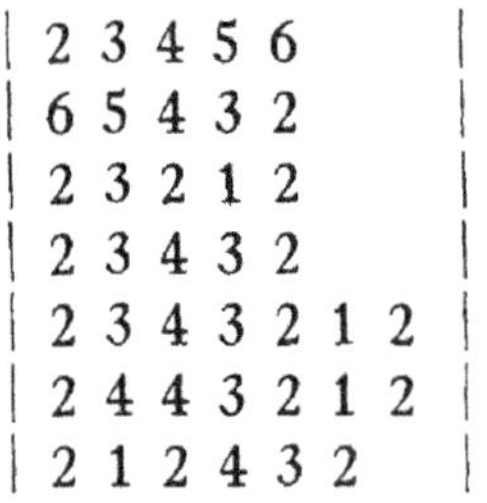

(*b*)
| 2 3 4 5 6 |
| 6 5 4 3 2 |
| 2 4 6 5 6 |
| 2 4 6 7̸ 6 |
| 2 6 7̸ 6 5 6 |
| 2 6 5 4 3 2 |
| 2 6 7̸ 6 5 4 3 2 |

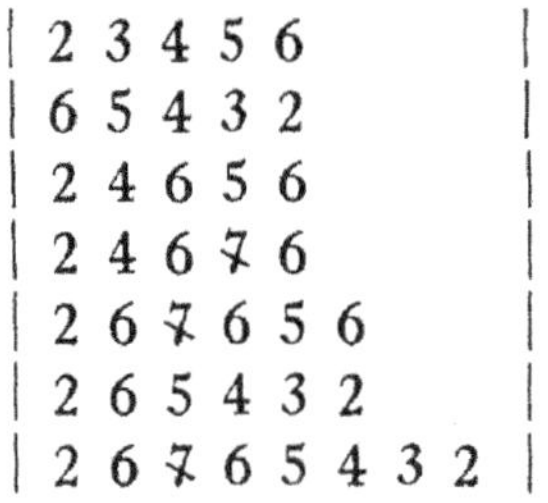

(*c*)
| 2 3 4 5 6 5 4 |
| 4 5 6 5 4 3 2 |
| 4 5 6 5 6 7̸ 6 |
| 6 7̸ 6 5 4 5 6 |
| 6 1̇ 1̇ 7 6 5 6 |
| 6 1̇ 6 5 6 5 4 |
| 6 1̇ 6 7̸ 6 5 4 |
| 4 5 4 3 2 1 2 |

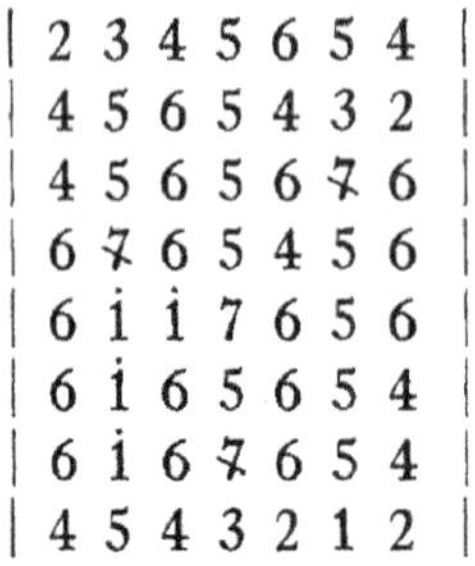

(*d*)
| 6 7 1̇ 7 6 7 6 |
| 6 1̇ 1̇ 2̇ 1̇ 7 6 |
| 6 7̸ 6 5 4 3 2 |
| 2 6 1̇ 6 5 6 6 |
| 2 6 1̇ 2̇ 1̇ 7 6 |
| 6 1̇ 2̇ 1̇ 6 7 6 |
| 6 7̸ 6 5 6 5 4 |
| 4 5 3 4 2 1 2 |

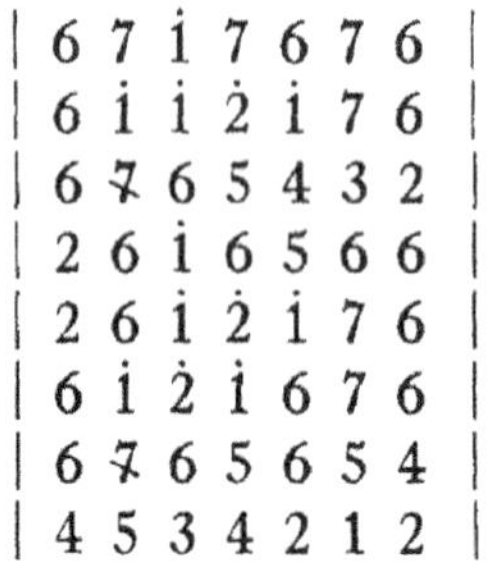

Visualization

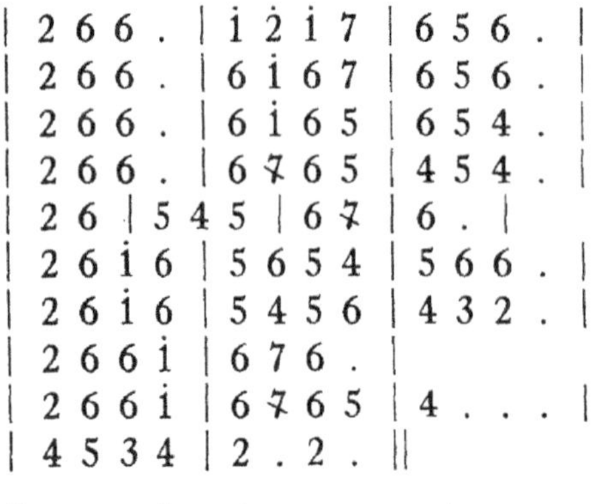

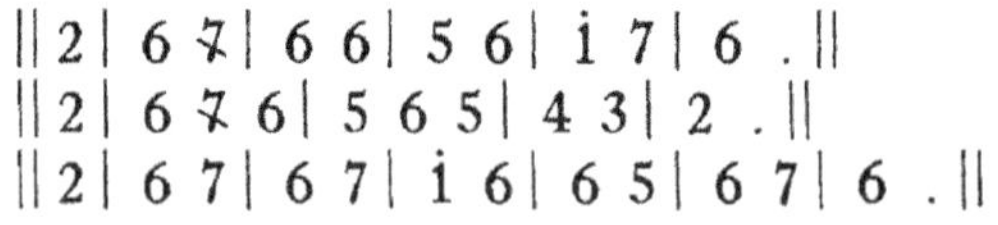

2 6 6 .	1̇ 2̇ 1̇ 7	6 5 6 .
2 6 6 .	6 1̇ 6 7	6 5 6 .
2 6 6 .	6 1̇ 6 5	6 5 4 .
2 6 6 .	6 7̸ 6 5	4 5 4 .
2 6	5 4 5	6 7̸	6 .
2 6 1̇ 6	5 6 5 4	5 6 6 .
2 6 1̇ 6	5 4 5 6	4 3 2 .
2 6 6 1̇	6 7 6 .
2 6 6 1̇	6 7̸ 6 5	4 . . .
4 5 3 4	2 . 2 .	

	2	6 7̸	6 6	5 6	1̇ 7	6 .	
	2	6 7̸ 6	5 6 5	4 3	2 .	
	2	6 7	6 7	1̇ 6	6 5	6 7	6 .	

Melody and Rhythm

	2 4 2 1	4 5 6 .
6 1̇ 6 5	4 5 6 .
6 7̸ 6 5	4 5 4 .
4 5 3 4	2 . 2 .	

	2 6 1̇ 6	5 6 6 .
4 5 6 5	4 . . x
2 6 1̇ 2̇	1̇ 7 6 .
1̇ 6 5 6	6 . . x
6 7 1̇ 7	1̇ 2̇ 6 x
6 2 4 3	2 . . x

|| 2 | 3 4 | 5 3 | 4 3 | 2 . | .
2 | 4 5 | 6 5 | 6 7̸ | 6 . | .
6 | 6 1̇ | 6 5 | 6 7̸ | 6 . | .
6 | 4 5 | 3 4 | 2 1 | 2 . | . ||

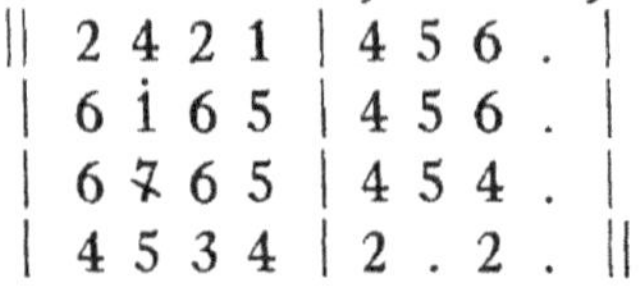

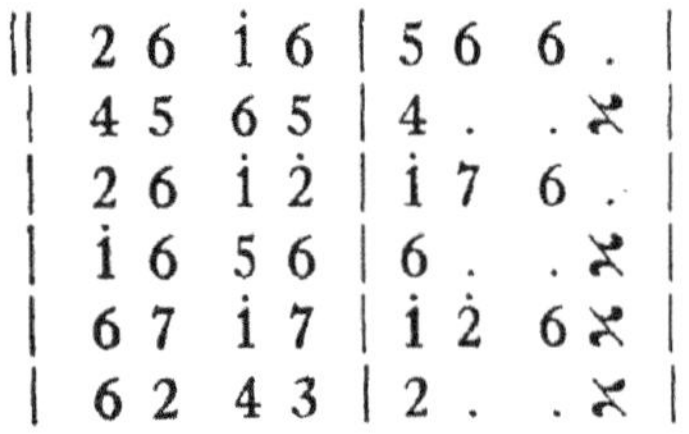

(*Use also for aural memory*)

CHAPTER TWENTY-NINE

Vocal Exercises || 6 3 | 5 6 | 6 . ||
No- a na- o nu

La = : *G*, *A*♭, *A*, *B*♭, *B*, *C*, *C*♯, *D*, *E*♭ and *E*.

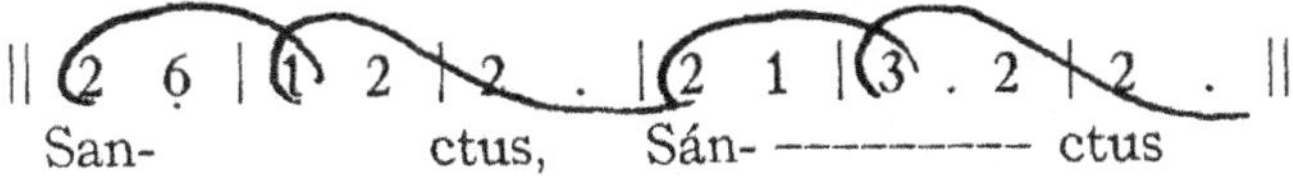

Re = : *G*, *A*♭, *A*, *B*♭, *B*, *C*, *C*♯, *D*, *E*♭ and *E*.

Intonation.—Mode of Re, Plagal Form (Mode II)

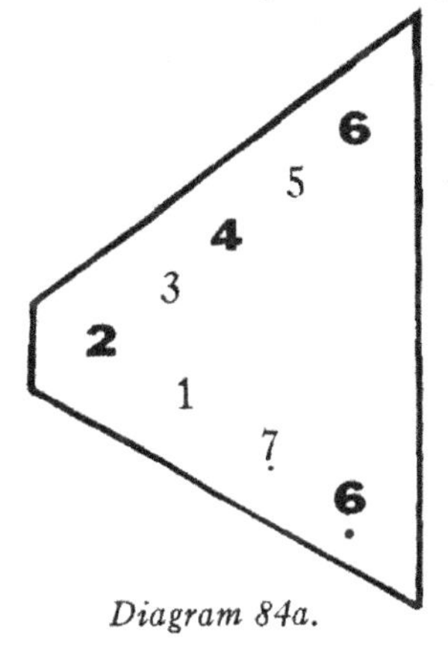

Diagram 84a.

Diagram 84b.

The Second Mode and the Minor Mode Compared:

Likeness: The Pentachord

2 34 5 6
6 71 2 3

Difference: The Tetrachords.

2 17 6
6 5 43
6$\not{5}$ 43

This tetrachord: 2 17 6 is not like anything in the *La Family*.

If we were to use $\not{7}$ (2 1 $\not{7}$6) the tetrachord would sound like 6 5 43. But this is never done. The $\not{7}$ is used only in the *upper* tetrachord (First Mode). We never find it in the tetrachord *below* the *Re*.

This tetrachord sounds like {5 43 2 / 2 17̣ 6̣}

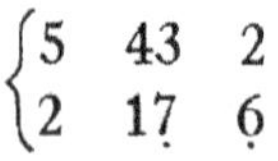

Intonation Exercise 162a (2 = A)

(Use Diagrams 84 *a* and *b*)

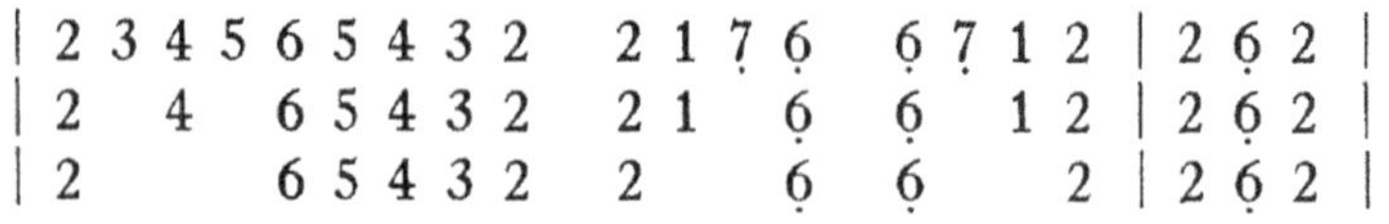

2 3 4 5 6 5 4 3 2 2 1 7̣ 6̣ 6̣ 7̣ 1 2	2 6̣ 2
2 4 6 5 4 3 2 2 1 6̣ 6̣ 1 2	2 6̣ 2
2 6 5 4 3 2 2 6̣ 6̣ 2	2 6̣ 2

Intonation Exercise 162b (2 = G)

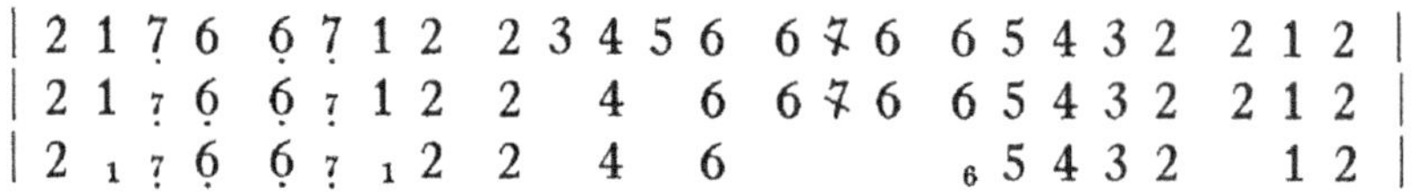

| 2 1 7̣ 6̣   6̣ 7̣ 1 2   2 3 4 5 6   6 7̸ 6   6 5 4 3 2   2 1 2 |
| 2 1 7̣ 6̣   6̣ 7̣ 1 2   2   4   6   6 7̸ 6   6 5 4 3 2   2 1 2 |
| 2 1 7̣ 6̣   6̣ 7̣ 1 2   2   4   6   6 5 4 3 2   1 2 |

Melody and Rhythm (2 = G)

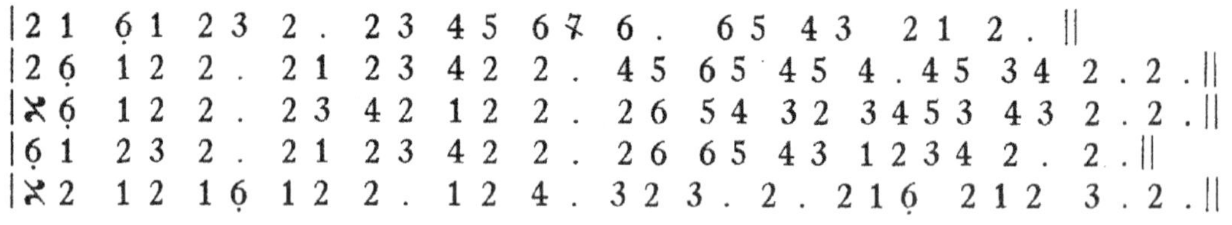

2 1 6̣ 1 2 3 2 . 2 3 4 5 6 7̸ 6 . 6 5 4 3 2 1 2 .	
2 6̣ 1 2 2 . 2 1 2 3 4 2 2 . 4 5 6 5 4 5 4 . 4 5 3 4 2 . 2 .	
x 6̣ 1 2 2 . 2 3 4 2 1 2 2 . 2 6 5 4 3 2 3 4 5 3 4 3 2 . 2 .	
6̣ 1 2 3 2 . 2 1 2 3 4 2 2 . 2 6 6 5 4 3 1 2 3 4 2 . 2 .	
x 2 1 2 1 6̣ 1 2 2 . 1 2 4 . 3 2 3 . 2 . 2 1 6̣ 2 1 2 3 . 2 .	

*Study the Sanctus,** Children's Manual, page 110.

Melody 235 Basque (2 = A)

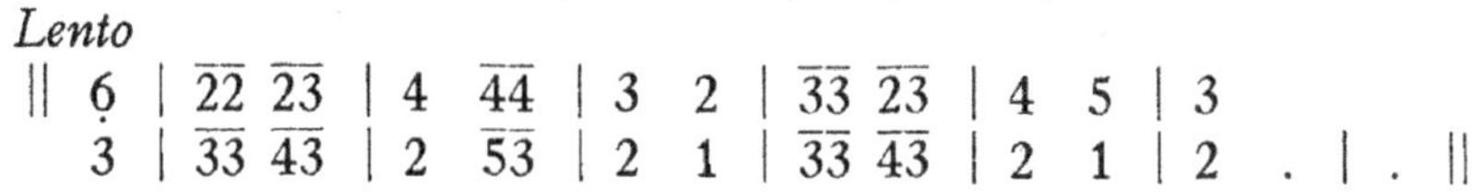

Lento

|| 6̣ | $\overline{22}$ $\overline{23}$ | 4 $\overline{44}$ | 3 2 | $\overline{33}$ $\overline{23}$ | 4 5 | 3
3 | $\overline{33}$ $\overline{43}$ | 2 $\overline{53}$ | 2 1 | $\overline{33}$ $\overline{43}$ | 2 1 | 2 . | . ||

Study Melodies 236, page **92**; *237*, *238*, *239*, *240*, page 93; *241*, *242*, *243*, page **94,** Children's Manual.

* This Sanctus is given in two forms: (a) with *La* as tonic, (b) with *Re* as tonic. With this particular melody, the intervals remain unchanged, and the presentation in the *Form a* makes it possible for the children to study this melody somewhat earlier in the year. The presentation in *Form b* should be used after the children have studied the Second Mode as presented in this chapter.

Vocal Exercises.—Special to this chapter. The exercise beginning 6 3 5 6 6 . prepares the pupil's mind for the intonation of the *Sanctus:* 2 6̣ 1 2 2 . which is characteristic of the Second Mode.

Intonation. The Mode of Re in Plagal Form.—The Pentachord 2 34 5 6 is similar to the minor Pentachord: 6 71̇ 2̇ 3̇. The latter should be sung as a preparation for the new mode, which will be studied from *Diagram 84a.* Taking intervals that are already familiar in the minor pentachord, we substitute *Re* for *La:*

Example (2 = A or G)

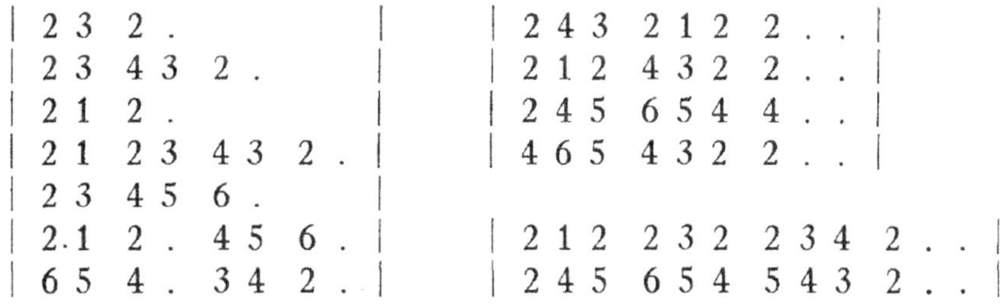

```
| 2 3  2 .            |     | 2 4 3  2 1 2  2 . . |
| 2 3  4 3  2 .       |     | 2 1 2  4 3 2  2 . . |
| 2 1  2 .            |     | 2 4 5  6 5 4  4 . . |
| 2 1  2 3  4 3  2 .  |     | 4 6 5  4 3 2  2 . . |
| 2 3  4 5  6 .       |
| 2.1  2 .  4 5  6 .  |     | 2 1 2  2 3 2  2 3 4  2 . . |
| 6 5  4 .  3 4  2 .  |     | 2 4 5  6 5 4  5 4 3  2 . . |
```

Phrases such as these should be used for observation and memory, for ear tests, etc. When *Diagram 84a* has served to lay a good foundation, *Diagram 84b* should be used in the same manner.

The *lower tetrachord:* 2 17̣ 6̣ is quite unlike the *minor mode*, and will need to be prepared carefully on the diagram. Going from the familiar to the unfamiliar, the teacher may begin as follows:

(2 = D)

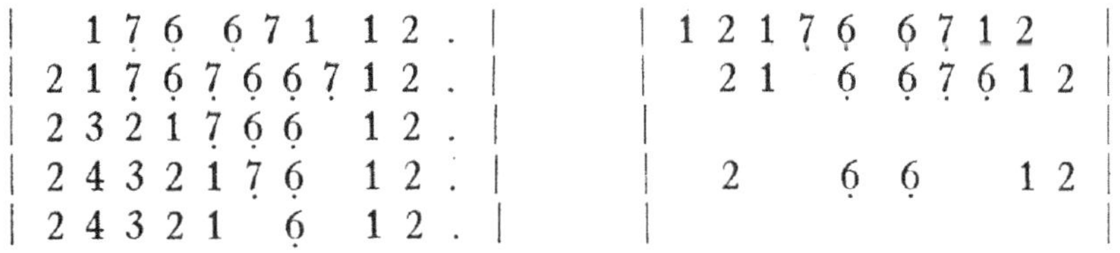

```
|   1 7̣ 6̣  6̣ 7̣ 1  1 2 . |     | 1 2 1 7̣ 6̣  6̣ 7̣ 1 2   |
| 2 1 7̣ 6̣ 7̣ 6̣ 6̣ 7̣ 1 2 . |     |   2 1   6̣  6̣ 7̣ 6̣ 1 2 |
| 2 3 2 1 7̣ 6̣ 6̣   1 2 . |     |                      |
| 2 4 3 2 1 7̣ 6̣   1 2 . |     |   2     6̣  6̣     1 2 |
| 2 4 3 2 1   6̣   1 2 . |     |                      |
```

Then unite the pentachord and tetrachord. (See *Intonation Exercise 162a and b.*) The phrases under *Melody and Rhythm* are typical of the mode. The "7̣" is often omitted in the lower tetrachord of the Second Mode.

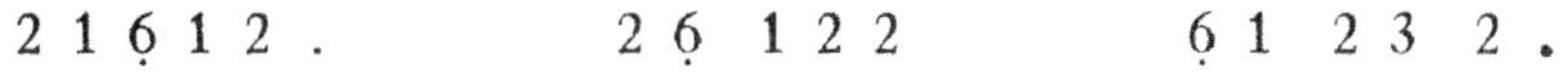

2 1 6̣ 1 2 .   2 6̣ 1 2 2   6̣ 1 2 3 2 .

As regards the Hexachord based on *Re*, the pupils should be able to sing both forms:

| 2 34 5 67̶ |
| 2 34 5 6 7 |

The former is considered less harsh than the latter. For the moment, the teacher will do well to avoid using the direct relation between *fa* and *ti*.

The direct relation between *fa* and *ti* can be avoided as follows:

(*a*) By substituting *teu* for *ti* (4 5 6 7̶ 6 rather than: 4 5 6 7 6).
(*b*) By using a melodic detour: (4 5 6 1̇ 7, 7 1̇ 6 5 4, etc.).
(*c*) By placing *fa* and *ti* on non-ictic notes:

|| 5 4 | 5 . | 6 7 | 6 . | 5 . ||

The direct relation is, in a sense, hidden, and the effect of the harsh relation between *fa* and *ti* is mitigated.

These general rules will be of use to the teacher when using the Diagrams, when giving ear tests or examples for visualization. These laws are not absolute. We will find many exceptions notably in Gregorian and Ambrosian melodies where the descending passage: 7 6 5 4 . is not only tolerated but used profusely.

Rhythm: 3/2 Time.—This is a slow ternary movement of which each unit is equal to a half-note. Thus we may analyse it into three groups of 2/4 time by inserting temporary bars, as in the first phrase of *Melody 240*, which follows:

|| 2 ‾.3 | 4 . ⁝ 2 . ⁝ 6̣ . | 2 ‾.3 ⁝ 2 . ⁝

When the melody has been grasped in 2/4 time, the bars represented by the dotted lines should be erased.

As a matter of fact, the chironomy brings out the phrasing so clearly that it makes little difference whether we write our subdivisions in terms of 3/2 or 2/4 time. Our purpose in including this example, is that the children may not feel puzzled should they find melodies with "3/2" at the clef.

Continue the study of the Mass.

CHAPTER THIRTY

Intonation.—Review the Modes studied during Music Second Year.

I. How do we recognize a melody in the *Major Mode?*

Make a Diagram of the *Do Family* showing the strong tones and the weak ones.

(*a*) in the range: 1 - 8 . *Authentic.*

(*b*) in the range: $\underset{\cdot}{5}$ - 5 *Plagal.*

Place each of these forms on the staff with the *C clef* in an appropriate position.

II. How do we recognize a melody in the *Minor Mode?*

Make a diagram of the *La Family* showing the strong tones and the weak ones.

(*a*) In the range: $\underset{\cdot}{6}$ - 6 *Authentic.*

(*b*) In the range: 3 - $\dot{3}$ *Plagal.*

Place each of these forms on the staff with the *C clef* in an appropriate position.

What tone do we find in the *modern minor mode* which we do not find in any of the other modes studied hitherto?

How do we write this tone in number notation? How do we cancel the "accidental"? In staff notation, how do we write this tone? and how do we cancel the "accidental"?

III. How do we recognize a melody in the *Mode of Sol?*

Make a diagram of the *Sol Family* showing the strong tones and the weak ones.

(*a*) In the range: $\underset{\cdot}{5}$ - 5 *Authentic. Mode VII.*

(*b*) In the range: 2 - $\dot{2}$ *Plagal. Mode VIII.*

What is the difference between the $\underset{\cdot}{5}$ - 5 range (Major Mode, Plagal) and the $\underset{\cdot}{5}$ - 5 range (*Mode of Sol, Authentic*)? The notes contained in these two scales are identical. What gives a different impression to the ear? Compare the two diagrams: are the strong notes in one of these forms the same as in the other?

IV. How do we recognize a melody in the *Mode of Re?*

Make a diagram of the *Re Family* showing the strong and weak tones:

(*a*) In the range: 2 – 2̇ *Authentic. Mode I.*
(*b*) In the range: 6̣ – 6 *Plagal. Mode II.*

What *accidental* tone do we find, at times, in the *Modes of Re*?

How do we write this "accidental" in number notation? and how do we cancel it? How do we write it on the staff? and how do we cancel it?

What is the difference between the range 6̣ – 6 in *Mode II*, *Plagal form*, and the range 6̣ – 6 in the Minor Mode, *authentic*. The notes are identical: what is it that gives a different impression to the ear? Compare the diagrams of the two: what are the strong tones in the minor mode? In the Plagal form of the *Re Mode*?

What is the difference between the 2 –2̇ range of Mode I and the 2 – 2̇ range of Mode VIII, plagal?

These Review questions should not take the form of a dry examination, but should be developed on the board in a living way. The musical facts in question have already been applied in the daily work. They are a matter of personal experience to the children. We can now draw their attention to what they already know, codify it, and make it available.

There are two things to notice in the study of modality: one is, the actual tones which make up a mode, and the extension of that mode. The other, and far the more important point, is to discern the functioning of these tones in relation to their surroundings. For instance: We have before us a melody in a range of *sol* – *sol*. (5̣ 6̣ 7̣ 1 2 3 4 5). It will contain the notes between brackets above. But this fact is relatively insignificant. What we need to know is the manner in which these tones *function*.

Is *sol* a *tonic*, or is it a *dominant?*

On the answer to this first question will depend the answer to all the others: what are the strong and weak tones of the mode? Are they *do* (*mi*) *sol* of the *major mode*, or *sol* (*si*) *re* of the *modes of sol?* Is the *Tonic* at the *base of the mode?* or *in its center*? Musically, there is a great difference between the two: in one case we radiate from a center, moving above and below it and being drawn back as by magnetism. This is the characteristic of the Plagal form of a mode. In the other case, our adventure consists in moving toward a central *dominant*; and from that point returning to a tonic either at the base or at the top of our range.

The utility of the *Diagrams* in this connection is evident. They not only give us the range, but—far more important—they give us a clear visual image of the function of each tone in relation to the others: the *tonic* and the *strong tones* along the central column; the dependent tones grouped about them. Thus: the *sol–sol range* in the *major mode* and in the *seventh mode* contains the same notes, materially; but the Diagrams show us the different importance of these notes and their function in the particular mode to which they belong.

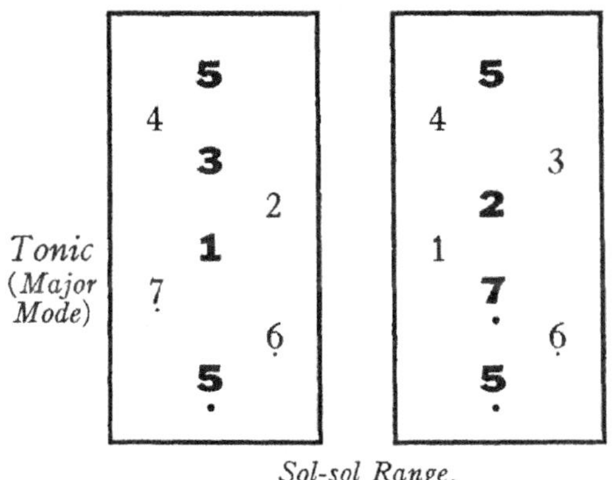

Tonic (Mode VII)

Sol-sol Range.

The central column contains the tones characteristic of the Mode.

The tones that are structural in one mode become secondary, dependent tones in the other.

In composition, to affirm clearly the modality in which we are writing, means to move along the central column of our modal diagram until the characteristic notes of the mode have become plain.

We do not need to affirm this *at once* unless we wish to. Some melodies leave us in suspense for a while, but always, at some time in the melody, we must bring out the modality quite definitely.

This may be done by *scale progression* or else by *chord progression.* When we wish to make the modality plain, we place one of tones of the central column on the first note of each group in our measures. For contrast, on the other hand, we avoid this use of the central column.

As a general rule, our melody should finish on the *tonic of the mode.* It need not *begin* on the tonic.

Exercise in Discerning the Modality

(*a*) *From the opening phrase**

|| 3 .2 34 5 | 1 5̣ 1 2 | 3 . . . |
|| 6 | 6 3 6 7 | 1̇ .2̇ 1̇
|| 56 77 27 66 | 1̇ 1̇ 7 . |
|| 24 65 | 43 2 |
|| 2 | 67 62 | 17 65 | 6

(*b*) *From the final cadence.*

| 5 1 7̣1 2 | 1 . . . ||
| 3 6 6 ♯5 | 6 . . . ||
| 5 6 7 6 | 5 . . . ||
2 | 1 2 4 3 | 2 . . . ||

*When the opening phrase of a melody does not disclose the modality plainly, the children should look at the final cadence which closes the last phrase. Here they will find the modality clearly affirmed.

The children will not require much *theoretical drill* on these points but will need to have their attention called to points which have already been applied. They may require some little steadying influence: for it is not a good thing to move from one modality to another *unintentionally*, as happens to the children, occasionally, for lack of proper guidance.

Dictation

To what mode do the following phrases belong?

This dictation should be given with the diagrams of the modes in plain view that the eye may aid the ear.

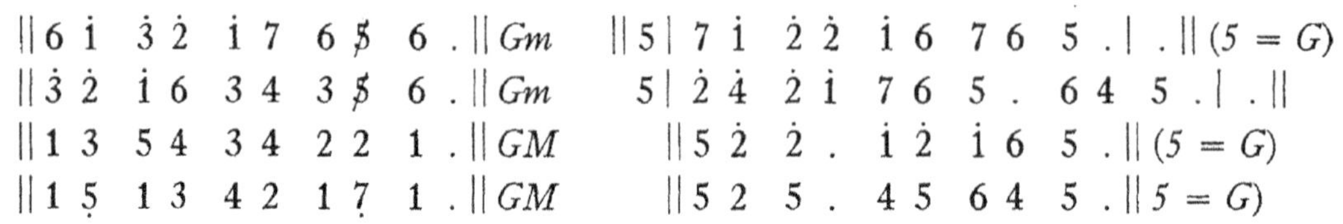

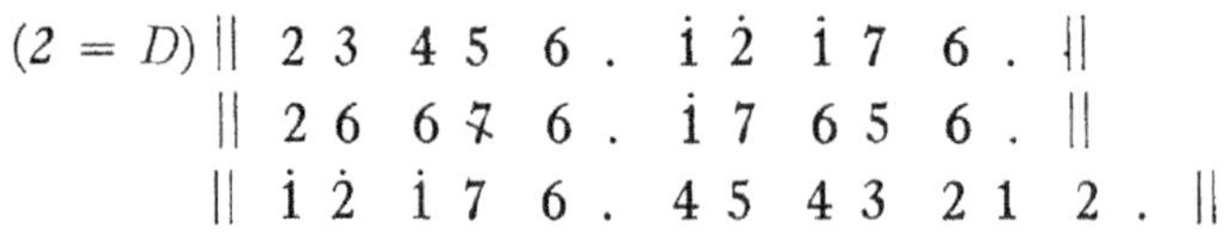

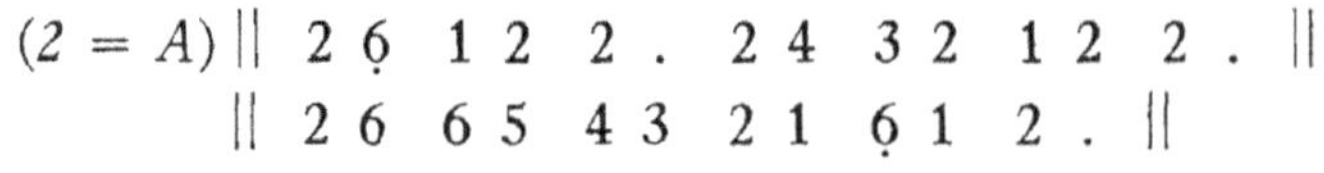

|| 6 1̇ 3̇ 2̇ 1̇ 7 6 5̸ 6 . || *Gm* || 5 | 7 1̇ 2̇ 2̇ 1̇ 6 7 6 5 . | . || *(5 = G)*
|| 3̇ 2̇ 1̇ 6 3 4 3 5̸ 6 . || *Gm* 5 | 2̇ 4̇ 2̇ 1̇ 7 6 5 . 6 4 5 . | . ||
|| 1 3 5 4 3 4 2 2 1 . || *GM* || 5 2̇ 2̇ . 1̇ 2̇ 1̇ 6 5 . || *(5 = G)*
|| 1 5̣ 1 3 4 2 1 7̣ 1 . || *GM* || 5 2 5 . 4 5 6 4 5 . || *5 = G)*

(2 = D) || 2 3 4 5 6 . 1̇ 2̇ 1̇ 7 6 . ||
|| 2 6 6 7̸ 6 . 1̇ 7 6 5 6 . ||
|| 1̇ 2̇ 1̇ 7 6 . 4 5 4 3 2 1 2 . ||

(2 = A) || 2 6̣ 1 2 2 . 2 4 3 2 1 2 2 . ||
|| 2 6 6 5 4 3 2 1 6̣ 1 2 . ||

The Ordinary of the Mass

The Kyrie

The directions for the singing of the *Kyrie* have already been given in *Music First Year, Chapter 30.* The children may sing the *Melody* given in *Music First Year* or they may substitute one of the two new melodies given in this volume.

The Gloria

Two melodies are included in this volume. The melody from Mass XV is the simpler of the two, but neither one should offer any difficulty from a melodic standpoint. The only difficulty is the study of the Latin words. The children must understand the meaning of what they are to sing. Then they must read the words distinctly, phrase by phrase. All this must precede any attempt to *sing* the *Gloria*.

The melody may be placed on the board by means of a few melodic formulae which are structural to the entire melody. When the children have become familiar with the structure of the melody and with the words, the two should be combined.

Structure of Gloria Mass XV

Inton.	*Recitation*	*Med. Cad.*	*Recitation*	*Final Cad.*
‖ 3 5	6 6 6 6 .	5 6 7 6 6 ’.	6 6 6	5 6 5 3 . ‖

Except for the "Amen," the whole *Gloria* is built on these little themes, representing a beginning, a middle and an end.

The structure of the *Gloria Mass XI* is somewhat less simple and regular than that of Mass XV. However, there are certain melodic themes that recur and that can be mastered before hand.

Phrases begin:	*Phrases end:*
‖ 2 5 | 4 3 | 4 5 | 4 3 | 2 . |	| 4 3 | 2 3 4 | 3 . | 2 . ‖
‖ 1 2 3 | 4 3 | 2 3 | 2 . |	| 2 3 4 | 3 . | 2 . ‖
‖ 2 1 3 | 4 3 | 2 . |	| 2 1 3 | 4 3 | 2 . | 2 . ‖
‖ 2 3 4 | 5 4 | 3 4 | 3 2 | 3 . | 2 . |	2 1 | 3 4 3 | 2 . | 2 . ‖

It is well to familiarize the children with this thematic material before they commence the study of the *Gloria*. They will find it relatively simple to follow the composition.

How to Sing the Gloria

The phrase "*Gloria in excelsis Deo*" is sung by the Celebrant of the Mass. The children begin to sing the words: "*Et in terra pax.*"

The singers should be divided into two groups which alternate at the double bar. This alternation can be effected between the two halves of the chorus, or else between a small group or *schola* which alternates with the whole chorus.

Usually the cantors sing the phrase: "*et in terra pax hominibus*," the full chorus singing "*bonae voluntátis.*" From that point on, the two groups alternate regularly until the end.

The Credo (No. 6)

The Credo should be studied like the Gloria: first the words and their meaning, then the melodic formulae or thematic material of the musical setting. Finally, the two should be combined.

Structure of the Credo

Phrases begin	*In the middle.*	*Phrases end.*
‖ 43 2 | 34 | 54 | 34 | 54 | 32 |		
2 | 34 | 54 | 34 | 54 | 34 |	| 26 | 66 | 66 | ———	| 56 | 54 | 343 | 2. ‖

This continues throughout save for the first phrase and the *Amen:*

| 6 7 | 6 6 | 6 6 | 5 6 | 5 4 | 3 4 3 | 2 . |
Pá- trem om-ní- po- ten- ——— tem ———

‖ 2 6 6 | 5 . | 4 5 6 | 5 . 4 | 3 . ‖
A- men ———————

These little themes can be committed to memory, so that the singing of the *Credo* becomes a mere question of placing the words where they belong.

The Sanctus and the Agnus Dei

Directions for the singing of the Sanctus and the Agnus Dei have been given in *Music First Year, Chapter 30*. The children may sing the melodies given in the First Year Book, or substitute one of those included in the present volume.

Study Melodies 244, 245, 246, 247, page 95; *248, 249, 250, 251,* page 96, Children's Manual.

Finish Study of the Mass, Children's Manual, pages 97-119.

TONALITIES IN MUSIC SECOND YEAR

(General Rules for Average Class)

Major Mode

Extension: 1 to $\dot{1}$ . . . . *Do* $= E^{\flat}$, *E or F.*
Extension: $\underset{\cdot}{5}$ to 5 . . . . *Do* $= A^{\flat}$ *or A.*
Extension: 3 to $\dot{3}$ . . . . *Do = C or B.*

Modes of Sol

Extension: $\underset{\cdot}{5}$ to 5 (Mode VII) . . . . *Sol* $= E^{\flat}$, *E or D.*
Extension: 2 to $\dot{2}$ (Mode VIII) . . . . *Sol* $= A^{\flat}$, *A, or G.*

Minor Mode and *First Mode tr. to La.*

Pentachord: 6 7 $\dot{1}$ $\dot{2}$ $\dot{3}$ . . . . *La = A or G.*
Hexachord: 6 7 $\dot{1}$ $\dot{2}$ $\dot{3}$ $\dot{4}$ . . . . *La = G or A.*
Tetrachord: 6 5 4 3 . . . . *La = C or B.*
Scale: 6 5 4 3 2 1 $\underset{\cdot}{7}$ $\underset{\cdot}{6}$ . . . . *La* $= E^{\flat}$ *or E.*
Triad: $\underset{\cdot}{6}$ 1 3 . . . . *La = A or G.*
Compass Exercise: $\underset{\cdot}{6}$ to 6 . . . . *La = D or E.*
Compass Exercise: 3 to $\dot{3}$ . . . . *La = G or A.*

Modes of Re

Pentachord: 2 3 4 5 6 . . . . *Re = A or G.*
Hexachord: 2 3 4 5 6 $\not{7}$ . . . . *Re = G.*
Tetrachord: $\dot{2}$ $\dot{1}$ 7 6 . . . . *Re = D.*
Scale: $\dot{2}$ $\dot{1}$ 7 6 5 4 3 2 . . . . *Re = E or D.*
Triad: 2 4 6 . . . . *Re = A or G.*
Extension: 2 to $\dot{2}$ (Mode I) . . . . *Re = E or D.*
Extension: $\underset{\cdot}{6}$ to 6 (Mode II) . . . . *Re = G or A.*

When an exercise moves in the upper extremity of the range, using the high tones constantly, it is best to choose the lower of the two tonalities indicated. When an exercise moves in the lower extremity of the range, it is best to select the higher tonality. The choice will also depend on the character of the voices in question, e.g.: the range of the boy's voice being higher than that of the girl.

As a general rule, an *exercise* should be placed at a lower pitch than a *song* or *melody* of similar extension, since the application required in order to find the intervals distracts the attention of the pupils from the concentration required for a beautiful tone production. Moreover, the exercise, insisting as it does on tones that are relatively difficult, tires the voices more than a melody.

TABLE OF CONTENTS

[1] Material will be found at the end of each chapter for appropriate dictation, melodic and rhythmic, with phrases for visualization and aural memory, graded in correlation with the intervals and rhythm of the chapter in question.

Printed in Dunstable, United Kingdom